THE GARLAND HOW-TO INDEX

GARLAND REFERENCE LIBRARY
OF THE HUMANITIES
(VOL. 573)

THE GARLAND HOW-TO INDEX

Grady Lynn Holt

GARLAND PUBLISHING INC. • NEW YORK & LONDON

1985

Library of Congress Cataloging in Publication Data

Holt, Grady Lynn, 1948–
　　The Garland how-to-index.

　(Garland reference library of the humanities ;
vol. 573)
　　1. Handicraft—Periodicals—Indexes. 2. Do-it-
yourself work—Periodicals—Indexes. 3. Woodworking—
Periodicals—Indexes. I. Title. II. Series: Garland reference
library of the humanities ; v. 573.
Z6152.H65　1985　016.684′08　　84-48761
[TT1]
ISBN 0-8240-8767-4 (alk. paper)

Cover design by Bonnie Goldsmith

Printed on acid-free, 250-year-life paper
Manufactured in the United States of America

CONTENTS

PREFACE

Like most do-it-your-selfers and woodworkers, I have subscribed over the years to several magazines designed for this type of reader. I enjoyed the articles and imagined building many of the interesting projects "someday." Previous commitments or more pressing needs usually required relegating these projects to a special list kept in the back of the mind of all do-it-yourselfers. Problems arose months or years later when "someday" arrived and it was time to gather information on a project. I could usually recall reading just the article I needed, but was not able to relocate it in the stacks of old magazines kept for just this reason.

The yearly indexes from December issues were not much help either. It always seemed that the publisher's method of indexing an article almost never used the descriptive key words that I used to look for information. What I needed was a list of project plans and how-to articles from the more popular magazines all combined into one index. This would make locating information in my magazine collection or that of the local library much easier. The problem was that such an index did not seem to exist. After two years of consideration and much encouragement from friends and fellow do-it-yourselfers, I decided that I would prepare the index myself. If I needed it, others might also.

The magazines selected for inclusion in this index are the more popular how-to and woodworking magazines: *Popular Mechanics*, *Fine Woodworking*, *Family Handyman*, *Woodsmith*, *Rodale's New Shelter*, and *Workbench*. Each issue of these magazines from 1972 through 1984 was reviewed and key descriptive words were selected for each article. Yearly magazine indexes were not used as a source. The key words selected were based on an estimation of possible routes a user might take in a search for information. One article might be indexed by three or four different key words. For example, an article describing how to build an Abraham Lincoln round marble top table made of mahogany is listed in the index under "Lincoln," "Table," "Marble top," and "Mahogany."

An effort was made to be as thorough as possible in preparing the index; however, some areas of information are included only in general reference rather than in detail.

Auto repair and gardening tips are two of these lightly
addressed categories. From personal observation, it seemed that
these areas are more than adequately covered in a variety of
publications.

I would like to thank Bobbie Pirrie for her encouragement
and prodding in tackling this project. Also, I would es-
pecially like to thank my wife, Melanie, for her patience and
support. This, the first of what I hope will be many editions,
is dedicated to Melanie and our daughters, Christy and Laura.

HOW TO USE THIS INDEX

The *How-to Index* has been prepared by reviewing each magazine article in issues from 1972 through 1984 and identifying key descriptive words. These key words usually include both general and specific terms for a subject or project: for example, an entry may include the popular name of the item, the wood from which it is made, and other descriptors for its use or design.

Symbols for magazines indexed were chosen to make the index as easy to use as possible. Magazine symbols used are FW (*Fine Woodworking*), HM (*Family Handyman*), NS (*Rodale's New Shelter*), PM (*Popular Mechanics*), WB (*Workbench*), and WS (*Woodsmith*). After key descriptive words are chosen and located in the index, the magazine, year, month and page number are read respectively.

Information on the magazines indexed is shown in the table which follows. I very much appreciate the valuable assistance and cooperation provided by these publications.

MAGAZINE INFORMATION TABLE

FW   *Fine Woodworking*
      Taunton Press, Inc.
      52 Church Hill Road
      Newtown, CT 06470

      Published 6/year @ $16/year
      Back issues available

HM   *Family Handyman*
      P.O. Box 2897
      Boulder, CO 80322

      Published 10/year @ $9.95/year
      Back issues available
      1999 Shepard Road
      St. Paul, MN 55108

NS   *Rodale's New Shelter*
      33 East Minor Street
      Emmans, PA 18099-0017

      Published 9/year @ $11/year
      Reprints available from
      Readers' Service Department

PM   *Popular Mechanics*
      P.O. Box 10060
      Des Moines, IA 50347-0060

      Published 12/year @ $11.97/year
      Popular Mechanics Plans Catalog
      available for $1. Photostat
      copies of any PM article, past or
      present, are available for .50/page
      from
      Popular Mechanics
      P.O. Box 1014
      Radio City Station
      New York, NY 10101

WB   *Workbench*
      Circulation Department
      4251 Pennsylvania
      Kansas City, MO 64111

      Published 10/year @ $9.95/year

WS   *Woodsmith*
      2200 Grand Avenue
      Des Moines, IA 50312

      Published 6/year @ $10/year
      Back issues available

THE INDEX

Abrasive planer, automatic feed   FW80/7-8:65
Abrasives   FW80/3-4:51
Abrasives, using   PM84/1:111
Acoustic tile, renewing   HM79/5-6:67
Acrylic, drilling and polishing   HM83/10:34
Acrylic, etching sculpture   PM73/2:80
Acrylic etagere   WB81/7-8:44
Acrylic lamp   HM83/10:34
Acrylic plant shelves, hanging   PM83/8:144
Acrylic plant stand   PM75/12:120
Acrylic sheet, removing scratches   PM81/2:143
Acrylic silverware drawer organizer   HM82/12:54
Acrylic wine server   PM75/11:62
Active solar house   NS82/4:20
Active solar house   NS83/3:30
Active solar system   NS81/1:46
Adding machine paper saver   WB78/9-10:53
Addition, attic   HM81/3:24
Addition, home   HM75/8:30
Addition, home   HM79/2:83
Addition, home   HM79/5-6:23
Addition, home   HM80/2:17
Addition, home   HM81/3:14
Addition, home   WB83/9-10:28
Addition, planning   PM76/4:148
Addition, remodeling second story   NS83/1:22
Addition, room part 1   WB77/5-6:42
Addition, room part 2   WB77/9-10:64
Addition, room part 3   WB77/11-12:78
Addition, room part 5 roof   WB78/3-4:72
Addition, room part 6   WB78/5-6:76
Addition, room part 7   WB78/7-8:56
Addition, room part 8   WB78/9-10:38
Addition, upstairs   HM79/10:53
Addition, wall framing part 4   WB78/1-2:40
Addition, warm/cool room   WB78/5-6:4
Adhesive, choosing and using   PM83/1:104
Adhesives   HM84/5-6:75
Adirondack lawn furniture   PM82/6:116
Adjustable wall light bracket   WS80/5:4
Adobe house   NS80/4:12
Advent candle holder   HM81/12:22
A-frame dog house   HM78/3:23
Airbrushes   WB79/1-2:77
Air cleaners, testing small   NS82/7-8:48
Air compressor   PM72/6:140
Air compressor plans to order $5.95   PM83/3:133
Air conditioner, installing in wall   HM79/5-6:64
Air conditioner, installing in wall   PM74/4:168
Air conditioner, installing room   PM77/4:114

Air conditioner, installing room   PM83/7:138
Air conditioner, solar   NS83/7-8:18
Air conditioner cover   PM80/11:196
Air conditioner guide, sizing   NS84/7-8:40
Air conditioner installation, central unit   HM77/5-6:14
Air conditioner maintenance, room   HM73/8:56
Air conditioner repair   PM73/7:72
Air conditioning ducts, insulating   HM84/1:20
Air cushion floater plans to order $9.95   PM84/1:62
Air cushion vehicle plans to order, $9.95   PM75/9:77
Air filter   WB77/3-4:84
Air gun target   PM78/11:208
Air hockey table top game   PM75/11:94
Air leaks   NS82/10:52
Airplane, biplane toy   WS84/9-10:8
Airplane, Fokker triplane tricycle   WB83/7-8:26
Airplane, radio controlled CO2 model   PM72/2:144
Airplane, toy   PM76/4:118
Airplane, toy SST   WB82/11-12:35
Airplane, ultralight plans to order $50   PM81/11:110
Airplane, wood toy   PM84/12:95
Airplane plans to order, $49.98   PM73/12:160
Airplane rocking toy   WB84/11-12:56
Airplane, motor and line toys   PM77/2:192
Airplane, wood   FW79/3-4:68
Airplane toy   WB79/11-12:70
Airplane weather vane, biplane   HM83/3:82
Air powered tools   FW79/1-2:70
Air quality, indoor   HM82/9:42
Alarm, basement water   PM80/7:56
Alarm, electronic Morse code auto beeper   PM84/1:76
Alarms, basement water   PM82/4:84
Alarms, burglar and fire   WB78/3-4:10
Alarms, smoke gas storm power   HM78/5-6:32
Alarm system, designing burglar   PM83/12:66
Alarm system, garage door opener   PM75/5:210
Alcove, bathroom   HM82/11:52
Alpine peasant furniture, carved   FW80/5-6:48
Aluminum can candle lantern   PM72/12:75
Aluminum can Christmas tree ornament   PM72/12:75
Aluminum can crusher   PM82/7:46
Aluminum door and screen repair   PM73/8:90
Aluminum seagull mobile   PM75/11:170
Ammeter, auto   PM77/10:68
Ammonia bending   FW81/9-10:87
Ammonia fumed oak finish   FW81/5-6:70
Ammunition, reloading   PM76/10:110
Amp, electronic headphone   PM74/1:133
AM radio antenna booster   PM82/8:28
Angel, copper tubing Christmas wall hanging   PM80/12:98

Angel Christmas tree ornament   PM80/12:98
Angled holes, drilling   FW84/5-6:76
Angled holes, drilling   PM73/6:158
Angle drilling guide   FW80/5-6:71
Angle drilling guide   PM83/11:106
Angle drilling guide, drill press   PM83/11:107
Angle drilling jig   WS79/7:10
Angles, compound   PM76/7:90
Animal candle holders   HM81/12:22
Animal cart   WB77/11-12:52
Animals, prehistoric   WB81/11-12:95
Animals and train, pull toy circus   PM72/12:108
Animal trap   PM76/5:86
Antenna, attic TV   HM80/10:58
Antenna, replacing broken TV   PM83/1:28
Antenna, shortwave   PM80/3:84
Antenna, TV installation   HM77/4:40
Antenna booster, AM radio   PM82/8:28
Antenna installation, TV   PM73/10:104
Antenna mast, conduit   PM72/12:186
Antenna mast installation   PM81/2:28
Antennas   PM84/12:88
Antennas, auto CB   PM76/3:86
Antennas, buying   PM73/10:156
Antennas, TV   PM79/6:102
Antiqued pine furniture   FW77/6:54
Antique tools   FW76/3:39
Antique wall mirror/coat rack (oak)   WS83/3-4:18
Antler mounting, deer   HM80/11:76
Anvil, small shop   PM84/5:101
Apolinere enameled bed, turned   FW84/7-8:56
Appliance cart, kitchen   PM76/4:126
Appliance finish repair   WB74/3-4:46
Appliance parts sources   WB80/1-2:124
Appliance repair   HM80/7-8:40
Appliance repair, electrical continuity   PM79/9:114
Appliance repair, small   PM79/8:98
Appliances, energy efficient   NS84/1:56
Appliance service contracts   HM83/5-6:108
Apron, leather shop   HM83/12:38
Aquaculture, solar fish pond   NS84/4:16
Aquarium, thirty inch   PM73/2:168
Aquarium end table, contemporary   WB81/5-6:82
Arbor, garden   PM82/3:132
Arbor, garden   PM84/6:74
Arbor, patio   HM79/5-6:50
Arbor, patio   HM80/5-6:18
Arbor, porch   NS81/5-6:23
Arched raised panels   WB77/3-4:94
Archimedes' marking gauge   FW83/3-4:14

Architectual scale, using   NS84/3:58
Architecture, regional houses   NS80/2:80
Arc welding   HM81/12:56
Arc welding, electric   WB80/9-10:114
Armchair, Chippendale 1765 (mahogany)   WB80/9-10:38
Armchair, Chippendale (mahogany)   WB80/5-6:97
Armchair, high back 17th century (walnut)   WB78/3-4:32
Armoire, carved girl's   WB83/3-4:27
Armoire (walnut)   PM81/3:140
Art deco lamps and table   PM81/12:106
Artist's easel   WB72/9-10:46
Asbestos advice   NS83/7-8:64
Asbestos floor coverings   HM83/7-8:54
Ash and canvas stool, folding   FW82/9-10:68
Ash and canvas tray, folding stand   FW82/9-10:68
Ash and cherry etagere, modern bentwood   WB84/11-12:74
Ash baseball bat   FW83/5-6:64
Ash basket, Shaker (black ash)   FW80/1-2:52
Ash swing, Jimmy Carter porch   FW84/5-6:68
Ash tray, cut glass bottle   PM72/12:104
Asphalt driveway repair   HM72/3:56
Asphalt driveway repair   HM80/4:60
Asphalt driveway repair   HM83/9:94
Asphalt driveway repair   HM84/3:88
Asphalt driveway repair   PM76/7:92
Asphalt driveway repair   PM79/4:151
Asphalt driveway repair   WB82/5-6:70
Asphalt driveway sealing   HM77/7-8:28
Assembly table, shop   PM84/11:160
Attic, finishing   HM81/3:24
Attic, insulating   NS80/7-8:33
Attic, remodeling   PM80/2:134
Attic, sealing access   PM80/9:145
Attic, solar   NS81/9:80
Attic, squirrels in   PM78/11:142
Attic, ventilating   PM75/7:100
Attic boy's room   WB75/3-4:58
Attic closet, cedar paneled   WB83/3-4:98
Attic dormers   PM76/5:110
Attic family room   PM74/4:152
Attic fan, electric   HM77/3:36
Attic fan, electronic control   PM81/7:27
Attic fan, installing   PM84/7:51
Attic inspection   HM72/10:40
Attic insulation   HM76/11:42
Attic insulation   WB83/11-12:86
Attic insulation and ventilation   NS84/9:78
Attic opening cover   PM81/4:175
Attic remodeling   HM84/10:93
Attic remodeling   NS84/2:32

Attic remodeling   WB74/3-4:34
Attic stairs   HM80/9:48
Attic stairway   HM75/10:28
Attic TV antenna   HM80/10:58
Attic ventilation   NS84/3:76
Attic ventilation   WB79/1-2:96
Attic ventilation, vent ridge   HM81/3:8
Attic ventilator, installing   PM73/4:166
Attic ventilator fan   PM72/4:139
Auctions   NS81/7-8:56
Auctions, country   HM81/2:46
Audio/video cable tester   PM84/3:154
Auger bits   FW84/1-2:62
Auto accident survival   PM79/10:106
Auto alarm, electronic Morse code beeper   PM84/1:76
Auto ammeter   PM77/10:68
Auto battery charge checker   PM79/5:84
Auto battery tester light, lighter   PM74/2:60
Auto brake repair, drum   PM76/9:116
Auto burglar alarm   PM82/3:24
Auto circuit checker   PM///3:184
Auto emergency kit   HM80/12:80
Auto emergency repair kit   HM84/7-8:108
Auto jacks, drive on   PM75/5:16
Auto kits   PM78/11:100
Auto maintenance, 1975   PM75/5:111
Auto maintenance, 1976   PM76/5:119
Auto maintenance guide, 1978   PM78/5:145
Auto painting   HM83/4:128
Auto painting, shopping for   PM75/10:56
Auto ramps   PM82/5:112
Auto security   HM79/9:98
Auto stereo, installing   PM79/10:24
Auto sunroof kit, installing   PM84/4:68
Auto tachometer, gear shifting   PM79/6:37
Auto voltmeter   PM80/5:42
Auto wheel blocks   HM84/5-6:150
Auto winch   PM81/3:128
Auto wind noises   PM73/12:146
Awnings, canvas   HM82/5-6:92
Ax handles (hickory)   FW83/7-8:40
Ax hewing   FW80/3-4:64
Aztec drum   FW77/9:72
Babbitt bearings   FW83/1-2:73
Baboon bank, wooden toy   PM81/1:94
Baby bed and playpen   HM81/10:24
Bachelor's chest four drawer contemporary   WS84/7-8:4
Backgammon and chess game table   WB79/7-8:70
Backgammon board and box   PM77/5:110
Backgammon/chess table   PM78/10:65

Backgammon game board   FW82/3-4:66
Background roll, photography   WB82/1-2:96
Back pack child carrier   WB75/5-6:53
Backsaw   FW83/3-4:96
Backyard play equipment   PM83/6:98
Bailey planes, restoring   FW79/1-2:55
Balance beam, 2X4s   PM76/4:18
Balance beam, toy   PM83/6:98
Balance scale, decorator   WB81/5-6:33
Balinese masks, carving   FW80/5-6:46
Ball, routed wood   FW84/1-2:8
Ball, wooden   FW79/1-2:61
Ball and claw feet, carving   FW78/3:58
Balloon, freedom   PM80/2:100
Balls, small wooden   FW80/7-8:10
Balusters, peeling paint   HM84/9:70
Bamboo fishing fly rods   FW82/5-6:68
Band saw   WB83/9-10:100
Band saw, 12 inch shop built   PM74/5:155
Band saw, shop built 42 inch   WB82/5-6:110
Band saw, straight cuts   FW81/3-4:84
Band saw, treadle   FW80/9-10:63
Band saw basics   FW81/3-4:82
Band saw basics   PM79/2:37
Band saw baskets   FW83/3-4:84
Band saw blade, welding   HM83/11:6
Band saw blade filing jig   PM76/10:28
Band saw blade installation   PM80/2:134
Band saw blade repair   FW83/5-6:82
Band saw blades   WB83/11-12:36
Band saw blade sharpening   FW83/5-6:83
Band saw boxes   FW80/11-12:64
Band saw capacity, increasing   FW82/5-6:16
Band saw circle cutting   FW79/5-6:16
Band saw circle cutting   FW81/7-8:16
Band saw circle cutting jig   PM80/11:182
Band saw dovetails   FW83/11-12:49
Band saw duster   PM84/11:140
Band sawed bowls   FW83/3-4:82
Band sawed miniature boxes   PM84/5:90
Band saw extension table   PM84/5:99
Band saw finger joints   FW83/3-4:14
Band sawing cylinders   PM75/11:34
Band saw kit   HM83/12:34
Band saw kit   WB78/9-10:96
Band saw pattern sawing   FW84/7-8:54
Band saw rip fence   FW84/5-6:14
Band saw rip fence   PM74/10:157
Band saw sawmill   FW81/3-4:86
Band saw speed reducer   PM75/2:140

Band saw speed reducer   WB78/5-6:100
Band saw speed reducer   WB81/1-2:9
Band saw stand, 12 inch shop built   PM74/5:155
Band saw table, king size   PM76/3:128
Band saw tips   HM84/9:12
Band saw tips   PM79/12:98
Band saw tips   PM80/1:116
Band saw wheel sweepers   WB76/9-10:79
Banjo, five string   WB72/5-6:28
Banjo/dulcimer   PM82/7:88
Banjo kit   PM82/7:105
Banjo kit   PM84/2:104
Banjo making   FW75/12:8
Banjo mother of pearl inlay   FW81/3-4:50
Banjo wall clock   WB72/7-8:34
Bank, boot   WB79/11-12:34
Banks, toy wooden cat clown and baboon   PM81/1:94
Bannister, turned stair   WB79/7-8:58
Bar, arched brick   WB76/5-6:40
Bar, barrel   PM72/1:130
Bar, basement   HM74/11:37
Bar, basement   WB73/11-12:34
Bar, basement   WB76/9-10:1
Bar, basement   WB81/11-12:4
Bar, Christmas tree   PM79/11:122
Bar, contemporary   PM74/1:178
Bar, home   WB75/1-2:38
Bar, kitchen cabinets   PM75/12:70
Bar, latticework patio   PM80/6:104
Bar, L-shaped   HM75/10:34
Bar, piano or roll around   PM72/9:74
Bar, portable refreshment   WB72/7-8:32
Bar, portable wet   PM73/8:78
Bar, split level for basement   PM72/1:128
Bar, wet   PM76/2:114
Bar and kitchen cabinet, mobile   PM82/4:142
Bar/barbecue, family room   PM79/5:148
Barbecue/bar, family room   PM79/5:148
Barbecue cart, butcher block top   WB84/3-4:8
Barbecue cart (redwood)   HM84/7-8:96
Barbecue cart (redwood)   PM84/7:94
Barbecue grill, installing indoor   PM81/4:168
Barbecue grill scraper   PM84/5:183
Barbecue skewers   PM80/7:91
Barbecue/smoker plans to order, $7.95   PM79/6:13
Barbecue table   PM77/5:107
Barbecue well   PM80/8:130
Barbecuing with hardwood scraps   PM80/8:114
Barber pole decoration   HM78/7-8:49
Barbie doll table and chair   WB80/11-12:42

Bar/bookcase, basement   HM72/6:44
Bar/buffet, family room   PM82/2:106
Bar/cart   HM82/5-6:50
Bar cart   WB76/5-6:70
Bar/cart, patio (redwood)   HM84/7-8:92
Bar clamps, edge gluing   WB84/9-10:32
Bar clamps, light duty   WB84/11-12:44
Bar clamps, wood   FW83/3-4:14
Bar clamps, wooden   WS79/9:3
Bar coffee table   WB81/1-2:16
Bar/entertainment unit fireplace   PM75/1:76
Bar icebox (oak)   PM84/12:102
Barn, backyard plans to order $10.50   PM83/3:102
Barn, Pennsylvania Dutch tobacco drying   FW80/5-6:60
Barn, red toy   WB79/5-6:31
Barn birdhouse   WB77/3-4:124
Barn/garage, country plans to order $30   PM84/9:90
Barn kit, storage   HM75/9:36
Barn plans to order, $7   PM80/8:96
Barn siding, making   PM79/1:99
Barn wood picture frames   PM77/2:184
Barometer, plexiglas water   PM74/9:142
Barometer frame, turned   WB73/9-10:39
Barometer weather station   WB74/7-8:32
Barrel, strawberry   PM73/5:88
Barrel bar   PM72/1:130
Barrel cradle   HM80/1:48
Barrel furniture   WB74/5-6:32
Barrel lily pool   HM83/5-6:64
Barrel planter   PM72/4:132
Barrel planter utility post cover   WB79/11-12:38
Barrister's bookcase (oak)   WS83/9-10:16
Bar top finish   WB75/11-12:24
Bar wall cabinet   HM73/6:50
Baseball bat, Louisville Slugger   FW83/5-6:64
Baseball board game   PM79/4:122
Baseboards, fitting   NS83/5-6:18
Basement, carpeting   PM84/4:22
Basement, finishing   HM77/3:16
Basement, finishing   HM78/10:20
Basement, finishing   WB81/11-12:4
Basement, finishing   WB83/9-10:10
Basement, keeping dry   HM72/10:54
Basement, outside entrance   HM77/3:56
Basement, remodeling contemporary   PM84/3:122
Basement, repairing wet   PM84/2:149
Basement, water leaks   PM80/2:163
Basement, waterproofing   WB84/5-6:51
Basement, wet   HM78/7-8:50
Basement, wet   HM79/7-8:85

Basement, wet   HM81/9:36
Basement, wet   HM83/9:74
Basement, wet   HM84/3:60
Basement, wet part 1   HM74/9:46
Basement, wet part 2   HM74/10:48
Basement, wet wall framing   HM77/3:58
Basement access, hinged deck   PM81/6:112
Basement access, outdoor   PM81/6:117
Basement bar   HM74/11:37
Basement bar   WB73/11-12:34
Basement bar   WB76/9-10:1
Basement bar   WB81/11-12:4
Basement bar, split level   PM72/1:128
Basement bar/bookcase   HM72/6:44
Basement bathroom   HM80/12:70
Basement bathroom   WB72/11-12:8
Basement bathroom   WB74/9-10:44
Basement bathroom   WB74/7-8:28
Basement bedroom   WB73/3-4:26
Basement ceiling   WB82/1-2:28
Basement ceilings, low   HM81/5-6:20
Basement circus decorations   PM75/4:128
Basement crack repair   WB80/11-12:82
Basement door, outside   PM72/4:144
Basement doors, outside   HM83/4:90
Basement duct soffits, three   HM84/7-8:74
Basement English pub   WB74/9-10:32
Basement fireplace   WB82/9-10:30
Basement flooding, gutter drainage   PM74/7:164
Basement insulation   WB80/9-10:86
Basement insulation, exterior   HM82/9:82
Basement light, sliding ceiling   PM84/3:128
Basement painting, airless sprayer   HM79/11:52
Basement remodeling   HM75/3:32
Basement remodeling   HM77/2:48
Basement remodeling   NS84/2:35
Basement remodeling   PM73/4:141
Basement remodeling   WB72/9-10:22
Basement remodeling, log cabin   WB77/11-12:118
Basement root cellar food storage, modern   PM82/8:94
Basement shop   WB77/11-12:100
Basement stairs, remodeling   HM74/1:48
Basement sump pump   HM80/1:46
Basement sump pump   PM79/4:162
Basement sump pump   WB80/3-4:78
Basement sump pump alarm   PM72/12:188
Basement tree, plumbing   WB73/11-12:34
Basement walls, framing   PM73/3:140
Basement walls, insulating   HM84/5-6:76
Basement walls, insulating exterior   WB82/9-10:38

Basement water alarm   PM80/7:56
Basement water alarms   PM82/4:84
Basement waterproofers   NS81/4:38
Basement waterproofing   PM73/10:92
Basement windows, framing   PM84/3:176
Basement window wells   HM84/9:84
Basket, barrel   WB74/5-6:32
Basket, folding plywood fruit   PM74/2:140
Basket, metal tubing   PM74/3:138
Basket, octagonal waste (maple)   WS80/1:5
Basket, Shaker (black ash)   FW80/1-2:52
Basketball goal, adjustable height   PM76/8:98
Baskets, bandsawn   FW83/3-4:84
Basket splints   FW78/9:64
Bas relief wood carving, pelican   WB84/11-12:82
Basswood eagle carving   FW76/3:24
Batch solar water heater   HM81/1:76
Batch water heater   NS81/7-8:27
Batch water heaters, solar   NS83/5-6:36
Bath, family   PM79/9:166
Bath, mini-half   PM79/9:165
Bath, solar   NS83/7-8:74
Bath, sunken   NS80/11-12:90
Bath and kitchen, Victorian remodeling   HM82/7-8:28
Bath and kitchen cleaning   HM84/5-6:117
Bath darkroom   HM73/3:52
Bath remodeling checklist   PM82/4:178
Bathroom   HM75/8:42
Bathroom, basement   HM80/12:70
Bathroom, basement   WB72/11-12:8
Bathroom, basement   WB74/9-10:44
Bathroom, basement   WB74/7-8:28
Bathroom, ceramic tile   HM82/7-8:57
Bathroom, one-piece   WB76/11-12:32
Bathroom, recessed towel rack and cabinet   HM76/9:46
Bathroom, remodeling   WB78/1-2:57
Bathroom, whirlpool tub   HM83/7-8:40
Bathroom accessories, wood   WB76/11-12:87
Bathroom alcove   HM82/11:52
Bathroom and kitchen remodeling   HM83/7-8:29
Bathroom built-ins   HM82/11:50
Bathroom cabinet   PM79/9:168
Bathroom ceramic shower   HM84/10:48
Bathroom linen cabinet   HM82/11:54
Bathroom magazine rack   HM82/11:52
Bathroom magazine rack/toilet tissue holder   PM75/4:134
Bathroom magazine/tissue rack, Colonial   WB84/1-2:79
Bathroom medicine cabinet   HM82/11:51
Bathroom medicine cabinet (oak)   HM84/5-6:136
Bathroom medicine chest (redwood)   WB81/3-4:72

Bathroom planter   PM76/5:106
Bathroom redesign   HM82/7-8:48
Bathroom remodeling   HM77/4:20
Bathroom remodeling   HM79/1:24
Bathroom remodeling   HM79/3:82
Bathroom remodeling   HM80/2:48
Bathroom remodeling   HM83/3:39
Bathroom remodeling   HM84/10:41
Bathroom remodeling   PM76/10:120
Bathroom remodeling   PM79/9:107
Bathroom remodeling   WB73/5-6:38
Bathroom remodeling   WB76/7-8:24
Bathroom remodeling   WB76/9-10:50
Bathroom remodeling   WB77/1-2:58
Bathroom remodeling, master   HM82/7-8:53
Bathroom remodeling, two from one   HM82/9:74
Bathroom rolltop wall cabinet (redwood)   WS81/9:10
Bathrooms, half   PM73/10:85
Bathroom scales, fold down   HM76/3:34
Bathroom shelf and cabinet, adjustable   WB79/3-4:111
Bathroom shelves   HM81/1:24
Bathroom shelves, ladder   PM76/4:135
Bathroom shower remodeling   HM72/6:42
Bathroom shower resurfacing   HM75/10:31
Bathroom shower stall, open   WB78/5-6:56
Bathroom sink rim   HM84/2:58
Bathroom tank top shelf   PM75/1:114
Bathroom tile, ceramic   PM78/6:134
Bathroom tile, ceramic   PM84/4:141
Bathroom toothbrush holder   WB80/7-8:59
Bathroom towel and cup holder, hand   PM79/11:122
Bathroom towel bar   HM82/11:52
Bathroom towel rack   PM78/3:128
Bathroom towel rack, recessed ladder   WB82/1-2:106
Bathroom towel rack, suspended   WB78/7-8:83
Bathroom towel rack, wall   WB79/5-6:66
Bathroom tub and shower kit   HM80/1:51
Bathroom tub to shower   WB83/1-2:94
Bathroom vanity   HM82/11:54
Bathroom vanity   WB76/11-12:64
Bathroom vanity, shop built   WB79/1-2:52
Bathroom vanity (redwood)   WB77/11-12:20
Bathroom whirlpool bath   WB83/1-2:49
Bath toothbrush holder, child's   WB83/1-2:86
Bathtub, stone walled   NS82/3:53
Bathtub, sunken   PM75/6:80
Bathtub and shower, fiberglass panels   HM76/9:40
Bathtub and shower unit installation   HM74/11:54
Bathtub recaulking   PM74/4:192
Bathtub valve replacement   WB80/5-6:92

Bathtub wall kit   HM84/10:58
Bathtub wall liners   NS81/10:16
Bath vanity   HM75/9:40
Bath vanity, two basin mirrored door island   WB81/9-10:46
Batter board, retaining wall   HM82/4:104
Batter boards, leveling with water   NS84/2:18
Batteries, drycell   HM84/11:82
Batteries, drycell   PM80/11:151
Battery charge checker, auto   PM79/5:84
Battery charger for NiCd batteries   PM82/2:62
Battery powered house   PM79/9:147
Battery tester, drycell   PM81/2:142
Battery tester and charger, drycell   PM80/11:20
Battery tester light, auto lighter   PM74/2:60
Bay window   WB79/7-8:18
Bay window   WB79/9-10:14
Bay window, installing   HM84/4:49
Bay windows, installing   PM84/4:130
BB gun target   PM78/11:208
Beaded edges, sanding   FW80/11-12:19
Beading tool, scratch stock   PM76/4:204
Beam ceiling   HM77/11-12:26
Beam ceiling   PM83/12:101
Beams, plastic decorative   PM73/4:195
Bean bag toss game   WB75/11-12:71
Bean trellis   PM84/3:130
Bear climbing toy   PM79/5:134
Bearings, babbitt   FW83/1-2:73
Bearing wall, removing   PM74/8:146
Bear napkin ring, carved   WB80/1-2:24
Bed   HM75/9:34
Bed   WB73/3-4:36
Bed, Apolinere enameled turned   FW84/7-8:56
Bed, bookcase headboard   WB81/9-10:92
Bed, bookcase headboard   WB81/9-10:111
Bed, boy's   WB72/9-10:28
Bed, boy's and loft   WB83/5-6:51
Bed, boy's trundle   PM79/9:112
Bed, built-in   WB74/7-8:39
Bed, cabinet headboard   PM72/9:74
Bed, canopy   WB72/3-4:30
Bed, captain's   HM81/7-8:20
Bed, carpeted platform   HM84/4:103
Bed, carved four poster   HM81/12:40
Bed, child's   WB82/9-10:48
Bed, child's Shaker   WB83/9-10:66
Bed, child's twin   HM73/3:38
Bed, contemporary platform   WB84/5-6:29
Bed, contemporary platform TV (maple)   PM84/5:92
Bed, double   WB76/3-4:48

Bed, floating   NS83/11-12:8
Bed, folding bookcase   WB78/3-4:42
Bed, four poster contemporary   PM79/9:110
Bed, French provincial four poster canopy   WB82/5-6:58
Bed, girls four poster   WB83/3-4:27
Bed, hidden (cherry)   FW76/9:24
Bed, high single   WB78/5-6:84
Bed, pencil post (cherry)   FW83/7-8:54
Bed, platform   NS81/2:61
Bed, platform   PM79/8:100
Bed, race car child's   WB79/7-8:5
Bed, sculptured modern   HM80/12:46
Bed, single (pine)   FW81/5-6:68
Bed, toy truck   PM72/4:160
Bed, traditional (pine)   HM81/9:54
Bed, water   WB81/9-10:86
Bed and desk, built-in   HM72/6:36
Bed and desk tree house, indoor   WB72/3-4:32
Bed and playhouse, fast plywood   HM78/11-12:28
Bed and playpen, baby   HM81/10:24
Bed and room divider, child's   HM72/12:30
Bed/bookcase/desk, twin   HM76/9:32
Bed/buffet table, rolling   PM74/6:156
Bed/carrier, pet   HM77/10:42
Bed/crib   WB82/9-10:48
Bed/desk, boy's   PM72/6:156
Bed/desk, family room   PM79/10:130
Bed/desk/chest, child's loft (plywood)   FW84/5-6:52
Bed headboard, child's bookcase   PM81/9:104
Bed headboard, contemporary   WS84/7-8:10
Bed headboard, master bedroom   PM79/9:111
Bedpost reeding   FW82/11-12:34
Bedposts, reeding   FW83/3-4:32
Bedposts, router reeding   FW83/1-2:4
Bedroom, basement   WB73/3-4:26
Bedroom, built-in bed and desk   HM72/6:36
Bedroom, child's   HM83/12:42
Bedroom, girl's armoire and four poster bed   WB83/3-4:27
Bedroom, modular   HM80/10:20
Bedroom desk   NS82/4:43
Bedroom divider   PM77/9:96
Bedroom furniture   WB73/3-4:36
Bedroom furniture   WS84/7-8:4
Bedroom light, clock and reading   PM79/11:154
Bedroom storage platform   HM76/6:26
Beds, bunk   HM72/9:36
Beds, bunk   PM77/9:99
Beds, bunk   WB73/9-10:26
Beds, bunk   WB78/11-12:58
Beds, bunk   WB84/1-2:38

Beds, bunk and chest   HM81/1:25
Beds, bunk and closet   HM73/12:36
Beds, bunk and closet   HM74/8:34
Beds, bunk tower   HM79/11:9
Beds, child's intermediate   WB79/3-4:114
Beds, platform   PM76/11:104
Beds, rope   HM79/4:6
Beds, simple stackable twins   PM81/4:154
Beds, triple bunks   PM78/10:136
Beds, water   NS81/11-12:11
Beds and desk, built-in bunk   HM77/5-6:56
Bed side stand (pine)   WS81/11:4
Bed sofa   WB79/11-12:68
Bed/sofa, caned   PM77/8:105
Bed/sofa, modern   HM81/4:18
Bed/sofa, rollaway built-in   PM80/2:134
Bedspread holder   WB76/5-6:24
Bed table   PM81/7:97
Bed table, footboard   PM75/9:79
Bed tusk tenon joint   FW83/1-2:14
Bee, bumble pull toy   PM73/12:166
Beehives (pine)   FW83/3-4:86
Bell holder   WB82/5-6:42
Bellows smoke gauge   HM81/3:93
Bells, door test and repair   PM73/6:84
Bells, wooden guest turned   WB82/7-8:85
Belt and tie rack, door mounted   WB80/11-12:80
Belt buckle, wooden   WS80/7:6
Belt grinder, homebuilt   WB77/5-6:26
Belt grinder, shop built   WB84/9-10:106
Belt sander, shop built   WB84/5-6:85
Belt sander, shop made   WB79/11-12:92
Belt sander, vertical   FW84/5-6:10
Belt sander counterbalance   FW82/3-4:16
Belt sander jig   PM83/11:112
Belt sander techniques   HM83/9:18
Belt sander thickness sander   FW82/11-12:22
Belt sander tips   PM79/9:113
Belt sander tips   PM82/12:112
Bench, assembly   PM82/11:106
Bench, carved hall (oak)   WB83/7-8:74
Bench, carving portable   FW82/9-10:91
Bench, concrete park   PM84/3:84
Bench, deck curved   HM83/5-6:56
Bench, drop leaf   WB73/5-6:26
Bench, English pub settle   WB78/9-10:50
Bench, exercise weight   PM73/12:152
Bench, garden   NS81/5-6:46
Bench, garden   WB78/3-4:56
Bench, garden (redwood)   WS79/5:8

Bench, garden (redwood and cedar)   WS83/5-6:12
Bench, hall storage   WB76/7-8:36
Bench, lattice door boot   NS83/5-6:54
Bench, log   HM79/4:73
Bench, log   PM83/6:104
Bench, long Lincoln (maple and pine)   PM80/2:126
Bench, long Shaker   HM72/12:58
Bench, low work   FW78/9:46
Bench, Mediterranean outdoor furniture   WB80/7-8:82
Bench, Mexican tile   WB72/5-6:8
Bench, mudroom   NS83/5-6:56
Bench, mudroom   PM77/9:109
Bench, park (metal and oak)   PM81/8:94
Bench, patio   PM78/9:113
Bench, patio storage   HM72/8:30
Bench, planter   PM77/3:97
Bench, plant potting   HM82/3:32
Bench, potting   PM79/5:140
Bench, potting   PM80/8:95
Bench, potting   PM82/3:149
Bench, potting   PM83/3:105
Bench, potting (redwood)   PM74/7:156
Bench, roll out   PM79/10:130
Bench, roofed flower box   PM74/7:139
Bench, Scandinavian   PM81/5:122
Bench, sketch   WB74/5-6:40
Bench, storage   HM73/2:46
Bench, storage   WB83/5-6:24
Bench, toy horse   PM78/11:121
Bench, trestle   WB83/9-10:32
Bench, trestle table   WS82/9:24
Bench, Victorian fireplace   HM83/11:32
Bench, wood carving   FW84/3-4:60
Bench, work   FW76/9:40
Bench and desk, plywood   HM80/12:16
Bench clamp   FW77/12:17
Bench clamp, wood   WB82/3-4:72
Bench dog collar   FW81/9-10:14
Benches, garden or deck   PM76/4:135
Benches, patio and park   PM84/6:78
Benches and table, outdoor   PM81/4:162
Benches and table, patio   WB80/5-6:32
Benches and table (redwood)   HM82/5-6:31
Bench/fireplace/desk   HM78/2:32
Bench/firewood box pass through   NS84/1:16
Bench grinder tips   HM84/12:18
Bench grinder tool rest   FW80/7-8:10
Bench plane   PM84/10:62
Bench plane basics   FW82/7-8:84
Bench planes   WS82/9:16

Bench plane tips   PM80/8:100
Bench plane tips   PM80/10:122
Bench plane tips   PM80/7:102
Bench plane use   WS82/9:20
Bench potting/plant stand   PM83/6:104
Bench press, veneer   FW84/7-8:41
Bench/stool, Colonial   PM80/11:128
Bench/storage, Colonial settle   WB84/9-10:116
Bench/storage boxes, garden or pool   HM84/5-6:40
Bench storage chest   WB82/11-12:22
Bench storage wall unit   HM75/1:30
Bench/table   HM75/3:42
Bench/table, foyer   PM79/6:112
Bench/table, Monk's   WB79/3-4:88
Bench top hold down   FW80/9-10:18
Bench/trellis (redwood)   HM84/5-6:36
Bench/workshop, two minis   PM76/1:98
Bending, ammonia   FW81/9-10:87
Bending cold, snowshoes   FW84/11-12:77
Bending compound curves, laminated staves   FW79/7-8:57
Bending fixture, steam   FW81/9-10:84
Bending iron   FW77/9:20
Bending irons   FW78/3:63
Bending jig, steam   FW78/9:16
Bending wood, hot pipe   FW78/3:62
Bending wood, kerf   PM72/10:167
Bending wood, laminating   FW83/3-4:58
Bending wood, steam   FW77/9:40
Bending wood steamer   FW78/6:9
Bending wood steamer   FW78/3:12
Bending wood without steam   FW82/11-12:22
Bent chair legs, cantilevered   FW84/7-8:16
Bent laminations   FW77/3:35
Bent serving tray (walnut and mahogany)   FW77/6:62
Bentwood coat rack   NS83/3:24
Bentwood cradle   WB84/11-12:4
Bentwood etagere, modern (ash and cherry)   WB84/11-12:74
Bentwood furniture   FW80/1-2:38
Bentwood rocker Christmas tree decoration   PM79/12:82
Bermudan dovetailing   FW82/7-8:71
Bevel/rip table saw technique   WS81/7:8
Bevel/taper table saw technique   WS81/7:11
Bicycle, motorizing   PM77/12:112
Bicycle built for two   PM77/6:43
Bicycle carrier, car top   HM81/4:80
Bicycle carrier, car top   PM73/9:154
Bicycle carrier rack   PM83/7:107
Bicycle cart, PVC   PM80/5:132
Bicycle cart, PVC   PM84/5:64
Bicycle Christmas tree ornament, high wheel   PM80/12:98

Bicycle commuting PM80/6:94
Bicycle exercise stand PM80/10:56
Bicycle fender taping tool PM83/7:96
Bicycle hang-up rack PM83/7:106
Bicycle maintenance HM83/5-6:42
Bicycle maintenance PM77/8:161
Bicycle maintenance PM79/7:118
Bicycle pedal spanner wrench PM83/7:96
Bicycle rack, bumper PM72/2:128
Bicycle rack, wall PM78/2:125
Bicycle repair shop PM83/7:96
Bicycle repair stand PM80/7:90
Bicycle repair stand PM83/7:96
Bicycle repair vise PM83/7:96
Bicycle speedometer, digital PM78/2:39
Bicycle storage racks NS80/4:49
Bicycle tire sharpening wheel FW83/7-8:14
Bicycle touring PM78/6:94
Bicycle tune up, ten speed HM81/7-8:68
Bicycle wheel trellis NS80/2:96
Bicycle wheel truing jig PM83/7:96
Billiard cue and ball rack PM72/7:145
Billiard pool cue rack PM76/5:224
Billiard table PM73/1:63
Billiard table, miniature WB81/11-12:60
Biplane, wood toy PM84/12:95
Biplane toy WB79/11-12:70
Birch campaign book/magazine case WS80/1:6
Birch desk, small modern writing WB84/7-8:62
Birch or maple kitchen cutting board WS79/1:1
Birch or maple letter opener WS80/7:7
Birch plywood book rack WS80/1:12
Birch plywood magazine binder WS80/1:4
Bird candleholder PM78/12:74
Bird carving PM78/1:94
Bird Christmas tree ornament PM80/12:98
Bird feeder PM72/6:151
Bird feeder WB75/11-12:22
Bird feeder WB77/9-10:74
Bird feeder WB82/9-10:92
Bird feeder, automatic PM74/2:148
Bird feeder, covered bridge WB72/3-4:42
Bird feeder, pagoda WB74/9-10:54
Bird feeder, peasant art WB84/11-12:67
Bird feeder, small birds WB83/9-10:144
Bird feeder, squirrel proof PM83/8:43
Bird feeder, squirrel proof PM83/3:109
Bird feeder (cedar) WB79/5-6:69
Bird feeders HM78/11-12:32
Birdhouse, barn WB77/3-4:124

Birdhouse, bluebird   WB74/3-4:42
Birdhouse, gourd and coconut wren   WB76/5-6:22
Birdhouse, round   WB79/3-4:28
Birdhouse mast, conduit   PM72/12:186
Birds, carved   FW82/1-2:77
Birds, carved sea gulls   PM78/2:24
Bit, expansion   FW77/3:27
Bit, improved spade   FW82/3-4:12
Black light, glowing wood   FW79/5-6:81
Black powder rifle kit   HM81/4:46
Blacksmith forge, homemade   HM81/5-6:102
Blacksmithing   FW77/12:58
Blacksmithing   PM78/6:130
Blanket chest, Colonial   HM82/7-8:24
Blanket chest, contemporary frame and panel   FW84/1-2:54
Blanket chest, contemporary (pine & redwood)   WS81/7:12
Blanket chest, country (cherry)   WS84/3-4:16
Blanket chest, Shaker (pine)   FW81/3-4:60
Blanket chest toy box   WB82/11-12:72
Blanket holder   WB76/5-6:24
Blanket rack   PM82/1:67
Blanket rack (cherry)   WS84/3-4:4
Blind finger joint   FW84/5-6:70
Blinds, covering verticle   HM77/10:74
Blinds, verticle window   WB80/5-6:64
Blockfront furniture   FW80/7-8:47
Block plane   FW83/3-4:65
Block plane   WB79/7-8:14
Block plane tips   PM80/6:116
Blocks, number toys   PM81/11:30
Blower   WB74/7-8:22
Blower, insulation   PM81/4:147
Blower, leaf   PM76/1:138
Blower, shop made insulation   WB78/5-6:92
Bluebird house   WB74/3-4:42
Boat, cedar guide plans to order $14   HM81/11:66
Boat, cedar strip sail   HM81/3:78
Boat, child's paddle   WB77/3-4:58
Boat, fishing plans to order $6.95   PM79/4:77
Boat, installing engine   PM78/10:254
Boat, lapstrake   FW82/11-12:82
Boat, paddle wheel   WB81/7-8:16
Boat, riding toy   WB79/11-12:72
Boat, sailboat kit   HM82/3:101
Boat, sailing rigging   PM77/4:104
Boat, toy freighter   WB82/9-10:45
Boat, toy herring fishing   WB82/11-12:48
Boat, toy lobster   WB82/11-12:48
Boat, toy tug   WB82/11-12:90
Boat, trolling motor inner tube bass   PM84/2:93

Boat, winterizing   PM77/11:116
Boat dock, portable   PM81/6:38
Boat dolly, dinghy   PM72/7:143
Boat floor, inflatable   PM74/7:140
Boat gas gauge, inexpensive   PM74/2:106
Boat kit, sail   PM77/6:106
Boat kits   PM78/10:100
Boat paints   PM80/4:124
Boat/raft   PM76/1:96
Boat repair, fiberglass   PM76/8:92
Boat roller tote   PM75/3:103
Boats, lapstrake   FW82/9-10:54
Boats, tug and barge toys   WB78/5-6:46
Boat safety   PM75/12:138
Boat safety   PM78/7:86
Boat seats, reclining   PM75/3:140
Boat trailer maintenance   PM72/4:90
Boat trailer mover, old mower chassis   PM84/3:30
Boat/utility trailer   HM80/11:60
Bobbin turning   FW80/7-8:70
Boiler, multifuel   PM79/10:122
Boiler maintenance   PM79/10:122
Bolection bowl turning   FW79/1-2:69
Bolt cutting   HM74/6:50
Bombe chest of drawers, Boston (mahogany)   FW84/3-4:52
Bonsai grooming turntable   PM80/3:174
Bonsai planter   PM77/7:97
Book caddy, table top   WB75/5-6:20
Bookcase   FW75/12:43
Bookcase   HM80/5-6:118
Bookcase   PM75/5:84
Bookcase   PM84/7:133
Bookcase, $60   HM79/4:30
Bookcase, boy's   HM72/3:36
Bookcase, boy's   WB72/9-10:31
Bookcase, brick and wood   WB79/3-4:66
Bookcase, built-in wall   WB80/1-2:87
Bookcase, chair side   WB76/3-4:8
Bookcase, contemporary arched window   HM84/9:32
Bookcase, cookbook caddy   PM74/9:139
Bookcase, corner   NS83/1:68
Bookcase, early American   WB72/3-4:56
Bookcase, lawyer's (oak)   HM84/1:62
Bookcase, lawyer's (oak)   WS83/9-10:16
Bookcase, plexiglas (walnut)   WB81/7-8:44
Bookcase, Sheraton   WB77/3-4:102
Bookcase, simple fastener   NS84/9:114
Bookcase, slotted   WB75/7-8:20
Bookcase, spiral   WB80/9-10:30
Bookcase, wall   HM73/3:34

Bookcase, wall   HM76/4:28
Bookcase, wall   PM84/2:106
Bookcase and display stand (pine)   WB80/5-6:52
Bookcase and wall cabinet, contemporary   PM84/4:136
Bookcase/bar, basement   HM72/6:44
Bookcase bed, folding   WB78/3-4:42
Bookcase/bed/desk, twin   HM76/9:32
Bookcase bed headboard   WB81/9-10:111
Bookcase bed headboard   WB81/9-10:92
Bookcase/cabinet, floor to ceiling   HM84/9:34
Bookcase/desk, wall hung contemporary (oak)   HM84/9:30
Bookcase divider   HM80/9:21
Bookcase/etagere, early American   WB72/7-8:38
Bookcase kits   PM84/2:110
Bookcases, easy building   WB82/5-6:34
Bookcases, two   WB77/3-4:6
Bookcase/secratary, (mahogany)   FW83/1-2:54
Bookcase shelf, wall (oak)   WS82/3:20
Bookcase storage cabinet   WB82/1-2:79
Bookcase unit   WB81/3-4:6
Bookcase unit, wall   PM74/4:166
Bookcase units, contemporary (oak)   WB82/9-10:96
Bookend, C-clamp   PM74/10:70
Bookends, child's Crayon   PM81/11:30
Bookends, glass insulator   HM82/1:52
Bookends, initial   PM73/11:161
Bookends, metal tubing   PM74/3:138
Bookends, picture cutouts   PM72/12:116
Bookends, planter   WB79/1-2:110
Bookends, sculptured scrap   PM76/11:150
Bookends, shelf   HM83/10:125
Bookends, sliding dovetail   FW80/1-2:19
Book/magazine case, campaign (birch)   WS80/1:6
Book matched box   FW82/1-2:14
Book rack, adjustable (pine)   HM80/11:32
Book rack, dog   PM72/3:136
Book rack, kitchen dowel   PM84/1:112
Book rack, plexiglas   PM73/11:162
Book rack, simple   PM84/7:131
Book rack, slip joint   PM76/4:200
Book rack, take apart   WB78/11-12:44
Book rack (birch plywood)   WS80/1:12
Book rack recipe holder   WB82/5-6:18
Books, antiqued display   WB75/11-12:17
Book shelf   WB78/3-4:4
Book shelves   HM81/1:16
Book shelves, anywhere   PM82/9:100
Book shelves, F. Scott Fitzgerald   HM81/2:20
Book shelves, gravity   PM84/4:103
Book shelves, hanging   PM78/11:130

Book shelves, low cost   PM78/1:88
Book shelves, wall   PM84/7:132
Book shelves and desk, rope nautical   PM76/1:73
Book stand   WB75/11-12:18
Book stand, Colonial   PM72/11:121
Book stand, table top   PM80/9:100
Book storage center, movable (pine)   NS80/2:59
Book trough table   WB78/7-8:44
Book turntable, desk   PM74/2:150
Boomerang   FW84/3-4:61
Boot and mitten dryer with blower   PM72/1:142
Boot bank   WB79/11-12:34
Boot bench, lattice door   NS83/5-6:54
Boot candy cane holder, Christmas   PM79/12:82
Bootjack, Lincoln   PM79/2:119
Boot shelves   WB79/3-4:98
Boring jig, horizontal   PM83/12:112
Boring machine, horizontal   FW82/11-12:98
Boston bombe chest of drawers, (mahogany)   FW84/3-4:52
Bottle display cabinet   WB82/1-2:74
Bottle houses   PM77/12:128
Bottle lamps, glass   WB82/3-4:58
Bottle lamps, turned wood   WB72/5-6:26
Bottle rack, wine   PM80/8:88
Bottles, cutting glass kit   PM72/12:104
Bottle/wine glass rack   WB83/9-10:124
Bowl, carved   WB79/9-10:46
Bowl, cut glass bottle   PM72/12:104
Bowl, laminated   PM76/11:126
Bowl, turned   FW82/1-2:54
Bowl, turned fruit   WS82/5:18
Bowl, turned inlaid fruit   PM75/2:116
Bowl, turned popcorn (koa)   WS83/1-2:24
Bowl, turning inlaid   FW79/1-2:69
Bowl blanks, freezing green   FW83/11-12:12
Bowl bottoms, turned   FW84/3-4:64
Bowl finish, salad   WB72/1-2:26
Bowl finish, walnut oil   FW83/1-2:71
Bowl gouges, bent   FW83/5-6:95
Bowl lathe   FW81/11-12:78
Bowl lathe chuck   FW80/5-6:17
Bowls, band sawed   FW83/3-4:82
Bowls, drying green   FW81/7-8:10
Bowls, laminated turning   FW78/3:70
Bowls, turned   WB79/5-6:4
Bowls, turned boards   WB74/5-6:50
Bowls, turned laminated   FW80/1-2:14
Bowls, turning giant   FW83/7-8:48
Bowls, turning spalted wood   FW78/6:54
Bowls, turning thin   FW80/7-8:60

Bowl set, turned salad   WB79/9-10:80
Bowl turning   FW81/1-2:28
Bowl turning, checkered   FW75/12:16
Bowl turning, Ethiopia   FW80/3-4:54
Bowl turning, green wood   FW76/6:37
Bowl turning, inside   FW77/6:41
Bowl turning, laminated   FW78/10:48
Bowl turning, matched set   FW83/1-2:70
Bowl turning, taped faceplate   FW79/5-6:14
Bowl turning chuck   FW84/9-10:10
Bowl turning depth gauge   FW79/11-12:18
Bowl turning gouge   FW76/12:55
Bowl turning grain designs   FW81/11-12:75
Bowl turning lathe toolrest   PM72/1:174
Bow reel, center shot   PM73/5:153
Bow saw   FW77/9:56
Bow saw, fold up (hardwood)   WS79/9:5
Bow saw, traditional   WB83/7-8:4
Box, book matched   FW82/1-2:14
Box, carved stamp (walnut)   FW75/12:42
Box, carved trinket   PM77/1:94
Box, contemporary jewelry (walnut)   WS82/11-12:20
Box, flip open one piece   FW80/11-12:63
Box, French fitted (Coco Bolo)   PM80/12:106
Box, inlaid music   WS83/7-8:4
Box, kerfing and bending   FW80/5-6:44
Box, Kleenex tissue   WS82/1:24
Box, music (walnut or cherry)   WS79/11:6
Box, planter (redwood)   WS79/5:9
Box, recipe (walnut and maple)   WS80/7:8
Box, rolltop bread (pine)   WS79/7:6
Box, routed jewelry   WS81/1:12
Box, routed jewelry   WS83/7-8:10
Box, router bit   PM81/3:160
Box, shadow   PM74/11:112
Box, shop storage   WS81/5:14
Box, slide top finger joint   WS81/9:14
Box, slope sided   FW84/3-4:57
Box, spice (pine)   WS79/11:3
Box, tissue cover (maple)   WS79/3:5
Box, torsion   FW82/1-2:96
Box, toy blocks   WB81/5-6:111
Box, treasure chest jewelry   WB73/9-10:47
Box, turned inlaid   WB75/7-8:48
Box, veneer   WB77/3-4:121
Box, wooden hinge jewelry   WS80/5:5
Box and finger joints, router jig   PM84/1:75
Box building   WS79/7:4
Boxcar toy box   WB80/11-12:45
Box/chest, plywood storage   PM74/2:146

Boxes, band saw   FW80/11-12:64
Boxes, band sawed miniatures   PM84/5:90
Boxes, clamping   FW78/9:14
Boxes, covered heirloom   WB73/7-8:58
Boxes, heart   HM82/2:32
Boxes, hexagonal (rosewood or walnut)   FW82/3-4:63
Boxes, kerf bent   FW80/5-6:36
Boxes, oyster shell veneer   FW79/11-12:66
Boxes, plant (cedar)   WS79/5:4
Boxes, planter   HM81/5-6:33
Boxes, plastic laminated   WB76/9-10:46
Boxes, quick and tricky little   FW83/11-12:32
Boxes, small   PM75/1:42
Boxes, small laminated   WB84/9-10:48
Boxes, small turned   FW77/12:72
Boxes, steambent Shaker oval   FW82/1-2:92
Boxes, turned music   FW84/9-10:78
Boxes and carriers, stacking garden   PM82/8:96
Box hinging, jewelry   FW84/11-12:52
Box joint   PM76/8:94
Box joint   WB78/7:040
Box joint   WS79/3:4
Box joint, parallel spline   WS80/5:9
Box joint, radial arm saw   FW81/5-6:76
Box joint, routed   FW81/9-10:18
Box joint, table saw   WS81/9:12
Box joint drawers   WS81/9:19
Box joint router jig   FW79/1-2:56
Box joints   WS84/9-10:14
Box lid panels   FW83/11-12:37
Box of drawers   WS79/7:5
Box or fingerlap joint   PM82/1:101
Box top, end grain   WS81/5:13
Boxwood microscope   FW78/10:43
Boy's bedroom furniture   WB78/11-12:58
Boy's bookcase   HM72/3:36
Boy's nightstand   WB78/9-10:106
Boy's room, attic   WB75/3-4:58
Boy's room furniture   WB72/9-10:28
Bracelet mandrel   FW81/5-6:14
Bracket, adjustable wall light   WS80/5:4
Bracket clock kit   PM75/12:98
Brake, sheet metal   PM73/1:170
Brake, sheet metal and workbench   WB80/9-10:50
Brake, small sheet metal   WB82/3-4:64
Brass, removing paint   HM75/11:56
Brass door catch   FW83/7-8:66
Brass etching, low voltage   WB82/7-8:9
Brass hardware   WB78/9-10:68
Brass hardware, hand worked   FW83/7-8:65

Brass hinges   NS82/5-6:62
Brazing   HM76/10:36
Breadboard, kitchen   HM83/11:80
Breadboard, kitchen (maple and cherry)   WS82/3:24
Breadboard, laminated   PM76/11:126
Breadbox, carved (oak)   WB83/5-6:14
Breadbox, fake rolltop   PM81/2:140
Breadbox, rolltop   WB82/3-4:48
Breadbox, rolltop (oak)   HM83/1:78
Breadbox, rolltop (pine)   WS79/7:6
Bread cupboard, French provincial   WB77/1-2:44
Bread cutting board   PM80/11:128
Bread cutting board   WB80/7-8:69
Breakfast counter addition, glass   HM83/5-6:54
Breakfast nook   WB80/3-4:123
Breakfast table   NS82/10:47
Briar pipe carving   FW80/3-4:82
Briar pipes   PM77/2:38
Brick, adobe   NS80/4:12
Brick, cleaning fireplace   HM78/10:62
Brick, decorative   HM72/3:49
Brick, fake   HM76/2:28
Brick, fake   PM73/4:168
Brick, patching fake   WB79/3-4:80
Brick, spalled   HM75/11:32
Brick, using   PM78/10:218
Brick and concrete steps   PM75/8:78
Brick and lumber entertainment center   WB81/5-6:109
Brick and sand patio   HM77/7-8:52
Brick and sand patio   PM73/7:78
Brick and sand patios and walks   HM72/4:56
Brick and stone, fake wall   WB78/11-12:134
Brick floor, plastic   HM74/9:48
Brick joint repair   HM83/9:98
Brick laying   HM75/11:59
Brick mowing strips   HM82/3:74
Brick paint, removing   HM75/4:52
Brick patio, three   HM84/3:54
Brick planter, raised   PM84/3:113
Brick planters   HM74/8:36
Brick repair   HM73/4-5:52
Brick repair   PM79/4:151
Brick repair, chimney   NS84/10:22
Brick repairs   HM84/9:88
Brick step repair   HM80/5-6:60
Brick walk, replacing bricks   PM82/12:52
Brick walks and patios   PM77/5:104
Brick wall, fake   HM72/12:56
Brick wall, insulating   HM75/10:30
Bridge, handmade   NS81/4:64

Bridge, trussed log   FW82/3-4:78
Bridge card holder, two decks   WS84/9-10:18
Bridges, covered   FW84/5-6:44
Bridle joint, beginner's   FW84/11-12:68
Brush, paint   HM83/4:46
Brush cleaner, paint   PM82/3:168
Brushes, cleaning paint   PM84/11:146
Brush holder, dust   PM78/8:47
Bucket, staved   FW79/3-4:74
Buckets, wood Swiss   FW83/5-6:73
Bucking horse toy   WB79/11-12:60
Buckle, belt   HM81/11:42
Buckle, wooden belt   WS80/7:6
Bud vase, cut glass bottle   PM72/12:104
Bud vase, turned   PM74/11:102
Bud vase, wall   WB80/5-6:119
Buffers, carpet   WB77/11-12:38
Buffet   PM72/9:74
Buffet, drop leaf   WB77/7-8:34
Buffet/bar, family room   PM82/2:106
Buffet/bed table, rolling   PM/4/6:156
Buffet/hutch, arched doors   WB78/5-6:48
Buffet storage wall unit   HM76/1:32
Buffet table, six gate leg (cherry)   WS82/3:14
Buffing machine   WB84/7-8:28
Buffing wheels and compounds   WB84/7-8:46
Bug box, screened   WB83/5-6:42
Bug vacuum, patio   PM74/7:107
Building codes   NS83/1:56
Building fasteners   HM80/2:104
Buildings, salvaging   HM82/1:22
Built-in bed   WB74/7-8:39
Built-in settee   WB80/1-2:131
Bulldozer, toy   WB79/11-12:26
Bullet catch, wooden   FW80/3-4:12
Bulletin and key board (oak)   WS81/11:24
Bulletin board, envelope   PM78/11:198
Bulletin/chalkboard, toy   PM81/5:118
Bull horn rack with leather decoration, wall   PM74/7:142
Bumble bee pull toy   PM73/12:166
Bumper pool cue rack   PM76/5:224
Bumper pool table   WB76/11-12:74
Bunk beds   HM72/9:36
Bunk beds   PM77/9:99
Bunk beds   WB73/9-10:26
Bunk beds   WB78/11-12:58
Bunk beds   WB84/1-2:38
Bunk beds, triple   PM78/10:136
Bunk beds and chest   HM81/1:25
Bunk beds and closet   HM73/12:36

Bunk beds and closet   HM74/8:34
Bunk beds and desk, built-in   HM77/5-6:56
Bunk bed tower   HM79/11:9
Bureau, four drawer 1848 (walnut)   WB84/5-6:74
Burglar alarm, auto   PM82/3:24
Burglar alarm, choosing   HM75/11:42
Burglar alarm system, designing   PM83/12:66
Burglar alarm systems, troubleshooting home   PM84/4:149
Burglar and fire alarms   WB78/3-4:10
Burglar bars, artistic   NS81/5-6:50
Burglar proofing   NS83/9:42
Burglar proofing, home   PM79/1:87
Burls   FW84/7-8:67
Bus stop, child's   WB78/3-4:50
Butcher block, kitchen   PM75/10:102
Butcher block clock   HM78/11-12:86
Butcher block coffee table, Parson's   WB83/5-6:72
Butcher block furniture   PM76/12:110
Butcher block kitchen cart   PM84/9:76
Butcher block mobile kitchen island   HM84/9:106
Butcher blocks, seven methods   PM84/9:76
Butcher block style chair with staves   WB82/11-12:4
Butcher block table   WB77/3-4:90
Butcher block table, extendable   WB82/11-12:84
Butcher block table (maple/walnut)   WB84/11-12:46
Butcher block top, rolling cabinet   WB82/5-6:106
Butcher block top barbeque cart   WB84/3-4:8
Butcher block top kitchen cart (oak/maple)   HM84/5-6:140
Butler's table and tray   PM75/3:90
Butler's table hinges   WS81/3:16
Butler's table hinges   WS81/3:16
Butler's tray (redwood)   WS79/5:9
Butler's tray table (walnut)   WS81/3:10
Butler tray table (walnut or mahogany)   WB76/1-2:41
Butterfly dropleaf table   WB72/5-6:48
Butterfly joint, double dovetails   FW80/11-12:72
Butterfly push action toy   WB84/11-12:122
Butterfly sculpture, wooden wall   PM82/2:60
Butt joints   PM81/11:118
Buttons, turning dowel   PM82/6:99
Buying hardwood   FW81/3-4:34
Cabin, owner built   WB80/7-8:42
Cabin, simple log   PM83/12:96
Cabin door latch lock   HM76/4:60
Cabinet, bar wall   HM73/6:50
Cabinet, bathroom   PM79/9:168
Cabinet, bathroom linen   HM82/11:54
Cabinet, cabinetmaker's tool   FW81/9-10:56
Cabinet, camera (cherry)   HM84/2:70
Cabinet, card table and chairs   WB82/3-4:26

```
Cabinet, China  WB77/1-2:66
Cabinet, Colonial corner (pine)  HM82/2:30
Cabinet, Colonial dry sink TV  WB84/3-4:122
Cabinet, Colonial home safe  PM79/1:84
Cabinet, Colonial spice  WB75/11-12:64
Cabinet, computer  NS82/9:51
Cabinet, computer rolltop contemporary (oak)  PM84/2:100
Cabinet, contemporary frame and panel record  FW84/1-2:54
Cabinet, contemporary gun (oak)  WB81/9-10:56
Cabinet, contemporary stereo (oak)  PM83/9:84
Cabinet, contemporary wall  HM84/2:70
Cabinet, curio  HM83/10:88
Cabinet, curio  WS82/5:12
Cabinet, curio, tall  WS83/3-4:12
Cabinet, curved sides  FW79/7-8:57
Cabinet, desk sewing (oak)  WB82/5-6:4
Cabinet, dowel  HM80/1:12
Cabinet, early American wall (oak)  HM82/10:32
Cabinet, file  HM83/2:37
Cabinet, file (oak)  HM84/1:63
Cabinet, four panel door chair side (walnut)  WS82/11-12:14
Cabinet, frame and panel (pine)  WS80/3:8
Cabinet, gun  PM75/2:120
Cabinet, hidden kitchen storage  WB77/3-4:50
Cabinet, highboy stereo  WB83/5-6:4
Cabinet, home office organizer (mahogany)  PM84/8:108
Cabinet, icebox (oak)  WS84/11-12:4
Cabinet, kitchen corner  WB84/9-10:14
Cabinet, kitchen pan rack  WB76/3-4:6
Cabinet, laundry  PM77/1:92
Cabinet, medicine (oak)  HM84/5-6:136
Cabinet, mobile shop tool  PM80/2:130
Cabinet, modular storage (plywood)  WS82/7:12
Cabinet, music center  HM78/3:38
Cabinet, portable dishwasher  PM75/5:84
Cabinet, punch pattern spice  HM82/2:32
Cabinet, raised panel corner  WB76/11-12:104
Cabinet, rolling butcher block top  WB82/5-6:106
Cabinet, rolltop glass door TV  WS83/1-2:14
Cabinet, rolltop stereo (maple plywood)  WS81/9:6
Cabinet, room divider planter  HM72/12:44
Cabinet, sandpaper  WB81/3-4:20
Cabinet, sewing  WB77/11-12:44
Cabinet, sewing (oak)  HM84/2:70
Cabinet, Shaker drop leaf work  HM72/9:48
Cabinet, Shaker (pine)  PM84/10:104
Cabinet, shoe and purse  WB74/7-8:42
Cabinet, shop storage  WS83/1-2:4
Cabinet, shop wall tool  HM81/12:20
Cabinet, small movable tool  PM78/3:126
```

Cabinet, small parts cardboard WB84/3-4:98
Cabinet, small stereo WB84/11-12:14
Cabinet, snack counter PM78/7:100
Cabinet, stationery desk caddy 1750 (cherry) PM84/3:74
Cabinet, stereo HM75/11:38
Cabinet, stereo HM84/2:38
Cabinet, stereo WB81/7-8:40
Cabinet, stereo speaker PM76/11:120
Cabinet, tape deck WB78/1-2:76
Cabinet, three drawer file WS83/9-10:10
Cabinet, trifold tool WB81/3-4:102
Cabinet, TV and firewood storage WB81/11-12:102
Cabinet, two drawer file (maple plywood) WS80/1:8
Cabinet, uses for old TV WB84/9-10:63
Cabinet, Victorian curved glass china (oak) WB84/9-10:56
Cabinet, video game PM84/3:110
Cabinet, wall bathroom rolltop (redwood) WS81/9:10
Cabinet, wall hung curio with drawer WB84/9-10:24
Cabinet, wall hung raised panel (plywood) WS80/3:7
Cabinet, wall spool PM80/3:62
Cabinet, wall spool display WS83/3-4:4
Cabinet and hutch, contemporary cane (oak) WS82/7:18
Cabinet and shelf, bathroom WB79/3-4:111
Cabinet and towel rack, recessed bathroom HM76/9:46
Cabinet arched raised panels WB77/3-4:94
Cabinet bookcase storage WB82/1-2:79
Cabinet coffee table WB77/11-12:48
Cabinet countertop joints, tight WB82/5-6:48
Cabinet countertops, installing HM84/7-8:61
Cabinet countertops, plastic laminates FW84/3-4:72
Cabinet/desk HM73/8:36
Cabinet doors, adjusting PM79/8:88
Cabinet doors, kitchen stained glass HM82/7-8:84
Cabinet doors, woven slats WB80/11-12:96
Cabinet furniture, kitchen PM75/12:70
Cabinet hanging prop FW80/5-6:14
Cabinet hinge, inlaid wooden FW82/7-8:52
Cabinet joints, carcase construction FW76/12:30
Cabinet/lamp table, Mediterranean WB78/9-10:70
Cabinetmaker's tool cabinet FW81/9-10:56
Cabinetmaker, working with HM83/7-8:110
Cabinet making, miniature models FW81/5-6:58
Cabinet making, stick measuring FW77/3:46
Cabinet plate butler PM79/11:212
Cabinet prop FW82/5-6:18
Cabinet refinishing, metal HM75/10:58
Cabinetry, desert FW76/6:30
Cabinets, contemporary drawer and door PM83/9:80
Cabinets, European style FW83/11-12:54
Cabinets, family room end PM79/10:130

Cabinets, finishing kitchen   WB74/7-8:8
Cabinets, garage storage   HM72/4:54
Cabinets, hanging wall units   HM84/7-8:53
Cabinets, installing base units   HM84/7-8:56
Cabinets, installing kitchen   NS82/7-8:32
Cabinets, installing kitchen   PM74/4:198
Cabinets, kitchen   HM78/3:14
Cabinets, kitchen   HM81/2:15
Cabinets, kitchen   PM78/4:141
Cabinets, kitchen   PM80/10:110
Cabinets, kitchen   PM82/2:100
Cabinets, kitchen extra   WB76/11-12:96
Cabinets, kitchen islands   HM84/7-8:25
Cabinets, low cost kitchen (pine)   HM82/7-8:40
Cabinets, mobile tool   PM81/10:122
Cabinets, refinishing kitchen   WB80/11-12:16
Cabinets, rolltop doors   WB80/9-10:34
Cabinets, rolltop kitchen   FW80/11-12:78
Cabinets, rosemaling kitchen   FW80/11-12:79
Cabinets, shop storage   WB83/3-4:98
Cabinets, showcase   FW79/9-10:44
Cabinets, stereo   FW82/5-6:76
Cabinets, wall mounting   FW84/9-10:10
Cabinets, wall shop tool   PM82/5:114
Cabinet scraper, homemade   FW78/10:13
Cabinet scraper, sharpening   PM82/1:60
Cabinet scraper tips   PM84/4:108
Cabinet stick, kitchen   FW83/7-8:42
Cabinet tops, tile and laminate   PM83/2:102
Cabinet wall unit   PM82/4:123
Cabinet wall unit, contemporary   PM84/4:136
Cabinet wall units, modular   WS84/5-6:8
Cable tester, audio/video   PM84/3:154
Cabriole leg desk (walnut)   WB84/11-12:48
Cabriole legs   FW79/9-10:80
Cabriole legs   FW83/9-10:36
Cabriole table legs   WB78/5-6:42
Cabriole templates   FW79/9-10:83
Calculator security stand   PM80/7:95
Calendar, perpetual desk   PM80/3:131
Calendar, perpetual wood   WB84/11-12:34
Calendar, slide rule   WB79/11-12:50
Calendar pinup   WB83/3-4:102
Calimba thumb piano   WB74/11-12:28
Caliper, giant sliding   WB83/3-4:84
Calipers   PM76/4:202
Calliope, mini pipe organ   PM82/12:102
Camel, turning split (walnut)   FW76/3:20
Camera, toy   WB77/7-8:20
Camera box, under/over water   PM79/7:60

Camera cabinet (cherry)   HM84/2:70
Camera flash extension bracket   PM81/3:88
Camera kit, video   PM81/5:22
Camera kits   PM79/5:126
Camera lens to telescope   PM74/11:138
Camera monopod   PM82/5:82
Camera stand, panoramic   PM81/8:134
Campaign book/magazine case (birch)   WS80/1:6
Campaign desk   WB74/3-4:32
Campaign desk, British military (cherry)   PM79/2:126
Campaign etagere   WB84/7-8:70
Camper, building 20 footer   PM72/7:136
Camper, pickup   PM73/3:178
Camper, pickup   WB79/5-6:46
Camper, truck   WB79/9-10:86
Camper, van   PM72/5:154
Camper dollhouse   WB76/11-12:88
Camper kitchen box   HM79/5-6:78
Camper ladder   PM78/4:57
Camper plans to order, pickup   PM78/1:76
Camper/tailgate party organizer   PM79/10:116
Camper van carpet   HM78/4:53
Camper van conversion   WB73/3-4:56
Camper van plans to order, $15   PM79/3:48
Camping, snow   PM76/11:100
Camping, snow survival   PM79/12:84
Camping pantry   HM84/5-6:130
Camping tips   PM76/3:108
Camp kitchen   WB83/7-8:16
Camp saw, folding   PM84/4:111
Can crusher   NS82/2:45
Can crusher   PM82/7:46
Candelabra, Chinese   FW80/11-12:60
Candelabra, turned table   WB77/5-6:36
Candle chandelier   NS80/11-12:63
Candle Christmas display, stained glass   WB82/11-12:106
Candle cubes, enameled   PM79/6:120
Candle cubes with Christmas cards   PM80/12:98
Candle flowerpot Christmas centerpiece   PM79/12:82
Candleholder, Advent   HM81/12:22
Candleholder, bird   PM78/12:74
Candleholder, block   HM81/11:42
Candleholder, candy cane   PM78/12:74
Candleholder, Christmas dove and partridge   HM81/12:22
Candleholder, flax spool   PM78/11:202
Candleholder, heart   HM82/2:32
Candleholder, mirror sconce   PM77/11:137
Candleholder, rocking horse   PM80/12:98
Candleholder, tree of life   PM78/12:74
Candleholder, turned   PM79/5:290

Candleholder centerpiece, tree   PM78/12:74
Candleholders   WB82/7-8:25
Candleholders, animal   HM81/12:22
Candleholders, coiled rope   PM79/11:76
Candleholders, cut glass bottle   PM72/12:104
Candleholders, dowels and macrame beads   WB82/1-2:100
Candleholders, glass jars   WB81/9-10:14
Candleholders, turned   PM78/11:198
Candleholders, turned (walnut)   HM82/12:64
Candle lantern, captain's   PM79/12:108
Candle lantern, English wall   WS84/11-12:16
Candle lantern, stained glass   WB81/5-6:44
Candle lantern, tin can   PM72/12:75
Candle lantern, town crier's   WB73/5-6:44
Candle pattern napkin holder   PM78/11:200
Candles   PM72/11:116
Candles, 3-D   WB75/1-2:52
Candles, freeform snow   PM73/12:70
Candles, glass molds   WB72/11-12:48
Candles, star shaped Christmas   PM81/10:52
Candle sconce   HM82/12:6
Candle sconce, Colonial (cherry)   WS79/11:5
Candle sconce, heart shaped   PM81/12:116
Candle sconce, wall   PM78/12:74
Candle sconces   HM78/11-12:86
Candle sconces, two   PM80/3:134
Candle sconce with mirror   PM74/11:100
Candle shaving console, Colonial   PM72/1:140
Candlestand   WB77/11-12:74
Candlestand   WB80/3-4:92
Candlestand, chard Oriental   PM72/6:149
Candlestand, Colonial   PM80/11:128
Candlestand, Shaker (cherry)   WS80/9:6
Candlestand, turned   PM77/11:146
Candlestand, turned adjustable   PM77/12:121
Candlestick, chamber   PM81/12:116
Candlestick, sparkplug   PM81/2:142
Candlestick, turned   PM74/11:102
Candlestick, turned floor   WB75/9-10:59
Candlestick and compote, turned   WB77/9-10:24
Candlesticks, flax spool   PM77/11:142
Candlesticks, stabilizing tall   FW84/5-6:12
Candlesticks, turned   WB77/9-10:41
Candlesticks, turned   WB79/11-12:112
Candlesticks, turned   WB79/5-6:4
Candlesticks, turned spiral   PM72/10:178
Candy cane candleholder   PM78/12:74
Cane, ladies walking   WB78/7-8:55
Cane, woven   FW80/1-2:49
Cane back dining chair   WB77/9-10:48

Cane bottom chairs, green oak   FW82/3-4:50
Cane bottom cherry chair, antique   WB72/9-10:42
Cane bottom corner chair   WB80/7-8:50
Cane cabinet and hutch, contemporary (oak)   WS82/7:18
Cane chair, contemporary laminate   PM74/9:64
Cane chair, Lincoln armless rocking (walnut)   PM84/2:60
Cane chair bottoms   WB80/5-6:87
Cane saddle seat   WB84/3-4:30
Cane sofa/bed   PM77/8:105
Caning chair seats   PM77/6:122
Caning chair seats   PM80/7:107
Canister, old time grocery bin   PM75/10:102
Canister, turned   WS81/3:14
Canisters, finger joint kitchen   WB80/5-6:48
Canister set, turned kitchen (walnut)   WS83/1-2:10
Cannon, muzzle loading miniature   WB77/11-12:4
Cannon kits, miniature   PM79/7:82
Canoe, knife   FW84/1-2:51
Canoe, stripper (cedar)   FW82/7-8:72
Canoe, twin paddle   PM72/6:138
Canoe kit, cedar strip   HM80/11:8
Canoe paddle brackets, auto   PM78/6:69
Canoe paddles, sanding   FW83/3-4:16
Canopy bed   WB72/3-4:30
Canopy gazebo   PM76/4:121
Can recycling   WB75/9-10:44
Canvas and ash stool, folding   FW82/9-10:68
Canvas and ash tray, folding stand   FW82/9-10:68
Canvas and dowel magazine rack   PM79/12:108
Canvas and redwood deck chair   WS79/5:6
Canvas and redwood deck stool   WS79/5:6
Canvas chair, (oak)   HM81/3:54
Canvas/redwood chair, sling   PM83/6:104
Canvas window awnings   HM82/5-6:92
Captain's bed   HM81/7-8:20
Captain's desk   HM78/11-12:48
Captain's lantern, candle   PM79/12:108
Car, cleaning   PM84/10:35
Car, electric   PM79/10:96
Car, funny toy   PM78/11:194
Car, model Stutz Bearcat from tin cans   PM79/3:118
Car, pedal toy plans to order $6   PM80/6:124
Car, solar powered toy   NS83/7-8:78
Car, toy 1915 Chevrolet   WB84/9-10:80
Car, toy race (plywood)   WS79/9:12
Car, toy racer   PM81/5:118
Car, toy Rolls Royce wood   PM84/12:94
Carbide blade, circular saw   HM84/7-8:79
Carbide tipped saw blades   FW80/7-8:72
Carbide tipped saw blades   PM77/5:59

Carbide tipped saw blades   WS83/5-6:16
Carbide tipped saw blade sharpening   WS83/7-8:19
Carbide tipped tools   WB82/1-2:82
Car care guide, 1973   PM73/5:153
Car care guide, 1974   PM74/5:169
Car care guide, 1977   PM77/5:121
Car care guide, 1979   PM79/5:151
Car care guide, 1980   PM80/10:123
Car care guide, 1980   PM80/5:141
Car care guide, 1981   PM81/5:135
Car care guide, 1982   PM82/5:125
Car care guide, 1983   PM83/5:113
Car care guide, 1984   PM84/5:105
Car care guide, fall 1981   PM81/10:119
Car care guide, fall 1982   PM82/10:125
Car carrier, trail bike   PM73/6:83
Card and pencil holder (scrap wood)   WS79/3:12
Cardboard cabinet, small parts   WB84/3-4:98
Cardboard carpentry   HM79/11:24
Cardboard cutting board   PM73/9:156
Cardboard sofa   NS83/11-12:38
Cardboard stereo speaker cabinets   HM78/9:76
Cardboard storage   WB83/9-10:81
Card holder, two decks   WS84/9-10:18
Card table, folding   WB82/11-12:26
Card table, Hepplewhite D-shaped (mahogany)   FW84/7-8:42
Card table and chairs, cabinet   WB82/3-4:26
Caribbean chair, 2X4   HM81/5-6:22
Car kits   PM81/10:96
Carousel, tool   FW80/9-10:53
Carousel horse carving   FW80/7-8:62
Carpenter's squares   WB73/9-10:50
Carpenter's toolbox, open top tray   PM81/11:128
Carpentry tips   FW77/3:20
Carpentry tips, finish   PM81/8:30
Carpentry tips, finish   PM81/9:106
Carpet   WB77/9-10:8
Carpet, choosing   WB72/7-8:40
Carpet, cleaning and repairing   PM78/5:138
Carpet, cutting with saber saw   PM84/3:144
Carpet, foam back   HM78/1:30
Carpet, installation   HM76/9:48
Carpet, installing   PM82/1:65
Carpet, measuring and buying   HM81/1:42
Carpet, removing   HM75/11:52
Carpet, seamless   PM72/5:144
Carpet, shag   WB75/7-8:16
Carpet buffers   WB77/11-12:38
Carpet buying   HM82/10:42
Carpet cleaning   HM82/10:84

Carpet clearing hinge   PM80/2:40
Carpeted box furniture   HM78/7-8:77
Carpeted garden   HM79/4:90
Carpeted platform bed   HM84/4:103
Carpeted walls   NS81/1:70
Carpeting, basement   PM84/4:22
Carpeting, camper van   HM78/4:53
Carpet maintenance   HM81/9:82
Carpet repair   HM75/4:42
Carport   PM78/9:111
Car ramps   PM82/5:112
Car repair tool cabinets, mobile   PM81/10:122
Carriage clock kit   PM75/12:98
Carriage table, spider leg (mahogany)   FW83/5-6:70
Carrier, casserole   PM77/11:140
Carrier, garden tools   WB78/5-6:36
Carrier, Shaker dovetail   FW82/1-2:94
Cars, block toys   PM75/12:96
Cars, fiberglass classic   HM83/1:93
Cars, wood toy   WB75/11-12:54
Cars and truck, toy   PM78/11:194
Car seat/sleigh, child's   PM79/12:64
Car security, auto alarm Morse code beeper   PM84/1:76
Car speakers, installing   PM73/9:122
Car stereo, installing   PM79/10:24
Cart, animal   WB77/11-12:52
Cart, appliance   PM76/4:126
Cart, bar   WB76/5-6:70
Cart, barbecue (redwood)   HM84/7-8:96
Cart, barbecue (redwood)   PM84/7:94
Cart, bench   PM77/3:97
Cart, bicycle PVC   PM84/5:64
Cart, butcher block kitchen   PM84/9:76
Cart, butcher block top barbecue   WB84/3-4:8
Cart, chain saw   HM83/9:102
Cart, Chinese Chippendale tea   WB79/5-6:52
Cart, collapsible leaf   PM82/9:64
Cart, Colonial serving   WB73/7-8:36
Cart, firewood   PM77/10:124
Cart, garbage can   HM80/12:60
Cart, garden   PM80/7:110
Cart, garden   PM83/10:69
Cart, garden   WB82/3-4:119
Cart, garden tool   NS80/7-8:41
Cart, heavy duty garden   PM82/11:158
Cart, heavy duty garden   PM82/6:123
Cart, kitchen butcher block top (oak/maple)   HM84/5-6:140
Cart, kitchen serving (walnut or fir)   FW77/3:58
Cart, laundry   PM75/4:126
Cart, microwave/serving kitchen (cherry)   WS82/9:8

```
Cart, plywood patio    HM80/12:19
Cart, PVC bicycle    PM80/5:132
Cart, PVC pipe garden    WB83/7-8:94
Cart, PVC pipe roll around    HM81/9:34
Cart, shop table saw    WS81/1:14
Cart, storage    HM75/11:46
Cart, tea and serving tray    WB83/9-10:4
Cart, traditional tea    WB76/3-4:60
Cart, TV    WB78/5-6:40
Cart and workbench, shop    WB84/9-10:101
Cart/bar    HM82/5-6:50
Cart/bar, patio (redwood)    HM84/7-8:92
Carter chairs, President Jimmy    PM84/8:73
Carter porch swing, Jimmy    FW84/5-6:68
Car top bicycle carrier    PM73/9:154
Car top bicycle carrier    HM81/4:80
Car top carrier    HM78/11-12:58
Cart plans to order, Mini Indy II    PM78/5:110
Cart/potting bench, garden (redwood)    HM83/3:60
Carved animal napkin rings    WB80/1-2:24
Carved bed, four poster    HM81/12:40
Carved bench, hall (oak)    WB83/7-8:74
Carved birds    FW82/1-2:77
Carved birds, sea gulls    PM78/2:24
Carved bowl    WB79/9-10:46
Carved box, trinket    PM77/1:94
Carved breadbox (oak)    WB83/5-6:14
Carved calendar pinup    WB83/3-4:102
Carved cat    PM77/1:96
Carved chest, Japanese    WB72/3-4:62
Carved chest (cedar)    WB72/11-12:58
Carved clock    WB74/1-2:48
Carved crocodile wall plaque    WB78/11-12:4
Carved dish, snack    PM77/1:94
Carved drawer pulls    WB76/5-6:26
Carved duck    WB75/1-2:44
Carved duck decoys    HM79/7-8:92
Carved furniture, Alpine peasant    FW80/5-6:48
Carved kitchen plaque    WB75/1-2:43
Carved kitchen utensils    WB82/1-2:32
Carved little man puzzle (walnut)    FW76/6:56
Carved low relief owl    WB75/1-2:44
Carved napkin rings, fish duck flower    PM83/10:98
Carved Nativity, musical rotating Creche    PM73/12:157
Carved partridge mirror    PM77/1:96
Carved pedestal, Indian    WB74/7-8:62
Carved pedestal table    WB80/1-2:64
Carved sculpture, wood hippo    WB76/3-4:100
Carved shells, Chippendale    FW79/3-4:76
Carved signs, Murphy knife    FW81/9-10:64
```

Carved stamp box (walnut)   FW75/12:42
Carver's stand   FW81/9-10:20
Carver's tricks, period furniture   FW81/9-10:67
Carving, chainsaw   FW78/3:76
Carving, chainsaw   PM74/7:42
Carving, chip   FW79/11-12:80
Carving, machine   PM83/10:96
Carving, power tool   WB78/1-2:86
Carving, traditional relief   FW78/10:56
Carving, wood   FW76/9:35
Carving, wood   FW77/12:64
Carving, wood   PM77/1:94
Carving, wood   WB75/1-2:40
Carving ball and claw feet   FW78/3:58
Carving bench, portable   FW82/9-10:91
Carving bench, wood   FW84/3-4:60
Carving birds   PM78/1:94
Carving board   PM82/1:159
Carving Carousel horse   FW80/7-8:62
Carving cupboard cockleshell   FW78/9:74
Carving design   FW75/12:28
Carving dough tray   FW82/7-8:80
Carving duck decoys   PM72/2:104
Carving eagle (basswood)   FW76/3:24
Carving eggs   FW81/3-4:36
Carving fans   FW77/6:60
Carving gouges   FW80/9-10:73
Carving holding fixture   WB84/11-12:84
Carving jewelry, animals etc.   PM73/11:89
Carving knife   FW83/1-2:84
Carving large sculptures   FW81/1-2:76
Carving letters   FW79/1-2:66
Carving linenfold   FW82/9-10:98
Carving masks, Balinese   FW80/5-6:46
Carving pipe, briar   FW80/3-4:82
Carving running patterns, picture frame   FW83/9-10:46
Carving Spanish molding   FW83/9-10:48
Carving spoon   FW83/1-2:84
Carving stacking   FW76/12:22
Carving tips, wood   FW84/3-4:58
Carving tool maintenance   FW82/3-4:18
Carving tools   NS80/11-12:20
Carving tray, kitchen   WB76/3-4:38
Carving wood, bas relief pelican   WB84/11-12:82
Car winch   PM81/3:128
Casablanca stained glass light box   PM80/7:96
Case, chess   PM81/2:161
Case, chisel (walnut)   WS82/11-12:20
Case, French fitted (Coco Bolo)   PM80/12:106
Case, in wall trophy   WB78/7-8:28

Case, violin   FW83/7-8:20
Case, wooden hinged wall display (oak)   WS80/5:11
Case fitting, French   FW80/7-8:79
Casserole cradle, kitchen dowel   PM84/1:112
Cassette recorder maintenance   PM79/11:34
Cassette recorder repairs   PM72/2:110
Cassette tape repair   PM76/1:95
Cassette tape storage cabinets   WB83/9-10:36
Casters   HM78/4:40
Casting, plaster   PM75/2:64
Castle puzzle   PM77/11:136
Cat's paw nail puller   PM82/1:60
Cat, carved   PM77/1:96
Catalogs, woodworking   WB81/1-2:108
Catalytic combustors, wood stove   NS83/9:50
Catalytic combustors, wood stove   NS84/9:90
Catalytic converter, wood stove   NS81/9:35
Cat and dog, pull toy   PM79/11:122
Cat and dog house, solar   HM83/9:46
Cat bank, wooden toy   PM81/1.94
Cat bed, A-frame   WB84/3-4:120
Cat cup rack, kitchen   WB84/9-10:113
Cat doorstop   PM81/11:32
Cathedral ceiling insulation   WB79/9-10:108
Cat stepstool, child's   WB79/7-8:53
Caulk   HM72/3:46
Caulk   PM74/11:132
Caulk   PM82/9:122
Caulk, silicone rubber sealers   HM72/12:40
Caulking   HM76/4:30
Caulking   HM80/9:56
Caulking   NS83/2:40
Caulking   WB72/5-6:58
Caulking, bathtub   PM74/4:192
Caulking, brown   HM75/4:16
Caulking and glazing   WB73/9-10:58
Caulking cracks   HM83/9:72
Caulking primer   NS80/4:18
Caulks and glues   WB77/9-10:54
Cedar, refinishing exterior   HM83/9:92
Cedar and pine coffee table   WB80/3-4:76
Cedar and redwood garden bench   WS83/5-6:12
Cedar and redwood patio chair   WS83/5-6:8
Cedar and redwood picnic table, folding   WS83/5-6:4
Cedar bird feeder   WB79/5-6:69
Cedar boat plans to order, $14   HM81/11:66
Cedar canoe, stripper   FW82/7-8:72
Cedar canoe kit, strip   HM80/11:8
Cedar chest   WB78/3-4:82
Cedar chest, carved   WB72/11-12:58

Cedar chest, raised panel   WB80/5-6:82
Cedar closet, freestanding   PM77/4:134
Cedar closet, stair   WB77/5-6:25
Cedar closet, walk in   WB83/5-6:86
Cedar closet lining   PM82/4:158
Cedar deck   WB76/7-8:6
Cedar flowerpot stand   WB79/3-4:86
Cedar jewelry box, heart shaped   WB82/7-8:80
Cedar or redwood planter   WS79/5:3
Cedar paneled attic closet   WB83/3-4:98
Cedar plant pillars   WS79/5:4
Cedar sail boat   HM81/3:78
Cedar sauna, home   WB82/5-6:76
Cedar shake roof   HM79/5-6:46
Cedar shingles, indoor   HM74/10:36
Cedar shingles, room   WB82/7-8:32
Cedar shower   NS81/2:12
Cedar swing, outdoor   NS82/7-8:43
Cedar table, sawbuck dining   HM81/1:50
Cedar yard screen   PM81/8:88
Ceiling, basement   WB82/1-2:28
Ceiling, beam   HM77/11-12:26
Ceiling, beam   PM83/12:101
Ceiling, garage   HM75/3:24
Ceiling, invisible grid suspended   HM73/1:56
Ceiling, luminous   PM72/1:116
Ceiling, sagging   HM82/1:44
Ceiling, seamless tile   PM74/8:142
Ceiling, sky   HM82/12:46
Ceiling, suspended   HM75/8:40
Ceiling, suspended   HM84/12:59
Ceiling, suspended   WB72/7-8:8
Ceiling, suspended   WB77/9-10:4
Ceiling, suspended   WB81/3-4:44
Ceiling, suspended with wood   PM83/12:102
Ceiling, water leak damage repair   HM79/5-6:62
Ceiling beams, installing   HM75/3:28
Ceiling beams, plastic decorative   PM73/4:195
Ceiling fan   PM76/4:102
Ceiling fan, balancing   PM83/8:26
Ceiling fan kit   WB79/11-12:94
Ceiling fans   HM79/7-8:14
Ceiling fans   WB82/7-8:22
Ceiling fixture replacement   HM77/9:42
Ceiling insulation, cathedral   WB79/9-10:108
Ceiling lamp, Colonial   WB74/7-8:54
Ceiling lamp installation   NS81/10:61
Ceiling lamps, fluorescent   WB84/11-12:124
Ceiling panel holder   WB81/11-12:82
Ceiling panel insulation   HM82/11:40

Ceiling repair   WB73/1-2:55
Ceiling repair, sheetrock   HM77/11-12:50
Ceiling repairs   PM76/4:114
Ceilings, low basement   HM81/5-6:26
Ceilings, repairing or hiding   HM82/10:48
Ceiling tile   HM74/1:46
Ceiling tile   HM75/3:18
Ceiling tile, renewing   HM79/5-6:67
Ceiling update   HM81/11:54
Ceiling vapor barrier   NS84/9:14
Cello, pitchfork   WB76/9-10:56
Center finder   PM79/3:79
Center finder   PM83/3:108
Center finder, shop   PM80/2:130
Center finders   FW83/11-12:8
Centerpiece, plexiglas Christmas tree   PM78/12:74
Centerpiece, tree candleholder   PM78/12:74
Central air conditioner installation   HM77/5-6:14
Ceramic counter top   PM77/12:114
Ceramic floor tile   HM80/11:20
Ceramic pot lamps   HM79/7-8:52
Ceramics, drilling   HM83/10:33
Ceramics, drilling   PM81/12:112
Ceramic shower   HM84/10:48
Ceramic tile   HM80/1:73
Ceramic tile   NS80/3:47
Ceramic tile, bathroom   PM78/6:134
Ceramic tile, bathroom   PM84/4:141
Ceramic tile, designer tips   HM84/3:68
Ceramic tile, glazed   PM84/6:84
Ceramic tile, grout   HM84/2:58
Ceramic tile, pregrouted   HM74/10:38
Ceramic tile, repair   HM74/3:46
Ceramic tile, repair   PM75/5:193
Ceramic tile, self-sticking   HM74/8:48
Ceramic tile, wall   HM73/3:50
Ceramic tile and mirror tables   HM81/1:36
Ceramic tile bathroom   HM82/7-8:57
Ceramic tile cheese tray   PM75/12:95
Ceramic tile countertops   PM83/2:102
Ceramic tile floor   HM72/4:44
Ceramic tile floor, installing   HM84/4:96
Ceramic tile floors   HM84/4:85
Ceramic tile repair   NS84/11-12:18
Ceramic tile repairs   HM84/2:54
Ceramic tile wall, wood stove   PM82/4:152
Chain saw   WB81/1-2:31
Chain saw, buying   PM79/10:129
Chain saw accessories   PM78/10:128
Chain saw cart   HM83/9:102

```
Chain saw carving    FW78/3:76
Chain saw carving    PM74/7:42
Chain saw cut benches and table, outdoor    PM81/4:162
Chain saw fuel mixing    PM78/10:192
Chain saw lumber cutting    HM83/11:53
Chain saw lumbering    FW77/9:50
Chain saw lumbermaking    FW82/9-10:60
Chain saw maintenance    HM79/3:62
Chain saw maintenance    HM82/3:60
Chain saw maintenance    HM82/9:96
Chain saw maintenance    NS82/9:41
Chain saw maintenance    PM75/6:118
Chain saw maintenance    PM81/10:108
Chain saw maintenance    WB73/3-4:34
Chain saw maintenance    PM78/10:130
Chain saw mill attachment    HM84/10:140
Chain saw miter box/sawhorse    PM75/11:112
Chain saw repair    HM81/1:14
Chain saw rip chain    FW77/9:53
Chain saws    HM76/8:32
Chain saws    HM78/4:48
Chain saw safety    WB84/1-2:64
Chain saw sharpening    WB81/1-2:98
Chain saw table, woodcutting    PM79/12:112
Chain saw tips    PM82/11:70
Chain saw tips    WB76/11-12:102
Chain saw tool box    HM79/10:106
Chain saw tote bucket    HM81/10:80
Chain saw tree trimming and climbing    PM79/10:126
Chair, 1675 painted Norwegian    WB76/9-10:28
Chair, Adirondack wooden lawn settee    PM82/6:116
Chair, antique cane bottom (cherry)    WB72/9-10:42
Chair, baby high    FW80/3-4:15
Chair, barrel    WB74/5-6:32
Chair, butcher block    PM76/12:110
Chair, butcher block styling with staves    WB82/11-12:4
Chair, cane bottom corner    WB80/7-8:50
Chair, canvas and aluminum tubing    PM77/4:128
Chair, canvas (oak)    HM81/3:54
Chair, canvas rocker with blind pivot joints    WB84/3-4:89
Chair, canvas sling (redwood)    PM83/6:104
Chair, Caribbean 2X4    HM81/5-6:22
Chair, child's animal    WB79/11-12:102
Chair, child's desk    PM80/10:212
Chair, child's folding rocking    WB83/11-12:40
Chair, child's high    WB83/11-12:49
Chair, child's rocking    WB82/11-12:58
Chair, child's rocking (oak)    FW83/9-10:55
Chair, child's straight with padded seat    WB84/9-10:97
Chair, child's Tinkertoy canvas    PM80/11:128
```

Chair, Chippendale arm 1765 (mahogany) WB80/9-10:38
Chair, Chippendale arm (mahogany) WB80/5-6:97
Chair, Chippendale Georgian side (mahogany) WB82/1-2:64
Chair, Colonial PM72/1:135
Chair, contemporary cane laminate PM74/9:64
Chair, contemporary (oak) WS81/5:8
Chair, deck (redwood) HM80/4:18
Chair, deck (redwood and canvas) WS79/5:6
Chair, designer rocking HM84/10:108
Chair, dining cane back WB77/9-10:48
Chair, director's canvas WB79/9-10:62
Chair, dowel HM79/5-6:54
Chair, dowel HM80/1:12
Chair, Duncan Phyfe WB79/5-6:14
Chair, folding canvas captain's PM79/3:146
Chair, folding canvas lounge PM79/3:146
Chair, folding canvas rocking PM79/3:146
Chair, folding straight WB84/3-4:100
Chair, German arm WB74/9-10:36
Chair, giant turned rocking WD74/1 0.00
Chair, high back 17th century (walnut) WB78/3-4:32
Chair, Laplander folding $16 HM79/5-6:54
Chair, lawn WB82/5-6:90
Chair, lawn webbing (redwood) HM72/6:52
Chair, leather sling seat contemporary WB82/9-10:52
Chair, Lincoln armless cane rocking (walnut) PM84/2:60
Chair, lounge (redwood) HM83/4:124
Chair, lounge (redwood) PM77/6:120
Chair, lounge (redwood) PM84/7:94
Chair, Mediterranean outdoor furniture WB80/7-8:82
Chair, modern upholstered WB76/1-2:36
Chair, modular HM84/10:114
Chair, one piece plywood FW80/1-2:46
Chair, outdoor lounger WB77/5-6:6
Chair, park bench style (metal and oak) PM81/8:94
Chair, patio lounge WB81/7-8:34
Chair, patio (redwood and cedar) WS83/5-6:8
Chair, plywood early American furniture WB82/5-6:95
Chair, PVC pipe HM81/9:30
Chair, Queen Anne WB75/7-8:36
Chair, Queen Anne side WB81/3-4:131
Chair, raw lumber HM79/10:56
Chair, reupholstering HM79/1:82
Chair, reupholstering PM77/11:128
Chair, rocking FW83/9-10:52
Chair, simple armless deck NS84/3:73
Chair, simple fastener NS84/9:114
Chair, split bottom Lincoln PM79/2:119
Chair, tree stump WB77/5-6:6
Chair, triangular folding plywood HM79/5-6:54

Chair, two board (maple)   FW81/7-8:44
Chair, upholstered   WB76/7-8:32
Chair, upholstered wing   WB80/9-10:6
Chair, V $13   HM79/5-6:54
Chair, veneer   FW79/5-6:52
Chair, webbing replacement   HM73/8:54
Chair, whale child's   WB78/11-12:74
Chair, Windsor   WB79/1-2:66
Chair, wood lawn lounge   HM80/5-6:42
Chair, woven bottom Shaker arm   HM72/6:38
Chair and desk, adjustable   WB73/7-8:38
Chair and desk, child's classic   WB83/11-12:122
Chair and desk, fast plywood   HM78/11-12:28
Chair and desk, telephone   WB81/3-4:90
Chair and love seat willow furniture, rustic   HM84/4:122
Chair and ottoman, outdoor (redwood)   HM83/4:116
Chair and sofa, modern   FW80/5-6:51
Chair and sofa, upholstered   WB78/1-2:52
Chair and stool, Spanish   WB75/5-6:44
Chair and table, child's   WB76/11-12:100
Chair and table, plastic laminate phone   PM78/6:142
Chair bottom, woven cane   FW80/1-2:49
Chair bottom, woven split sapling   WB81/3-4:106
Chair bottoms, cane   WB80/5-6:87
Chair bottom scoop, drill press   WB76/11-12:8
Chair critique   FW79/1-2:58
Chair design   FW79/5-6:58
Chair design   FW81/11-12:56
Chair design   FW82/1-2:68
Chair design   FW82/5-6:80
Chair design and construction   FW84/5-6:72
Chair joint, dowel   FW80/3-4:68
Chair joints   FW80/11-12:54
Chair kit, Chippendale corner   PM84/8:101
Chair kit, Shaker rocking   HM82/1:42
Chair kit, Shaker rocking   PM82/11:114
Chair legs, bent cantilevered   FW84/7-8:16
Chair rail, wainscoting   PM84/6:83
Chair repair   WB83/5-6:78
Chair repair, wooden   FW80/1-2:79
Chair restoring   HM76/6:46
Chair/rocker, child's high (maple)   FW84/7-8:72
Chair rung lathe chuck   FW81/3-4:22
Chair rung tenons, band saw   FW81/3-4:18
Chairs, contemporary (oak)   WS79/3:6
Chairs, designer plywood   HM79/5-6:54
Chairs, gluing   HM83/1:52
Chairs, green Sawyer's (oak)   FW82/3-4:50
Chairs, President Jimmy Carter (hickory)   PM84/8:73
Chairs, stenciling   FW83/7-8:22

Chairs and table, card cabinet   WB82/3-4:26
Chairs and table, Colonial drop leaf   PM82/4:116
Chairs and table, Contemporary trestle   PM76/9:104
Chairs and table, hexagonal patio   PM79/5:142
Chair seat, cowhide   FW80/5-6:54
Chair seat, restoring antique rocker   WB79/3-4:18
Chair seat, reupholstering   HM83/4:18
Chair seat caning   PM77/6:122
Chair seat caning   PM80/7:107
Chair seat drilling   FW80/5-6:71
Chair seats, leather   FW84/1-2:70
Chair side bookcase   WB76/3-4:8
Chair side cabinet, four panel door (walnut)   WS82/11-12:14
Chair side table, ship hatch cover   WB79/11-12:130
Chair table, child's   WB83/7-8:50
Chair/table/hutch, Colonial   PM73/7:96
Chair/table unit with umbrella, outdoor   HM83/4:122
Chair wood   FW76/3:50
Chaise lounge chair willow furniture, rustic   HM84/4:122
Chamber candlestick   PM81/1?:116
Chandelier, candle   NS80/11-12:63
Chandelier, Christmas   WB82/11-12:79
Chandelier, classical turned   PM74/2:158
Chandelier, eleven tier   NS81/10:59
Chandelier, ready made turnings   WB72/1-2:50
Chandelier, turned   WB77/9-10:6
Charcoal grill   NS81/5-6:47
Charcoal starter   HM84/4:155
Char finishing wood   HM80/5-6:122
Charger for NiCd batteries   PM82/2:62
Chebec model sailboat plans to order, $12.50   PM83/1:6
Checkerboard puzzle   WB83/11-12:92
Checkerboard table   PM81/2:161
Checker/chessboard   FW80/5-6:16
Checkered bowl turning   FW75/12:16
Checkers, wooden   FW81/3-4:14
Checker table, butcher block   WB82/11-12:100
Check valve, hot water   NS83/3:54
Cheese board, enameled   PM79/6:120
Cheese cutting board   HM78/11-12:90
Cheese knife, wood   PM75/5:207
Cheese slicer   PM81/3:74
Cheese tray, ceramic tile   PM75/12:95
Cherry and ash etagere, modern bentwood   WB84/11-12:74
Cherry and maple bread board   WS82/3:24
Cherry bed, pencil post   FW83/7-8:54
Cherry blanket chest, country   WS84/3-4:16
Cherry blanket rack   WS84/3-4:4
Cherry cabinet, camera   HM84/2:70
Cherry chair, antique cane bottom   WB72/9-10:42

Cherry Colonial candle sconce   WS79/11:5
Cherry desk, British military campaign   PM79/2:126
Cherry desk, rolltop miniature   FW81/5-6:58
Cherry desk, slant top Shaker   WS80/11:4
Cherry desk caddy, 1750 stationery cabinet   PM84/3:74
Cherry goblet, turning   WS82/9:4
Cherry lowboy, Massachusetts 1720   WB82/3-4:100
Cherry microwave/serving cart, kitchen   WS82/9:8
Cherry mirror, antique dressing   PM83/7:52
Cherry or pine Shaker lap desk   FW76/3:48
Cherry or walnut music box   WS79/11:6
Cherry quilt rack   WS84/3-4:4
Cherry Shaker candle stand   WS80/9:6
Cherry Shaker stand, round   FW77/12:68
Cherry spindle cradle   FW81/11-12:72
Cherry spinning wheel   FW78/6:40
Cherry step stand, Shaker   WS82/1:20
Cherry table, coffee   HM81/1:57
Cherry table, living room   FW81/11-12:63
Cherry table, Shaker dining   HM84/10:104
Cherry table, Shaker side   WS80/9:4
Cherry table, six gate leg buffet   WS82/3:14
Cherry toolbox   PM81/11:128
Cherry toolbox   PM83/4:108
Cherry tool chest   PM79/11:132
Chess and backgammon game table   WB79/7-8:70
Chess/backgammon table   PM78/10:65
Chessboard   HM80/3:86
Chessboard, veneered   WB83/11-12:44
Chessboard and case   PM81/2:161
Chessboard/coffee table (walnut)   WB84/1-2:4
Chess/checkerboard   FW80/5-6:16
Chess computers   PM79/5:118
Chess/lamp table, inlaid veneer   WB84/11-12:15
Chessmen, child's   WB75/11-12:82
Chessmen drawer pulls   WB74/3-4:12
Chess set, deluxe   WB76/11-12:78
Chess table   PM81/2:159
Chess table, butcher block   WB82/11-12:100
Chess table, marquetry game   WB72/1-2:36
Chest, carved (cedar)   WB72/11-12:58
Chest, carved Japanese   WB72/3-4:62
Chest, Colonial toy   PM79/1:94
Chest, contemporary blanket (pine & redwood)   WS81/7:12
Chest, contemporary frame and panel blanket   FW84/1-2:54
Chest, country blanket (cherry)   WS84/3-4:16
Chest, five drawer bedroom   WB78/11-12:58
Chest, four drawer 1848 (walnut)   WB84/5-6:74
Chest, four drawer contemporary bachelor's   WS84/7-8:4
Chest, ice (oak)   HM82/1:30

```
Chest, joiner's tool    FW80/9-10:76
Chest, machinist's    WB74/5-6:42
Chest, mahogany tool    NS81/7-8:45
Chest, Norwegian    WB77/3-4:14
Chest, one drawer Shaker linen (pine)    HM72/8:38
Chest, one drawer Shaker storage    HM72/3:52
Chest, painted 1850 Norwegian    WB78/11-12:20
Chest, pirate treasure    WB80/11-12:30
Chest, post and panel    FW80/7-8:53
Chest, raised panel (cedar)    WB80/5-6:82
Chest, seven drawer    WB81/7-8:22
Chest, Shaker blanket (pine)    FW81/3-4:60
Chest, silverware    HM83/7-8:94
Chest, silverware    WB84/1-2:48
Chest, simple toy    WB77/5-6:4
Chest, six drawer contemporary (pine)    WS81/9:16
Chest, small Queen Anne highboy    FW83/9-10:32
Chest, small Spanish    WB78/9-10:3
Chest, telephone (walnut)    FW76/3:56
Chest, tool (cherry)    PM79/11:132
Chest, toy    NS81/3:59
Chest, toy    WS83/9-10:4
Chest, trinket    PM77/11:140
Chest, wagon seat    WB75/3-4:60
Chest, wine    WB76/3-4:54
Chest, wooden hinged sweater (maple plywood)    WS80/5:8
Chest, wood molding    WB77/9-10:84
Chest/bed/desk, child's loft (plywood)    FW84/5-6:52
Chest bench, storage    WB82/11-12:22
Chest/box, plywood storage    PM74/2:146
Chest (cedar)    WB78/3-4:82
Chest drawer, family room    PM79/10:130
Chest lid stop    FW81/11-12:20
Chest lock    FW84/11-12:54
Chest of drawers    FW82/11-12:78
Chest of drawers, bedroom    PM78/10:136
Chest of drawers, Boston bombe (mahogany)    FW84/3-4:52
Chest of drawers, boy's    WB83/5-6:50
Chest of drawers, closet    HM79/2:34
Chest of drawers, French provincial    WB82/7-8:70
Chest of drawers, Hepplewhite (mahogany)    FW84/9-10:42
Chest of drawers, highboy (curly maple)    WB73/1-2:36
Chest of drawers, inlaid 1740 Norwegian    WB80/9-10:61
Chest of drawers, Shaker    HM72/2:58
Chest of drawers (walnut)    WB84/7-8:57
Chests, alphabet pirate trunk Pa. Dutch    PM78/1:100
Chests, tall    FW77/12:38
Chest wall mirror, contemporary    WS84/7-8:20
Cheval mirror, full length arched (oak)    WS83/11-12:4
Chick, hatching pull toy    PM74/11:108
```

Chicken and egg pull toy   WB83/3-4:70
Chicken wire shop light protector   WB81/11-12:90
Child's bed   WB82/9-10:48
Child's bed, race car   WB79/7-8:5
Child's bed, Shaker   WB83/9-10:66
Child's bed, twin   HM73/3:38
Child's bed and desk tree house, indoor   WB72/3-4:32
Child's bed and room divider   HM72/12:36
Child's bed headboard, bookcase   PM81/9:104
Child's bedroom   HM83/12:42
Child's beds, bunk   WB73/9-10:26
Child's beds, intermediate   WB79/3-4:114
Child's bus stop   WB78/3-4:50
Child's car seat/sleigh   PM79/12:64
Child's cat stepstool   WB79/7-8:53
Child's chair, animal   WB79/11-12:102
Child's chair, straight with padded seat   WB84/9-10:97
Child's chair, Tinkertoy canvas   PM80/11:128
Child's chair and desk, adjustable   WB73/7-8:38
Child's chair table   WB83/7-8:50
Child's chessmen   WB75/11-12:82
Child's closet   HM81/11:60
Child's coat rack   PM78/10:242
Child's coat rack   PM81/9:199
Child's desk   NS81/3:58
Child's desk, dog   PM73/5:94
Child's desk, drawing   PM80/9:98
Child's desk, game chest/lap   WB84/5-6:72
Child's desk, rolltop   PM80/3:124
Child's desk, wall hung   PM75/9:78
Child's desk and chair, classic   WB83/11-12:122
Child's desk chair   PM80/10:212
Child's desk/drawing table   PM83/6:80
Child's desk/wall unit   PM80/6:118
Child's easel, two way   WB77/11-12:124
Child's easel/display stand   HM82/11:63
Child's giraffe clothes tree   PM75/11:141
Child's high chair   WB83/11-12:49
Child's lemonade stand   PM79/8:86
Child's paddle boat   WB77/3-4:58
Child's play area, indoor   WB81/9-10:62
Child's play center, $250   HM79/10:60
Child's plywood desk   WB75/5-6:32
Child's pool deck   HM83/5-6:90
Child's rocking chair   WB82/11-12:58
Child's rocking chair, folding   WB83/11-12:40
Child's rocking chair (oak)   FW83/9-10:55
Child's rocking horse, toddler's   WB78/1-2:97
Child's rocking horse, toddler's   WB81/11-12:98
Child's rocking horse, toddler's chair   WB79/5-6:20

47

Child's room storage, plastic pan storage   HM72/4:37
Child's sandbox   HM80/5-6:32
Child's sleigh, Russian troika   WB83/1-2:20
Child's snow sled, wood   WB76/1-2:81
Child's step stool   WS84/9-10:12
Child's stool   NS81/3:59
Child's stool, two legs   WB77/3-4:34
Child's stroller   WB77/11-12:52
Child's table, Lincoln's   HM83/11:38
Child's table, tough   HM79/10:21
Child's table and chair   WB76/11-12:100
Child's table and stools, lion   PM74/2:144
Child's table and stools, round   WB83/9-10:45
Child's teaching box, counting   PM73/11:175
Child's toothbrush holder   WB83/1-2:86
Child's toy box, 18 wheeler   WB83/11-12:94
Child's toy soldier lamp   WB77/11-12:16
Child's treehouse   PM80/8:92
Child's workbench   PM80/11:115
Child's workbench, adjustable   WB70/J-4.PN
Child carrier back pack   WB75/5-6:53
Children, woodworking for   HM83/12:62
Chimes, cut glass bottle   PM72/12:104
Chimes, door   PM76/5:107
Chimney, cleaning   HM84/9:78
Chimney, cleaning   PM80/1:110
Chimney, installing new flue   PM84/10:170
Chimney, rain cap   HM80/4:40
Chimney, solar thermal   NS80/7-8:25
Chimney, wood stove   NS80/2:98
Chimney brick repair   NS84/10:22
Chimney brush   HM74/4:26
Chimney care   NS84/10:80
Chimney cleaner   PM83/2:55
Chimney cleaning   HM80/1:94
Chimney cleaning   NS81/9:18
Chimney cleaning   WB81/5-6:92
Chimney creosote   NS81/9:40
Chimney flashing repair   HM83/9:87
Chimney leaks   HM75/4:32
Chimney repair   HM84/9:68
Chimneys, backdrafting   NS84/11-12:32
Chimneys, installing metal prefab   PM84/9:30
Chimneys, solar   NS84/7-8:10
China cabinet   WB77/1-2:66
China cabinet, Victorian curved glass (oak)   WB84/9-10:56
China repair   HM82/11:18
Chinese candelabra   FW80/11-12:60
Chinese Chippendale tea cart   WB79/5-6:52
Chinese jewelry, wood   WB72/11-12:44

Chinese planter, concrete   WB78/3-4:58
Chip carving   FW79/11-12:80
Chippendale armchair 1765 (mahogany)   WB80/9-10:38
Chippendale armchair (mahogany)   WB80/5-6:97
Chippendale carved shells   FW79/3-4:76
Chippendale chair, corner   PM84/8:101
Chippendale Chinese tea cart   WB79/5-6:52
Chippendale Georgian side chair (mahogany)   WB82/1-2:64
Chippendale mirror, wall (mahogany)   PM83/7:52
Chippendale molding, reproductions   PM84/8:122
Chippendale room furnishings   PM84/8:98
Chippendale sofa, upholstered (walnut)   FW84/11-12:60
Chippendale tilt top table   WB81/5-6:20
Chippendale tilt top table (mahogany)   PM84/8:98
Chisel, pare   FW81/3-4:71
Chisel case   WB75/1-2:41
Chisel case (walnut)   WS82/11-12:20
Chisel handle cap   WB81/9-10:95
Chisel holder   PM79/3:70
Chisel making   FW78/6:17
Chisel protector   PM84/3:44
Chisel rack, turning   WB80/9-10:107
Chisel routing jig   PM77/8:110
Chisels   HM73/9:48
Chisels, cold   WB73/7-8:8
Chisels, lathe   PM76/4:202
Chisels, making six wood lathe   PM82/2:106
Chisels, sharpening   FW84/9-10:47
Chisels, sharpening   PM75/2:114
Chisels, small turning   PM78/2:122
Chisels, turning   FW79/9-10:70
Chisels, turning   WB75/5-6:61
Chisels, wood   HM83/4:10
Chisels, wood   PM78/1:93
Chisels, wood tips   PM84/5:97
Chisels and gouges   WB73/9-10:10
Chisels and plane irons, sharpening   FW81/7-8:67
Chisel sharpening   FW78/9:70
Chisel sharpening techniques   WS82/3:8
Chisel tool box, lathe   WB82/3-4:70
Chisel turning tool sharpening   WS82/5:22
Chord harp kit   PM84/2:104
Christmas angel, copper tubing wall hanging   PM80/12:98
Christmas bentwood rocker tree decoration   PM79/12:82
Christmas boot candy cane holder   PM79/12:82
Christmas candle display, stained glass   WB82/11-12:106
Christmas candle holder, dove and partridge   HM81/12:22
Christmas candle lantern, tin can   PM72/12:75
Christmas candlestick, chamber   PM81/12:116
Christmas card holder, Swedish cradle   PM81/12:114

Christmas cards, photo   PM74/10:80
Christmas cards, printing   PM77/11:110
Christmas centerpiece, candle flowerpot   PM79/12:82
Christmas chandelier   WB82/11-12:79
Christmas cookie cutters, tin can   WB83/11-12:90
Christmas Creche, musical rotating Nativity   PM73/12:157
Christmas decorations   PM81/12:114
Christmas decorations, eleven   PM79/12:82
Christmas decorations, fourteen   PM78/12:74
Christmas decorations, fourteen   PM80/12:98
Christmas decorations, inexpensive   PM72/12:75
Christmas decorations, window Santa Claus   PM78/12:74
Christmas decorations, wreath   PM78/12:74
Christmas display, outdoor greeting card   PM73/11:182
Christmas doorstop, mouse   PM80/12:98
Christmas fireplace, fake   PM75/11:148
Christmas garland, pine cone   PM72/12:75
Christmas gifts   HM78/11-12:52
Christmas gifts, mailing   PM78/11:16
Christmas gifts, nineteen   PM77/11:131
Christmas gifts, seven   PM75/12:94
Christmas gifts, shop made   HM81/11:40
Christmas gifts, twelve   PM80/11:128
Christmas gifts to make, twelve   PM79/11:122
Christmas horse tree decoration   PM79/12:82
Christmas lighting, outdoor   PM81/12:30
Christmas lights, traveling outdoor   PM75/11:172
Christmas mobile, snowball   WB73/11-12:52
Christmas mobile, stained glass   PM72/12:75
Christmas nativity picture, laminated 3D   WB84/9-10:4
Christmas rainbow mobile   PM79/12:82
Christmas reindeer   HM81/12:22
Christmas Santa, waving   PM72/11:109
Christmas Santa display, animated   WB74/11-12:34
Christmas Santa door decoration   PM79/12:82
Christmas sleigh, child's Russian troika   WB83/1-2:20
Christmas sleigh, horse   WB77/11-12:56
Christmas star shaped candles   PM81/10:52
Christmas Swedish star   HM81/12:22
Christmas table decorations, reindeer   PM79/12:82
Christmas toys, six   PM75/11:118
Christmas tree, tin can   PM73/12:72
Christmas tree, wall (wooden)   WS79/11:12
Christmas tree, wooden wall coasters   PM81/12:114
Christmas tree bar   PM79/11:122
Christmas tree centerpiece, plexiglas   PM78/12:74
Christmas tree decorations   PM76/12:114
Christmas tree decorations   PM77/12:122
Christmas tree decorations, Mexican style   PM81/12:116
Christmas tree donkey and rider   PM80/12:98

Christmas tree ornament, aluminum can   PM72/12:75
Christmas tree ornament, doves   PM80/12:98
Christmas tree ornament, high wheel bicycle   PM80/12:98
Christmas tree ornament, rocking chair   PM78/12:74
Christmas tree ornament, stained glass   PM80/12:98
Christmas tree ornaments, angel and tree   PM80/12:98
Christmas tree ornaments, cookie cutter   PM78/12:74
Christmas tree ornaments, gingerbread   PM79/12:82
Christmas tree ornaments, hot air balloon   PM78/12:74
Christmas tree ornaments, poured resin   PM78/12:74
Christmas tree ornaments, tin   PM81/12:116
Christmas tree ornaments, toy tops   PM78/12:74
Christmas tree ornaments, veneer   PM78/12:74
Christmas tree ornaments, wooden   WS79/11:10
Christmas tree stand, live   NS82/11-12:42
Christmas tree train decoration   PM79/12:82
Christmas tree wall hanging, tinsel   PM79/12:82
Christmas village mantel decorations   PM81/12:114
Christmas wrapping paper center   HM83/11:70
Christmas wreaths   PM72/12:75
Christmas xylophone toy, Noel   PM79/11:122
Cider press   PM78/9:120
Circle, drawing large   PM79/7:85
Circle, sanding   WS80/9:12
Circle cutter   PM76/1:104
Circle cutter, table saw   PM81/7:130
Circle cutting   FW77/3:12
Circle cutting, bandsaw   FW79/5-6:16
Circle cutting, band saw   FW81/7-8:16
Circle cutting, saber saw   PM81/2:150
Circle cutting guide, scroll saw   PM83/2:98
Circle cutting jig   PM80/11:182
Circle cutting jig, radial arm saw   PM81/5:52
Circle cutting jig, saber saw   PM81/1:122
Circle guide, router   FW82/11-12:22
Circle jig, router   WB79/7-8:57
Circles, cutting perfect   PM78/3:129
Circle sander   PM81/12:144
Circuit board processing   PM79/3:14
Circuit checker, auto   PM77/3:184
Circular saw, portable   HM74/1:38
Circular saw bench for portable   PM79/11:136
Circular saw blade, carbide tipped   HM84/7-8:79
Circular saw crosscut platform   PM83/11:107
Circular saw cutting jig   PM84/6:82
Circular saw guides, homemade   HM80/5-6:50
Circular saw lumber cutting tips   NS84/10:20
Circular saw maintenance   FW78/3:80
Circular saw mount   PM79/11:140
Circular saw paneling cutting jigs   PM83/3:65

Circular saw radial arm saw   FW84/5-6:12
Circular saw techniques   HM82/12:20
Circular saw techniques   HM83/1:12
Circular saw tips   PM75/9:96
Circular saw tips   PM80/11:126
Circular stairway   FW79/5-6:76
Circus decorations, basement   PM75/4:128
Circus train and animals, pull toy   PM72/12:108
Circus wagon toy box   PM75/11:120
Circus wagon toy box   WB80/11-12:64
Circus wagon toy chest   HM79/1:21
Cistern, above ground   HM82/9:60
Cistern, decorative well   WB79/3-4:56
Cistern, rain   WB77/7-8:48
Cistern rain water   NS80/4:34
Clamp, bench   FW77/12:17
Clamp, clothespin   FW79/7-8:17
Clamp, deep throat   FW80/7-8:12
Clamp, double bar   WB79/1-2:30
Clamp, earring miniature   WB81/11-12:93
Clamp, extended clothespin   PM81/2:68
Clamp, fast setting homemade bench   FW79/1-2:14
Clamp, gluing   PM79/8:136
Clamp, improved C   PM84/4:32
Clamp, inexpensive   FW80/11-12:23
Clamp, multicorner miter   WB79/3-4:113
Clamp, picture frame   FW78/10:16
Clamp, picture frame   FW80/1-2:16
Clamp, picture frame   FW80/9-10:22
Clamp, picture frame   FW80/5-6:18
Clamp, picture frame   HM81/7-8:92
Clamp, simple channel iron   PM84/2:154
Clamp, Spanish luthier's guitar top   FW80/1-2:18
Clamp, toolmaker's   FW79/7-8:13
Clamp, V-block   PM82/8:89
Clamp, wood bench   WB82/3-4:72
Clamping boxes   FW78/9:14
Clamping dogs   FW80/9-10:68
Clamping tips   PM79/6:124
Clamping wide boards   FW80/7-8:12
Clamps   NS80/9:16
Clamps   WB74/1-2:10
Clamps   WB78/11-12:30
Clamps   WB84/1-2:30
Clamps, bar   PM72/11:165
Clamps, edge gluing bar   WB84/9-10:32
Clamps, glue   HM80/9:90
Clamps, light duty bar   WB84/11-12:44
Clamps, shop made   WB77/1-2:71
Clamps, shop tips   PM80/12:102

```
Clamps, table saw hold down    WS79/1:6
Clamps, wooden    FW77/3:10
Clamps, wooden    FW77/9:64
Clamps, wooden    WB78/5-6:68
Clamps, wooden bar    FW82/1-2:66
Clamps, wooden bar    FW83/3-4:14
Clamps, wooden bar    WS79/9:3
Clamp spur dogs, angle iron miter    FW83/3-4:22
Clamps rack    PM78/4:130
Clamp storage    FW78/3:18
Clamp storage rack, shop    PM83/12:158
Clamp tips, pipe    FW84/3-4:43
Cleaner, parts    PM76/1:91
Cleaning, kitchen and bath    HM84/5-6:117
Cleaning, metal    WB76/7-8:14
Cleaning aluminum siding    HM73/4-5:59
Cleaning everything    HM82/3:90
Cleaning tips    HM84/7-8:115
Cleaning water damage    HM83/3:88
Cleaving wood    FW78/9:64
Cloche, caterpillar    PM83/3:105
Cloche, garden plant cover    PM78/3:155
Clock, backward    WB82/11-12:71
Clock, banjo wall    WB72/7-8:34
Clock, butcher block    HM78/11-12:86
Clock, carved    WB74/1-2:48
Clock, ceramic tile    WB82/11-12:63
Clock, clown    WB82/11-12:97
Clock, Colonial wall    PM72/11:118
Clock, cutting board    PM77/11:188
Clock, desk/wall (walnut and maple)    WS80/7:4
Clock, garden    WB82/11-12:66
Clock, handsaw    PM78/11:196
Clock, mantel    WB82/1-2:87
Clock, mantel    WS82/11-12:8
Clock, mantel wood and crystal (walnut)    HM84/11:70
Clock, modern pendulum (walnut)    HM83/1:82
Clock, oil can    WB82/11-12:68
Clock, pendulum mantle    NS80/11-12:62
Clock, Regulator    WS84/11-12:12
Clock, round wall    WS83/11-12:10
Clock, schoolhouse    HM80/10:64
Clock, schoolhouse (oak)    PM81/6:145
Clock, schoolhouse wall (oak)    WS82/5:4
Clock, ship dial    WB82/11-12:70
Clock, tall case 18th century    FW81/1-2:67
Clock, wall octagonal frame    WS80/11:8
Clock, wood plaque    WB82/11-12:96
Clock and spool house    WB73/9-10:24
Clock case, scrap wood    WB72/11-12:18
```

Clock coffee table, slab   WB84/3-4:74
Clock finishing   FW77/6:15
Clock gears, wooden   WB78/7-8:70
Clock kit, digital grandfather   WB82/5-6:93
Clock kit, grandfather   PM73/8:162
Clock kit, grandfather   WB74/5-6:28
Clock kit, grandfather   WB76/11-12:56
Clock kits   HM78/2:17
Clock kits   HM80/5-6:40
Clock kits   PM81/2:134
Clock kits   WB79/9-10:4
Clock kits, buying   HM79/2:78
Clock kits, grandfather   HM75/4:44
Clock kits, parts, and plans   WB80/1-2:69
Clock kits, six   PM75/12:98
Clock moldings, radial arm saw   FW82/9-10:82
Clock overhaul, antique   HM81/2:60
Clocks, maintenance   HM79/1:44
Clocks, slab   WB83/5-6:74
Clocks, two Lincoln mantels   PM81/2:130
Clock/thermometer, desk   WS84/5-6:18
Clockworks, wooden   FW78/3:44
Clogs and leaks, plumbing repair   PM73/2:156
Closet   HM75/11:36
Closet, building   HM77/9:34
Closet, cedar paneled attic   WB83/3-4:98
Closet, cedar walk-in   WB83/5-6:86
Closet, child's   HM81/11:60
Closet, double corner   HM73/6:62
Closet, enlarging   WB77/1-2:78
Closet, entry   WB74/7-8:38
Closet, freestanding (cedar)   PM77/4:134
Closet, lining with cedar   PM82/4:158
Closet, peninsular   PM72/4:130
Closet, sewing   HM72/2:34
Closet, sewing   HM73/2:36
Closet, stair   WB80/5-6:67
Closet, stair (cedar)   WB77/5-6:25
Closet, winter clothes   HM73/2:52
Closet and bunk beds   HM73/12:36
Closet and bunk beds   HM74/8:34
Closet chest of drawers   HM79/2:34
Closet compartments   PM76/4:133
Closet dining room   HM81/2:24
Closet doors, folding   HM74/4:46
Closet garden workshop   HM81/3:67
Closet office   HM79/2:34
Closet pantry   HM79/2:34
Closet planning   HM77/7-8:39
Closet remodeling   HM79/2:34

Closet rods   HM81/11:92
Closets   WB79/9-10:66
Closet storage shelves   PM72/4:129
Closet workshop, mobile   HM83/12:20
Clothes, handyman   HM77/11-12:52
Clothes hamper   PM84/4:102
Clothes hangers, kids'   PM77/11:144
Clothesline organizer   HM83/7-8:115
Clothes rack, child's   PM81/11:30
Clothes tree   PM77/11:142
Clothes tree, child's giraffe   PM75/11:141
Cloverleaf table, drop leaf   WB83/1-2:110
Cloverleaf top x-leg table (pine)   WB80/11-12:124
Clown bank, wooden toy   PM81/1:94
Clown clock   WB82/11-12:97
Clown pull toy, jumping   PM80/11:130
Clown puppet toy   PM81/11:32
Coal, buying and storing   NS80/9:50
Coal and firewood mixing   NS80/9:44
Coal bin, back yard   PM81/10:190
Coal/wood bin   NS80/9:53
Coaster Christmas tree   PM81/12:116
Coaster set, enameled   PM79/6:120
Coat hangers, (plywood)   PM79/11:122
Coatings, solar panels   NS83/4:68
Coat rack, bentwood   NS83/3:24
Coat rack, child's   PM78/10:242
Coat rack, child's   PM81/9:199
Coat rack, Colonial   PM79/12:108
Coat rack, floor   WB76/9-10:44
Coat rack, giraffe   WB78/11-12:68
Coat rack, initialed   WB82/1-2:116
Coat rack, Shaker-peg Colonial   WS79/3:3
Coat rack, wall   WB76/9-10:44
Coat rack and hall mirror   HM80/1:80
Coat rack and mirror, antique wall (oak)   WS83/3-4:18
Coat rack/hat shelf, plexiglas   PM75/5:72
Coat rack hooks, forged   PM78/6:130
Coat rack (mahogany)   HM81/11:97
Coat rack/mirror, hallway   PM84/7:132
Coat racks, heart   HM82/2:32
Coat tree   WB81/3-4:88
Cobbler's bench coffee table   WB80/5-6:112
Cobbler's bench lamp, table   PM73/5:92
Cockleshell, carving   FW78/9:74
Cocobolo case, French fitted   PM80/12:106
Cocobolo flute, six hole   FW84/1-2:64
Coffee cup tree   WB79/9-10:104
Coffee/dining table, Scandinavian   PM81/5:122
Coffee/dining table, two height   WB79/3-4:4

Coffee/game table   HM80/1:70
Coffee grinder   WS84/9-10:16
Coffee maker repair   HM79/7-8:26
Coffee mill   PM78/11:196
Coffee mill, kitchen   HM82/7-8:72
Coffee mill kit   HM77/2:46
Coffee mill kit   PM75/12:142
Coffee percolator, repair   PM76/6:102
Coffee table   HM76/10:34
Coffee table, butcher block   PM76/12:110
Coffee table, cabinet   WB77/11-12:48
Coffee table, clear plastic   HM77/7-8:36
Coffee table, cobbler's bench   WB80/5-6:112
Coffee table, contemporary cube   PM82/2:106
Coffee table, contemporary (oak/glass)   PM83/12:148
Coffee table, contemporary three drawer   WS82/1:14
Coffee table, cube   PM81/1:96
Coffee table, drum   PM73/2:164
Coffee table, glass top contemporary   WB79/11-12:153
Coffee table, glass top (walnut)   HM81/1:56
Coffee table, glass top wrought iron   HM76/4:44
Coffee table, grid (pine)   NS80/5-6:43
Coffee table, kerfed oval   WB82/7-8:56
Coffee table, low cost massive   HM78/7-8:74
Coffee table, mirror top   HM81/11:74
Coffee table, modern (oak and smoked glass)   WS79/1:7
Coffee table, Parson's butcher block   WB83/5-6:72
Coffee table, plank top   WB75/7-8:52
Coffee table, plexiglas   PM75/5:72
Coffee table, plywood modern   HM80/12:15
Coffee table, round with mail order parts   HM78/2:52
Coffee table, rustic willow furniture   HM84/4:122
Coffee table, scrap wood   WB77/5-6:66
Coffee table, simple block strips (oak)   PM80/11:130
Coffee table, slab with clock   WB84/3-4:74
Coffee table, tile top   WB79/9-10:24
Coffee table, tray (mahogany)   FW84/1-2:72
Coffee table, trestle   WB72/3-4:70
Coffee table, veneer   FW78/6:70
Coffee table, wagon seat   WB72/9-10:44
Coffee table, wood strips   PM80/9:103
Coffee table, woven top   WB77/11-12:96
Coffee table and terrarium, contemporary   WB81/1-2:4
Coffee table (cherry)   HM81/1:57
Coffee table/chessboard (walnut)   WB84/1-2:4
Coffee table modules   HM80/2:28
Coffee table (oak)   WS83/1-2:20
Coffee table (pine and cedar)   WB80/3-4:76
Coffee table/slide viewer, lighted   PM75/9:102
Coin counter   WB77/3-4:77

Coin sorter   WS81/7:9
Coin sorter tray   WS80/7:6
Cold, surviving it   PM81/12:164
Cold cellar food storage, basement   PM82/8:94
Cold frame, garden   NS83/1:76
Cold frame, garden   PM78/3:152
Cold frame, roll around   WB80/3-4:46
Cold frame and greenhouse, lean-to   PM82/3:128
Cold frame and hot bed   HM78/2:26
Cold frames, garden   PM76/3:92
Cold frame/solar dryer   PM84/3:112
Cold water survival   PM78/8:76
Colimba thumb piano, Sansa   WB74/3-4:40
Colonial bathroom magazine/tissue rack   WB84/1-2:79
Colonial bench, Lincoln (maple and pine)   PM80/2:126
Colonial blanket chest   HM82/7-8:24
Colonial book stand   PM72/11:121
Colonial cabinet, dry sink TV   WB84/3-4:122
Colonial cabinet home safe   PM79/1:84
Colonial candle sconce (cherry)   WS79/11:5
Colonial candlestand   PM80/11:128
Colonial chair   PM72/1:135
Colonial coat rack   PM79/12:108
Colonial coat rack, Shaker-peg   WS79/3:3
Colonial corner cabinet (pine)   HM82/2:30
Colonial cradle   PM80/5:128
Colonial cradle   WB81/11-12:122
Colonial cradle (pine)   HM84/12:64
Colonial cradle (pine)   PM83/12:130
Colonial cupboard   PM75/6:102
Colonial desk, small corner   WB84/11-12:26
Colonial desk, trestle (pine)   PM74/10:77
Colonial desk/hutch   WB82/9-10:104
Colonial desk plans to order, $4.95   HM83/2:86
Colonial doughbox lamp table/magazine rack   WB84/3-4:4
Colonial drop leaf table and chairs, plywood   PM82/4:116
Colonial dry sink   PM72/2:138
Colonial dry sink   WB74/9-10:66
Colonial dry sink   WB80/9-10:74
Colonial dry sink   WS81/11:12
Colonial entry, stock moldings   HM82/1:56
Colonial fireplace mantel, molding   WB82/1-2:76
Colonial firewood box   PM77/10:125
Colonial footstool   PM72/7:130
Colonial footstool (walnut)   PM75/1:110
Colonial hall stand and arched mirror   WB82/1-2:92
Colonial hutch/table/chair   PM73/7:96
Colonial kitchen   NS82/10:86
Colonial lamp, ceiling   WB74/7-8:54
Colonial lap desk, wooden hinged (pine)   WS80/5:6

Colonial letter holder   PM79/6:118
Colonial milk paint   FW79/3-4:67
Colonial mirror   PM78/12:102
Colonial pie safe, pierced tin panels   PM82/8:90
Colonial serving cart   WB73/7-8:36
Colonial settle storage bench   WB84/9-10:116
Colonial sewing table, Sheraton   WB74/3-4:36
Colonial Shaker trestle table (pine)   WS79/1:3
Colonial shaving console   PM72/1:140
Colonial shelf, hanging   WB83/5-6:63
Colonial shelf, whatnot   PM73/5:96
Colonial spice cabinet   WB75/11-12:64
Colonial spoon rack   WB79/1-2:88
Colonial Stool/bench   PM80/11:128
Colonial storage chest   PM77/11:109
Colonial table, drop leaf (mahogany)   PM82/6:132
Colonial table, end   WB74/7-8:37
Colonial table, tilt top reeded pedestal   WB84/3-4:36
Colonial table, trestle $75   HM79/2:36
Colonial tavern table, elliptical top   WB82/1-2.22
Colonial towel rack   PM78/3:128
Colonial toy chest   PM79/1:94
Colonial wall hutch   WS81/11:16
Colonial wall shelf   PM72/3:138
Colonial wall shelf with drawer   WB84/11-12:118
Colonial washstand, harp rack   WB82/3-4:67
Coloring with penetrating oils   FW81/3-4:65
Color selection, house exterior   HM82/4:70
Columns, coopered   FW81/5-6:78
Columns, fluted   FW80/11-12:22
Columns and rails, wrought iron   HM77/7-8:60
Combination machines, sources   FW80/9-10:84
Commode, 18th century green and gold   WB79/9-10:54
Compactor, homebuilt   PM72/11:162
Compass, beam   FW79/3-4:16
Compass, large wooden   WS80/1:3
Compass/trammel, oval scribing   PM82/12:94
Compost bin   HM82/9:54
Compost box   PM77/3:98
Composting toilets   HM82/9:48
Compost sifter   PM81/3:155
Compote and candlestick, turned   WB77/9-10:24
Compressor, air   PM72/6:140
Computer, workshop   FW83/5-6:96
Computer cabinet   NS82/9:51
Computer cabinet, rolltop contemporary (oak)   PM84/2:100
Computer care and repair   PM82/4:112
Computer controlled house   NS84/11-12:56
Computer controllers   HM82/2:86
Computer desk   HM83/2:34

Computer desk   HM84/1:63
Computer desk, office   PM81/5:114
Computerized homes   NS82/9:31
Computer office   PM81/4:135
Computer printer stand   HM83/2:36
Computer program, cooling   NS84/7-8:60
Computer program, firewood switch   NS84/10:28
Computer program, framing lumber   NS84/9:30
Computer program, fuel switching   NS82/9:39
Computer program, stairs design   NS84/11-12:22
Computer programs, free by phone   NS84/9:119
Computers, buying   HM84/1:27
Computers, home work   NS83/9:74
Computer sketch pad kit   PM80/2:88
Computer word processor   PM80/7:78
Computer workstation   PM83/8:92
Concrete   WB77/9-10:88
Concrete   WB80/3-4:56
Concrete, dry pack   WB73/7-8:28
Concrete, patching   NS82/9:58
Concrete, pouring   HM78/7-8:80
Concrete, pouring   PM72/6:152
Concrete and brick steps   PM75/8:78
Concrete balusters, peeling paint   HM84/9:70
Concrete bench, park   PM84/3:84
Concrete bench and temple lantern   WB78/3-4:56
Concrete block and wood picnic table   PM73/6:76
Concrete block laying   HM83/3:36
Concrete block making mold   NS81/5-6:41
Concrete blocks, insulating   WB77/7-8:4
Concrete blocks, laying with Surewall   HM80/3:52
Concrete blocks and door desk   WB77/9-10:58
Concrete block wall covering   WB80/1-2:54
Concrete crack repair   PM79/4:151
Concrete crack repair   WB80/11-12:82
Concrete deicers   WB84/3-4:72
Concrete driveway, <$1000   HM83/3:34
Concrete driveway repair   HM80/4:92
Concrete fence, privacy   HM78/4:78
Concrete floors and slabs   PM73/8:92
Concrete forms and pouring   HM79/11:92
Concrete fountain pool   HM78/4:78
Concrete pads, fix sinking   HM84/9:94
Concrete painting   HM80/3:40
Concrete painting   PM78/6:144
Concrete patio   WB81/3-4:34
Concrete planter, Chinese   WB78/3-4:58
Concrete problems   HM81/3:90
Concrete repair   HM72/6:46
Concrete repair   HM73/4-5:52

59

Concrete repair   HM83/9:84
Concrete repair   PM83/6:112
Concrete repairs   HM81/9:108
Concrete repairs   WB79/3-4:35
Concrete slab, insulating   NS84/11-12:12
Concrete slab, sinking   HM73/4-5:28
Concrete stepping stones   WB81/3-4:70
Concrete step repair   HM80/3:56
Concrete steps   HM72/8:42
Concrete steps   WB76/3-4:32
Concrete steps, worn   HM73/4-5:26
Concrete walk   WB79/5-6:72
Concrete walk and driveway repair   HM75/3:24
Condensation cures   NS84/4:74
Conductor's stepstool   WB79/11-12:133
Conduit, electrical   HM80/11:80
Conduit mast, antenna or birdhouse   PM72/12:186
Cones, staved   FW78/3:75
Console and mirror, early American   WB83/1-2:37
Console table, Spanish   WB/4/11-12:44
Construction contract   NS84/9:86
Contemporary bar   PM74/1:178
Contemporary basement, remodeling   PM84/3:122
Contemporary bed, four poster   PM79/9:110
Contemporary bed, platform   WB84/5-6:29
Contemporary bed, platform TV (maple)   PM84/5:92
Contemporary blanket chest, frame and panel   FW84/1-2:54
Contemporary bookcase, arched window   HM84/9:32
Contemporary cabinet, rolltop computer (oak)   PM84/2:100
Contemporary cabinet, wall   HM84/2:70
Contemporary cabinets, drawer and door   PM83/9:80
Contemporary cane cabinet and hutch (oak)   WS82/7:18
Contemporary chair, cane laminate   PM74/9:64
Contemporary chair, leather sling seat   WB82/9-10:52
Contemporary chair (oak)   WS81/5:8
Contemporary chairs (oak)   WS79/3:6
Contemporary chest, blanket (pine & redwood)   WS81/7:12
Contemporary chest, four drawer bachelor's   WS84/7-8:4
Contemporary coffee table, cube   PM82/2:106
Contemporary coffee table and terrarium   WB81/1-2:4
Contemporary desk, plywood   WB78/11-12:86
Contemporary desk/bookcase, wall hung (oak)   HM84/9:30
Contemporary desk/center hobby   HM84/2:70
Contemporary entertainment wall unit   PM84/4:136
Contemporary gate leg table (oak)   FW76/6:42
Contemporary gun cabinet (oak)   WB81/9-10:56
Contemporary hammock stand   HM83/5-6:66
Contemporary headboard   WS84/7-8:10
Contemporary hutch   PM74/1:67
Contemporary hutch (maple)   WS81/1:4

Contemporary kitchen island   HM84/7-8:25
Contemporary lamps, hanging (plexiglas)   PM80/1:112
Contemporary letter holder, plexiglas   PM79/6:118
Contemporary light fixture (teak)   PM82/4:166
Contemporary magazine rack   PM79/12:108
Contemporary mirror   PM80/11:130
Contemporary mirror, half round molding   PM78/12:102
Contemporary nightstand   WS84/7-8:16
Contemporary oak and smoked glass tables   WS79/1:7
Contemporary planter, tree   WB81/9-10:78
Contemporary playhouse   WB84/5-6:42
Contemporary record cabinet frame and panel   FW84/1-2:54
Contemporary shelf units (oak)   WB82/9-10:96
Contemporary six drawer chest (pine)   WS81/9:16
Contemporary spice rack   PM78/11:198
Contemporary spice shelf, mirror   WB81/5-6:96
Contemporary stereo cabinet, (oak)   PM83/9:84
Contemporary table, aquarium end   WB81/5-6:82
Contemporary table, coffee (oak/glass)   PM83/12:148
Contemporary table, end   WB81/3-4:66
Contemporary table, glass top   WB79/11-12:153
Contemporary table, laminated legs   WB84/7-8:54
Contemporary table, trestle   WS82/9:12
Contemporary table and chairs, trestle   PM76/9:104
Contemporary table and stools   WB84/5-6:20
Contemporary table/desk, drop leaf dining   PM82/11:112
Contemporary table (oak)   WS81/5:4
Contemporary three drawer coffee table   WS82/1:14
Contemporary TV stand   HM81/9:84
Contemporary wall mirror   WS84/7-8:20
Contemporary wastebasket   WB81/1-2:6
Continuity tester   PM78/11:60
Contour tracer   FW79/9-10:83
Contract, construction   NS84/9:86
Contractor, being your own   NS84/5-6:18
Contractor, working with solar   HM84/2:88
Contractors   HM81/2:58
Contractors, antagonizing   HM79/2:54
Contractors, home   PM78/4:178
Contractors, house repair   NS80/4:88
Contractors, working with   HM80/2:94
Conversation pit   HM79/9:14
Cookbook caddy   PM74/9:139
Cookbook/recipe shelf (maple)   WS79/11:4
Cookbook shelf   WB80/9-10:21
Cooker plans to order, gas $3.00   NS83/5-6:81
Cookie cutter Christmas tree ornaments   PM78/12:74
Cookie cutters, tin can   WB83/11-12:90
Cooking, woodstove   NS84/10:84
Cook out center, mobile with refrigerator   PM73/8:72

Cool house   NS82/7-8:29
Cool house   NS82/7-8:25
Cooling, air conditioning guide   NS84/7-8:40
Cooling, home   HM79/5-6:43
Cooling, home   PM81/7:88
Cooling, misting air conditioner   NS83/5-6:52
Cooling, naturally   NS80/7-8:20
Cooling, naturally   NS81/7-8:49
Cooling, naturally   NS82/7-8:17
Cooling, roof cupola   PM80/6:106
Cooling, solar   NS83/7-8:18
Cooling, underground tubes   NS81/11-12:48
Cooling computer program   NS84/7-8:60
Cooling cost reduction   NS82/7-8:17
Cooling costs, lowering   HM84/4:66
Cooling costs, lowering   PM74/6:116
Cooling design tips   NS84/7-8:44
Cooling energy savings   NS80/3:36
Cooling fan, whole house   NS80/7-8:29
Cooling fans, portable house   PM/8/6:132
Cooling insulation   NS83/5-6:64
Cooling mobile home, landscape   NS80/9:33
Cooling rack, kitchen   WB79/5-6:42
Cooling rack, kitchen (pine)   WS79/1:2
Cooling tips   NS84/7-8:22
Cooling with shade   HM80/5-6:18
Cooling with vines   NS84/3:50
Cool tubes   NS80/7-8:22
Cool tubes   NS84/7-8:57
Cool/warm room   WB78/5-6:4
Cooperage, wood Swiss buckets   FW83/5-6:73
Coopered columns   FW81/5-6:78
Copper pipe   PM74/2:76
Copper pipe firewood basket   WB82/9-10:94
Copper plumbing   HM75/2:36
Copper plumbing, cutting and soldering   HM84/12:62
Copper tubing, soldering   NS82/1:36
Copying stand, photo   PM82/12:140
Copy photography   PM76/3:90
Copyright laws   FW80/5-6:78
Copy stand, photo   PM73/7:14
Cord reel, electric extension   PM72/12:182
Corner cabinet, Colonial (pine)   HM82/2:30
Corner cabinet, kitchen   WB84/9-10:14
Corner cabinet, raised panel   WB76/11-12:104
Corner chair, cane bottom   WB80/7-8:50
Corner chair kit, Chippendale   PM84/8:101
Corner cupboard   WB80/11-12:22
Corner desk   WB80/7-8:40
Corner desk, small Colonial   WB84/11-12:26

Corner shelf   WB75/3-4:22
Corner shelf, plywood early American   WB82/5-6:95
Corner sofa, cushioned   PM79/2:134
Corner whatnot   WB84/3-4:88
Cornice shelf   WB84/3-4:97
Corrugated nails, tips   PM82/7:91
Costs, figuring   FW81/1-2:38
Couch, cardboard   NS83/11-12:38
Counter, family room   PM79/10:130
Counter, snack   PM78/7:100
Countertop, ceramic tile   PM77/12:114
Countertop, kitchen   HM81/12:64
Countertop, kitchen   WB74/3-4:28
Countertop, plastic laminate   WB78/9-10:115
Countertop joints, tight   WB82/5-6:48
Countertop organizer, kitchen   HM83/7-8:95
Countertops, installing   HM84/7-8:61
Countertops, kitchen   HM77/3:44
Countertops, plastic laminates   FW84/3-4:72
Countertops, plastic laminates   HM79/1:60
Countertops, tile and laminate   PM83/2:102
Country snack tables, nested   HM83/7-8:26
Cove, cutting on table saw   WS84/11-12:11
Cove cutting jig, table saw   WS80/11:16
Cove molding   WB78/7-8:39
Cowhide chair seat   FW80/5-6:54
Cracked finish, repairing   FW84/11-12:74
Cracker tray   PM76/4:172
Crack repair   FW77/9:22
Cradle   HM81/10:28
Cradle, antique (walnut)   HM78/11-12:84
Cradle, barrel   HM80/1:48
Cradle, bentwood   WB84/11-12:4
Cradle, Colonial   WB81/11-12:122
Cradle, Colonial doll   PM81/5:118
Cradle, Colonial (pine)   HM84/12:64
Cradle, Colonial (pine)   PM83/12:130
Cradle, cratewood   FW82/3-4:42
Cradle, curved end   WB75/7-8:54
Cradle, doll   WB81/3-4:99
Cradle, Dutch   WB83/3-4:46
Cradle, fast plywood   HM78/11-12:28
Cradle, heritage   WB73/9-10:30
Cradle, Hoover doll   WB84/11-12:89
Cradle, pioneer doll   WB80/11-12:36
Cradle, pioneer (spruce)   WB72/5-6:66
Cradle, rocking doll   WB81/11-12:112
Cradle, routered spindles   WB79/3-4:99
Cradle, spindle (cherry)   FW81/11-12:72
Cradle, Swedish Christmas card holder   PM81/12:114

Cradle and crib safety   WB81/3-4:116
Cradle (oak)   HM82/11:62
Cradles, hanging and Colonial   PM80/5:128
Crane, high rise toy   WB79/11-12:96
Crate furniture   HM77/4:74
Crawl space, weatherizing   HM84/9:86
Crayon holder, heart   PM80/2:124
Crayon holders, bunny elephant duck   PM78/11:194
Crayon wall/desk unit, child's   PM80/6:118
Creche, musical rotating Nativity   PM73/12:157
Creosote   HM81/11:78
Creosote, chimney   NS81/9:40
Creosote, chimney   PM81/9:116
Crib, 1879   WB76/3-4:52
Crib, doll   WB74/5-6:26
Crib, doll   WB79/11-12:30
Crib, doll   WB81/5-6:90
Crib, folding   WB80/9-10:130
Crib and cradle safety   WB81/3-4:116
Cribbage board table, two drawer   WB83/11-12:116
Cribbage table, butcher block   WB82/11-12:100
Crib/bed   WB82/9-10:48
Crib dropside mechanism   FW81/11-12:74
Cricket stool   WB80/11-12:94
Crocodile wall plaque, carved   WB78/11-12:4
Crosscut platform, circular saw   PM83/11:107
Crosscut sawing firewood   PM80/10:106
Crosscut saw sharpening tools   PM82/12:146
Crown molding mitering jig   PM83/12:107
Crystal radio   PM77/1:60
Cube coffee table   PM81/1:96
Cube coffee table, contemporary   PM82/2:106
Cube puzzle   PM82/1:66
Cucumber trellis   PM84/3:114
Cupboard, 1800 kitchen   WB81/1-2:33
Cupboard, Colonial   PM75/6:102
Cupboard, corner   WB80/11-12:22
Cupboard, French provencial bread   WB77/1-2:44
Cupboard, painted 1850 Norwegian   WB78/11-12:20
Cupboard cockleshell, carving   FW78/9:74
Cupboard plate butler   PM79/11:212
Cupola   HM78/7-8:34
Cupola, roof   PM80/6:106
Cup rack/rooster parrot cat squirrel   WB84/9-10:113
Curio cabinet   HM83/10:88
Curio cabinet   WS82/5:12
Curio cabinet, tall   WS83/3-4:12
Curio cabinet, wall hung with drawer   WB84/9-10:24
Curio shelf   PM75/1:112
Curio stand, mirrored Victorian   WB84/5-6:46

Current checker with alarm   PM72/8:119
Curtain retainers for patio doors   PM84/5:192
Curve, adjustable   FW82/3-4:14
Curve, cyma   WB73/7-8:42
Curve, cyma   WB74/1-2:51
Curved edge joint   FW78/10:15
Curved joints   FW82/7-8:46
Curved slot mortise and tenon   FW81/1-2:60
Curved wall   PM84/3:122
Cushion waterproofing, outdoor furniture   PM73/10:108
Cutoff machine, portable saw   PM74/11:150
Cutoff saw, economical   PM76/2:109
Cutter, paper   PM79/4:133
Cutting board   PM77/11:137
Cutting board   WS84/3-4:10
Cutting board, bowl type   PM79/11:122
Cutting board, bread   WB80/7-8:69
Cutting board, bread (maple and cherry)   WS82/3:24
Cutting board, cheese   HM78/11-12:90
Cutting board, kitchen (maple or birch)   WS79/1:1
Cutting board, multipurpose   PM73/9:156
Cutting board, plexiglas   PM75/5:72
Cutting board, small   HM81/11:42
Cutting board and knife set, kitchen   WB75/3-4:35
Cutting board clock   PM77/11:188
Cutting circles, table saw   FW80/9-10:24
Cutting glass   PM80/7:100
Cutting table   HM79/5-6:48
Cutting table, folding   FW79/9-10:16
Cylinder assemble, staved   FW80/11-12:26
Cylinders, bandsawing   PM75/11:34
Cyma curve   WB73/7-8:42
Cyma curve   WB74/1-2:51
Cyma curve leg and drum top table   WB80/5-6:104
Dado and rabbet joints   PM81/11:118
Dado guide   FW81/7-8:10
Dado guide, router   WB84/11-12:113
Dado spacing   FW80/11-12:23
Damper, adding to fireplace   PM84/10:189
Darkroom, bathroom   HM73/3:52
Darkroom, portable   PM75/4:106
Darkroom, suitcase   PM74/7:130
Darkroom sink   PM73/3:42
Darkroom wall organizer   PM77/3:72
Deadman switch, drill press   PM73/6:66
Decal wall plaques   WB75/5-6:10
Deck   HM79/3:18
Deck   HM80/5-6:98
Deck, cedar   WB76/7-8:6
Deck, child's pool   HM83/5-6:90

Deck, circular second story   HM83/5-6:68
Deck, curved   HM82/3:36
Deck, gluing   HM84/5-6:79
Deck, hinged to basement   PM81/6:112
Deck, hot tub   PM79/3:134
Deck, mini   WB79/3-4:95
Deck, pool   PM78/3:137
Deck, redwood   PM75/4:114
Deck, refinishing and staining   HM84/9:91
Deck, roofed (redwood)   WB77/3-4:68
Deck, screened and covered   HM83/3:28
Deck, sloped   HM82/5-6:28
Deck, two level   PM80/4:156
Deck and greenhouse   PM81/4:142
Deck and hot tub kit   WB81/7-8:46
Deck and patio ideas, nine   PM78/6:138
Deck and screen house   HM84/4:60
Deck bench, curved   HM83/5-6:56
Deck benches   PM76/4:135
Deck building   HM81/7-8:54
Deck chair, simple armless   NS84/3:73
Deck chair (redwood)   HM80/4:18
Deck chair (redwood and canvas)   WS79/5:6
Deck construction   NS83/5-6:24
Deck cover, fiberglass   HM79/3:22
Deck cover, lightweight   WB82/7-8:46
Deck design   HM81/4:34
Deck firepit   HM83/5-6:52
Deck furniture, canvas and aluminum tubing   PM77/4:128
Deck grill   HM82/5-6:26
Deck hot tub   HM84/5-6:34
Deck ideas   PM73/7:100
Deck lattice work   PM80/6:102
Deck lumber   WB82/5-6:38
Deck/patio planter   PM80/8:88
Deck planters   PM76/4:134
Deck planters (redwood)   HM80/4:20
Deck planters (redwood)   PM82/6:104
Deck/porch, double decker   PM82/10:118
Deck railing joint   PM80/11:184
Deck (redwood)   HM82/5-6:22
Deck (redwood)   PM82/6:104
Deck (redwood)   PM84/6:90
Deck (redwood)   WB75/5-6:26
Deck (redwood)   WB84/3-4:106
Deck roof, hyperbolic paraboloid   WB79/7-8:79
Decks, building   HM80/4:30
Decks, wood   PM79/4:156
Decks, wood   WB72/5-6:32
Decks and walkways   HM84/5-6:45

Deck seats (redwood)   PM82/6:104
Deck squares   WS79/5:10
Deck stool (redwood and canvas)   WS79/5:6
Deck sun screens   WB79/7-8:38
Deck table and chairs, hexagonal   PM79/5:142
Deck table (redwood)   HM80/4:18
Deck table (redwood)   HM84/5-6:32
Deck with storage   WB83/7-8:8
Decorating   HM82/10:37
Decoupage   PM78/10:241
Decoupage jewelry box   WB72/9-10:52
Decoys, carved ducks   HM79/7-8:92
Decoys, duck   PM72/2:104
Deer antler mounting   HM80/11:76
Deer weather vane   PM83/3:98
Dehumidifiers   PM77/6:114
Deicers   WB82/3-4:57
Deicers, concrete   WB84/3-4:72
Dentil, cutting   WS84/11-12:3
Derringer, wooden 1849 pepperbox   PM81/3:72
Design, chair   FW79/5-6:58
Desk, bedroom   NS82/4:43
Desk, boy's   HM75/4:32
Desk, boy's   WB72/9-10:31
Desk, British military campaign   PM79/2:126
Desk, cabriole legs (walnut)   WB84/11-12:48
Desk, campaign   WB74/3-4:32
Desk, cantilevered light duty   PM77/11:147
Desk, captain's   HM78/11-12:48
Desk, child's   NS81/3:58
Desk, child's dog   PM73/5:94
Desk, child's drawing   PM80/9:98
Desk, child's plywood   WB75/5-6:32
Desk, child's roll top   PM80/3:124
Desk, closet   HM79/2:34
Desk, Colonial plans to order $4.95   HM83/2:86
Desk, Colonial trestle (pine)   PM74/10:77
Desk, compact   WB79/3-4:75
Desk, computer   HM83/2:34
Desk, computer   HM84/1:63
Desk, computer   PM83/8:92
Desk, computer cabinet   NS82/9:51
Desk, computer office   PM81/5:114
Desk, concrete blocks and door   WB77/9-10:58
Desk, contemporary plywood   WB78/11-12:86
Desk, corner   WB80/7-8:40
Desk, corner and storage   HM73/1:36
Desk, drawing table   WB79/9-10:74
Desk, drop lid   WB81/1-2:44
Desk, fast plywood two faced   HM78/11-12:28

Desk, four drawer modern   WB72/1-2:44
Desk, French provincial   WB82/9-10:99
Desk, gateleg   WB75/9-10:34
Desk, hobby/work   PM74/1:70
Desk, inlaid lap   FW81/3-4:52
Desk, Jefferson secretary   PM76/6:86
Desk, kitchen cabinets   PM75/12:70
Desk, lacquered circa 1715   WB72/11-12:30
Desk, lap   WB73/9-10:65
Desk, lap   WB83/3-4:90
Desk, lap Colonial wooden hinged (pine)   WS80/5:6
Desk, large office   PM73/9:80
Desk, Mark Twain lap (mahogany)   PM83/10:100
Desk, merchants   HM73/2:54
Desk, pigeonhole   HM83/2:66
Desk, pigeonhole (mahogany)   FW80/1-2:74
Desk, plywood   WB84/5-6:56
Desk, rolltop   HM75/10:60
Desk, rolltop   PM76/1:80
Desk, rolltop   WB77/3-4:64
Desk, rolltop miniature (cherry)   FW81/5-6:58
Desk, satinwood secretary 1795   WB77/5-6:38
Desk, Shaker lap (pine or cherry)   FW76/3:48
Desk, Shaker sewing   HM72/4:52
Desk, six ft. trestle (pine)   WB82/3-4:20
Desk, slant top Newport style   FW80/7-8:41
Desk, slant top Shaker (cherry)   WS80/11:4
Desk, small corner Colonial   WB84/11-12:26
Desk, small Hepplewhite   WB76/1-2:49
Desk, small modern writing (birch)   WB84/7-8:62
Desk, small rolltop (oak)   WB84/7-8:4
Desk, spiral spindles   WB80/9-10:8
Desk, standing Lincoln   WB76/5-6:34
Desk, standing Lincoln   WB76/7-8:28
Desk, standing Scandinavian   PM81/5:122
Desk, traditional   WB79/3-4:38
Desk, two built in   HM73/3:36
Desk, two people   WB82/1-2:62
Desk, wall   PM73/3:86
Desk, wall drop leaf   PM73/9:73
Desk, wall hung child's   PM75/9:78
Desk, wall length   PM80/2:134
Desk, writing (oak)   FW82/5-6:67
Desk and bed, built in   HM72/6:36
Desk and beds, built in bunk   HM77/5-6:56
Desk and bed tree house, indoor   WB72/3-4:32
Desk and bench, plywood   HM80/12:16
Desk and bookshelves, rope nautical   PM76/1:73
Desk and chair, adjustable   WB73/7-8:38
Desk and chair, child's classic   WB83/11-12:122

Desk and chair, fast plywood   HM78/11-12:28
Desk and chair, telephone   WB81/3-4:90
Desk/bed, boy's   PM72/6:156
Desk/bed, family room   PM79/10:130
Desk/bed/chest, child's loft (plywood)   FW84/5-6:52
Desk/beds, bunk tower   HM79/11:9
Desk/bench/fireplace   HM78/2:32
Desk/bookcase, wall hung contemporary (oak)   HM84/9:30
Desk/bookcase/bed, twin   HM76/9:32
Desk book turntable   PM74/2:150
Desk/cabinet   HM73/8:36
Desk caddy, 1750 stationery cabinet (cherry)   PM84/3:74
Desk caddy, turned   WB81/11-12:24
Desk caddy, two drawer   WS84/1-2:12
Desk calendar, perpetual   PM80/3:131
Desk/center, contemporary hobby   HM84/2:70
Desk chair, child's   PM80/10:212
Desk clock/thermometer   WS84/5-6:18
Desk/drawing table, adjustable height   WS84/1-2:4
Desk/drawing table, child's   PM83/6:80
Desk/game chest, child's lap   WB84/5-6:72
Desk/hutch, Colonial   WB82/9-10:104
Desk in/out box   WS84/1-2:10
Desk kit, Queen Anne secretary   HM76/11:38
Desk laminate, plastic   HM83/2:32
Desk mail basket   PM72/7:146
Desk organizer   HM80/3:88
Desk organizer   WB78/9-10:34
Desk organizer, diamond inlay   WB80/11-12:126
Desk paper spike   HM82/10:22
Desks, his and her office center   PM81/7:97
Desk set   HM82/11:63
Desk set, pencil and stamp   PM73/5:91
Desk sewing cabinet (oak)   WB82/5-6:4
Desk/storage, built in   HM76/8:30
Desk/storage, two plywood   HM74/2:34
Desk/storage unit   PM77/9:98
Desk/table, drop leaf dining   PM82/11:112
Desk top organizer   PM77/4:116
Desk toy, swinging balls   PM74/6:152
Desk/wall clock (walnut and maple)   WS80/7:4
Desk/wall storage unit   HM77/4:19
Desk/wall unit, child's   PM80/6:118
Dial indicators   WB75/11-12:50
Diamond sharpening stones   WS82/11-12:7
Dice, electronic   PM79/3:14
Dice game, box   WB75/1-2:62
Dice jumbler   WB81/1-2:66
Die cutter attachment   PM74/11:42
Dimmer switch   PM76/5:227

Dining chair, cane back   WB77/9-10:48
Dining/coffee table, Scandinavian   PM81/5:122
Dining/coffee table, two height   WB79/3-4:4
Dining/game table   WB83/9-10:50
Dining/kitchen remodeling   HM82/7-8:35
Dining room greenhouse   WB78/5-6:96
Dining room in a closet   HM81/2:24
Dining room pass through   WB76/3-4:40
Dining room remodeling   HM81/10:19
Dining server, Victorian marble top (oak)   PM83/5:102
Dining sideboard   WB77/9-10:32
Dining sideboard, Spanish   WB79/5-6:43
Dining sideboard, tile top (oak)   WB78/9-10:62
Dining table   WB74/5-6:20
Dining table   WB77/9-10:36
Dining table, Dutch pull-out extension   FW77/12:34
Dining table, expandable two to twelve   WB80/11-12:111
Dining table, modern   WB81/5-6:52
Dining table, round contemporary (mahogany)   WS83/11-12:16
Dining table, round traditional   WB79/11-12:134
Dining table, simple long drop leaf   PM82/9:104
Dining table and chairs, Colonial drop leaf   PM82/4:116
Director's chair   WB79/9-10:62
Director's movie slate   PM79/11:122
Directors chair, folding canvas   PM79/3:146
Disc and drum sander   PM80/10:29
Disc sander   FW80/7-8:68
Dish dryer, no drip wall   HM84/7-8:71
Dishwasher, installation   PM76/9:108
Dishwasher, portable cabinet   PM75/5:84
Dishwasher, raised built-in   PM76/4:126
Dishwasher, save energy   NS80/2:46
Dishwasher decorating   HM80/2:86
Dishwasher decorating   HM82/10:64
Dishwasher hutch   PM75/4:126
Dishwasher repair   PM73/8:96
Dishwasher replacement   HM74/11:50
Disk/drum sander   WB81/3-4:22
Display cabinet, small bottle   WB82/1-2:74
Display cabinets   FW79/9-10:44
Display case, 2X4 and glass   WB80/5-6:100
Display case, collector's   WB82/7-8:38
Display case, doll   WB82/7-8:14
Display case, lighted wall   WB76/11-12:4
Display case, wooden hinged wall (oak)   WS80/5:11
Display case table   WB81/9-10:54
Display racks   WB75/11-12:68
Display stand and bookcase (pine)   WB80/5-6:52
Display stand/easel   HM82/11:63
Display table, Mediterranean octagonal   WB76/3-4:86

Display wall cabinet, spool   WS83/3-4:4
Distressing furniture finish   WB75/1-2:48
Divider, folding photo display   PM73/12:48
Divider, folding room screen   HM83/10:94
Divider, folding screen   WB78/7-8:32
Divider, folding screen   WB79/1-2:82
Divider, kitchen cabinets   PM75/12:70
Divider, room   WB78/3-4:36
Divider, Scandinavian screen   WB75/5-6:2
Divider, see through   HM81/1:21
Divider, see through with blinds   HM81/11:32
Divider, storage   HM81/1:20
Divider, wall room   PM75/2:84
Divider bookcase   HM80/9:21
Divider/planter, lighted   PM76/10:116
Diving scooter plans to order, $9.95   PM81/9:78
Diving scuba tow plans to order, $8.95   PM79/8:74
Diving/snorkeling tow, battery powered   PM83/8:68
Diving speargun stirrups   PM73/9:109
Diving tow plans to order, $7.95   PM74/7:69
Diving tow rig, trolling motor powered   PM73/4:96
Do-it-yourself commandments   NS82/5-6:48
Dock, portable boat   PM81/6:38
Dock, swimming   WB78/5-6:70
Dog, pull toy   HM83/11:76
Dog, pull toy   PM73/11:168
Dog, self-locking workbench   FW83/1-2:12
Dog, wooden workbench   FW83/11-12:10
Dog and cat, pull toy   PM79/11:122
Dog and cat house, solar   HM83/9:46
Dog collar, workbench   FW81/9-10:14
Dog desk, child's   PM73/5:94
Dog grooming   PM74/6:85
Dog house   WB79/9-10:34
Dog house, A-frame   HM78/3:23
Dog house, insulated   WB83/1-2:70
Dog kennel   HM79/9:106
Dogs, security   HM78/5-6:28
Dogs, wood workbench   FW83/1-2:20
Dogs, workbench   FW80/1-2:15
Dog sled, Alaskan   WB82/11-12:30
Doll clothes closet chest   WB81/11-12:110
Doll cradle   WB81/3-4:99
Doll cradle, Colonial   PM81/5:118
Doll cradle, Hoover   WB84/11-12:89
Doll cradle, pioneer   WB80/11-12:36
Doll cradle, rocking   WB81/11-12:112
Doll crib   WB79/11-12:30
Doll crib   WB81/5-6:90
Doll crib/toy box   WB74/5-6:26

Doll display case   WB82/7-8:14
Doll furniture   WB76/11-12:52
Doll high chair   WB84/11-12:86
Dollhouse   PM75/11:122
Dollhouse, Borden   WB80/11-12:50
Dollhouse, camper   WB76/11-12:88
Dollhouse, gingerbread $10   HM79/1:84
Dollhouse, solar   WB80/11-12:62
Dollhouse, substitute materials   WB83/1-2:32
Dollhouse bookcase cabinet   WB82/11-12:50
Dollhouse furniture   WB77/11-12:86
Dollhouse furniture   WB83/11-12:4
Dollhouse/jewelry chest, Victorian   WB79/1-2:113
Dollhouse kit   WB80/11-12:4
Dollhouse lights   WB80/11-12:68
Dollhouse plans to order   PM76/12:116
Dollhouse roof, Victorian   WB73/9-10:42
Dollhouse shake shingles   FW81/9-10:14
Dollhouse shingles, miniature   FW80/9-10:19
Dollhouse siding   FW83/11-12.12
Dollhouse/toy box   PM81/6:94
Dollies, four Shopsmith attachment   PM81/12:172
Dollies, plywood   FW82/3-4:12
Doll table and chair, Barbie   WB80/11-12:42
Dolly, garage tools   PM82/10:132
Dolly, retractable drill press   PM84/3:115
Dolly, table saw   PM74/8:56
Dolly, tip proof vacuum   PM80/5:55
Dolly, tool   PM81/3:52
Dolly (oak)   PM79/11:132
Dome home   NS83/7-8:72
Dome home, foam   HM83/1:28
Dome home kits   HM79/7-8:8
Dome house school   HM83/5-6:32
Dome kit, geodesic   HM73/9:34
Dominoes, big   WB78/1-2:48
Domino planter   PM74/8:176
Domino rack   WB78/11-12:100
Donkey and rider Christmas tree ornament   PM80/12:98
Door, building paneled entry   WB82/7-8:26
Door, Colonial entry from stock moldings   HM82/1:56
Door, entry   PM78/4:174
Door, entry   WB72/9-10:10
Door, entry   WB82/5-6:44
Door, entry facelift   WB76/1-2:57
Door, entry update   WB76/9-10:8
Door, entry with molding   WB76/11-12:70
Door, frame and panel   WS80/3:6
Door, hanging   FW77/12:48
Door, hanging   HM77/4:14

Door, hanging   PM73/4:174
Door, hollow core construction   WB79/3-4:68
Door, installing patio   HM82/4:53
Door, installing storm   HM84/9:66
Door, insulating entry   NS83/10:62
Door, latticework   PM80/6:105
Door, mosaic entry   FW81/1-2:56
Door, refinishing exterior   HM84/9:82
Door, repairing hollow core   HM84/2:64
Door, repairing hollow core   PM84/2:133
Door, repairing panel   HM83/9:92
Door, repairing veneer   HM75/11:62
Door, replacing entry with insulated   HM84/10:69
Door, replacing patio   HM79/4:33
Door, replacing storm   HM78/2:54
Door, rustic entry   NS83/3:56
Door, shed   HM82/12:76
Door, sliding   HM75/4:50
Door, sliding   WB82/3-4:36
Door, sliding glass   WB77/3-4:99
Door, sliding glass replacement   WB82/9-10:36
Door, steel entry   HM81/9:50
Door, steel entry   WB78/9-10:80
Door, sticking   PM73/2:158
Door, storm   WB75/9-10:24
Door, stylish screen   WB73/5-6:24
Door, two surface wall patio   WB83/9-10:52
Door and room trim   HM75/8:44
Door and screen repair, aluminum   PM73/8:90
Door and window drip caps   NS84/11-12:26
Door bells, test and repair   PM73/6:84
Door bottom seal, custom   WB79/11-12:16
Door bumpers   FW82/9-10:18
Door catch, brass   FW83/7-8:66
Door chimes   PM76/5:107
Door Christmas Santa   PM79/12:82
Door cutting gauge, bottom   WB77/5-6:29
Door frame, cutting for raised panel door   WS79/3:11
Door grooving frame, router   WB77/9-10:92
Door hanging   FW78/6:74
Door hanging   WB81/5-6:78
Door hinges, buying   HM77/3:54
Door insulation, sliding glass   PM82/1:64
Door jamb repair   WB81/1-2:125
Door joint, decorative   FW83/5-6:16
Door knob rack   WB82/3-4:9
Door knocker, hand forged iron   HM83/10:82
Door latch lock, cabin   HM76/4:60
Door lock   WB75/7-8:25
Door lock, installing   PM74/11:154

Door lock, installing deadbolt   HM84/2:62
Door lock, keyless   WB73/11-12:54
Door lock, seven bolt   WB78/7-8:4
Door lock protectors   WB83/7-8:32
Door locks   HM73/6:54
Door locks   HM78/5-6:40
Door locks   WB82/9-10:4
Door locks, replacing   HM75/3:54
Door moldings, entry   WB75/11-12:32
Door muntins, stops and hinges   WS81/1:9
Door openers, garage   WB74/3-4:38
Door organizer, kitchen   PM81/9:100
Door panel, cutting for raised panel door   WS79/3:10
Door repair, plexiglas storm   HM72/12:54
Door replacement, front   PM82/2:167
Door replacement, patio   WB81/5-6:97
Doors, board and batten   FW82/5-6:26
Doors, concealed hinged   FW83/11-12:59
Doors, entry   FW77/12:44
Doors, etched glass cabinet   HM83/7-8:62
Doors, folding closet   HM74/4:46
Doors, frame and panel   FW84/11-12:44
Doors, French   PM84/12:104
Doors, glass   WS81/1:8
Doors, grooving   WB76/3-4:84
Doors, handcrafted entry   NS80/9:86
Doors, handcrafted entry   NS82/11-12:79
Doors, installing sliding glass   PM77/4:142
Doors, insulated garage   WB82/7-8:4
Doors, Japanese sliding   FW82/5-6:50
Doors, kitchen cabinet stained glass   HM82/7-8:84
Doors, leaded glass   PM84/12:110
Doors, louvered   FW78/3:84
Doors, outside basement   HM83/4:90
Doors, screen slides smoothly   WB79/7-8:48
Doors, solid wood   FW79/7-8:78
Doors, tempered glass storm   PM75/2:46
Doors, wood   FW79/9-10:4
Doors, woven slat cabinet   WB80/11-12:96
Doors and walls, planed paneled   FW79/9-10:84
Doorstop, cat   PM81/11:32
Doorstop, mouse   PM80/12:98
Doors/windows, weatherizing   PM78/9:158
Door trim finishing   WB82/11-12:108
Door wreath, wooden Christmas   PM81/12:114
Dormers, attic   PM76/5:110
Double shell solar house   NS82/4:28
Double shell solar house   NS84/7-8:84
Double wall solar house   NS81/2:82
Dough box lamp table/magazine rack, Colonial   WB84/3-4:4

Dough tray   FW82/7-8:80
Dove and partridge Christmas candle holder   HM81/12:22
Dove Christmas tree ornament   PM80/12:98
Dovetail, chiseling   FW81/3-4:74
Dovetail, curved   FW81/1-2:58
Dovetail, sliding   FW83/5-6:18
Dovetail, tapered sliding   FW79/9-10:51
Dovetail bookends, sliding   FW80/1-2:19
Dovetail drawers   WS82/1:18
Dovetail hand tools   WS82/1:4
Dovetailing, Bermudan   FW82/7-8:71
Dovetail jigs, tests   FW82/11-12:69
Dovetail joint, hand   FW76/3:28
Dovetail joint, hand cut lap   WS82/7:4
Dovetail joint, router   WS82/7:6
Dovetail joints   FW80/3-4:73
Dovetail joints   PM77/8:102
Dovetail joints   PM82/1:98
Dovetail joint with hand tools   WS82/1:6
Dovetail marking setup   FW80/3-4:15
Dovetail pins   WS82/1:8
Dovetail router jig, false   WB82/1-2:104
Dovetails   FW79/9-10:56
Dovetails, bandsaw   FW83/11-12:49
Dovetails, hand shaped   WB80/3-4:30
Dovetails, scroll saw   FW79/7-8:15
Dovetails, table saw   FW83/11-12:50
Dovetail square   FW77/6:14
Dovetail step stand, Shaker (cherry)   WS82/1:20
Dovetail table lamp   WS82/7:24
Dovetail tails   WS82/1:10
Dovetail template   FW81/3-4:68
Dovetail tongue and groove joint, glueless   WS82/3:22
Dovetail tongue and groove wall shelf (oak)   WS82/3:20
Dovetail trimming with router   FW80/3-4:13
Dowel, end-drilling vise   FW81/3-4:14
Dowel and canvas magazine rack   PM79/12:108
Dowel and macrame bead candle holders   WB82/1-2:100
Dowel and molding rack, shop   PM83/12:154
Dowel bookrack, kitchen   PM84/1:112
Dowel buttons, turning   PM82/6:99
Dowel casserole cradle, kitchen   PM84/1:112
Dowel centering jig   PM78/11:131
Dowel chair   HM79/5-6:54
Dowel cutter, lathe   PM81/5:53
Dowel cutting jig   WB77/11-12:85
Dowel cutting jig, table saw   HM84/4:155
Dowel decorations   WB81/11-12:86
Dowel drilling jig   WB82/11-12:99
Doweled miter joint jig, drill press   PM80/11:119

Dowel end smoothing guide   PM78/9:56
Dowel furniture, Selbermachen   HM80/1:11
Dowel holder   WB83/9-10:117
Doweling   WB76/9-10:92
Doweling jig, radial arm saw   HM81/9:126
Doweling jigs, testing nine   FW84/3-4:48
Doweling tips   PM83/5:110
Dowel joint   FW80/3-4:68
Dowel joints   FW77/6:46
Dowel joints   PM81/12:108
Dowel joints   PM83/4:112
Dowel joints   PM83/6:83
Dowel joint T-jig   FW80/5-6:15
Dowel kerfing   PM76/8:96
Dowel magazine rack   PM75/12:106
Dowel maker   FW77/9:67
Dowel maker   HM82/7-8:103
Dowel making   FW80/3-4:14
Dowel making, router   FW80/11-12:22
Dowel making, router   PM70/5:54
Dowel planter, hanging   PM80/8:88
Dowel quiver   WB78/9-10:9
Dowel rack   WB75/9-10:48
Dowels, finding center   PM78/2:38
Dowels, reducing diameter   FW82/3-4:20
Dowels, router   FW81/11-12:16
Dowels, table saw   FW81/11-12:16
Dowels, working with   FW84/9-10:40
Dowel sawing jig   WB82/11-12:99
Dowel stock cutter   PM84/5:101
Dowel storage   PM80/3:82
Dowel swing   PM77/7:96
Dowel trellis plant box   PM80/8:88
Dowel turning, drill press   PM77/6:174
Dowel utensil rack, kitchen   PM84/1:112
Dowel wall storage unit   HM80/3:48
Downspout well   WB79/9-10:44
Draft air leak detector   PM79/2:194
Drafting machine, clipboard   WB73/1-2:48
Drafting table   WB80/9-10:62
Drafting table, folding   PM77/5:39
Drafting table, workbench   PM79/3:126
Drafting table/desk   WB79/9-10:74
Drafting table (oak)   HM84/12:68
Drafting tools   NS83/1:20
Dragonfly pull toy   FW79/11-12:61
Dragonfly stained glass mirror   PM80/7:96
Drain, unclogging   NS82/3:60
Drainage system, plumbing   HM79/4:80
Drain heat recovery system   NS84/1:68

Drain repair, tub   HM77/3:32
Drains, clogged   HM78/7-8:46
Drains, clogged   HM78/5-6:53
Drains, clogged plumbing   HM74/2:50
Drains, connectors   WB81/3-4:114
Drains, plastic plumbing   HM79/7-8:94
Drains, plastic plumbing   HM79/5-6:85
Drains, tub and sink   WB80/3-4:87
Drains, unclogging   PM73/11:98
Drains, unclogging   PM83/11:54
Drains, unclogging water powered plunger   PM84/6:51
Draped wall   WB77/9-10:18
Drapery, hanging rods   PM73/3:144
Drapery retainers for patio doors   PM84/5:192
Drapery rings, PVC pipe   PM82/3:167
Drawer bottom, band saw   FW81/11-12:16
Drawer bottoms, six   FW77/12:49
Drawer chest, family room   PM79/10:130
Drawer construction   WS84/1-2:20
Drawer glide, toy marbles   FW84/9-10:4
Drawer guides, wooden   WS81/11:22
Drawer joint   FW80/5-6:18
Drawer joint, lap dovetail   WS82/7:4
Drawer kits   HM77/9:40
Drawer making   FW78/6:50
Drawer pull, integral   FW83/7-8:14
Drawer pull, routed   FW79/9-10:18
Drawer pull, routed   FW82/7-8:50
Drawer pulls, carved   WB76/5-6:26
Drawer pulls, chess men   WB74/3-4:12
Drawers   FW84/3-4:32
Drawers   PM74/9:74
Drawers   WB72/7-8:18
Drawers   WB79/11-12:122
Drawers   WS84/7-8:13
Drawers, box   WS79/7:5
Drawers, box joint   WS81/9:19
Drawers, dovetail   WS82/1:18
Drawers, rabbet and groove joint   WS81/11:20
Drawers, slide out   WB74/3-4:10
Drawers, vanity   WB77/5-6:16
Drawer stops, three   FW84/3-4:36
Drawing, transferring patterns   PM84/7:134
Drawing aids, four   PM84/4:106
Drawing board and typing table   WB81/5-6:4
Drawing board/cabinet, shop   PM82/5:114
Drawing desk, child's   PM80/9:98
Drawing/desk table, child's   PM83/6:80
Drawing grid ruling tool   PM80/7:93
Drawing lightbox   PM72/12:112

Drawing machine, doodles and designs   PM76/3:174
Drawing multi sided shapes   WB84/7-8:34
Drawing numbers   PM81/1:103
Drawing pad kit, computer   PM80/2:88
Drawing pantograph   WB83/1-2:58
Drawing plans, enlarging by squares   WB81/11-12:94
Drawing projector, opaque letter enlarging   WB83/11-12:14
Drawings, measured   FW76/12:46
Drawing shapes, tips   PM81/7:86
Drawing table   FW84/3-4:32
Drawing table   WB80/9-10:62
Drawing table, desk   WB79/9-10:74
Drawing table, folding   PM77/5:39
Drawing table, lighted   WB80/5-6:68
Drawing table, workbench   PM79/3:126
Drawing table/desk, adjustable height   WS84/1-2:4
Drawing table (oak)   HM84/12:68
Drawknife   FW76/9:50
Drawknife   FW80/11-12:92
Drawknife, mini   FW82/9-10:22
Dremel hand grinder trammel point   PM81/1:120
Dremel Moto Shop accessory sanding table   PM82/8:88
Dresser, bedroom   WB73/3-4:36
Dresser, French provincial   WB82/3-4:4
Dresser, teenager's double   WB72/5-6:38
Dresser caddy   WB73/11-12:30
Dresser mirror, lighted three way movie star   PM81/12:174
Dresser wall storage unit   HM76/3:30
Dressing mirror, antique (cherry)   PM83/7:52
Dressing mirror, antique (pine)   PM83/7:52
Dressing table, wall   HM79/12:68
Drill, hand   FW83/1-2:16
Drill, portable   HM84/12:45
Drill, portable   PM78/5:142
Drill, repair or replace electric   NS83/3:48
Drill accessories   PM81/4:132
Drill accessories, portable   NS84/11-12:60
Drill accessories, portable   PM78/8:98
Drill accessories tips, portable   PM81/3:148
Drill angle guide   PM83/11:106
Drill bit, auger   FW84/1-2:62
Drill bit, expansion   FW77/3:27
Drill bit holder   PM81/5:53
Drill bit holder   WB73/11-12:20
Drill bit lazy Sam   WS79/7:9
Drill bits   NS81/4:18
Drill bits, modified spade   FW84/7-8:76
Drill bits, spoon   FW83/11-12:70
Drill guide, portable   PM78/9:200
Drilling angled holes   FW78/10:14

Drilling angled holes   FW80/5-6:71
Drilling angled holes   FW84/5-6:76
Drilling angled holes   PM73/6:158
Drilling angled holes   PM82/3:70
Drilling ceramics   HM83/10:33
Drilling glass   HM78/4:24
Drilling glass and ceramics   PM81/12:112
Drilling hard materials   PM81/12:112
Drilling holes, tips   PM82/5:122
Drilling jig, angle   WS79/7:10
Drilling jig, center locator   WB79/9-10:43
Drilling jig, horizontal   WS80/11:13
Drilling tips, portable   PM82/4:120
Drilling tools   WB83/5-6:59
Drill lathe, small   PM75/4:104
Drill lathe, small portable   HM81/10:110
Drill press, beginners   PM76/1:90
Drill press accessories chest   PM84/3:115
Drill press accessory board   PM80/7:94
Drill press accessory table   HM80/2:56
Drill press angle guide   PM83/11:107
Drill press auxiliary table   PM83/12:110
Drill press bit holder   PM81/5:53
Drill press bit stand   PM84/3:115
Drill press centering guide   PM84/3:116
Drill press chair bottom scoop   WB76/11-12:8
Drill press clamping panel   PM84/3:115
Drill press dolly, retractable   PM84/3:115
Drill press dowel turning   PM77/6:174
Drill press drilling table, small parts   PM75/10:43
Drill press dust fan   PM84/11:145
Drill press elevator   WB78/1-2:66
Drill press end-boring jig   FW78/10:72
Drill press fence   PM73/3:150
Drill press fly cutter   WB77/3-4:109
Drill press hold down   PM73/1:146
Drill press honer   HM77/5-6:55
Drill press indexer   WB73/1-2:20
Drill press indexing head   WB81/7-8:28
Drill press jig, doweled miter joints   PM80/11:119
Drill press mortising table   FW83/11-12:10
Drill press overarm router   WB84/11-12:128
Drill press paper boring tool   PM81/10:37
Drill press punch   PM80/2:130
Drill press router adapter   PM76/1:162
Drill press routing   WS80/7:11
Drill press safety switch   FW83/9-10:10
Drill press switch, deadman   PM73/6:66
Drill press table, swing away   FW84/5-6:58
Drill press table elevator   PM73/11:178

Drill press table lifter   PM78/10:55
Drill press table truing   FW78/3:26
Drill press thickness sander   WB82/9-10:87
Drill press tips   PM79/10:71
Drill press tips   PM79/11:60
Drill press tips   PM80/5:138
Drill press tool tray   PM84/3:115
Drill press tray   PM76/5:226
Drill press turning jig   PM83/12:106
Drill press wood lathe   PM72/12:164
Drill repair, electric   PM79/1:102
Drill repairs, electric   HM76/1:36
Drills, hand   WB76/9-10:32
Drill stand, multi use   WB74/5-6:35
Drill stand, portable   WB84/11-12:102
Drip caps   NS84/11-12:26
Driveway, concrete <$1000   HM83/3:34
Driveway, repairing asphalt   HM84/3:88
Driveway and walk repair, concrete   HM75/3:24
Driveway repair   HM75/11:34
Driveway repair   PM79/4:151
Driveway repair, asphalt   HM72/3:56
Driveway repair, asphalt   HM83/9:94
Driveway repair, asphalt   PM76/7:92
Driveway repair, asphalt   WB82/5-6:70
Driveway repair, concrete   HM80/4:92
Driveway sealing, asphalt   HM77/7-8:28
Driveway water channel   PM80/6:22
Driving, snow   PM79/12:87
Driving, visual exercises   PM84/8:138
Driving, winter   PM72/12:98
Driving, winter   PM77/12:82
Driving, winter emergency kit   PM80/10:150
Driving in snow   PM78/12:70
Driving on ice   PM77/11:92
Driving over frozen water   PM83/12:88
Driving safety   PM80/11:87
Driving schools, professionals   PM84/8:128
Driving tips, winter   PM75/11:74
Drop leaf and gate leg tables   FW79/9-10:62
Drop leaf bench   WB73/5-6:26
Drop leaf buffet   WB77/7-8:34
Drop leaf cabinet, Shaker work   HM72/9:48
Drop leaf desk, wall   PM73/9:73
Drop leaf hinge   FW79/9-10:66
Drop leaf hinges   WS81/3:8
Drop leaf Pembroke table (mahogany/walnut)   WS81/3:4
Drop leaf table   WB77/3-4:4
Drop leaf table   WB78/9-10:6
Drop leaf table, butterfly   WB72/5-6:48

Drop leaf table, Colonial (mahogany)   PM82/6:132
Drop leaf table, Duncan Phyfe (mahogany)   PM82/3:140
Drop leaf table, Shaker   WS80/9:8
Drop leaf table, simple long dining   PM82/9:104
Drop leaf table, snack   WB83/3-4:62
Drop leaf table, triangular   FW80/11-12:61
Drop leaf table, triangular   WB72/9-10:40
Drop leaf table, triangular   WB83/1-2:110
Drop leaf table and chairs, plywood Colonial   PM82/4:116
Drop leaf table/desk, dining   PM82/11:112
Drop leaf table joint   WS80/9:10
Drop leaf tables, radial arm saw   PM82/3:76
Drowning, cold water   PM78/8:76
Drum, Aztec   FW77/9:72
Drum and disc sander   PM80/10:29
Drum/disk sander   WB81/3-4:22
Drum footrest   WB72/3-4:54
Drum grill   HM80/3:92
Drum sander, inflatable   FW80/3-4:48
Drum table, coffee   PM73/2:164
Drum top and cyma curve leg table   WB80/5-6:104
Dryer, boot and mitten with blower   PM72/1:142
Dryer, firewood solar   HM81/10:89
Dryer, fruit and vegetable   PM76/5:112
Dryer, heat to solar room   WB84/1-2:56
Dryer, solar food   NS81/5-6:76
Dryer, solar food   PM79/1:100
Dryer and washer installation   HM84/2:47
Dryer heat recovery   HM79/10:34
Dryer heat recovery box   WB81/1-2:148
Dryer repair   HM78/3:59
Dryer repair, clothes   NS80/3:64
Dryer repair, electric   PM73/11:92
Dryer repair, gas   PM73/12:78
Dryer repair, solid state   PM79/8:102
Dryer venting, clothes   HM73/9:40
Drying barn, Pennsylvania Dutch tobacco   FW80/5-6:60
Drying cabinet, lumber   WB82/7-8:6
Drying kiln   FW77/3:39
Drying kiln, dehumidifier   FW84/3-4:40
Drying kiln, solar   FW77/6:59
Drying kiln, solar lumber   PM77/5:273
Drying lumber   HM80/9:68
Drying lumber   WB77/1-2:86
Drying lumber, air   FW82/3-4:88
Drying oven, tin-can   FW79/7-8:12
Drying wood   FW76/12:40
Drying wood, solar   FW80/5-6:56
Dry sink, Colonial   PM72/2:138
Dry sink, Colonial   WB74/9-10:66

Dry sink, Colonial   WB80/9-10:74
Dry sink, Colonial   WS81/11:12
Dry sink, early American (oak)   HM82/10:32
Dry sink, Shaker   HM73/3:48
Dry sink cabinet, Colonial TV   WB84/3-4:122
Dry sink plans to order, $7.95   HM83/4:27
Drywall   HM75/8:34
Drywall   HM83/7-8:76
Drywall   PM74/5:90
Drywall, finishing   WB73/5-6:16
Drywall, installing   PM81/7:32
Drywall clip fasteners   NS84/10:41
Drywall crack repair   PM73/1:72
Drywall elevator   HM74/4:43
Drywall installation   HM77/7-8:22
Drywall patching   PM79/12:95
Drywall patching   PM81/6:104
Drywall repair   HM73/4-5:66
Drywall repair   HM77/5-6:24
Drywall repair   HM83/2:54
Drywall repair   NS83/7-8:24
Drywall repair   PM76/4:30
Duck, carved   WB75/1-2:44
Duck, flying weather vane   PM72/3:144
Duck, laminated   PM76/11:126
Duck, waddling toy   NS82/11-12:46
Duckbill spoon joint   FW83/11-12:70
Duck crayon holder   PM78/11:194
Duck decoy lamp   PM74/9:140
Duck decoys   PM72/2:104
Duck decoys, carved   HM79/7-8:92
Duck head wall hanger   PM80/8:51
Duck napkin ring, carved   WB80/1-2:24
Duck note holder   WB73/11-12:63
Ducks, pull toy   PM73/11:166
Ducts, insulating   HM84/1:20
Duct soffits, three   HM84/7-8:74
Dulcimer   FW82/3-4:68
Dulcimer   WB75/5-6:22
Dulcimer/banjo   PM82/7:88
Dulcimer kit, hammered   PM84/2:104
Dulcimer kit, teardrop   PM84/2:104
Dulcimer peg box   FW78/6:77
Duncan Phyfe chair   WB79/5-6:14
Duncan Phyfe table, drop leaf (mahogany)   PM82/3:140
Duplicate sawing   FW84/7-8:54
Duplicate turning gauge   FW80/11-12:24
Duplicating wood parts   FW80/11-12:20
Duplicator, lathe   FW82/11-12:92
Dustboard   FW80/11-12:6

Dust collecting router attachment   PM76/3:129
Dust collection system   WB82/9-10:82
Dust collection system, shop   FW80/11-12:58
Dust collector, cardboard box   WB80/7-8:63
Dust collector, lathe box   FW83/11-12:69
Dust collector, shop   FW78/9:76
Dust collector, shop   WB75/11-12:40
Dust collector, shop   WB77/9-10:91
Dust collector, shop   WB78/9-10:59
Dust collector system, plastic pipe   WB82/1-2:38
Dust collector/table, radial arm saw   WB77/3-4:116
Dust collector tool stand   WB78/3-4:90
Dust control, router   WS84/11-12:3
Dust control, shop   FW84/7-8:60
Dust exhaust fan, portable   FW83/3-4:14
Dust hazards, wood   FW83/7-8:36
Dust slot, radial arm saw   PM84/2:116
Dutch cradle   WB83/3-4:46
Dutchman inlay patching   FW81/3-4:16
Dyes, stains and pigments   FW78/9:58
Eagle carving, power tool   WB78/1-2:86
Eagle carving (basswood)   FW76/3:24
Early American dry sink (oak)   HM82/10:32
Early American hutch/table/chair   PM73/7:96
Early American shelf and mirror   WB83/1-2:37
Early American wall cabinet (oak)   HM82/10:32
Easel, artist's   WB72/9-10:46
Easel, borderless photo enlarging   PM73/2:46
Easel, child's two way   WB77/11-12:124
Easel/display stand   HM82/11:63
Easels, table   HM78/11-12:20
Easter egg, classic   PM77/4:102
Edge banding, plywood   FW78/3:14
Edge finishing, plywood   FW80/11-12:18
Edge gluing bar clamps   WB84/9-10:32
Edge gluing panels   WS84/3-4:13
Edge gluing without clamps   FW82/3-4:14
Edge joint, routed   FW77/12:66
Edge jointing, beginner   FW84/9-10:46
Edge lap joint   PM81/12:108
Edges, sixteen plywood   PM74/5:96
Edges, squaring   PM76/4:204
Edge sander   PM82/8:86
Edge sanding   FW82/5-6:20
Edge treatments, plywood   PM84/12:52
Edge truing jig, table saw   WB84/1-2:84
Edging plywood   HM78/7-8:37
Editor's movie slate   PM79/11:122
Educational toy, learning frames   PM81/11:30
Egg, Easter classic   PM77/4:102

Egg carving   FW81/3-4:36
Egg cups, England India Belgium Germany   WB82/1-2:52
Eggshell mosaic   WB73/3-4:60
Egg timer, electronic   PM75/5:209
Electrical capacity, home   HM82/7-8:79
Electrical circuit update   HM79/10:46
Electrical conduit   HM80/11:80
Electrical emergencies   PM73/12:88
Electrical extension cord, shock proof   HM81/10:64
Electrical fuses   WB79/11-12:117
Electrical hardware, installing   HM83/11:45
Electrical hazards   HM83/9:126
Electrical plug repair   PM78/7:94
Electrical rewiring, house   WB74/11-12:8
Electrical soldering   PM74/7:104
Electrical system mapping, home   HM82/9:106
Electrical tool tote   PM72/6:116
Electrical volt ohm meter   HM79/7-8:24
Electrical wiring, aluminum   HM81/3:20
Electrical wiring, shockproofing   HM80/1:100
Electrical wiring repairs   PM83/10:34
Electric auto voltmeter   PM80/5:42
Electric car   PM79/10:96
Electric ceiling fixture replacement   HM77/9:42
Electric circuit checker, auto   PM77/3:184
Electric cord reel, extension   PM72/12:182
Electric cord suspension arm   FW80/1-2:18
Electric current checker with alarm   PM72/8:119
Electric drill repair   HM76/1:36
Electric drill repair   PM79/1:102
Electric game, number guessing   PM73/1:134
Electric guitar amp, portable   PM79/9:29
Electrician's toolkit   NS83/2:18
Electric iron repair   PM74/8:82
Electricity, photovoltaic   NS83/9:10
Electric light fixture, moving   WB81/3-4:85
Electric lighting, low voltage   HM82/1:58
Electric lights, wiring   HM83/10:37
Electric meter, reading   NS80/2:49
Electric mower cord reel   PM83/5:73
Electric outlet checker   PM76/6:42
Electric outlets, wiring   PM73/2:154
Electric power, selling   NS81/5-6:54
Electric range, repairing   PM75/4:144
Electric receptacles, outdoor   PM81/6:114
Electric shaver repair   PM83/2:112
Electric shock detector   PM78/2:120
Electric slide projector dissolve control   PM74/3:120
Electric switches, four way   WB73/1-2:44
Electric wall receptacle, installing   NS81/9:58

Electric wires, splicing   PM73/3:138
Electric wiring, light and power circuits   HM84/9:104
Electric wiring, surface mounted   WB83/9-10:75
Electric wiring, switches and outlets   HM84/7-8:72
Electric wiring, using GFI's   HM84/5-6:88
Electronic air leak detector   PM79/2:194
Electronic alarm, basement water   PM80/7:56
Electronic AM radio antenna booster   PM82/8:28
Electronic auto alarm, Morse code beeper   PM84/1:76
Electronic auto battery charge checker   PM79/5:84
Electronic battery tester and charger   PM80/11:20
Electronic cable tester, audio/video   PM84/3:154
Electronic charger for NiCd batteries   PM82/2:62
Electronic coin toss   PM78/5:45
Electronic controller, attic fan   PM81/7:27
Electronic dice   PM79/3:14
Electronic egg timer   PM75/5:209
Electronic game, hand coordination   PM81/2:141
Electronic garage door lock   PM81/5:132
Electronic guitar fuzz box   PM79/2:22
Electronic headphone amp   PM74/1:133
Electronic heat shrink tubing   PM83/5:152
Electronic light switch on reminder   PM81/1:60
Electronic phone speaker amp   PM74/2:132
Electronic power meter/stylus timer, stereo   PM81/11:85
Electronic printed circuit board processing   PM79/3:14
Electronic project tools   PM82/1:106
Electronic saltmeter   PM83/2:158
Electronic solder splice   PM83/5:152
Electronic sound effects machine   PM82/1:68
Electronic transistor tester   PM74/3:124
Electronic TV commercial silencer   PM80/1:162
Electronic voltmeter/burglar alarm, auto   PM82/3:24
Elephant, rocking   HM81/10:32
Elephant chair, child's   WB79/11-12:102
Elephant crayon holder   PM78/11:194
Elephant toy, old tire   NS80/5-6:68
Elephant toy box   WB79/1-2:94
Elipse drawing   WS81/3:3
Ellipse   WB76/3-4:82
Ellipse, drawing   FW80/5-6:72
Ellipse, drawing   WS79/9:8
Ellipse, lath and framing square   FW83/9-10:8
Ellipse, super   FW84/3-4:14
Ellipse picture frame   WS79/9:9
Ellipse scribing trammel compass   PM82/12:94
Emergencies, electrical   PM73/12:88
Emergencies, home   HM80/10:28
Emergencies, plumbing   HM79/10:92
Emergencies, power outage   PM77/11:99

Emergencies, winter   HM75/1:34
Emergency cutoff valves   HM74/10:50
Emergency gear, home   PM73/9:106
Emergency kit, auto   HM80/12:80
Emergency kit, winter driving   PM80/10:150
Emergency repair kit, auto   HM84/7-8:108
Emergency repairs   HM81/10:34
Enameled candle cubes   PM79/6:120
Enameled cheese board   PM79/6:120
Enameled coaster set   PM79/6:120
Enameling craft   PM79/6:120
End boring jig   FW78/10:72
End cabinets, family room   PM79/10:130
End grain box top   WS81/5:13
End table   WB78/5-6:34
End table, Colonial   WB74/7-8:37
End table, contemporary   WB81/3-4:66
End table, contemporary aquarium   WB81/5-6:82
End table, crate furniture   HM77/4:74
End table, low cost massive   HM78/7-8:74
End table, modern (oak and smoked glass)   WS79/1:7
End table, rustic   HM78/11-12:84
End table, tape and record   WB79/7-8:22
End table, trestle   WB72/3-4:70
End table, triangular storage   PM82/2:106
End table, turned (walnut)   WB74/3-4:66
End table, two drawer and secret compartment   WB83/9-10:102
End table/magazine rack, Colonial doughbox   WB84/3-4:4
End tables, kitchen cabinets   PM75/12:70
End table/sofa, built-in   HM76/10:34
Energy, drain heat recovery system   NS84/1:68
Energy, saving   PM84/9:84
Energy audit, home   NS82/2:70
Energy conservation, house   NS82/3:36
Energy cost reduction   NS80/3:33
Energy efficient appliances   NS84/1:56
Energy efficient lighting   NS81/10:71
Energy management   NS80/3:31
Energy monitor   NS83/10:8
Energy product ripoffs   NS82/11-12:59
Energy ripoffs   HM78/10:26
Energy savers, trees   HM79/5-6:38
Energy saving   HM80/5-6:81
Energy saving   HM80/2:38
Energy saving   HM81/9:90
Energy saving   NS80/4:76
Energy saving   NS81/3:61
Energy saving   WB79/1-2:72
Energy saving, appliance   HM79/9:76
Energy saving, dryer heat recovery   HM79/10:34

Energy saving, dryer heat recovery box   WB81/1-2:148
Energy saving, electricity   NS80/2:45
Energy saving, heat less area   HM81/11:58
Energy saving, home   NS81/10:44
Energy saving, home   WB76/5-6:43
Energy saving, home   WB76/11-12:22
Energy saving, home   WB76/7-8:48
Energy saving, home   WB76/9-10:80
Energy saving, light switch on reminder   PM81/1:60
Energy saving, lowering cooling costs   HM84/4:66
Energy saving air leak detector   PM79/2:194
Energy saving computer   HM80/7-8:84
Energy saving guide   PM82/9:109
Energy saving house maintenance   NS82/1:47
Energy saving houses   PM77/7:88
Energy saving methods, simple low cost   WB82/9-10:76
Energy saving rip-offs   NS82/9:78
Energy saving rip-offs   HM80/9:76
Energy savings, cooling   NS80/3:36
Energy saving tips   HM84/10:86
Energy saving tips   NS80/11-12:82
Energy saving tips   PM73/1:70
Energy saving tips   PM77/11:124
Energy saving tips   PM77/9:115
Energy saving tips   PM78/9:142
Energy saving tips   PM83/10:48
Energy use index worksheet   NS84/4:34
Engine hoist, garage   PM83/4:168
Engine repair, small   HM80/3:98
English pub addition   WB79/9-10:106
English pub basement   WB74/9-10:32
English pub settle bench   WB78/9-10:50
English sewing stand, turned   WB83/9-10:74
English treen   FW76/12:58
English wall lantern, candle   WS84/11-12:16
Enlarging easel, borderless photo   PM73/2:46
Enlarging plans by squares   WB81/11-12:94
Entertainment center   PM76/11:120
Entertainment center   WB80/9-10:20
Entertainment center, brick and lumber   WB81/5-6:109
Entertainment center, contemporary   PM83/1:108
Entertainment center, home   PM81/7:95
Entertainment unit/bar fireplace   PM75/1:76
Entertainment wall unit   HM81/12:26
Entertainment wall unit   WB84/9-10:66
Entertainment wall unit, contemporary   PM84/4:136
Entry, adding air lock   PM83/11:100
Entry, remodeling   PM73/4:148
Entry step   PM78/4:172
Entryway mirror/coat rack   PM84/7:132

Entryway remodeling   PM79/6:112
Epoxy paints   WB76/5-6:50
Escutcheon plate, wood   PM80/3:32
Etagere, campaign   WB84/7-8:70
Etagere, clear plastic   HM77/7-8:36
Etagere, early American   WB72/7-8:38
Etagere, French   HM80/5-6:118
Etagere, modern bentwood (ash and cherry)   WB84/11-12:74
Etagere, plexiglas (walnut)   WB81/7-8:44
Etched glass   HM83/7-8:62
Etching, low voltage brass   WB82/7-8:9
Etching acrylic sculptures   PM73/2:80
Etching glass   WB76/1-2:16
Etching kit, glass   PM79/11:16
Ethiopian bowl turning   FW80/3-4:54
European style kitchen cabinets   FW83/11-12:54
Exercise center, outdoor Parcours   PM79/9:116
Exercise equipment   PM77/1:50
Exercise equipment   PM78/8:64
Exercise equipment, indoor   NS82/1:43
Exercise jump rope   PM79/3:170
Exercise stand, bicycle   PM80/10:56
Exercise weight bench   PM73/12:152
Exhaust fan, portable   FW83/3-4:14
Exhaust system, shop   FW78/9:76
Extension cord, shock proof   HM81/10:64
Extension cord reel   HM83/10:125
Extension cord reel, lawnmower   PM83/5:73
Eyeglass frames, wood   FW83/7-8:68
Eyeglass holder   PM78/11:196
Eye protection   WB73/7-8:65
Eye protection   WB81/11-12:26
Fabric covers, outdoor   NS83/7-8:82
Fabrics, solar home   NS80/11-12:92
Fabrics, solar home   NS83/1:48
Faceplate chuck turnings without screw holes   FW80/11-12:82
Family room builtins   PM79/10:130
Fan, balancing ceiling   PM83/8:26
Fan, ceiling   HM84/4:145
Fan, ceiling   PM76/4:102
Fan, electronic attic control   PM81/7:27
Fan, installing attic   PM84/7:51
Fan, whole house   HM79/5-6:43
Fan, whole house   HM84/4:144
Fan, whole house   NS80/7-8:29
Fan, whole house attic   WB81/5-6:61
Fan air leak detector   HM81/10:60
Fan cover, whole house   NS84/5-6:6
Fan destratifier   NS81/1:12
Fan kit, ceiling   WB79/11-12:94

Fans, carving on furniture   FW77/6:60
Fans, ceiling   HM79/7-8:14
Fans, ceiling   WB82/7-8:22
Fans, portable house   PM78/6:132
Fans, solar installations   NS82/10:38
Fastener furniture, simple   NS84/9:114
Fasteners   PM82/10:35
Fasteners   WB79/11-12:40
Fasteners, building   HM80/2:104
Fasteners, framing   WB78/9-10:74
Fasteners, metal   WB78/11-12:110
Fasteners, power tool   WB78/5-6:54
Fasteners, rivet techniques   WB72/1-2:28
Fasteners, wall   PM76/9:120
Fasteners, wall   PM80/4:164
Fastening anchors, sheetrock   NS82/1:14
Faucet, extra outdoor   PM81/6:121
Faucet, freeze proof   PM84/12:64
Faucet, modern   WB82/1-2:58
Faucet, repairing leaking   PM83/4:149
Faucet repair   HM72/9:44
Faucet repair   HM79/10:78
Faucet repair   NS82/2:49
Faucet repair   PM75/5:11
Faucet replacement   HM76/6:42
Faucets   WB72/7-8:50
Faucets and showerheads, new   HM83/7-8:56
Feather board   WB78/7-8:41
Feather board   WB80/7-8:80
Feeder, bird   WB75/11-12:22
Feeder, covered bridge bird   WB72/3-4:42
Feeder, squirrel   WB72/1-2:30
Feeder, squirrel proof bird   PM83/8:43
Feeder, squirrel proof bird   PM83/3:109
Feet, carving ball and claw   FW78/3:58
Feet, ogee bracket   FW80/3-4:62
Fence, brick and lattice   PM84/5:88
Fence, concrete privacy   HM78/4:78
Fence, fiberglass   HM72/6:50
Fence, fiberglass   HM77/9:52
Fence, garden   PM78/10:170
Fence, lattice   PM81/8:88
Fence, lattice and post   PM84/5:88
Fence, patio   NS80/9:12
Fence, patio   PM75/8:92
Fence, picket   PM84/5:88
Fence, privacy   HM83/5-6:58
Fence, round picket   HM82/4:38
Fence, rustic basket weave (cedar)   PM84/5:88
Fence, scalloped picket   HM82/4:36

Fence, scroll picket   HM82/4:42
Fence, square picket   HM82/4:40
Fence, stockade   WB82/3-4:98
Fence, stone New England   PM82/7:84
Fence, wood   HM80/5-6:34
Fence, wood   PM80/3:152
Fence gates, wood   WB76/5-6:28
Fence planter, verticle   PM84/3:112
Fence post ferrules   WB83/3-4:113
Fence posts   HM75/2:53
Fence posts   WB80/3-4:96
Fence posts, removing   HM83/9:131
Fence repairs   HM72/3:44
Fences, four   PM84/5:88
Fences, installing   PM74/3:82
Fences, nine wooden   PM78/3:140
Fences, picket   NS81/7-8:63
Fences, wood   HM76/8:34
Fences, wood   PM75/7:62
Fences, wooden country picket   PM83/6:89
Fence screen, patio (redwood)   HM80/4:26
Fence stop, self locking table saw   PM83/11:106
Fern stand   WB79/1-2:70
Fern stand, antique (oak)   WB82/5-6:80
Fern stand, spiral pedestal   WB81/1-2:60
Ferruled handles, turned   WB74/9-10:42
Ferrules, tool   FW80/9-10:22
Fiberboard   FW81/7-8:76
Fiberglass, insulation protection   WB83/5-6:82
Fiberglass, using   PM76/8:92
Fiberglass deck cover   HM79/3:22
Fiberglass fence   HM72/6:50
Fiberglass fence   HM77/9:52
Fiberglass greenhouse, $350   HM79/7-8:20
Fiberglass insulation, cutting   PM79/9:145
Fiberglass patches   PM80/4:130
Fiberglass patio cover   WB80/5-6:54
Fiberglass patio screen   WB73/5-6:23
Fiberglass screen, outdoor   HM72/8:52
Fiberglass tool holder   WB83/1-2:107
Fiberglass truck cap, wood   WB82/3-4:44
Fiberglass tub and shower panels   HM76/9:40
Fiber optics   WB73/1-2:50
Fiber optics lamp   PM73/12:67
Fiddleback footstool   WB76/1-2:12
Field saw, compact   PM84/4:112
File, breaking safely   PM84/5:230
File cabinet   HM83/2:37
File cabinet, home   WB72/3-4:36
File cabinet, three drawer   WS83/9-10:10

File cabinet, two drawer (maple plywood)   WS80/1:8
File cabinet (oak)   HM84/1:63
File caddy, two drawer   WS84/1-2:12
File cleaning   FW80/5-6:18
File handle from old paint brush   PM84/12:167
Files, woodshop   FW84/5-6:40
Files and rasps   PM77/10:132
Files and rasps, tips   HM84/3:12
Files and rasps, tips   HM84/4:18
Filing stand   PM80/5:55
Filler, auto body   HM82/2:70
Fillers, wood   WB73/1-2:42
Fillet knife   PM73/6:58
Film dryer, photo   PM72/12:56
Film repair, movie   PM83/11:158
Films, window   NS84/5-6:56
Film washer   PM74/8:12
Film washer   PM81/9:63
Filter, air   WB77/3-4:84
Filter, refrigerated water   PM84/11:48
Filters, water   HM82/11:30
Financing owner built home   NS81/2:52
Finger and box joints, router jig   PM84/1:75
Finger joint, blind   FW84/5-6:70
Finger joint jig, adjustable   WB81/11-12:91
Finger joint jig, table saw   FW80/1-2:13
Finger joints, band saw   FW83/3-4:14
Finger joint slide top box   WS81/9:14
Fingerlap or box joint   PM82/1:101
Finish, ammonia fumed oak   FW81/5-6:70
Finish, antiqued furniture   FW77/6:54
Finish, bar top   WB75/11-12:24
Finish, char   HM80/5-6:122
Finish, distressing furniture   WB75/1-2:48
Finish, French polish   FW75/12:44
Finish, French polish   FW80/1-2:66
Finish, furniture   HM83/4:103
Finish, marbleizing   WB75/7-8:10
Finish, oil/varnish   FW79/11-12:76
Finish, oil/varnish mix   FW76/3:46
Finish, outdoor varnish   WB73/9-10:22
Finish, piano   FW84/1-2:58
Finish, repairing cracked   FW84/11-12:74
Finish, tortoiseshell paint   WB74/11-12:66
Finish, tung oil   FW78/10:55
Finish, varnish   PM78/2:134
Finish, varnish rubbed on   FW84/3-4:39
Finish, water based varnish   FW84/7-8:65
Finishes   WB76/11-12:84
Finishes   WB76/9-10:76

Finishes, clear   WB80/5-6:72
Finishes, clear Watco Minwax Deft   FW81/1-2:64
Finishes, decorative   HM81/3:26
Finishes, fine tuning color   FW82/11-12:101
Finishes, furniture   NS83/2:30
Finishes, lacquer   WB73/3-4:54
Finishes, metal on wood   WB79/7-8:61
Finishes, oil   WB75/9-10:8
Finishes, oil   WS83/11-12:12
Finishes, oil stain   WB72/3-4:40
Finishes, old   FW82/3-4:71
Finishes, old time   FW81/7-8:28
Finishes, outdoor   FW83/9-10:66
Finishes, outdoor   WS83/5-6:14
Finishes, stain   PM77/12:120
Finishes, water stains   WB72/5-6:56
Finishes, wood   NS81/3:16
Finishing, coloring with penetrating oils   FW81/3-4:65
Finishing, lacquer   FW81/11-12:90
Finishing, polymerized tung oil   WS84/3-4:7
Finishing, rustproof   WB73/5-6:40
Finishing, smoke   FW83/1-2:97
Finishing, stain   WB78/11-12:88
Finishing, wax French polishing   FW82/3-4:73
Finishing, wood graining kit   WB83/7-8:34
Finishing and sanding, lathe   FW81/7-8:58
Finishing furniture guide   PM77/2:115
Finishing kitchen cabinets   WB74/7-8:8
Finishing materials   FW79/7-8:72
Finishing notes   FW78/6:64
Finishing pigments, dyes and stains   FW78/9:58
Finishing problems, spray   FW81/11-12:94
Finishing sander techniques   HM83/10:16
Finishing screw holes   WB74/9-10:8
Finishing sealers   WB72/11-12:50
Finishing stains and dyes   FW82/3-4:75
Finishing techniques, hand rubbed sheen   WS81/3:9
Finishing tips   PM82/2:112
Finishing tips, applying   PM82/3:150
Finishing toys   WB73/7-8:44
Finishing unfinished furniture   WB76/1-2:64
Finishing walnut   WB78/1-2:98
Finishing wood   WB76/3-4:22
Finishing wood fillers   WB73/1-2:42
Finish preparation   FW79/9-10:75
Finish preparation   FW79/5-6:69
Finish repair   FW82/5-6:92
Fire alarms   PM76/12:74
Fire alarms, installation   HM77/5-6:36
Fire and burglar alarms   WB78/3-4:10

Fire damage repair   NS81/7-8:76
Fire damage repair   WB82/5-6:26
Fire engine, mini pumper/motorbike   PM74/10:92
Fire extinguishers   HM78/5-6:44
Fire extinguishers   HM83/1:84
Fire extinguishers   WB81/7-8:39
Firepit, deck   HM83/5-6:52
Fireplace   WB75/7-8:44
Fireplace   WB80/1-2:34
Fireplace, adding a damper   PM84/10:189
Fireplace, basement   WB82/9-10:30
Fireplace, customizing prefab   PM79/1:92
Fireplace, decorative   WB75/11-12:60
Fireplace, fake   PM75/11:148
Fireplace, Finland   NS83/1:50
Fireplace, forced air   WB79/11-12:82
Fireplace, freestanding   HM73/10:44
Fireplace, masonry high efficiency   NS84/10:77
Fireplace, outdoor   HM79/9:112
Fireplace, prefab   HM82/11:92
Fireplace, prefab   WB78/1-2:58
Fireplace, Rumford   NS81/9:26
Fireplace, smoke problems   HM78/3:46
Fireplace, smoking   PM73/1:76
Fireplace, tile customizing   PM79/4:160
Fireplace, zero clearance prefab   HM84/11:48
Fireplace bar/entertainment unit   PM75/1:76
Fireplace bench, Victorian   HM83/11:32
Fireplace boiler/solar heated home   PM80/9:117
Fireplace brick, cleaning   HM78/10:62
Fireplace chimney, backdrafting   NS84/11-12:32
Fireplace chimney, cleaning   PM80/1:110
Fireplace chimney repair   HM84/9:68
Fireplace cover, aluminum   PM80/1:63
Fireplace/desk/bench   HM78/2:32
Fireplace furnance grate   PM74/10:154
Fireplace hearth, raised   PM78/7:102
Fireplace heat exchanger   WB81/3-4:84
Fireplace heating tips   PM80/9:122
Fireplace improvements   NS81/9:29
Fireplace insert, installing   PM82/9:148
Fireplace inserts   NS81/9:37
Fireplace kit   HM75/9:52
Fireplace kit   HM77/10:14
Fireplace kit, prefab   HM81/10:54
Fireplace mantel   HM73/6:56
Fireplace mantel, Colonial molding   WB82/1-2:76
Fireplace mantel Christmas village   PM81/12:114
Fireplace noise   HM75/11:61
Fireplace remodeling   PM72/11:110

Fireplace remodeling   WB76/9-10:38
Fireplace repairs   HM72/9:38
Fireplace restoration   NS81/3:14
Fireplaces, modern   WB81/9-10:26
Fireplace tools   NS81/9:53
Fireplace tool set and rack   PM81/3:26
Fireplace tube heaters   HM79/12:14
Fireplace wall   PM78/7:101
Fireplace water heater and radiator   HM74/3:38
Fireplace wood box   WB78/9-10:92
Fire protection   WB75/3-4:28
Fires, woodstove   HM80/9:60
Fire safety, home   PM78/9:96
Firewood   PM77/10:120
Firewood   WB78/5-6:62
Firewood, buying   HM80/10:92
Firewood, buying   HM83/10:120
Firewood, crosscut sawing   PM80/10:106
Firewood, cutting   HM82/11:74
Firewood, cutting and burning   PM75/10:60
Firewood, heating with   HM81/10:83
Firewood, lathe turning   PM83/12:70
Firewood, newspaper log roller   HM75/10:46
Firewood, seasoning   WB79/9-10:89
Firewood, splitting and storing   HM78/1:40
Firewood and coal mixing   NS80/9:44
Firewood basket   WB81/11-12:92
Firewood basket, copper pipe   WB82/9-10:94
Firewood box, Colonial   PM77/10:125
Firewood box/window seat pass through   NS84/1:16
Firewood buggy and storage rack   WB80/1-2:40
Firewood canvas carrier   PM82/1:102
Firewood carrier   PM78/10:217
Firewood cart   PM77/10:124
Firewood co-ops   NS80/3:41
Firewood cutting, tree felling   PM73/9:90
Firewood cutting tips   PM82/11:70
Firewood cutting tote bucket   HM81/10:80
Firewood double deck bench   HM79/10:111
Firewood dryer, solar   NS81/9:30
Firewood dryers, solar   PM83/9:122
Firewood heating switch worksheet   NS84/10:78
Firewood holder, indoor (oak)   PM82/1:102
Firewood holder, wrought iron indoor   PM82/1:102
Firewood holders, three   PM82/1:102
Firewood kiln, solar   WB81/9-10:82
Firewood rack, aluminum bar   HM83/11:94
Firewood rack, indoor   HM80/11:34
Firewood rack, indoor A-frame   WB84/3-4:120
Firewood rack, octagonal outdoor   HM79/10:103

Firewood rack, outdoor   HM79/10:104
Firewood sawbuck   HM75/10:58
Firewood sawbuck   HM79/10:102
Firewood sawbuck   PM80/10:187
Firewood sawbuck, portable   HM84/9:136
Firewood sawing crib   HM80/11:30
Firewood shed   PM78/10:132
Firewood sling cable   PM81/12:55
Firewood solar dryer   HM81/10:89
Firewood splitter, buying   PM82/11:178
Firewood splitter plans to order $8.95   PM77/10:123
Firewood splitter plans to order, $8.95   PM78/10:142
Firewood splitters   NS80/10:18
Firewood storage and TV cabinet   WB81/11-12:102
Firewood storage bin   PM77/10:125
Firewood storage box   HM79/10:108
Firewood/storage shed   HM82/9:92
Firewood storage shed   PM81/10:114
Firewood substitute, newspaper   NS81/10:86
Firewood switch computer program   NS84/10:28
Firewood tips   PM80/9:124
Firewood tote, green wood   FW83/11-12:39
Fir or maple knockdown Oriental table   FW80/1-2:59
Fir or walnut kitchen serving cart   FW77/3:58
Fish, catfish in greenhouse   HM82/3:25
Fish, stained glass   HM81/11:97
Fishhooks, sharpening tips   PM81/8:82
Fishing bow reel, center shot   PM73/5:153
Fishing fly rods (bamboo)   FW82/5-6:68
Fishing gear rack   WB74/5-6:22
Fishing knots   PM80/6:178
Fishing net, laminated (walnut and maple)   FW80/1-2:56
Fishing plugs   PM76/4:93
Fishing pole, ice   PM84/2:160
Fishing rod, custom   PM79/4:120
Fishing rod and gun travel case, PVC   PM74/11:178
Fishing rod brackets, auto   PM78/6:69
Fishing rod carrier, auto   PM77/7:103
Fishing rod holder, wall   PM78/2:125
Fishing rod repair   PM73/10:151
Fish plaques   HM80/11:56
Fish pond, solar   NS84/4:16
Fitting, French   FW80/7-8:79
Flageolet, turning a woodwind   FW77/9:80
Flag poles   PM76/6:90
Flagstone, sealing patio   HM84/9:74
Flagstone designs, cutting   HM74/4:50
Flash, close up macro light   PM81/11:25
Flash extension bracket   PM81/3:88
Flashing, roof   NS82/3:30

Flashing repair, roof   HM83/9:87
Flashlight, with beacon   PM79/2:18
Flat roof repair   HM83/9:96
Flax spool candleholder   PM78/11:202
Flintlock rifle replica kit   WB72/5-6:50
Float, planemaker's   FW81/9-10:63
Floor, ceramic tile   HM72/4:44
Floor, ceramic tile   HM84/4:85
Floor, clay tile   PM76/12:106
Floor, flagstone design cutting   HM74/4:50
Floor, hardwood   NS83/11-12:20
Floor, hardwood   PM80/4:137
Floor, hardwood parquet   WB73/5-6:20
Floor, installing ceramic tile   HM84/4:96
Floor, installing sub   HM84/5-6:78
Floor, kitchen   HM83/7-8:48
Floor, painted   PM78/7:101
Floor, painted design on wood   PM83/1:108
Floor, parquet   HM72/10:42
Floor, parquet   HM77/4:26
Floor, parquet   HM82/7-8:38
Floor, parquet   PM76/2:118
Floor, parquet   PM84/6:88
Floor, parquet   WB81/9-10:72
Floor, patching hardwood   HM84/2:60
Floor, patching sheet   PM73/3:142
Floor, plastic brick   HM74/9:48
Floor, quarry tile   PM76/4:144
Floor, quarry tile   PM84/6:87
Floor, reclaim hardwood   HM83/1:64
Floor, refinishing hardwood   PM83/1:100
Floor, sagging   HM82/1:44
Floor, slate entry   WB82/7-8:36
Floor, solar   NS82/3:88
Floor, solar heated house   NS83/3:30
Floor, solar radiant   NS84/9:38
Floor, squeaky   HM75/2:46
Floor, squeaky   NS83/2:52
Floor, squeaky   PM73/5:98
Floor, tile   HM74/3:34
Floor, vinyl   HM75/10:50
Floor, vinyl   HM78/1:43
Floor, vinyl   HM79/1:18
Floor, vinyl   HM81/1:44
Floor, vinyl   HM83/7-8:50
Floor, vinyl   HM84/9:45
Floor, vinyl   PM75/9:100
Floor, vinyl   PM84/4:121
Floor, vinyl   WB84/3-4:86
Floor, wood   HM80/2:77

Floor, wood   PM77/1:102
Floor and stair repair   HM76/2:30
Floor boards, salvaging   HM82/1:70
Floor candlesticks, turned spiral   PM72/10:178
Floor care, hardwood   HM83/1:67
Floor covering, resilient tile   WB80/11-12:73
Floor covering, sheet   PM77/8:18
Floor covering, sheet   PM77/12:126
Floor coverings, asbestos   HM83/7-8:54
Floor framing   WB77/11-12:78
Flooring, sheet   WB81/9-10:130
Floor lamp   NS81/10:58
Floor lamp, turned   WB84/5-6:38
Floor lamp (walnut)   WB77/5-6:68
Floor mirror   WB76/3-4:90
Floor mirror, antique   WB84/1-2:34
Floor refinishing, hardwood   HM76/10:38
Floor refinishing, hardwood   PM75/10:92
Floor refinishing, hardwood   WB77/1-2:12
Floor repair   HM73/3:46
Floor repair, hardwood   HM73/4-5:25
Floor repair, sagging   HM77/7-8:56
Floor repair, warped   HM83/2:65
Floor safe   PM79/11:85
Floor safe, installing   PM79/1:86
Floor sanding   HM75/4:51
Floor sanding, hardwood   HM74/6:42
Floors and slabs, concrete   PM73/8:92
Floors and walls, insulating   NS80/9:90
Floor scraper, hook and floorman's holder   FW84/11-12:67
Floor squeaks   HM74/4:48
Floor squeaks   HM77/11-12:25
Floor tile   HM75/8:36
Floor tile   HM76/6:44
Floor tile   HM78/1:26
Floor tile   WB74/11-12:48
Floor tile, ceramic   HM80/11:20
Floor tile graphics   PM79/2:134
Flower box, aluminum gutter   PM83/6:104
Flower box bench, roofed   PM74/7:139
Flowerpot A-frame   HM79/3:32
Flowerpot stand (cedar)   WB79/3-4:86
Flower pot tree   WB78/5-6:74
Flowerpot wall planter   WB79/11-12:89
Flue, installing in chimney   PM84/10:170
Fluorescent ceiling lamps   WB84/11-12:124
Fluorescent lamp repair   WB77/1-2:72
Fluorescent lamps   PM76/3:120
Flute, six hole (coco bolo)   FW84/1-2:64
Flute, turning   FW77/9:80

Flute, turning   FW83/7-8:12
Flute boring   FW82/7-8:16
Fluted columns   FW80/11-12:22
Flute hole boring   FW83/1-2:20
Flute playing   FW84/1-2:67
Fluting, miniature   WB84/3-4:32
Fluting jig   FW81/3-4:20
Fly cutter, drill press   WB77/3-4:109
Flying on air cushion, plans to order $9.95   PM84/1:62
Fly rods (bamboo)   FW82/5-6:68
Foamboard shelf/mantel   HM78/3:31
Folding chair, straight   WB84/3-4:100
Folding deck chair and stool (redwood)   WS79/5:6
Folding saw, camp   PM84/4:111
Folding sawhorse   FW83/1-2:14
Folding table, picnic (redwood and cedar)   WS83/5-6:4
Folding table, spider leg carriage   FW83/5-6:70
Folding tables, IV tray (oak)   WS81/7:4
Food and wine cellar, underground   HM82/9-114
Food center, portable   HM82/5-6:56
Food dryer, solar   NS81/5-6:76
Food dryer, solar   PM79/1:100
Food mixer repair   PM74/3:76
Food mixer repair   PM76/12:104
Food pantry, roll out   PM83/4:145
Food processor rack   PM78/9:72
Food processor repair   PM78/6:56
Food storage, basement root cellar   PM82/8:94
Foosball table soccer game   PM78/11:124
Footboard bed table   PM75/9:79
Footrest, drum   WB72/3-4:54
Footstool, canvas and aluminum tubing   PM77/4:128
Footstool, Colonial   PM72/7:130
Footstool, Colonial (walnut)   PM75/1:110
Footstool, fiddleback   WB76/1-2:12
Footstool, fireside   WB78/7-8:30
Footstool sewing and magazine rack   WB80/1-2:44
Forge   PM76/5:22
Forge, blacksmith   FW77/12:58
Forge, blacksmith   HM81/5-6:102
Forge, blacksmith   PM78/6:130
Forged coat rack hooks   PM78/6:130
Forging techniques, hand   FW84/1-2:51
Fork, scissor salad   WB79/9-10:80
Formaldehyde, neutralizing   HM83/3:24
Form gauge   NS81/7-8:16
Forstner bit sharpening   HM84/11:10
Forstner bit storage case   WB84/3-4:33
Foundation, insulating   NS80/10:66
Foundation, low cost   NS83/7-8:54

Foundation, wood   NS84/5-6:66
Foundation, wood   WB75/3-4:50
Foundation, wood   WB77/3-4:54
Foundation batter boards, water leveling   NS84/2:18
Foundation crack repair   HM83/9:96
Foundation insulation   NS83/9:64
Foundries   FW81/1-2:86
Fountain pool, concrete   HM78/4:78
Foyer remodeling   PM79/6:112
Foyer table/bench   PM79/6:112
Frame, deep needlework   PM73/12:154
Frame and panel   FW80/7-8:55
Frame and panel cabinet (pine)   WS80/3:8
Frame and panel door   WS80/3:6
Frame and panel doors   FW84/11-12:44
Frame and panel joint, stub tenon and groove   WS83/9-10:22
Frame and panel variations   FW81/7-8:59
Frame clamping jig   FW79/9-10:59
Frame holder, painting picture   PM82/12:132
Frame joint, mortise and tenon   WS83/3-4:7
Frame miter jig, picture   PM82/12:98
Frame production   FW79/9-10:59
Frames, barn wood picture   PM77/2:184
Frames, molding picture   PM79/8:96
Frames, needlepoint working   PM83/2:72
Frames, picture   HM75/11:56
Frames and framing pictures   HM83/10:65
Framing, addition   HM81/3:14
Framing, basement walls   PM73/3:140
Framing, estimating lumber   NS84/9:26
Framing, house   NS83/4:8
Framing, metal connectors   HM84/5-6:82
Framing, stud straightening   HM83/3:106
Framing, toenailing tips   NS84/4:18
Framing, truss   PM79/6:164
Framing, two foot spacing   PM72/12:62
Framing, using plywood   NS84/7-8:32
Framing, wall   WB78/1-2:40
Framing, wider studs   WB76/7-8:66
Framing and matting, picture   PM73/2:77
Framing construction   FW78/6:68
Framing fasteners   WB78/9-10:74
Framing fasteners, building   HM80/2:104
Framing lumber computer program   NS84/9:30
Framing square, trueing   FW79/7-8:15
Framing square protractor   WB79/11-12:20
Framing walls   NS84/1:18
Freezer repair   PM74/1:72
French doors   PM84/12:104
French fitting   FW80/7-8:79

```
French polish finish    FW75/12:44
French polishing, wax   FW82/3-4:73
French polishing finish    FW80/1-2:66
French provencial bread cupboard    WB77/1-2:44
French provincial bed, four poster canopy    WB82/5-6:58
French provincial chest of drawers    WB82/7-8:70
French provincial desk    WB82/9-10:99
French provincial dresser    WB82/3-4:4
French provincial gun cabinet    WB73/3-4:46
French provincial nightstand    WB82/9-10:99
French provincial sewing cabinet    WB75/1-2:30
Freon solar system    NS81/4:76
Fretsaw, treadle powered    WB79/3-4:42
Fretsaw for marquetry    FW83/11-12:60
Froe, homemade    FW79/5-6:16
Froe handle    FW79/3-4:21
Front, door, adding air lock    PM83/11:100
Front door replacement    PM82/2:167
Froozen plumbing    HM73/1:42
Frosted glass, glue chipping glass    PM75//:136
Fruit basket    WB78/5-6:44
Fruit basket, folding plywood    PM74/2:140
Fruit basket, metal tubing    PM74/3:138
Fruit bowl    PM72/3:142
Fruit bowl, cut glass bottle    PM72/12:104
Fruit bowl, pewter    PM79/8:92
Fruit bowl, turned    WB73/5-6:63
Fruit bowl, turned    WS82/5:18
Fruit dryer    PM76/5:112
Fuel, oil or gas    NS81/9:92
Fuel costs    NS81/3:23
Fuel switching computer program    NS82/9:39
Fumed oak finish, ammonia    FW81/5-6:70
Furnace, cleaning oil    NS83/10:26
Furnace, gas    NS82/5-6:12
Furnace, HSHSA garbage plans to order $20    PM81/8:32
Furnace, improving    PM80/9:130
Furnace, metalworking    PM77/11:126
Furnace, multifuel    PM79/10:122
Furnace, oil    HM81/2:50
Furnace, oil    HM81/1:68
Furnace, oil    HM81/3:92
Furnace, oil    HM81/4:48
Furnace, use less oil    NS80/10:49
Furnace, warm air    HM77/10:28
Furnace, wood    HM78/3:32
Furnace, wood    WB78/9-10:16
Furnace booster fan    HM76/10:44
Furnace chimney damper    PM78/11:14
Furnace humidifier    HM76/3:38
```

Furnace maintenance   HM77/2:40
Furnace maintenance   HM80/12:64
Furnace maintenance   PM77/2:104
Furnace maintenance, gas   NS83/11-12:24
Furnace maintenance, oil   PM84/10:56
Furnace maintenance   PM78/10:120
Furnace noise   HM80/11:50
Furnace repair, gas   HM76/1:38
Furnaces, new minis   NS82/10:66
Furnace update   WB80/3-4:58
Furnace vent damper   HM79/2:44
Furnace/wood stove piggyback   HM77/10:38
Furniture, Adirondack wooden lawn   PM82/6:116
Furniture, antiqued finish   FW77/6:54
Furniture, barrel   WB74/5-6:32
Furniture, bedroom   WB73/3-4:36
Furniture, bedroom   WS84/7-8:4
Furniture, bentwood   FW80/1-2:38
Furniture, blockfront   FW80/7-8:47
Furniture, built-in   HM79/9:14
Furniture, butcher block   PM76/12:110
Furniture, carpeted boxes   HM78/7-8:77
Furniture, carved Alpine peasant   FW80/5-6:48
Furniture, clear plastic   HM77/7-8:34
Furniture, conserving   FW82/7-8:60
Furniture, crate   HM77/4:74
Furniture, cushion waterproofing   PM73/10:108
Furniture, fast plywood   HM78/11-12:28
Furniture, folding canvas lawn   PM79/3:146
Furniture, kitchen cabinet   PM75/12:70
Furniture, knockdown   FW84/3-4:44
Furniture, low cost lawn   HM79/3:50
Furniture, mass produced   FW84/1-2:32
Furniture, Mediterranean outdoor   WB80/7-8:82
Furniture, miniature   WB83/9-10:76
Furniture, modular   PM74/1:63
Furniture, modular office   HM83/2:34
Furniture, outdoor   WS79/5:11
Furniture, outdoor block/wood picnic table   PM73/6:76
Furniture, painted   FW77/9:48
Furniture, paper   PM72/6:132
Furniture, park bench   PM81/8:94
Furniture, platform   HM81/9:42
Furniture, refinishing   FW77/12:32
Furniture, refinishing   PM83/11:108
Furniture, refinishing outdoor   WB77/3-4:82
Furniture, restoring antique   HM83/1:51
Furniture, restoring wicker   HM84/5-6:123
Furniture, rewebbing patio   HM77/7-8:43
Furniture, rustic willow patio   HM84/4:122

Furniture, scratch repair   PM73/11:102
Furniture, Selbermachen dowel   HM80/1:11
Furniture, shipping   FW84/11-12:84
Furniture, simple fastener   NS84/9:114
Furniture, Sonotube   HM79/9:115
Furniture, Taos (pine)   FW83/5-6:79
Furniture, unfinished   PM79/12:96
Furniture, unfinished   WB76/1-2:64
Furniture arrangement   NS83/11-12:60
Furniture buying   HM82/10:40
Furniture care   HM81/11:106
Furniture cleaning and polishing   HM83/1:55
Furniture crack repair   FW77/9:22
Furniture distressing finish   WB75/1-2:48
Furniture finishes   NS83/2:30
Furniture finishing guide   PM77/2:115
Furniture finish repair   FW82/5-6:92
Furniture from anything   NS80/2:89
Furniture from photographs   FW79/7-8:61
Furniture gluing   PM79/8:90
Furniture hardware   FW82/5-6:86
Furniture hardware   WB81/5-6:70
Furniture kits   HM77/11-12:20
Furniture kits   HM80/7-8:20
Furniture kits   HM82/1:38
Furniture kits   WB78/7-8:6
Furniture kits   WB81/9-10:4
Furniture kits   WB84/9-10:85
Furniture kits, Shaker   PM76/7:98
Furniture kits, Shaker   PM84/10:108
Furniture maintenance   HM80/10:34
Furniture making tips   HM80/2:78
Furniture marquetry   FW83/1-2:61
Furniture painting   WB79/7-8:46
Furniture refinishing   HM75/3:64
Furniture refinishing   HM78/1:36
Furniture refinishing   HM81/9:94
Furniture refinishing   NS83/2:24
Furniture refinishing   NS83/2:27
Furniture refinishing   PM75/12:76
Furniture refinishing, finish   HM83/4:103
Furniture refinishing, stripping   HM83/2:80
Furniture refinishing, stripping/staining   PM75/11:114
Furniture refinishing, surface preparation   HM83/3:98
Furniture repair   HM74/4:38
Furniture repair   NS83/2:20
Furniture repair   WB80/1-2:92
Furniture repair, cracks   HM83/1:57
Furniture repair, metal patio   HM75/4:46
Furniture repair, old   FW83/5-6:66

Furniture repair, patch   WB74/1-2:16
Furniture repair, warping   HM83/1:56
Furniture repair with glue   HM81/4:56
Furniture restoring   FW80/5-6:65
Furniture restoring   HM77/9:55
Furniture restoring   WB75/3-4:12
Furniture stripping   HM72/9:52
Furniture stripping   HM75/2:42
Furniture stripping, professional   HM79/12:24
Fuses, electrical   WB79/11-12:117
Game, air hockey table top   PM75/11:94
Game, backgammon board and box   PM77/5:110
Game, baseball board   PM79/4:122
Game, basketball goal with adjustable height   PM76/8:98
Game, bean bag bull's eye   PM74/9:138
Game, bean bag toss   WB75/11-12:71
Game, chess set   WB76/11-12:78
Game, child's chessmen   WB75/11-12:82
Game, dice box   WB75/1-2:62
Game, dominoes   WB78/1-2:48
Game, electronic coin toss   PM78/5:45
Game, electronic hand coordination   PM81/2:141
Game, hearts cubes   WB83/1-2:26
Game, marble balancing board   PM74/5:162
Game, marble ramps   WB80/11-12:78
Game, marble travel   PM76/4:210
Game, number guessing electric   PM73/1:134
Game, paddle ball   WB81/11-12:96
Game, puzzle   WB76/3-4:16
Game, ring   WB81/11-12:96
Game, solo ping pong   WB81/11-12:96
Game, Swiss cheese mountain   PM72/7:147
Game, table soccer   PM78/11:124
Game, tee   PM76/2:34
Game, tee solution   PM76/7:6
Game, tetherball   PM76/8:99
Gameboard, backgammon   FW82/3-4:66
Gameboard, cross   WB78/5-6:59
Gameboard, fox and geese   WB78/5-6:59
Gameboard, friends   WB78/5-6:59
Gameboard, marble trap   WB78/5-6:59
Gameboard, migration   WB78/5-6:59
Gameboard, nine puzzle   WB78/5-6:59
Gameboard cabinet   WB78/5-6:58
Game cabinet, video   PM84/3:110
Game card holder, two decks   WS84/9-10:18
Game chest/lap desk, child's   WB84/5-6:72
Game/coffee table   HM80/1:70
Game/dining table   WB83/9-10:50
Game rack, domino   WB78/11-12:100

Game table, backgammon/chess   PM78/10:65
Game table, butcher block checkers   WB82/11-12:100
Game table, butcher block cribbage   WB82/11-12:100
Game table, chess   PM81/2:159
Game table, chess and backgammon   WB79/7-8:70
Game table, cribbage board two drawer   WB83/11-12:116
Game table, marquetry   WB72/1-2:36
Game table, shuffleboard   PM73/12:154
Gaming dice, electronic   PM79/3:14
Garage   PM78/9:111
Garage, building   HM78/7-8:44
Garage, workshop   WB72/9-10:26
Garage back-up mirror   HM82/10:81
Garage/barn, country plans to order $30   PM84/9:90
Garage ceiling   HM75/3:24
Garage door, double panes and panels   PM81/12:158
Garage door, insulated   WB82/7-8:4
Garage door insulation kit   WB84/11-12:100
Garage door lock, electric   WB80/9-10:46
Garage door lock, electronic   PM81/5:132
Garage door maintenance   HM83/9:76
Garage door opener   PM78/2:130
Garage door opener   WB74/3-4:38
Garage door opener, buying   HM79/10:113
Garage door opener, emergency release   PM80/10:40
Garage door opener, installation   HM73/2:40
Garage door opener, installation   HM77/3:50
Garage door opener, installation   HM84/9:117
Garage door opener, installation   PM73/4:170
Garage door opener alarm system   PM75/5:210
Garage door open warning light   WB82/9-10:109
Garage door painting   HM84/9:79
Garage door repair   HM73/8:58
Garage door repair   PM78/8:102
Garage door safety block   PM82/4:22
Garage engine hoist   PM83/4:168
Garage entry remodeling   HM83/4:40
Garage family room   HM79/2:88
Garage kitchen conversion   WB81/7-8:36
Garage parking guide   WB80/1-2:129
Garage parts washer   HM82/9:120
Garage remodeling   HM81/11:19
Garage remodeling   NS84/2:37
Garage remodeling   PM74/10:162
Garage screen   WB76/5-6:33
Garage shop, designing   PM82/5:126
Garage storage   HM78/11-12:68
Garage storage   PM76/2:120
Garage storage   PM77/2:122
Garage storage   WB77/3-4:74

Garage storage, increasing   PM82/11:170
Garage storage cabinets   HM72/4:54
Garage storage cabinets, between cars   HM74/6:34
Garage tool cabinets, mobile   PM81/10:122
Garage tool dolly   PM82/10:132
Garage tree playhouse   HM81/5-6:14
Garage tune-up bench   PM75/4:105
Garage workbench   PM82/10:128
Garage workshop/utility room   HM83/12:26
Garbage bag holder   PM84/5:224
Garbage can cart   HM80/12:60
Garbage can pit   PM81/6:119
Garbage can rack   HM81/5-6:60
Garbage can retainer   HM82/4:116
Garbage can shed, lean-to   PM82/6:112
Garden, carpeted   HM79/4:90
Garden, food and landscaping   NS83/2:89
Garden, indoor   HM81/3:64
Garden, indoor   PM75/4:120
Garden, indoor light   HM81/3:77
Garden, Oriental   NS81/5-6:30
Garden, Oriental   WB78/3-4:54
Garden, raised bed   PM82/3:132
Garden arbor   PM82/3:132
Garden barrel, strawberry   PM73/5:88
Garden basket   WB78/5-6:44
Garden bench   NS81/5-6:46
Garden bench   WB78/3-4:56
Garden bench, roofed   PM74/7:139
Garden benches   PM76/4:135
Garden benches, patio and park   PM84/6:78
Garden bench (redwood)   WS79/5:8
Garden bench (redwood and cedar)   WS83/5-6:12
Garden caddy   WB78/5-6:36
Garden cart   PM77/3:97
Garden cart   PM80/7:110
Garden cart   PM83/10:69
Garden cart   WB82/3-4:119
Garden cart, heavy duty   PM82/11:158
Garden cart, heavy duty   PM82/6:123
Garden cart, PVC pipe   WB83/7-8:94
Garden cart/potting bench (redwood)   HM83/3:60
Garden center (redwood)   HM80/4:22
Garden clean-up table   HM79/3:31
Garden cloche, mini greenhouse   PM83/3:105
Garden cold frame   NS83/1:76
Garden cold frame   PM76/3:92
Garden cold frame   PM78/3:152
Garden cold frame/solar dryer   PM84/3:112
Garden fence   PM78/10:170

Garden frame, raised bed   NS83/1:76
Garden gazebo   PM76/4:121
Garden gazebo, canopy   PM76/4:121
Garden gazebo, square   PM84/6:74
Garden hotbed   PM78/3:154
Garden house, lattice   PM84/6:74
Gardening, greenhouse   NS84/11-12:88
Gardening with rocks and pebbles   PM78/3:144
Garden irrigation, drip   NS84/9:68
Garden kneeler   WB77/7-8:57
Garden lettuce shader   PM83/3:105
Garden planter   NS81/5-6:46
Garden planter, verticle fence   PM84/3:112
Garden planters   PM76/4:134
Garden pool, stone and concrete   WB81/3-4:56
Garden pools, four   PM84/8:94
Garden potting bench   PM79/5:140
Garden potting bench   PM80/8:95
Garden rake, wooden   NS83/4:30
Gardens, French and Chinese vegetable   HM83/3:50
Garden screen house   PM76/4:121
Garden seed starter, indoor   NS84/1:87
Garden shears, buying   PM79/3:142
Garden shed, small contemporary   PM83/8:80
Garden shed, solar   PM81/3:136
Garden shelter (redwood)   HM78/7-8:14
Garden soil mixer   PM73/4:122
Garden stacking boxes and carriers   PM82/8:96
Garden storage/bench boxes   HM84/5-6:40
Garden storage chest   WB73/3-4:52
Garden temple lantern   WB78/3-4:56
Garden tiller maintenance   WB74/3-4:22
Garden tiller tips   PM78/3:160
Garden tool cart   NS80/7-8:41
Garden tool maintenance   PM78/3:168
Garden tool shed/mini greenhouse lean-to   PM82/6:110
Garden trailer   HM84/3:99
Garden trellis   NS83/1:79
Garden trellis   PM83/6:104
Garden trellis, A-frame   HM79/3:30
Garden trellis, arched lattice   PM84/6:74
Garden wagon, mower pulled   WB78/5-6:80
Garden waterfall and rock garden, $50   HM78/9:93
Garden workshop, closet   HM81/3:67
Garland, pine cone Christmas   PM72/12:75
Gas cooker plans to order, $3.00   NS83/5-6:81
Gas furnace   NS82/5-6:12
Gas furnace maintenance   NS83/11-12:24
Gas furnace repair   HM76/1:38
Gas gauge, inexpensive boat   PM74/2:106

Gas or oil fuel   NS81/9:92
Gas range, connecting   HM84/2:66
Gas tank, auto auxiliary   PM74/6:148
Gas welding and cutting   WB80/11-12:102
Gate, wood   PM80/3:176
Gate, wooden country   PM81/8:88
Gate, wood no sag   HM83/4:64
Gate latch, pioneer latch   WB81/3-4:59
Gate leg and drop leaf tables   FW79/9-10:62
Gate leg buffet table, six (cherry)   WS82/3:14
Gate leg contemporary table (oak)   FW76/6:42
Gate leg table   PM82/4:123
Gate leg table   WB75/9-10:34
Gate leg table   WB78/9-10:6
Gate leg table   WB79/5-6:95
Gate leg table, mini/maxi   PM72/10:172
Gates, wooden fence   PM83/6:90
Gates, wooden fence   PM84/5:88
Gates, wooden fence   WB76/5-6:28
Gauge, Archimedes' marking   FW83/3-4:14
Gauge, cutting   FW82/1-2:82
Gauge, cutting   FW82/5-6:8
Gauge, form   NS81/7-8:16
Gauge, marking   FW82/3-4:97
Gauges, pencil   FW78/6:76
Gazebo   HM80/5-6:23
Gazebo   HM80/5-6:98
Gazebo   NS81/5-6:26
Gazebo   WB82/3-4:84
Gazebo, canopy   PM76/4:121
Gazebo, garden   PM76/4:121
Gazebo, large screened   NS84/4:52
Gazebo, Oriental   WB80/3-4:4
Gazebo, square garden   PM84/6:74
Gazebo storage building   PM75/8:90
Gazebo/teahouse   WB83/5-6:64
Gear cutting, wood lathe   WB76/9-10:90
Gears, wooden   FW78/3:44
Gears, wooden   WB78/7-8:70
Gem polisher   PM76/1:102
Generator, installing emergency   PM78/8:18
Generators, portable power   HM78/4:88
Geodesic dome kit   HM73/9:34
Geometric turnings   FW81/7-8:54
Geometry, shop   WB77/11-12:114
Georgian side chair, Chippendale (mahogany)   WB82/1-2:64
Geothermal heat exchanger   NS84/10:14
German armchair   WB74/9-10:36
GFI   NS83/1:80
GFI, ground fault interrupter   HM77/9:30

GFI, ground fault interrupter   HM84/5-6:88
GFI, ground fault interruptor   WB75/1-2:35
GFI extension cord, shock proof   HM81/10:64
Gilding   HM83/1:53
Gilding, gold leaf   FW79/3-4:80
Gilding, gold water   FW84/5-6:82
Gilding, metal leaf   FW82/9-10:77
Gingerbread Christmas tree ornaments   PM79/12:82
Gingerbread doll house, $10   HM79/1:84
Giraffe clothes tree, child's   PM75/11:141
Giraffe coat rack   WB78/11-12:68
Glass, cutting   WB79/3-4:82
Glass, cutting circles   PM78/3:129
Glass, drilling   HM78/4:24
Glass, drilling   PM81/12:112
Glass, efficient window   NS81/9:43
Glass, etched   HM83/7-8:62
Glass, glue chipping   PM75/7:136
Glass, repairing broken window   HM84/10:24
Glass, repairing broken windows   PM84/9.110
Glass, replacing   HM79/4:74
Glass, safety   WB74/3-4:58
Glass, sanding   HM78/1:39
Glass, sanding   PM80/11:196
Glass, sanding   WS81/1:3
Glass, solar installation   NS82/5-6:52
Glass, stained   HM79/9:28
Glass, stained   WB81/5-6:40
Glass and oak modern tables   WS79/1:7
Glass blocks   NS82/10:92
Glass block windows   WB72/9-10:25
Glass bottle lamps   WB82/3-4:58
Glass/bottle rack wine   WB83/9-10:124
Glass bottles, cutting kit   PM72/12:104
Glass cutter, circles and nibbler   WB82/5-6:20
Glass cutting   HM83/10:71
Glass cutting   PM72/10:156
Glass cutting   PM80/7:100
Glass cutting   WS81/1:16
Glass cutting board   HM77/9:44
Glass cutting board   PM73/9:156
Glass cutting frame   WB76/5-6:56
Glass cutting setup   PM82/12:101
Glass door, sliding   WB77/3-4:99
Glass doors   WS81/1:8
Glass doors, leaded   PM84/12:110
Glass etching   WB76/1-2:16
Glass etching kit   PM79/11:16
Glass installation in frames   FW81/9-10:16
Glass insulator bookends   HM82/1:52

Glass jar candle holders   WB81/9-10:14
Glass/oak table, contemporary coffee   PM83/12:148
Glass rack, hanging wine   WB83/3-4:45
Glass rack, wine   PM77/11:144
Glass repair, window   PM73/2:152
Glass replacement, window   HM73/12:44
Glass terrarium, Tiffany   PM78/5:66
Glass top coffee table (walnut)   HM81/1:56
Glass top table, contemporary   WB79/11-12:153
Glass top table, wine rack base   WB80/1-2:70
Glass top table, wrought iron   HM76/4:44
Glass window repair   HM77/7-8:58
Glass/wine rack   WB83/1-2:99
Glazing and caulking   WB73/9-10:58
Glider swing, porch (oak)   HM84/5-6:70
Globe, wooden world   FW79/1-2:61
Gloves   PM77/8:108
Glue   NS82/4:10
Glue   PM76/6:104
Glue, choosing and using   PM83/1:104
Glue, furniture repair   HM81/4:56
Glue, high temperature   HM83/1:20
Glue, hot melt   WB76/9-10:74
Glue, removing excess   FW79/3-4:21
Glue, wood   FW83/11-12:62
Glue bottle   FW81/11-12:22
Glue chipping glass   PM75/7:136
Glue clamps   HM80/9:90
Glue gun caddy   PM74/8:152
Glue gun holder   WB77/3-4:93
Glue kit   WB74/5-6:52
Glue press   FW80/1-2:48
Glues   HM78/4:64
Glues   HM84/5-6:75
Glues, woodworking   FW84/1-2:48
Glues and caulks   WB77/9-10:54
Glues and gluing   FW77/6:28
Glue spreader, laminate   FW81/11-12:22
Gluing chairs   HM83/1:52
Gluing clamp   PM79/8:136
Gluing clamps, shop tips   PM80/12:102
Gluing edge without clamps   FW82/3-4:14
Gluing frame   FW78/3:24
Gluing furniture   PM79/8:90
Gluing panels, edge   WS84/3-4:13
Gluing rack   FW81/11-12:18
Gluing table   FW78/10:14
Gluing table, hot water   FW80/11-12:19
Gluing tips   PM82/8:93
Gluing tips   PM83/8:46

Gluing tips   PM83/7:104
Gluing up   FW81/11-12:86
Goblet, turning   FW83/1-2:72
Goblet, turning (cherry or koa)   WS82/9:4
Go cart plans to order, Mini Indy II   PM78/5:110
Gold, panning for   PM74/7:82
Gold leaf gilding   FW79/3-4:80
Gold leather inlay   FW78/6:61
Gold picture frames, guilding   WB78/7-8:52
Gold water gilding   FW84/5-6:82
Golf cart, two hp mini   HM78/7-8:67
Golf green, patio putting   PM75/8:55
Gophers, protecting plants   PM82/3:52
Gothic tracery   FW76/12:44
Gothic trim, house   WB79/3-4:62
Gouge, bowl turning   FW76/12:55
Gouge, carving   FW80/9-10:73
Gouge, turning   FW78/9:60
Gouge and chisels   WB73/9-10:10
Grading lumber   FW78/10:77
Grain, reading   FW83/11-12:45
Grain mill   HM83/9:103
Grandfather clock, 18th century   FW81/1-2:67
Grandfather clock kit   HM75/4:44
Grandfather clock kit   PM73/8:162
Grandfather clock kit   WB74/5-6:28
Grandfather clock kit   WB76/11-12:56
Grandmother clock case, pocket watch   WB76/9-10:62
Green bowl blanks, freezing   FW83/11-12:12
Greenhouse   HM78/2:65
Greenhouse   HM80/7-8:50
Greenhouse   HM82/3:88
Greenhouse   NS80/2:25
Greenhouse   NS81/11-12:21
Greenhouse   NS84/1:90
Greenhouse   PM76/8:80
Greenhouse   PM81/1:96
Greenhouse   WB77/7-8:36
Greenhouse   WB78/3-4:60
Greenhouse   WB84/1-2:22
Greenhouse, A-frame   HM80/3:28
Greenhouse, fiberglass $350   HM79/7-8:20
Greenhouse, gambrel roof   HM80/3:28
Greenhouse, Gothic   HM80/3:28
Greenhouse, Gothic   WB76/3-4:66
Greenhouse, indoor   WB77/1-2:4
Greenhouse, lean-to   HM80/3:28
Greenhouse, less than $175   HM78/5-6:66
Greenhouse, miniature   NS81/11-12:29
Greenhouse, monitoring   HM82/3:23

Greenhouse, simple modular   WB75/3-4:6
Greenhouse, stone pillared   WB83/5-6:64
Greenhouse, sun pit   HM80/3:28
Greenhouse, window   HM77/7-8:49
Greenhouse, window   HM82/4:64
Greenhouse, window   NS82/3:45
Greenhouse, window   PM75/9:54
Greenhouse, window   WB79/5-6:56
Greenhouse, with catfish   HM82/3:25
Greenhouse and cold frame, lean-to   PM82/3:128
Greenhouse and deck   PM81/4:142
Greenhouse dining room   WB78/5-6:96
Greenhouse gardening   NS81/11-12:33
Greenhouse gardening   NS84/11-12:88
Greenhouse greens   NS81/11-12:30
Greenhouse hydroponics   NS81/11-12:34
Greenhouse kit   PM74/7:154
Greenhouse kits   PM78/3:148
Greenhouse kits, real cost   NS80/3:14
Greenhouse living room   HM82/3:26
Greenhouse over brick planter   WB77/5-6:30
Greenhouse/storage shed   HM72/9:40
Greenhouse sunspace   NS80/11-12:75
Greenhouse sunspace   NS82/7-8:78
Greenhouse table   NS81/11-12:27
Greenhouse/tool shed lean-to, mini   PM82/6:110
Greenhouse window box   HM81/9:28
Green lumber   NS84/5-6:64
Green lumber construction   FW78/6:68
Green wood   FW79/5-6:48
Green wood, PEG 1000   WB82/3-4:106
Green wood, polyethylene glycol   WB72/3-4:48
Green wood and PEG   FW79/11-12:68
Green wood bowl turning   FW76/6:37
Green woodworking   FW82/3-4:50
Grenno interlock joint   FW81/3-4:16
Grid ruling drawing tool   PM80/7:93
Grill, charcoal   NS81/5-6:47
Grill, concrete   HM78/4:78
Grill, deck   HM82/5-6:26
Grill, drum   HM80/3:92
Grill, indoor cabinet   PM72/2:134
Grill, installing indoor   PM81/4:168
Grill, outdoor   HM79/9:112
Grill, outdoor brick   NS83/3:22
Grill, wishing well   WB80/7-8:24
Grill scraper, barbecue   PM84/5:183
Grill shelter, weatherproof   PM73/6:80
Grill work   PM80/6:102
Grill work, hardboard   HM76/1:42

Grill work, window   WB74/5-6:48
Grinder, shop built belt   WB77/5-6:26
Grinder, shop built belt   WB84/9-10:106
Grinder cabinet   HM83/12:28
Grinder sander belt guard   WB78/9-10:88
Grinder/sander/sharpener, shop made   PM82/3:93
Grinder/sander techniques   PM83/5:98
Grinder stand   HM80/4:104
Grinder tips, bench   HM84/12:18
Grinding   FW81/7-8:66
Grooves, router jig for   WS83/11-12:22
Grooving frame, router   WB77/9-10:92
Ground covers   NS80/5-6:29
Ground fault interrupter, GFI   HM84/5-6:88
Grout, ceramic tile   HM84/2:58
Growing frame, solar   NS81/11-12:29
Guest cottage/playhouse   HM82/5-6:66
Guest house cabana   WB74/7-8:44
Guilding picture frames   WB78/7-8:52
Guitar   WB74/7-8:34
Guitar, rosette   FW81/5-6:51
Guitar amp, portable   PM79/9:29
Guitar binding and purfling   FW81/5-6:52
Guitar fuzz box   PM79/2:22
Guitar joints   FW76/12:52
Guitar (lute) roses   FW77/6:38
Guitar making school   FW79/1-2:36
Guitar mosaic rosettes   FW76/9:53
Guitar top clamp, Spanish luthier's   FW80/1-2:18
Gumball machine   HM78/11-12:84
Gun, muzzle loader kits   PM79/10:30
Gun, wooden 1849 pepperbox derringer   PM81/3:72
Gun ammunition, reloading   PM76/10:110
Gun and rod travel case, PVC   PM74/11:178
Gun cabinet   PM75/2:120
Gun cabinet, contemporary (oak)   WB81/9-10:56
Gun cabinet, French provincial   WB73/3-4:46
Gun case, French fitted (Coco Bolo)   PM80/12:106
Gun practice box, target shooting   PM74/6:141
Gun rack   HM79/9:22
Gun rack, oil proof   PM82/2:110
Gun replica kit, flintlock   WB72/5-6:50
Gun restocking   WB72/1-2:46
Gun shooting bench rest   PM77/11:152
Gun shooting tips, pistol   PM76/4:84
Gun stock refinishing   WB78/3-4:69
Gun toy, cardboard shooter   PM80/8:36
Gutter, wooden maintenance   HM72/4:50
Gutter cleaners   PM81/10:58
Gutter downspout well   WB79/9-10:44

Gutter drainage, underground   PM74/7:164
Gutter flower box, aluminum rain   PM83/6:104
Gutter heaters   PM76/11:118
Gutter ice dams   PM73/1:74
Gutter maintenance   HM77/5-6:20
Gutter maintenance   HM83/9:78
Gutter maintenance   HM83/9:65
Gutter maintenance   NS82/10:60
Gutter maintenance   PM73/10:100
Gutter repair   HM73/4-5:46
Gutter repair   HM80/5-6:59
Gutter repair   PM76/4:34
Gutter repair   PM78/4:170
Gutter repair   PM79/4:151
Gutters   HM78/4:44
Gutters, cleaning and repairing   HM84/9:80
Gutters, frozen   HM75/1:40
Gutters, iced   PM84/11:203
Gutters, ice dams   HM79/2:64
Gutters, plastic   HM80/4:36
Gutters, rain   WB77/7-8:44
Gutters, vinyl   WB80/7-8:72
Gutters, vinyl   WB83/7-8:22
Gutter substitutes   HM83/9:82
Gym, child's play center   HM79/10:60
Gym, indoor   NS82/1:43
Gym, indoor toy   PM79/7:80
Gym equipment   PM77/1:50
Gym equipment   PM78/8:64
Gym equipment, child's backyard   PM83/6:98
Gym exercise center, outdoor Parcours   PM79/9:116
Hacksaw, power   WB77/7-8:30
Half lap joint   WS83/5-6:22
Hall butler, Victorian (oak)   HM83/11:24
Hall mirror, round top   WS82/5:16
Hall stand and arched mirror, Colonial   WB82/1-2:92
Hall storage bench   WB76/7-8:36
Hall tree   WB81/3-4:88
Hall tree, traditional turned   WB84/11-12:40
Hall tree, wall and floor   WB76/9-10:44
Hallway mirror/coat rack   PM84/7:132
Hammer, claw   PM77/6:119
Hammer, offset   PM84/5:102
Hammer, veneering   FW78/3:52
Hammered dulcimer kit   PM84/2:104
Hammer handle, replacing   PM83/2:146
Hammers   HM74/1:52
Hammers   HM80/3:44
Hammers   HM83/12:10
Hammers   NS82/2:16

Hammers   WB73/5-6:52
Hammers   WB84/1-2:10
Hammers, make special purpose   PM83/7:46
Hammers, part 1   HM82/4:44
Hammers, part 2   HM82/5-6:100
Hammer safety   WB77/1-2:62
Hammock   PM80/6:110
Hammock stand, contemporary   HM83/5-6:66
Hamper, hippo   WB78/11-12:66
Hamper, laundry   PM84/4:102
Hand and paper towel rack   PM81/2:136
Hand bathroom towel cup holder   PM79/11:122
Hand forging techniques   FW84/1-2:51
Hand grinder trammel point   PM81/1:120
Handicapped home modifications   WB84/3-4:16
Handle, file from old paint brush   PM84/12:167
Handle, handsaw   PM78/1:99
Handle, replacing hammer   PM83/2:146
Handle replacing, splitting mall   PM78/11:132
Handles, ax (hickory)   FW83/7-8:40
Handles, replacing   NS84/7-8:28
Handles, small tool   PM76/4:204
Handles, turned ferruled   WB74/9-10:42
Handles, turning tool   PM83/12:104
Hand planes   FW75/12:22
Handrail, steps   PM79/2:44
Hand ring caddy   PM80/2:124
Handsaw, toy   PM78/11:196
Handsaw basics   HM77/11-12:58
Handsaw clock   PM78/11:196
Handsaw depth stop guide   PM81/7:87
Handsaw handle   PM78/1:99
Handsawing   WB79/7-8:47
Handsaws   NS81/5-6:16
Handsaws   WB73/3-4:10
Handsaws, storing   PM81/4:121
Handsaws, tips   PM84/8:141
Handsaw storage rack   FW83/9-10:10
Handsaw techniques   PM77/11:8
Hand tool mistakes   PM80/9:190
Hangers, coat (plywood)   PM79/11:122
Hangers, kids' clothes   PM77/11:144
Hanging lamp (veneer strips)   WS79/3:9
Hanging planter (scrap wood)   WS79/5:12
Hanging shelves   PM78/11:130
Hanging technique   WS79/7:12
Hang-it-up fasteners   NS82/1:14
Hardboard, storage wall, perforated   HM74/1:36
Hardboard grillwork   HM76/1:42
Hardboard projects   WB81/9-10:32

Hardness metal tester, shop built   PM80/2:80
Hardware, furniture   WB81/5-6:70
Hardware, hand worked brass   FW83/7-8:65
Hardwood buying   FW81/3-4:34
Hardwood floor, reclaiming   HM83/1:64
Hardwood floor, sanding   HM74/6:42
Hardwood floor care   HM83/1:67
Hardwood floors   PM80/4:137
Hardwood parquet flooring   WB73/5-6:20
Hardwoods, myths   HM80/3:82
Harp, American (mahogany)   FW81/11-12:70
Harp kit, chord   PM84/2:104
Harp rack washstand, Colonial   WB82/3-4:67
Harpsichord   WB74/1-2:34
Hasp, hinge   PM78/5:288
Hat rack, scissors   PM81/6:147
Hauling building materials   HM78/4:14
Hauling lumber, car   WB77/9-10:38
Hauling materials   HM78/9:75
Haunched mortise and tenon joint   FW79/9-10:52
Haunched mortise and tenon joint   WS81/11:8
Headboard, child's bookcase   PM81/9:104
Headboard, contemporary bed   WS84/7-8:10
Headphone amp, electronic   PM74/1:133
Health hazards, hobby   NS82/5-6:28
Health hazards in woodworking   FW77/12:54
Hearse, horse drawn model   WB73/5-6:28
Heart boxes   HM82/2:32
Heart crayon holder   PM80/2:124
Hearth, raised   PM78/7:102
Heart jewelry box   PM80/2:124
Heart letter holder   HM82/2:32
Heart sconce, candle   PM81/12:116
Heart shape jewelry box (cedar)   WB82/7-8:80
Heart shape mirror   PM80/2:124
Heater, hiding radiator   NS81/9:49
Heater, installing wall   PM81/9:142
Heater maintenance checklist   PM82/9:111
Heater repair, portable room   PM78/12:30
Heaters, kerosene   NS80/11-12:44
Heaters, kerosene   NS81/10:94
Heaters, new vented   NS82/10:66
Heaters, radiant   NS80/11-12:45
Heat exchanger   HM82/1:48
Heat exchanger   HM84/10:128
Heat exchanger   NS80/5-6:50
Heat exchanger   NS84/1:58
Heat exchanger   PM82/9:138
Heat exchanger, air to air   NS82/5-6:26
Heat exchanger, geothermal   NS84/10:14

Heating, picture panels   HM78/1:46
Heating, task   NS80/11-12:42
Heating, underground tubes   NS81/11-12:48
Heating, using less   NS81/1:100
Heating, zoned home   PM74/10:142
Heating system ducts, insulating   HM84/1:20
Heating system improvements   NS81/1:61
Heat loss, measuring   HM84/10:122
Heat pump   NS81/11-12:45
Heat pump   WB78/11-12:16
Heat pump, ground water coupled   WB84/5-6:96
Heat pump, solar assisted   NS84/2:6
Heat pump, solar assisted   WB81/11-12:76
Heat pump, water source   PM80/9:155
Heat pump cover   PM82/12:148
Heat pump water heater   HM84/12:50
Heat pump water heater   NS83/4:54
Heat pump water heater   NS83/9:12
Heat pump water heater   WB83/7-8:78
Heat recovery system from drain   NS84/1:68
Heat shields, stove   NS80/10:87
Heat shrink tubing, electronic   PM83/5:152
Heat storage, indoor pool   NS83/11-12:46
Heat storage, solar   NS81/10:26
Heat storage, solar   NS82/4:24
Heat treating   FW76/9:50
Hedgetrimmer maintenance   HM82/3:64
Helicopter, flying toy   HM82/11:27
Helicopter, large toy   WB82/11-12:10
Helicopter, toy   WB79/11-12:66
Helicopter, wood toy   HM84/12:72
Hepplewhite chest of drawers, (mahogany)   FW84/9-10:42
Hepplewhite desk, small   WB76/1-2:49
Hepplewhite secretary,1809   WB73/7-8:26
Hepplewhite table, D-shaped card (mahogany)   FW84/7-8:42
Herb drying   NS82/1:74
Herb rack, Shaker   NS82/1:70
Hewing, ax   FW80/3-4:64
Hexagonal mortising chisel   PM82/3:70
Hexagonal table, veneered   WB79/5-6:82
Hickory ax handles   FW83/7-8:40
Hickory chairs, President Jimmy Carter   PM84/8:73
Highboy, Philadelphia   WB83/3-4:114
Highboy chest, small Queen Anne   FW83/9-10:32
Highboy (curly maple)   WB73/1-2:36
Highboy stereo cabinet   WB83/5-6:4
High chair, baby   FW80/3-4:15
High chair, child's   WB83/11-12:49
High chair, doll   WB84/11-12:86
High chair/rocker, child's (maple)   FW84/7-8:72

Hinge, brass   NS82/5-6:62
Hinge, brass   WB78/9-10:68
Hinge, Butler's table   WS81/3:16
Hinge, buying   HM77/3:54
Hinge, carpet clearing   PM80/2:40
Hinge, drop leaf   WS81/3:8
Hinge, fall flap   FW83/7-8:66
Hinge, inlaid wooden cabinet   FW82/7-8:52
Hinge, knife   FW83/7-8:66
Hinge, knife   FW84/11-12:53
Hinge, laminated leather   FW81/1-2:22
Hinge, miniature   WB77/1-2:10
Hinge, two-way wooden   FW78/3:69
Hinge, wood   WB79/5-6:9
Hinge, wooden 18th century   FW84/7-8:45
Hinge edge, plywood   PM84/2:116
Hinging, jewelry box   FW84/11-12:52
Hippo carving, chain saw   PM74/7:42
Hippo hamper   WB78/11-12:66
Hippo sculpture, wood   WB76/3-4:100
Hobby, health hazards   NS82/5-6:28
Hobby center hideaway   HM78/7-8:54
Hobby corner worktable   HM76/11:34
Hobby desk/center, contemporary   HM84/2:70
Hobby horse, auto spring   WB84/5-6:16
Hobby horse, toy   PM79/11:122
Hobby horse, toy stick   WB82/5-6:53
Hobby horse swing   WB78/11-12:77
Hobby storage trays   PM76/6:114
Hobby tray   HM84/11:78
Hobby workbench   WB83/9-10:57
Hoist, engine   PM83/4:168
Hold down arm   PM81/4:120
Hold down clamps, table saw   WS79/1:6
Hold downs and push sticks, table saw   WB72/7-8:16
Hold in, rubber tire   FW81/1-2:24
Hold in, table saw   FW82/9-10:20
Hollow turnings   FW79/5-6:62
Holly wreath, wooden Christmas   PM81/12:116
Home, adobe   NS80/4:12
Home, affordable solar   NS83/7-8:36
Home, battery powered   PM79/9:147
Home, computer controlled   NS84/11-12:56
Home, computerized   NS82/9:31
Home, dome   NS83/7-8:72
Home, double wall   NS80/5-6:47
Home, double wall solar   NS81/2:82
Home, earth sheltered   WB83/1-2:38
Home, earth sheltered   WB83/1-2:4
Home, factory built   NS84/1:38

Home, factory built panelized   NS84/2:46
Home, financing owner built   NS81/2:52
Home, foam dome   HM83/1:28
Home, guest/playhouse   HM82/5-6:66
Home, insulating   HM81/11:45
Home, insulating   NS84/10:56
Home, kit   NS84/3:62
Home, large screened gazebo   NS84/4:52
Home, log   HM79/1:86
Home, log   HM81/3:30
Home, log   HM83/1:40
Home, log   NS83/4:28
Home, low cost   NS82/11-12:88
Home, low cost solar   NS81/2:102
Home, manufactured   HM83/1:36
Home, new high tech   NS84/4:46
Home, octagonal   NS82/3:50
Home, owner built   NS81/2:66
Home, owner built   NS83/4:22
Home, owner built   NS83/10:90
Home, owner built   NS83/5-6:82
Home, owner built   NS83/9:102
Home, owner built   WB84/7-8:10
Home, owner built   WB84/5-6:12
Home, owner built   WB84/3-4:50
Home, owner built precut   HM79/11:14
Home, owner built savings   NS81/2:22
Home, owner built solar   NS82/9:68
Home, post and beam cottage   NS80/3:57
Home, precut   HM83/1:34
Home, precut   WB84/5-6:80
Home, prefabricated   PM84/2:112
Home, recycling   HM79/10:12
Home, remodeling   NS83/2:69
Home, restoring   HM78/10:16
Home, salvaged materials   NS81/2:92
Home, selling   NS84/10:32
Home, small   NS81/2:30
Home, small   NS81/2:28
Home, small then add-on   NS81/2:34
Home, small vacation   HM82/7-8:87
Home, solar   HM83/5-6:101
Home, solar   NS80/3:22
Home, solar   NS80/7-8:68
Home, solar   NS83/2:8
Home, solar   WB77/1-2:34
Home, solar double shell   NS80/9:72
Home, solar retrofit   NS80/5-6:36
Home, solar saltbox   NS81/11-12:69
Home, super insulated   NS83/11-12:68

Home, trisol solar   NS80/3:76
Home, underground   HM80/7-8:44
Home, underground   HM80/2:12
Home, underground   HM82/11:120
Home, underground   NS80/10:44
Home, underground   NS81/5-6:60
Home, underground   NS82/5-6:84
Home, underground   NS82/1:18
Home, underground   NS83/9:98
Home, underground   NS84/1:46
Home, underground   WB79/3-4:92
Home, underground   WB79/1-2:104
Home, underground   WB81/1-2:80
Home, underground guidelines   NS80/2:74
Home, underground home   HM83/1:30
Home, underground twelve   PM80/5:114
Home, vacation   HM79/7-8:80
Home addition   HM81/3:14
Home addition   WB83/9-10:28
Home addition, upstairs   HM79/10:53
Home additions   HM75/8:30
Home additions   HM79/2:83
Home additions   HM79/5-6:23
Home additions   HM80/2:17
Home air leaks   NS80/4:76
Home air leaks   NS82/10:52
Home architecture, regional designs   NS80/2:80
Home building   NS83/3:60
Home building, 37 cost cutting innovations   NS84/2:52
Home building, designer   NS81/2:39
Home building, finding subcontractors   NS84/10:68
Home building books   NS81/2:78
Home building energy saving tips   PM77/11:124
Home building kits   NS81/2:42
Home building mistakes   HM79/4:22
Home building schools, owner built   NS81/2:72
Home buyer checklist   HM79/5-6:68
Home buying, old   NS80/3:44
Home caused illnesses   NS80/4:54
Home color, exterior   HM82/4:70
Home computers   NS83/9:74
Home cooling design tips   NS84/7-8:44
Home cooling naturally   NS80/7-8:20
Home cooling tips   PM81/7:88
Home decorating, mobile   WB83/7-8:88
Home designing, cost effectiveness   NS84/5-6:72
Home electrical capacity   HM82/7-8:79
Home electrical system mapping   HM82/9:106
Home emergencies   HM80/10:28
Home emergency gear   PM73/9:106

Home energy audit   NS82/2:70
Home energy conservation   NS82/3:36
Home energy leaks   NS80/11-12:82
Home energy saving   NS81/10:44
Home energy saving   WB76/5-6:43
Home energy saving   WB76/9-10:80
Home energy saving   WB76/7-8:48
Home energy saving   WB76/11-12:22
Home energy saving maintenance   NS82/1:47
Home entertainment center   PM81/7:95
Home fix up   HM79/2:24
Home frame   NS83/4:8
Home framing, 2 foot spacing   PM72/12:62
Home from commercial buildings   NS81/4:23
Home heating, zoned   PM74/10:142
Home improvement, old   HM78/11-12:38
Home in a bottle   PM77/12:128
Home inspecting   WB79/3-4:60
Home inspection   PM76/3:122
Home inspection   WB81/3 4:36
Home inspection checklist   PM79/4:179
Home insulation guide   PM84/9:86
Home kits, dome   HM79/7-8:8
Home maintenance manual   NS83/4:32
Home moisture problems   NS80/5-6:71
Home mortgage, early payoff   NS84/11-12:28
Home moving   HM83/1:32
Home moving   NS81/5-6:12
Home noises, quieting   PM80/5:235
Home numbers, lighted   PM75/11:152
Home office   HM83/2:28
Home office   PM81/4:135
Home office, built-ins   HM84/1:41
Home office center, his and her desks   PM81/7:97
Home office organizer (mahogany)   PM84/8:108
Home offices   PM73/9:73
Home painting, exterior   HM77/7-8:15
Home painting, exterior   HM81/5-6:40
Home painting, exterior   HM83/4:30
Home painting, exterior   PM83/4:115
Home painting problems guide, exterior   PM83/6:84
Home paint vs. stain   HM82/4:77
Home plans, solar   NS81/2:56
Home plans, solar   NS82/4:13
Home remodeling   HM78/3:9
Home remodeling   HM80/1:20
Home remodeling   HM82/4:18
Home remodeling   NS80/2:64
Home remodeling   NS80/5-6:58
Home remodeling   NS83/10:56

Home remodeling   PM77/10:128
Home remodeling, 1900 duplex   WB79/9-10:38
Home remodeling, exterior update   HM78/4:10
Home remodeling, fifty year old   HM79/3:46
Home remodeling, opening up small house   HM78/9:16
Home remodeling, replacing load bearing beam   WB83/11-12:82
Home remodeling, small   WB82/3-4:74
Home remodeling, wall removal   NS80/2:71
Home remodeling and additions   PM84/4:115
Home remodeling financing   NS82/4:80
Home renovation   HM80/12:22
Home renovation   HM81/7-8:30
Home renovation   HM81/9:68
Home repair contractors   NS80/4:88
Home repair manual   HM82/2:37
Home repair manual   HM83/9:71
Home repair manual   HM83/2:47
Home repair manual   HM84/2:53
Home repairs   PM75/11:108
Home restoring   NS81/11-12:36
Home safety   HM82/2:74
Home security   HM82/4:85
Home security   NS83/9:42
Home security   PM82/1:110
Home security   WB82/9-10:4
Home security alarm system, designing burglar   PM83/12:66
Home security part 2, locks   WB78/5-6:50
Home security system, installing   WB84/7-8:36
Home security systems, troubleshooting   PM84/4:149
Home siding   HM78/4:28
Home siding   HM84/1:46
Home siding   PM79/4:144
Home siding   WB78/3-4:24
Home siding   WB78/5-6:30
Home siding, installing   PM74/6:96
Home siding, recycling   HM83/4:56
Home siding maintenance, wood   HM72/8:40
Home siding products   HM83/4:35
Home soffit repair   HM80/4:44
Homesteaders   NS81/10:78
Home sunspace   NS80/2:25
Home sunspace construction   NS80/2:37
Home trim, Gothic   WB79/3-4:62
Home ventilation   HM81/11:82
Home weatherizing   WB80/1-2:4
Home winterizing checklist   NS83/10:46
Hone, portable drill   FW84/7-8:10
Hone, shop built   FW84/9-10:52
Honeycomb panel   FW82/1-2:96
Hood, oven over range   PM74/10:158

Hook scraper and floorman's holder   FW84/11-12:67
Horizontal boring jig   FW80/3-4:17
Horizontal boring jig   PM83/12:112
Horizontal drilling jig   WS80/11:13
Horn, Swiss alphon   FW80/5-6:4
Horn rack with leather decoration, wall   PM74/7:142
Horse, auto spring hobby   WB84/5-6:16
Horse, shaving   FW78/9:46
Horse, stick toy   PM80/11:128
Horse, toy rocking   HM84/11:74
Horse, toy rocking   WB84/11-12:8
Horse, toy stick   WB82/5-6:53
Horse and wagon, toy   FW80/11-12:61
Horse bench, toy   PM78/11:121
Horse Christmas tree decoration   PM79/12:82
Horse drawn model hearse   WB73/5-6:28
Horse swing   PM79/4:131
Hose bib, extra outdoor faucet   PM81/6:121
Hotbed, garden   PM78/3:154
Hotbed, plant   PM78/8:92
Hot bed and cold frame   HM78/2:26
Hot tub   HM82/5-6:24
Hot tub, deck   HM84/5-6:34
Hot tub, deck   PM79/3:134
Hot tub, solar   PM79/3:137
Hot tub kit   HM79/5-6:15
Hot tub kit   WB81/7-8:46
Hot tubs, saunas and spas   NS82/2:20
Hot water cost reduction   NS80/9:63
Hot water dispenser, installing   WB84/9-10:38
Hot water heater, batch solar   NS80/10:96
Hot water heater sediment cleaner   PM82/4:138
Hourglasses, light bulb   WB73/3-4:40
HSHSA garbage furnace plans to order $20   PM81/8:32
Humidifier   HM81/12:60
Humidifier   WB80/9-10:60
Humidifier, furnace   HM76/3:38
Humidifier installation   WB77/3-4:122
Humidifiers   HM75/1:38
Humidifiers   PM78/12:98
Humidity, controlling   WB73/11-12:8
Humidity and condensation   WB78/7-8:34
Humidity control   HM77/10:22
Humidor/pipe rack   PM75/12:95
Huntboard, Southern   FW83/3-4:74
Hutch   WB77/1-2:66
Hutch, Colonial   PM75/6:102
Hutch, Colonial wall   WS81/11:16
Hutch, contemporary   PM74/1:67
Hutch, contemporary (maple)   WS81/1:4

Hutch, dishwasher   PM75/4:126
Hutch, frame and panel stained glass   WB81/5-6:62
Hutch, rabbit   WB80/3-4:60
Hutch and cabinet, contemporary cane (oak)   WS82/7:18
Hutch/buffet, arched doors   WB78/5-6:48
Hutch/desk, Colonial   WB82/9-10:104
Hutch plans to order, $7.95   HM82/11:28
Hutch plant display   PM81/1:96
Hutch table, 1700's (pine)   PM82/7:92
Hutch/table/chair, Colonial   PM73/7:96
Hutch top   FW75/12:43
Hutch waterer, rabbit   WB81/7-8:12
Hydraulic press   PM75/10:85
Hydraulic press   WB76/1-2:26
Hydroelectric plant, miniature   PM81/2:122
Hydroponics   NS81/11-12:34
Hyperbolic paraboloid patio roof   WB79/7-8:79
Ice, driving on   PM77/11:92
Ice, driving over water   PM83/12:88
Icebox, restoring   WB78/11-12:118
Icebox bar (oak)   PM84/12:102
Icebox cabinet (oak)   WS84/11-12:4
Icebox (oak)   HM82/1:30
Iced gutters   PM84/11:203
Ice fishing pole   PM84/2:160
Ice maker servicing   WB82/5-6:82
Ice problems, ten   PM84/10:187
Ice skates, sharpening   PM74/2:75
Ice skating rink, back yard   PM77/11:74
Ice skating Sunfish   PM79/2:52
Impact driver tool   NS80/7-8:16
Indexer, drill press   WB73/1-2:20
Indexing attachment, lathe   PM76/2:117
Indexing head   WB81/7-8:28
Indexing jig, router   WB81/3-4:54
Indian carved pedestal   WB74/7-8:62
Indian kerf-bent boxes   FW80/5-6:36
Indian weather vane   PM83/3:98
Indoor air contaminates   NS82/5-6:20
Indoor air quality   HM82/9:42
Indoor air quality   HM84/10:128
Indoor air quality   HM84/9:132
Indoor air quality   HM84/11:94
Indoor air quality   NS80/4:54
Indoor air quality   NS84/9:42
Indoor air quality, improving   NS82/5-6:29
Indoor air quality, radon gas   NS84/5-6:28
Inflatable boat floor   PM74/7:140
Initialed case, French fitted (Colo Bolo)   PM80/12:106
Inlaid bowl, turned fruit   PM75/2:116

Inlaid box, turned   WB75/7-8:48
Inlaid chest of drawers, 1740 Norwegian   WB80/9-10:61
Inlaid lap desk   FW81/3-4:52
Inlaid music box   WB80/1-2:74
Inlaid music box   WS83/7-8:4
Inlaid serving tray   FW75/12:41
Inlaid table, round top (pine)   WB80/9-10:72
Inlaid table, veneer chess/lamp   WB84/11-12:15
Inlaid tables, nestled (walnut)   WS83/7-8:12
Inlaid turnings   FW81/7-8:56
Inlaid wooden cabinet hinge   FW82/7-8:52
Inlay, leather and gold   FW78/6:61
Inlay, routing   HM80/12:74
Inlaying mother of pearl   FW81/3-4:50
Inlay jigsaw, foot powered   FW81/3-4:53
Inlay making   FW81/3-4:46
Inlay patching, Dutchman   FW81/3-4:16
Inlays   WS83/7-8:8
Inlays, routing for   FW79/7-8:68
Insect box, screened   WB83/6 6:12
Insects, wood   NS82/4:56
Insect vacuum, patio   PM74/7:107
Inspection checklist, house   PM79/4:179
Instrument form, musical   FW83/5-6:100
Instruments, wooden scientific   FW78/10:40
Insulated garage doors   WB82/7-8:4
Insulate gas water heater   NS83/2:60
Insulating, house   NS84/10:56
Insulating attic   NS80/7-8:33
Insulating block walls   HM84/5-6:76
Insulating brick wall   HM75/10:30
Insulating ceiling panels   HM82/11:40
Insulating concrete slab   NS84/11-12:12
Insulating door, entry   NS83/10:62
Insulating ducts   HM84/1:20
Insulating exterior basement walls   WB82/9-10:38
Insulating foundations   NS80/10:66
Insulating garage door, double panes/panels   PM81/12:158
Insulating masonry   WB77/7-8:4
Insulating post and beam houses   NS84/9:96
Insulating walls   HM81/11:45
Insulating water heater   HM76/10:50
Insulating windows   NS80/10:26
Insulation   HM77/9:20
Insulation   HM79/9:46
Insulation   WB74/11-12:22
Insulation, attic   WB83/11-12:86
Insulation, attic opening cover   PM81/4:175
Insulation, basement   WB80/9-10:86
Insulation, basement exterior   HM82/9:82

Insulation, buying   NS82/11-12:29
Insulation, cooling   NS83/5-6:64
Insulation, cutting fiberglass   PM79/9:145
Insulation, foundation   NS83/9:64
Insulation, home   PM78/9:132
Insulation, installing   NS82/11-12:25
Insulation, installing   PM73/4:178
Insulation, low cost window   WB81/11-12:72
Insulation, needs analysis   NS82/11-12:20
Insulation, outside   NS80/4:41
Insulation, pipe   NS81/11-12:82
Insulation, roof   NS82/4:36
Insulation, sliding glass doors   PM82/1:64
Insulation, solar   NS81/3:41
Insulation, stress skin panels   NS84/9:96
Insulation, super   NS83/7-8:48
Insulation, wall   HM78/9:22
Insulation, walls and floors   NS80/9:90
Insulation, water heater   NS80/9:63
Insulation, water heater and pipe   HM77/10:46
Insulation, window   NS80/10:36
Insulation, window   NS82/2:8
Insulation and vapor barriers   WB78/1-2:32
Insulation and ventilation, attic   NS84/9:78
Insulation blower   PM81/4:147
Insulation blower, shop made   WB78/5-6:92
Insulation guide, home   PM84/9:86
Insulation kit, garage door   WB84/11-12:100
Insulation mistakes   HM78/9:66
Insulation protection, fiberglass   WB83/5-6:82
Insulation scars, painting exterior   HM79/4:58
Intercom, home   HM77/2:50
Inventor's patents   PM84/5:172
Iron decorations, hand forged   HM83/10:80
Iron door knocker, hand forged   HM83/10:82
Ironing board, kitchen   HM83/2:67
Ironing board wall cabinet   WB84/11-12:96
Ironing center, movable builtin   PM80/4:146
Iron pan, reclaiming cast   HM82/1:80
Iron railings, installing   PM73/7:82
Iron repair, electric   PM74/8:82
Irrigation, drip   NS84/9:68
Irrigation, trickle   PM79/3:140
Island, kitchen   NS81/1:57
Island kitchen cabinet, mobile   PM82/4:142
Island vanity, two basin mirrored doors   WB81/9-10:46
Jack plane   PM82/6:97
Japanese blade sharpening   FW81/7-8:71
Japanese chest, carved   WB72/3-4:62
Japanese gift wrapping tying   HM83/12:58

Japanese joinery   FW79/11-12:89
Japanese measuring and marking tools   FW84/9-10:68
Japanese planes   FW80/1-2:60
Japanese resaws   FW83/5-6:84
Japanese saw and plane   HM82/12:36
Japanese saws   FW80/3-4:77
Japanese sharpening equipment and tips   PM84/1:104
Japanese sharpening water stones   WS82/11-12:4
Japanese shutters, Shoji indoor   WB80/3-4:42
Japanese sliding doors   FW82/5-6:50
Japanese tools   PM76/11:114
Japanese tools, hand   HM82/12:32
Japanese woodworking tools   WB83/1-2:75
Jardiniere plant stand (oak)   PM81/10:104
Jefferson's designs, Thomas   PM76/6:84
Jelly paddle   PM75/8:116
Jet, toy bouncing   WB72/11-12:22
Jewelry, animals etc.   PM73/11:89
Jewelry, bracelet mandrel   FW81/5-6:14
Jewelry, bracelet wood burn design   PM78/2·36
Jewelry, kitchen   WB76/9-10:16
Jewelry, silver   PM80/12:94
Jewelry, wood   WB74/11-12:54
Jewelry, wood Chinese   WB72/11-12:44
Jewelry, wood pendent mirror   WB83/9-10:56
Jewelry, wood rings   WB79/3-4:81
Jewelry box   WB76/9-10:47
Jewelry box, contemporary (walnut)   WS82/11-12:20
Jewelry box, decoupage   WB72/9-10:52
Jewelry box, heart   PM80/2:124
Jewelry box, heart shaped (cedar)   WB82/7-8:80
Jewelry box, needlepoint   WB81/11-12:35
Jewelry box, routed   WS81/1:12
Jewelry box, routed   WS83/7-8:10
Jewelry box, train   HM82/12:63
Jewelry box, treasure chest   PM75/12:97
Jewelry box, treasure chest   WB73/9-10:47
Jewelry box, wooden hinge   WS80/5:5
Jewelry box hinging   FW84/11-12:52
Jewelry box (oak)   HM83/12:74
Jewelry box (redwood)   WB83/11-12:8
Jewelry chest, Oriental   WB73/11-12:48
Jewelry chest, rolltop door   WB83/5-6:104
Jewelry chest/doll house, Victorian   WB79/1-2:113
Jig, radial arm saw mortise   WS81/7:18
Jig, table saw taper   WS79/1:6
Jigsaw, foot powered   FW81/3-4:53
Jigsaw cutting guide   WB79/9-10:96
Jigsaw puzzles   WB84/11-12:32
Jigsaw sander   PM84/2:116

Joiner's tool chest   FW80/9-10:76
Joiner   FW79/11-12:92
Joiner knives, sharpening   FW81/9-10:14
Joiner maintenance   FW81/9-10:72
Joinery, Japanese   FW79/11-12:89
Joinery, pole and wire   FW81/7-8:74
Joint, bed tusk tenon   FW83/1-2:14
Joint, beginner's bridle   FW84/11-12:68
Joint, blind finger   FW84/5-6:70
Joint, box   PM76/8:94
Joint, box   WS79/3:4
Joint, box   WS81/9:19
Joint, butt   PM81/11:118
Joint, curved edge   FW78/10:15
Joint, curved slot mortise and tenon   FW81/1-2:60
Joint, deck railing   PM80/11:184
Joint, decorative door   FW83/5-6:16
Joint, double dovetail butterfly   FW80/11-12:72
Joint, dovetail hand tools   WS82/1:4
Joint, dovetail pins   WS82/1:8
Joint, dovetail router   WS82/7:6
Joint, dovetail tails   WS82/1:10
Joint, dovetail tongue and groove glueless   WS82/3:22
Joint, dovetail with hand tools   WS82/1:6
Joint, dowel   FW80/3-4:68
Joint, dowel T-jig   FW80/5-6:15
Joint, drawer   FW80/5-6:18
Joint, drop leaf hinge   FW79/9-10:66
Joint, drop leaf table   WS80/9:10
Joint, duckbill spoon   FW83/11-12:70
Joint, finger   WS81/9:14
Joint, frame and panel stub tenon and groove   WS83/9-10:22
Joint, Grenno interlock   FW81/3-4:16
Joint, half lap   WS83/5-6:22
Joint, hand cut lap dovetail   WS82/7:4
Joint, hand dovetail   FW76/3:28
Joint, haunched mortise and tenon   FW79/9-10:52
Joint, haunched mortise and tenon   WS81/11:8
Joint, invisible nails   PM84/4:160
Joint, locked miter   WS80/5:10
Joint, locking   WS79/11:8
Joint, miter and spline   WS82/5:8
Joint, mitered mortise and tenon   WS81/7:16
Joint, molded mortise and tenon   WS82/11-12:12
Joint, mortise and tenon   FW76/6:16
Joint, mortise and tenon   FW79/3-4:46
Joint, mortise and tenon   WS81/1:10
Joint, mortise and tenon frame   WS83/3-4:7
Joint, open mortise and tenon   FW80/9-10:14
Joint, open mortise and tenon   WS82/11-12:18

Joint, open spline miter   WS84/11-12:22
Joint, plate   FW82/5-6:95
Joint, plywood and solid wood   WS84/5-6:20
Joint, precision   FW80/11-12:68
Joint, rabbet and dado   WS80/7:9
Joint, rabbet and groove   WS81/11:20
Joint, radial arm saw box   FW81/5-6:76
Joint, radial arm saw slip   FW82/1-2:71
Joint, routed box   FW81/9-10:18
Joint, routed edge   FW77/12:66
Joint, routed miter   FW82/3-4:12
Joint, rule   FW79/9-10:66
Joint, scribed   FW82/3-4:76
Joint, slot mortise   WS83/3-4:8
Joint, spline mitered   FW81/3-4:62
Joint, stave   WS83/1-2:8
Joint, stretcher-to-post   FW81/7-8:10
Joint, table saw box   WS81/9:12
Joint, table saw finger jig   FW80/1-2:13
Joint, table saw jig for tenoner   FW79/9-10:16
Joint, tenon   WS83/3-4:10
Joint, three member lap   FW81/11-12:16
Joint, tusked-pegged-wedged locked   FW79/5-6:45
Joint, twin tenon   WS80/11:12
Joint, wedged loom   FW82/5-6:16
Joint, wedge/tenon   FW79/9-10:10
Jointer, hold down   FW81/5-6:18
Jointer, model makers   WB79/5-6:91
Jointer, sanding disk   FW80/3-4:47
Jointer, thickness planing   FW84/9-10:8
Jointer, wooden   FW81/5-6:44
Jointer blade sharpening   WB82/3-4:9
Jointer blade sharpening jig   PM82/3:66
Jointer guide   PM84/11:140
Jointer knife mini drawknife   FW82/9-10:22
Jointer knife setting jig, magnetic   PM72/6:162
Jointer knife sharpening fixture   FW81/3-4:14
Jointer knife sharpening jig   FW82/5-6:14
Jointer knives, installing   FW83/7-8:12
Jointer knives, sharpening   FW80/7-8:15
Jointer nick repair   FW82/1-2:14
Jointer safety   FW81/5-6:50
Jointer stand, six inch   PM80/10:27
Jointer techniques   PM77/12:116
Jointer toolbox   WB83/1-2:87
Jointer use tips   PM76/9:118
Jointing, radial arm saw   FW82/1-2:14
Jointing decorative strips   FW78/10:16
Jointing wide planks   FW82/1-2:14
Joint jig, adjustable finger   WB81/11-12:91

Joint router jig, box   FW79/1-2:56
Joints, 28 wood   PM74/8:130
Joints, 36 wood   WB78/11-12:92
Joints, bandsaw finger   FW83/3-4:14
Joints, box   WS84/9-10:14
Joints, cabinet carcase construction   FW76/12:30
Joints, curved   FW82/7-8:46
Joints, decorative   FW81/5-6:72
Joints, decorative   FW82/7-8:68
Joints, dovetail   FW80/3-4:73
Joints, dovetail   PM77/8:102
Joints, dovetail   PM82/1:98
Joints, dowel   FW77/6:46
Joints, dowel   PM81/12:108
Joints, dowel   PM83/6:83
Joints, dowel   PM83/4:112
Joints, edge lap   PM81/12:108
Joints, fingerlap or box   PM82/1:101
Joints, guitar   FW76/12:52
Joints, interlocking   PM83/2:140
Joints, miter and spline   WS80/1:11
Joints, mortise and tenon   WS80/3:3
Joints, mortising sloping wedges and shims   FW79/11-12:95
Joints, parallel spline (plywood)   WS80/5:9
Joints, part 1   PM81/11:118
Joints, part 2   PM81/12:108
Joints, part 3   PM82/1:98
Joints, rabbet and dado   PM81/11:118
Joints, routing splined miter   FW82/7-8:14
Joints, slot mortise   WS80/3:4
Joints, table saw mortise and tenon   WB77/9-10:28
Joints, tenon   WS80/3:5
Joints, tight countertop   WB82/5-6:48
Joints, wedged mortise and tenon   WS81/5:12
Joints, wood   PM80/3:127
Joints, wood   PM80/4:134
Joints jig, router   PM84/1:75
Jump rope   PM79/3:170
Kaleidoscope, toy   PM81/1:100
Kennel, dog   HM79/9:106
Kerf bending, wood   PM72/10:167
Kerf bent boxes   FW80/5-6:36
Kerfed table, oval coffee   WB82/7-8:56
Kerfing and bending a box   FW80/5-6:44
Kerosene heater   NS82/10:74
Kerosene heaters   NS80/11-12:44
Kerosene heaters   NS81/10:94
Key and bulletin board (oak)   WS81/11:24
Key chain wrench, multi one piece tool   PM82/8:87
Key hanger, heart   HM82/2:32

Keyhole cutter, blind   PM84/12:14
Key hole escutcheon plate, wood   PM80/3:32
Kid made toys   FW79/11-12:98
Kiln, dehumidifier dryer   FW84/3-4:40
Kiln, drying   FW77/3:39
Kiln, solar drying   FW77/6:59
Kiln, solar lumber drying   PM77/5:273
Kitchen, buying for   NS84/5-6:34
Kitchen, camp   WB83/7-8:16
Kitchen, Colonial   NS82/10:86
Kitchen, improving   WB84/1-2:88
Kitchen and bath, Victorian remodeling   HM82/7-8:28
Kitchen and bath cleaning   HM84/5-6:117
Kitchen and bathroom remodeling   HM83/7-8:29
Kitchen appliance cart   PM76/4:126
Kitchen barbecue grill scraper   PM84/5:183
Kitchen barbecue skewers   PM80/7:91
Kitchen book rack, dowel   PM84/1:112
Kitchen book rack recipe holder   WB82/5-6:18
Kitchen box, camper   HM79/5-6:78
Kitchen breadboard   HM83/11:80
Kitchen breadboard (maple and cherry)   WS82/3:24
Kitchen breadbox, carved (oak)   WB83/5-6:14
Kitchen breadbox, rolltop   WB82/3-4:48
Kitchen breadbox, rolltop (oak)   HM83/1:78
Kitchen bread cupboard, French provincial   WB77/1-2:44
Kitchen bread cutting board   PM80/11:128
Kitchen butcher block   PM75/10:102
Kitchen butcher block table   WB77/3-4:90
Kitchen cabinet, corner   WB84/9-10:14
Kitchen cabinet, hidden storage   WB77/3-4:50
Kitchen cabinet, rolling butcher block top   WB82/5-6:106
Kitchen cabinet doors, stained glass   HM82/7-8:84
Kitchen cabinet doors, woven slats   WB80/11-12:96
Kitchen cabinet furniture   PM75/12:70
Kitchen cabinetmaker, working with   HM83/7-8:110
Kitchen cabinet plate butler   PM79/11:212
Kitchen cabinet refinishing, metal   HM75/10:58
Kitchen cabinets   HM78/3:14
Kitchen cabinets   HM81/2:15
Kitchen cabinets   PM78/4:141
Kitchen cabinets   PM82/2:100
Kitchen cabinets, European style   FW83/11-12:54
Kitchen cabinets, extra   WB76/11-12:96
Kitchen cabinets, finishing   WB74/7-8:8
Kitchen cabinets, installing   NS82/7-8:32
Kitchen cabinets, installing   PM74/4:198
Kitchen cabinets, low cost (pine)   HM82/7-8:40
Kitchen cabinets, refinishing   WB80/11-12:16
Kitchen cabinets, rolltop   FW80/11-12:78

Kitchen cabinets, rolltop   FW80/11-12:78
Kitchen cabinets, rolltop doors   WB80/9-10:34
Kitchen cabinets, rosemaling   FW80/11-12:79
Kitchen canister, old time grocery bin   PM75/10:102
Kitchen canisters, finger joints   WB80/5-6:48
Kitchen canisters, turned   WS81/3:14
Kitchen canister set, turned (walnut)   WS83/1-2:10
Kitchen cart, butcher block   PM84/9:76
Kitchen cart, butcher block top (oak/maple)   HM84/5-6:140
Kitchen carving board   PM82/1:159
Kitchen casserole carrier   PM77/11:140
Kitchen casserole cradle, dowel   PM84/1:112
Kitchen center, mobile with refrigerator   PM73/8:72
Kitchen cheese slicer   PM81/3:74
Kitchen cheese tray, ceramic tile   PM75/12:95
Kitchen cleaning supplies tote   PM78/4:112
Kitchen coffee cup tree   WB79/9-10:104
Kitchen coffee grinder   WS84/9-10:16
Kitchen coffee mill   HM82/7-8:72
Kitchen cookbook caddy   PM74/9:139
Kitchen cookbook/recipe shelf (maple)   WS79/11:4
Kitchen cookbook shelf   WB80/9-10:21
Kitchen cooling rack   WB79/5-6:42
Kitchen cooling rack (pine)   WS79/1:2
Kitchen countertop   HM81/12:64
Kitchen countertop   WB74/3-4:28
Kitchen countertop, ceramic   PM77/12:114
Kitchen countertop organizer   HM83/7-8:95
Kitchen countertops   HM77/3:44
Kitchen countertops, tile and laminate   PM83/2:102
Kitchen cracker tray   PM76/4:172
Kitchen cupboard, 1800   WB81/1-2:33
Kitchen cup rack/rooster parrot cat squirrel   WB84/9-10:113
Kitchen cutting board, bowl type   PM79/11:122
Kitchen cutting board, bread   WB80/7-8:69
Kitchen cutting board, plexiglas   PM75/5:72
Kitchen cutting board (maple or birch)   WS79/1:1
Kitchen cutting boards   WS84/3-4:10
Kitchen design   HM84/7-8:66
Kitchen design   NS84/9:102
Kitchen design   NS84/7-8:88
Kitchen design   PM78/4:133
Kitchen/dining remodeling   HM82/7-8:35
Kitchen dish dryer, no drip wall   HM84/7-8:71
Kitchen door organizer   PM81/9:100
Kitchen doors, etched glass cabinet   HM83/7-8:62
Kitchen floor   HM83/7-8:48
Kitchen food processor rack   PM78/9:72
Kitchen garage conversion   WB81/7-8:36
Kitchen glass rack, hanging wine   WB83/3-4:45

Kitchen grain mill   HM83/9:103
Kitchen hangups, seven   PM81/2:136
Kitchen herb rack, Shaker   NS82/1:70
Kitchen ironing board   HM83/2:67
Kitchen island   HM82/5-6:56
Kitchen island   NS81/1:57
Kitchen island, birch plywood and gray tile   HM84/7-8:30
Kitchen island, butcher block mobile   HM84/9:106
Kitchen island, contemporary   HM84/7-8:25
Kitchen island, mobile   PM82/4:142
Kitchen island, paneled doors   HM84/7-8:36
Kitchen island, three   HM84/7-8:25
Kitchen jelly paddle   PM75/8:116
Kitchen jewelry   WB76/9-10:16
Kitchen knife block   HM84/9:114
Kitchen knife block   PM77/11:142
Kitchen knife block   WB79/11-12:140
Kitchen knife block holder   WB82/11-12:117
Kitchen knife case (walnut and maple)   WS80/7:7
Kitchen knife handle refinishing   HM83/7-8:20
Kitchen knife holder, plexiglas   PM73/11:162
Kitchen knife rack   PM81/2:136
Kitchen knife racks   PM80/12:110
Kitchen knife set and cutting board   WB75/3-4:35
Kitchen knife storage   WB82/3-4:9
Kitchen knives   HM78/11-12:26
Kitchen knives   PM77/2:108
Kitchen knives, choosing and maintaining   PM78/11:122
Kitchen lazy Susan (oak)   WS82/5:10
Kitchen lights   PM73/4:160
Kitchen microwave, built-in   HM80/2:52
Kitchen microwave/serving cart (cherry)   WS82/9:8
Kitchen noise   PM80/5:235
Kitchen office   PM80/12:100
Kitchen office organizer   PM78/4:112
Kitchen pan rack   WB72/9-10:20
Kitchen pan rack cabinet   WB76/3-4:6
Kitchen pan rack (pine)   HM80/11:32
Kitchen pantry   NS83/2:78
Kitchen pantry   NS84/3:14
Kitchen pantry, closet   HM79/2:34
Kitchen pantry, roll out   PM83/4:145
Kitchen pantry door   HM81/1:23
Kitchen pantry storage   WB79/9-10:48
Kitchen paper and hand towel rack   PM81/2:136
Kitchen paper towel holder   PM74/8:174
Kitchen pass through, louver doors   HM74/4:34
Kitchen pasta rack   HM82/12:70
Kitchen pepper mill and salt shaker, hexagon   PM82/1:158
Kitchen phone organizer, wall   PM81/2:136

Kitchen phone shelf, rolltop (oak)   PM84/8:107
Kitchen plaque, carved   WB75/1-2:43
Kitchen planning   HM75/4:16
Kitchen planning   NS84/4:38
Kitchen pot and pan rack   PM82/4:166
Kitchen pot hanger   HM81/2:18
Kitchen pot hanger   HM83/2:67
Kitchen pot rack plans to order   NS83/2:80
Kitchen potting shed   HM81/3:66
Kitchen rack, vertical deli containers   PM81/2:136
Kitchen recipe box (walnut and maple)   WS80/7:8
Kitchen recipe file box   HM83/7-8:95
Kitchen recipe holder, turned   WB79/7-8:28
Kitchen recycling center   HM82/9:66
Kitchen redesign   HM82/7-8:45
Kitchen remodeling   HM78/11-12:12
Kitchen remodeling   HM79/1:78
Kitchen remodeling   HM81/9:22
Kitchen remodeling   HM83/10:44
Kitchen remodeling   HM84/7-8:40
Kitchen remodeling   NS81/1:24
KItchen remodeling   NS84/2:40
Kitchen remodeling   NS84/1:34
Kitchen remodeling   PM80/10:110
Kitchen remodeling   WB78/11-12:38
Kitchen remodeling   WB84/9-10:8
Kitchen remodeling, country   HM81/2:14
Kitchen remodeling, country   WB75/1-2:32
Kitchen remodeling tips   NS81/9:16
Kitchen remodeling tips   NS84/3:56
Kitchen rolling pin   PM77/11:140
Kitchen rolling pin   PM80/11:130
Kitchen rolltop bread box, fake rolltop   PM81/2:140
Kitchen safe, pierced tin panel Colonial   PM82/8:90
Kitchen salt and pepper shakers   PM84/4:104
Kitchen serving cart (walnut or fir)   FW77/3:58
Kitchen shelf, corner   PM81/7:96
Kitchen shelves   HM75/9:44
Kitchen shelves   HM81/2:19
Kitchen shelves, built-in   WB84/9-10:12
Kitchen silverware drawer organizer, acrylic   HM82/12:54
Kitchen silverware tote   WB79/7-8:32
Kitchen spice box, four drawer (maple)   PM79/11:122
Kitchen spice box of drawers (pine)   WS79/11:3
Kitchen spice cabinet, Colonial   WB75/11-12:64
Kitchen spice cabinet, punch pattern   HM82/2:32
Kitchen spice rack   NS82/11-12:48
Kitchen spice rack   PM84/7:133
Kitchen spice rack   WB77/3-4:78
Kitchen spice rack   WB81/7-8:53

Kitchen spice rack, contemporary   PM78/11:198
Kitchen spice rack, dowel   PM81/2:136
Kitchen spice rack, latticework   WB79/9-10:84
Kitchen spice rack, over oven   WB79/5-6:7
Kitchen spice rack, swivel   PM78/4:114
Kitchen spice shelf, contemporary mirror   WB81/5-6:96
Kitchen stained glass light box   PM82/8:54
Kitchen stemware rack   WB78/9-10:44
Kitchen step stool   HM82/7-8:74
Kitchen stool   WB83/9-10:32
Kitchen storage   PM76/11:116
Kitchen storage, hidden   PM75/4:124
Kitchen storage, overhead shelves   HM83/7-8:34
Kitchen storage bin   WB80/5-6:76
Kitchen storage projects   PM78/4:112
Kitchen table   HM81/1:54
Kitchen table   WB74/5-6:20
Kitchen table, butcher block (maple/walnut)   WB84/11-12:46
Kitchen table, cutting   HM81/3:94
Kitchen table, drop down   HM72/12:38
Kitchen table napkin holder   PM83/2:74
Kitchen tableware caddy   PM78/4:114
Kitchen tableware/napkin caddy   PM75/10:102
Kitchen telephone tower, built-in (maple)   PM84/8:102
Kitchen tile, ceramic   PM84/6:87
Kitchen tongs   PM76/3:188
Kitchen tool rack   PM81/2:136
Kitchen towel holder (pine)   HM80/11:34
Kitchen towel holders, paper   WB81/1-2:72
Kitchen towel rack   HM83/7-8:94
Kitchen towel rack   PM78/3:128
Kitchen triangle   NS81/1:29
Kitchen trivets, molding   PM74/2:147
Kitchen utensil holder   WB81/5-6:110
Kitchen utensil rack, dowel   PM84/1:112
Kitchen utensils, carved wood   WB82/1-2:32
Kitchen vegetable bin, country   HM82/9:58
Kitchen wall rack   WB74/5-6:62
Kitchen workcenter   HM83/7-8:34
Kites   PM77/8:96
Kites, bicentennial   PM76/3:98
Kites, building   PM75/3:114
Kite winder   HM82/5-6:98
Kit houses   NS81/2:42
Kleenex tissue box cover (maple)   WS79/3:5
Kleenex tissue box (maple)   WS82/1:24
Kneeler, garden   WB77/7-8:57
Knife, buying a personal   PM82/8:78
Knife, canoe   FW84/1-2:51
Knife, carving   FW83/1-2:84

Knife, fillet   PM73/6:58
Knife, wood cheese   PM75/5:207
Knife block   PM77/11:142
Knife block holder, kitchen   WB82/11-12:117
Knife blocks, kitchen   HM84/9:114
Knife blocks, kitchen   WB79/11-12:140
Knife care kits   HM83/3:20
Knife case, kitchen (walnut and maple)   WS80/7:7
Knife handle refinishing, kitchen   HM83/7-8:20
Knife hinge   FW84/11-12:53
Knife holder, plexiglas   PM73/11:162
Knife kits, customizing   PM78/6:106
Knife making   WB82/3-4:52
Knife rack, kitchen   PM81/2:136
Knife racks, kitchen   PM80/12:110
Knife set and cutting board, kitchen   WB75/3-4:35
Knife sheath, custom leather   PM79/5:29
Knife storage, kitchen   WB82/3-4:9
Knitting yarn bin, family room   PM79/10:130
Knives, choosing and maintaining kitchen   PM78/11:122
Knives, kitchen   HM78/11-12:26
Knives, kitchen   PM77/2:108
Knives from saw blades   FW83/11-12:8
Knockdown furniture   FW84/3-4:44
Knockdown Oriental table (fir or maple)   FW80/1-2:59
Knockdown tabletops with dovetails   FW80/1-2:57
Knot, treeman's   PM80/2:6
Knots, fishing   PM80/6:178
Koa goblet, turning   WS82/9:4
Koa table, cove cuts   FW79/1-2:65
Koa turned popcorn bowl   WS83/1-2:24
Labeling tools and valuables   PM84/3:118
Lacquered desk, circa 1715   WB72/11-12:30
Lacquer finishes   WB73/3-4:54
Lacquer finishing   FW81/11-12:90
Ladder, camper   PM78/4:57
Ladder, folding   FW83/5-6:14
Ladder, plant   WB77/5-6:40
Ladder and scaffolding safety   HM83/4:42
Ladder bench   HM82/5-6:110
Ladder know how   HM77/7-8:20
Ladder paint tray   HM83/5-6:126
Ladder repair   HM76/8:40
Ladder repair   PM79/4:151
Ladders   WB78/5-6:102
Ladders, using   PM73/6:92
Ladder stilt, adjustable   PM80/6:20
Ladder tips   WB84/3-4:103
Ladder use and safety   PM83/4:119
Lambrequins, covered window frame   HM77/11-12:75

Laminate, plastic   HM83/2:32
Laminate, plastic countertop   WB78/9-10:115
Laminate and tile countertops   PM83/2:102
Laminate countertops   FW84/3-4:72
Laminated boomerang   FW84/3-4:61
Laminated bowls, turned   FW80/1-2:14
Laminated bowls, turning   FW78/3:70
Laminated bowl turning   FW78/10:48
Laminated boxes, plastic   WB76/9-10:46
Laminated boxes, small   WB84/9-10:48
Laminated fishing net (walnut and maple)   FW80/1-2:56
Laminated leather hinge   FW81/1-2:22
Laminated leg table, contemporary   WB84/7-8:54
Laminated sculpture   FW83/7-8:34
Laminated spindles, turning   FW81/7-8:52
Laminated staves, bending compound curves   FW79/7-8:57
Laminated table legs, tapered   FW79/1-2:48
Laminate glue spreader   FW81/11-12:22
Laminate strip cutting, table saw   WB79/5-6:76
Laminating   PM76/11:124
Laminations, bent   FW77/3:35
Laminations, gluing up   WS80/7:9
Lamp, acrylic   HM83/10:34
Lamp, art deco hanging   PM81/12:106
Lamp, art deco table   PM81/12:106
Lamp, ceiling Colonial   WB74/7-8:54
Lamp, ceiling installation   NS81/10:61
Lamp, ceramic   HM83/10:32
Lamp, child's toy soldier   WB77/11-12:16
Lamp, cobbler's bench table   PM73/5:92
Lamp, dovetail table   WS82/7:24
Lamp, duck decoy   PM74/9:140
Lamp, early American table   WB74/1-2:40
Lamp, eleven tier chandelier   NS81/10:59
Lamp, fiber optics   PM73/12:67
Lamp, fiber optics   WB73/1-2:50
Lamp, floor   NS81/10:58
Lamp, floor (walnut)   WB77/5-6:68
Lamp, hanging end grain (oak)   FW81/11-12:60
Lamp, hanging (veneer strips)   WS79/3:9
Lamp, hanging Venetian blind   HM83/10:30
Lamp, hardboard hanging   WB81/9-10:34
Lamp, lighthouse night light   PM76/7:102
Lamp, nautical block and tackle   WB84/11-12:79
Lamp, patio lantern   HM81/2:82
Lamp, patio post   PM75/8:92
Lamp, patio (redwood)   HM80/4:22
Lamp, patio (redwood)   PM75/8:91
Lamp, post   HM84/3:40
Lamp, scissor wall   WB82/1-2:42

Lamp, spiral   WB81/1-2:60
Lamp, table   NS81/10:60
Lamp, thimble or spoon collection   WB83/1-2:14
Lamp, turned floor   WB84/5-6:38
Lamp, turning tree   WB77/3-4:118
Lamp, walkway   HM84/3:52
Lamp, wall exterior   HM84/3:46
Lamp, wall exterior   HM84/3:48
Lamp, wood block   WB75/9-10:52
Lamp, wood post   HM78/2:34
Lamp base, turned   WB82/1-2:68
Lamp bases, turning   FW80/11-12:24
Lamp/cabinet table, Mediterranean   WB78/9-10:70
Lamp chandelier, ready made turnings   WB72/1-2:50
Lamp/chess table, inlaid veneer   WB84/11-12:15
Lamppost, yard   PM76/5:108
Lamp (redwood)   HM75/10:42
Lamp repair   NS81/11-12:56
Lamp repair, fluorescent   WB77/1-2:72
Lamps   HM75/10:30
Lamps, contemporary hanging (plexiglas)   PM80/1:112
Lamps, create your own   HM79/7-8:52
Lamps, fluorescent   PM76/3:120
Lamps, fluorescent ceiling   WB84/11-12:124
Lamps, glass bottles   WB82/3-4:58
Lamps, table square or turned   WB79/9-10:59
Lamps, turned   WB79/5-6:4
Lamps, turned wood bottles   WB72/5-6:26
Lamps, wall   HM73/2:56
Lamp table, modern (oak and smoked glass)   WS79/1:7
Lamp table, round   WB79/7-8:62
Lamp table, turned pedestal   WB83/11-12:66
Lamp table/magazine rack, Colonial dough box   WB84/3-4:4
Land, buying rural   NS81/3:92
Land buying   NS80/10:16
Landscape lighting   HM78/5-6:68
Landscape lighting   HM78/5-6:73
Landscape lighting, low voltage   HM82/5-6:60
Landscape steps   NS83/5-6:35
Landscaping checklist   PM81/8:92
Landscaping walls, retaining   NS82/7-8:84
Landscaping with rocks and pebbles   PM78/3:144
Lantern, captain's candle   PM79/12:108
Lantern, English wall candle   WS84/11-12:16
Lantern, garden   WB78/3-4:56
Lantern, patio light   HM81/2:82
Lantern, pine strip   HM82/5-6:40
Lantern, stained glass candle   WB81/5-6:44
Lantern, tin can   PM79/3:118
Lantern, tin can candle   PM72/12:75

Lantern, town crier's candle   WB73/5-6:44
Lap desk   WB73/9-10:65
Lap desk   WB83/3-4:90
Lap desk, Colonial wooden hinged (pine)   WS80/5:6
Lap desk, inlaid   FW81/3-4:52
Lap desk, Mark Twain (mahogany)   PM83/10:100
Lap desk, Shaker (pine or cherry)   FW76/3:48
Lap desk/game chest, child's   WB84/5-6:72
Lapidary shop   WB72/7-8:22
Lapidary tumbler, wind driven   WB77/9-10:46
Lap joint, three member   FW81/11-12:16
Lapstrake boat   FW82/11-12:82
Lapstrake boat   FW82/9-10:54
Laser engraving   FW83/9-10:98
Laser woodworking   FW81/5-6:56
Lathe, bowl   FW81/11-12:78
Lathe, deep boring jig   HM82/1:92
Lathe, drill press   PM83/12:106
Lathe, drill press wood   PM72/12:164
Lathe, freewheel drive   FW79/3-4:65
Lathe, metal boring bar set   PM78/2:72
Lathe, metal steady rest   PM78/11:8
Lathe, miniature   PM80/8:98
Lathe, outboard   FW84/9-10:8
Lathe, simple shop made wood   WB79/11-12:100
Lathe, small drill   PM75/4:104
Lathe, small portable drill   HM81/10:110
Lathe, treadle   FW79/3-4:60
Lathe, turning miniatures   PM78/2:123
Lathe, wood   FW80/11-12:80
Lathe, wood   WB84/1-2:60
Lathe, wood from washing machine motor   PM81/3:158
Lathe ABC's   WB73/1-2:32
Lathe bowl turning tool rest   PM72/1:174
Lathe box dust collector   FW83/11-12:69
Lathe bull nose tailstock   FW82/1-2:22
Lathe chisel, molding head cutter   PM75/7:108
Lathe chisels, making 6   PM82/2:106
Lathe chisels from files   PM76/4:202
Lathe chisel tool box   WB82/3-4:70
Lathe chuck, bowl   FW80/5-6:17
Lathe chuck, expansion   FW82/5-6:14
Lathe chuck, hose clamp   FW79/11-12:26
Lathe chuck, napkin ring   WB82/7-8:67
Lathe dowel maker   PM81/5:53
Lathe duplicating holder   PM81/5:54
Lathe duplicating jig   PM83/12:106
Lathe duplicator   FW82/11-12:92
Lathe extension   WB76/5-6:32
Lathe faceplate   PM80/11:185

Lathe fundamentals   WB79/5-6:33
Lathe gear cutting, wood   WB76/9-10:90
Lathe indexing attachment   PM76/2:117
Lathe indexing head   WB81/7-8:28
Lathe kit   HM83/12:34
Lathe plans to order   PM78/6:66
Lathe projects   WB79/5-6:4
Lathe reverse, sanding   FW83/9-10:8
Lathe sanding and finishing   FW81/7-8:58
Lathe sanding attachments   PM83/12:109
Lathe sanding drum   FW80/3-4:14
Lathe screw chuck   FW80/11-12:84
Lathe semaphore jig   PM83/12:106
Lathe spoke hole jig   FW79/3-4:18
Lathe stand, steel pipe   PM80/5:53
Lathe steady rest, wood   PM83/12:108
Lathe steady rest, wood   WB75/3-4:34
Lathe steady rests   FW81/5-6:14
Lathe techniques   PM78/7:96
Lathe thickness sander   FW82/11-12:22
Lathe tips   FW84/1-2:40
Lathe tool bit holder, metal   PM80/7:92
Lathe toolpost, adjustable metal   PM84/5:59
Lathe tool rack   PM75/5:206
Lathe tool rest, long   WB76/11-12:50
Lathe tool stand   WB81/3-4:129
Lathe turning firewood   PM83/12:70
Lathe turning head, tapered   FW78/9:16
Lathe turning speeds, pulleys   FW82/11-12:93
Lathe turning wood, metal   FW82/5-6:98
Lathe work supports   PM80/8:109
Lattice door boot bench   NS83/5-6:54
Lattice fence   PM81/8:88
Lattice garden house   PM84/6:74
Lattice trellis, arched garden   PM84/6:74
Latticework   PM80/6:102
Latticework deck screen   WB82/3-4:84
Latticework door and window treatment   PM80/6:105
Latticework patio bar   PM80/6:104
Latticework shutters and wall panels   PM80/6:103
Latticework spice rack, wall   WB79/9-10:84
Latticework wall shelf   WB79/1-2:48
Laundry cabinet   PM77/1:92
Laundry cart   PM75/4:126
Laundry center   HM81/1:22
Laundry center   HM84/7-8:48
Laundry center   PM76/4:126
Laundry center   PM76/5:106
Laundry center closet   PM80/4:142
Laundry chute   HM78/11-12:36

Laundry chute   HM82/1:95
Laundry hamper   PM84/4:102
Laundry room, built-in washer and dryer   HM77/10:20
Laundry room planning tips   HM84/7-8:122
Laundry room remodeling   HM80/10:24
Laundry room remodeling   PM77/1:92
Lavatory sink rim   HM84/2:58
Lawn, grassless   WB83/9-10:92
Lawn, wildflowers and grasses   NS80/5-6:20
Lawn chair   WB82/5-6:90
Lawn chair, webbing (redwood)   HM72/6:52
Lawn chair, webbing replacement   HM73/8:54
Lawn chair, wood   HM80/5-6:42
Lawn furniture, Adirondack wooden   PM82/6:116
Lawn furniture, folding canvas   PM79/3:146
Lawn furniture, low cost   HM79/3:50
Lawn furniture repair, replacing webbing   PM84/3:44
Lawn mower, electric cord reel   PM83/5:73
Lawn mower, engine replacement   WB84/3-4:87
Lawn mower maintenance   HM74/8.40
Lawn mower maintenance   HM75/3:52
Lawn mower maintenance   HM82/11:46
Lawn mower maintenance   HM82/3:57
Lawn mower maintenance   NS83/4:60
Lawn mower maintenance   PM75/3:111
Lawn mower maintenance   PM79/6:169
Lawn mower maintenance   PM82/4:71
Lawn mower maintenance   PM83/6:52
Lawn mower maintenance, hand   PM80/3:146
Lawn mower pulled garden wagon   WB78/5-6:80
Lawn mower repair   HM75/4:30
Lawn mower repair   HM83/4:83
Lawn mower repair school   PM78/5:92
Lawn mower tune-up   HM77/5-6:50
Lawn sprinkler, automatic   HM77/4:68
Lawn sprinkler system   PM77/7:92
Lawn sprinkler system   PM80/5:131
Lawyer's bookcase (oak)   HM84/1:62
Lawyer's bookcase (oak)   WS83/9-10:16
Lazy Susan, kitchen (oak)   WS82/5:10
Lazy Susan, shop   WB76/3-4:43
Lazy Susan, veneer   WB73/3-4:69
Lazy Susan routed snack tray   WS83/7-8:16
Leaded glass doors   PM84/12:110
Lead melting stand   PM75/7:108
Lead miniature figures, painting   PM82/4:104
Leaf blower   PM76/1:138
Leaf blower snowblower   PM76/11:57
Leaf cart, collapsible   PM82/9:64
Leak detector, electronic air   PM79/2:194

Leaks and clogs, plumbing repair   PM73/2:156
Learning toy, counting   PM73/11:175
Leather chair seats   FW84/1-2:70
Leather edging tool   FW81/11-12:24
Leather hinge, laminated   FW81/1-2:22
Leather inlay, gold   FW78/6:61
Leather knife sheath, custom   PM79/5:29
Leather shop apron   HM83/12:38
Leather sling chair seat, contemporary   WB82/9-10:52
Lectern   HM74/4:52
Lectern, portable   PM80/9:100
Legs, Cabriole   FW83/9-10:36
Leg vise   FW78/6:16
Leg vise   FW80/9-10:66
Leg vise adjustment   FW81/7-8:10
Lemonade stand, child's   PM79/8:86
Lemonade stand/puppet theater, toy   HM84/7-8:86
Lens, low cost 762mm   PM75/5:86
Letter bookends   PM73/11:161
Letter enlarging, opaque projector   WB83/11-12:14
Letter holder   WB84/1-2:50
Letter holder, heart   HM82/2:32
Letter holder, plexiglas   PM73/11:162
Letter holders, contemporary and Colonial   PM79/6:118
Lettering, incised   FW79/1-2:66
Letter opener, plywood early American   WB82/5-6:95
Letter opener (maple or birch)   WS80/7:7
Letter openers   HM83/11:83
Letter rack/planter   WB74/3-4:56
Letters   PM80/12:109
Letters, drawing   PM77/9:174
Letters, plans for   WB82/1-2:116
Letters, sign   HM80/3:104
Lettuce shader, garden   PM83/3:105
Level, truing   FW83/7-8:22
Level, water   PM76/3:187
Leveling batter boards with water   NS84/2:18
Leveling jack, screw type   PM79/2:131
Leveling shims   PM76/4:50
Levels   NS82/9:10
Levels   WB74/7-8:50
Levels, tips on using   PM84/3:120
Library step stool   FW79/7-8:80
Life jacket, survival   PM79/12:14
Light, bedroom clock and reading   PM79/11:154
Light, dimmer controlled shop   PM84/4:65
Light, installing yard post lamp   PM74/4:176
Light, sliding basement ceiling   PM84/3:128
Light, wiring and installing yard   PM73/5:100
Light and power circuits, installation   HM84/9:104

Light box, drawing   PM72/12:112
Light box, kitchen stained glass   PM82/8:54
Light bracket, adjustable wall   WS80/5:4
Light bulb wrench   WB77/5-6:73
Light dolly, photo   PM72/8:14
Lighted house numbers   PM75/11:152
Lighted mirror, three-way movie star   PM81/12:174
Lighted planter, contemporary tree   WB81/9-10:78
Lighter, turned table   WB74/11-12:32
Lighter auto battery tester light   PM74/2:60
Light fixture, contemporary (teak)   PM82/4:166
Light fixture, large overhead   PM72/4:142
Light fixture, moving   WB81/3-4:85
Lighthouse night light   PM76/7:102
Lighting, energy efficient   NS81/10:71
Lighting, landscape   HM78/5-6:73
Lighting, landscape   HM78/5-6:68
Lighting, low voltage   HM82/1:58
Lighting, low voltage interior   PM84/1:108
Lighting, low voltage landscaping   HM82/5-6:60
Lighting, outdoor Christmas   PM81/12:30
Lighting, outdoor security   NS83/5-6:76
Lighting, track   HM75/1:36
Lighting, track   HM78/9:84
Lighting, track   PM76/9:100
Lighting, track   WB75/11-12:85
Lighting, wiring   PM76/9:102
Lightning   PM76/8:49
Lightning, equipment protection   HM82/2:66
Lightning rod, trees   HM78/7-8:64
Lightning rods   HM77/9:69
Light protector, chicken wire shop   WB81/11-12:90
Lights, four yard   HM84/3:39
Lights, kitchen   PM73/4:160
Lights, landscape   PM75/6:58
Lights, repair flickering   HM83/2:49
Lights, wall and built-in sofa   HM75/4:36
Lights, wiring   HM83/10:37
Light stand, lowboy   PM84/12:71
Light stand, shop   FW80/3-4:17
Light switch on reminder   PM81/1:60
Lily pool   HM78/2:74
Lily pool barrel   HM83/5-6:64
Lincoln, Mary's vanity mirror   PM78/2:102
Lincoln bench, long (maple and pine)   PM80/2:126
Lincoln bootjack   PM79/2:119
Lincoln chair, split bottom   PM79/2:119
Lincoln child's table   HM83/11:38
Lincoln clocks, two mantel   PM81/2:130
Lincoln desk, standing   WB76/5-6:34

Lincoln desk, standing   WB76/7-8:28
Lincoln post, turned newel stair rail   PM82/5:60
Lincoln rocking chair, armless cane (walnut)   PM84/2:60
Lincoln shaving mirror   PM78/2:102
Lincoln shaving mirror, wall (mahogany)   PM83/2:116
Lincoln table, round marble top (mahogany)   WB84/1-2:72
Linen cabinet, bathroom   HM82/11:54
Linen chest, one drawer Shaker (pine)   HM72/8:38
Linenfold carving   FW82/9-10:98
Lion paw pedestal table   FW80/11-12:74
Lion planter box   WB80/1-2:46
Lion table and stools, child's   PM74/2:144
Lion toy box   WB78/11-12:72
Living room, greenhouse   HM82/3:26
Living room table (cherry)   FW81/11-12:63
Lock, cabin door latch   HM76/4:60
Lock, cam   FW83/7-8:66
Lock, chest   FW84/11-12:54
Lock, door   WB75/7-8:25
Lock, electric garage door   WB80/9-10:46
Lock, electronic garage door   PM81/5:132
Lock, installing deadbolt   HM84/2:62
Lock, installing door   PM74/11:154
Lock, keyless door   WB73/11-12:54
Lock, lubricating sticky   HM84/2:68
Lock, seven bolt door   WB78/7-8:4
Locked miter joint   WS80/5:10
Locking joint   WS79/11:8
Locking joint, tusked-pegged-wedged   FW79/5-6:45
Lock protectors, door   WB83/7-8:32
Locks   WB78/5-6:50
Locks, door   HM73/6:54
Locks, door   HM78/5-6:40
Locks, door   WB82/9-10:4
Locks, replacing   HM75/3:54
Locks, wooden   FW83/9-10:60
Locomotive weather vane   WB73/9-10:40
Log basket, fireplace   WB81/11-12:92
Log bench   HM79/4:73
Log bench   PM83/6:104
Log bridge, trussed   FW82/3-4:78
Log cabin, simple   PM83/12:96
Log cabin basement   WB77/11-12:118
Logging with horse   FW81/9-10:98
Log home   HM79/1:86
Log home   HM81/3:30
Log home   HM83/1:40
Log home   NS83/4:28
Log home school   HM83/5-6:33
Log roller, newspaper   HM75/10:46

Logs, miniature building   FW84/5-6:12
Logs, toy building   WB84/5-6:4
Log section patio   WB77/5-6:64
Log splitter, buying   PM82/11:178
Lollipop tree centerpiece   PM80/12:98
Loom, weaving   PM77/2:118
Loom joint, wedged   FW82/5-6:16
Looseleaf notebook binder (birch plywood)   WS80/1:4
Lounge chair, folding canvas   PM79/3:146
Lounge chair, patio   WB81/7-8:34
Lounge chair, wood lawn   HM80/5-6:42
Lounge chair (redwood)   PM77/6:120
Louver, wood   FW82/9-10:16
Louvered doors   FW78/3:84
Louvers, solar house   NS80/7-8:45
Louver walls, solar   NS83/5-6:10
Love seat, fast plywood   HM78/11-12:28
Love seat and chair willow furniture, rustic   HM84/4:122
Love seat sofa, upholstered   WB82/11-12:80
Lowboy, Massachusetts 1720 (cherry)   WB82/3-4:100
Lowboy, Philadelphia   WB83/3-4:114
Lubrication   HM74/10:40
Lucite sculpturing, etching   PM73/2:80
Luggage stand, folding   PM84/4:105
Lumber, air drying   FW82/3-4:88
Lumber, buying   PM84/1:137
Lumber, car hauling   WB77/9-10:38
Lumber, chain sawing   FW77/9:50
Lumber, cutting and curing   WB74/11-12:58
Lumber, cutting and curing   WB74/9-10:16
Lumber, cutting and planing   HM83/11:53
Lumber, drying   HM80/9:68
Lumber, drying   WB72/11-12:52
Lumber, drying   WB77/1-2:86
Lumber, green   NS84/5-6:64
Lumber, pine   FW84/5-6:62
Lumber, pressure treated   PM80/3:162
Lumber, pressure treated   WB80/7-8:97
Lumber, quartersawn   FW84/9-10:76
Lumber, recycled   WB84/1-2:82
Lumber, salvaged   HM81/11:16
Lumber, salvaged   HM81/7-8:82
Lumber, treating with preservative   PM84/4:170
Lumber, twisted   FW80/5-6:16
Lumber cutting tips, circular saw   NS84/10:20
Lumber drying   FW76/12:40
Lumber drying, solar   FW80/5-6:56
Lumber drying barn, Pennsylvania Dutch   FW80/5-6:60
Lumber drying cabinet, shop   WB82/7-8:6
Lumber drying kiln, dehumidifier   FW84/3-4:40

Lumber drying kiln, solar   PM77/5:273
Lumber grading   FW78/10:77
Lumbermaking, chainsaw   FW82/9-10:60
Lumber planers   HM83/11:62
Lumber rack   HM75/2:64
Lumber rack   PM81/11:122
Lumber rack, post and spar   FW80/9-10:70
Lumber storage rack   PM75/7:108
Lumber storage rack, shop   PM84/11:160
Lumber storage shed   HM84/2:41
Lumber surfacing, router   PM78/9:20
Lunch box, heated   PM73/4:207
Lute roses   FW77/6:38
Lyre table, round   WB83/9-10:69
Machines, ancient   PM79/11:108
Machinist's chest   WB74/5-6:42
Macrame bead and dowel candle holders   WB82/1-2:100
Magazine binder (birch plywood)   WS80/1:4
Magazine/bookcase, campaign (birch)   WS80/1:6
Magazine rack   WB76/9-10:64
Magazine rack   WB77/7-8:60
Magazine rack   WB81/5-6:2
Magazine rack, bathroom   HM82/11:52
Magazine rack, dowel   PM75/12:106
Magazine rack, dowel and canvas   PM79/12:108
Magazine rack, hardboard   WB81/9-10:34
Magazine rack, plexiglas   PM73/11:162
Magazine rack and sewing footstool   WB80/1-2:44
Magazine rack (oak)   HM81/11:86
Magazine rack/table, Colonial dough box lamp   WB84/3-4:4
Magazine rack/toilet tissue holder, bathroom   PM75/4:134
Magazine/tissue rack, Colonial bathroom   WB84/1-2:79
Magnets, ten uses   PM82/1:108
Mahogany and walnut serving tray, bent   FW77/6:62
Mahogany armchair, Chippendale   WB80/5-6:97
Mahogany armchair, Chippendale 1765   WB80/9-10:38
Mahogany bookcase/secratary   FW83/1-2:54
Mahogany chair, Chippendale Georgian side   WB82/1-2:64
Mahogany chest of drawers, Boston bombe   FW84/3-4:52
Mahogany chest of drawers, Hepplewhite   FW84/9-10:42
Mahogany clock, Lincoln mantle   PM81/2:130
Mahogany coat rack   HM81/11:97
Mahogany Desk, Mark Twain lap   PM83/10:100
Mahogany desk, pigeonhole   FW80/1-2:74
Mahogany harp, American   FW81/11-12:70
Mahogany mirror, Chippendale wall   PM83/7:52
Mahogany mirror, Mary Lincoln's vanity   PM78/2:102
Mahogany office, home organizer cabinet   PM84/8:108
Mahogany or walnut table, butler's tray   WB76/1-2:41
Mahogany serving tray, glass top   HM84/9:110

Mahogany shaving mirror, Lincoln's   PM78/2:102
Mahogany shaving mirror, Lincoln wall   PM83/2:116
Mahogany table, Chippendale tilt top   PM84/8:98
Mahogany table, Colonial drop leaf   PM82/6:132
Mahogany table, Duncan Phyfe drop leaf   PM82/3:140
Mahogany table, Hepplewhite D shaped card   FW84/7-8:42
Mahogany table, Lincoln round marble top   WB84/1-2:72
Mahogany table, lyre rotating top 1825   WB81/3-4:78
Mahogany table, round contemporary dining   WS83/11-12:16
Mahogany table, spider leg carriage   FW83/5-6:70
Mahogany table, tilt top reeded pedestal   WB84/3-4:36
Mahogany table, tray coffee   FW84/1-2:72
Mahogany tool chest, woodworker's   NS81/7-8:45
Mahogany/walnut drop leaf Pembroke table   WS81/3:4
Mailbox, giant   WB79/3-4:30
Mailbox, lighted   NS82/5-6:43
Mailbox, pentagonal   PM79/4:132
Mailbox, rustic   WB80/5-6:114
Mailboxes, eye catching   HM83/5-6:40
Mailbox flag, automatic rear   PM77/12:152
Mailbox/planter post   PM78/7:112
Mailbox stand and planter   HM80/5-6:30
Mailbox update, painted   HM80/3:59
Mailbox update, tile   HM80/3:59
Maintenance, woodworking machines   FW78/10:66
Mallet, tree   WB75/11-12:83
Mallet, wooden   FW80/3-4:12
Manometer vacuum gauge   HM81/3:93
Mantel, Colonial molding fireplace   WB82/1-2:76
Mantel, fireplace   HM73/6:56
Mantel Christmas village decorations   PM81/12:114
Mantel clock   WB82/1-2:87
Mantel clock   WS82/11-12:8
Mantel clock, pendulum   NS80/11-12:62
Mantel clock, wood and crystal (walnut)   HM84/11:70
Mantel clock kit   PM75/12:98
Mantel clocks, two Lincoln   PM81/2:130
Mantel/shelf, foamboard   HM78/3:31
Maple and cherry bread board   WS82/3:24
Maple and pine bench, long Lincoln   PM80/2:126
Maple and walnut desk/wall clock   WS80/7:4
Maple and walnut fishing net, laminated   FW80/1-2:56
Maple and walnut kitchen knife case   WS80/7:7
Maple and walnut recipe box   WS80/7:8
Maple and walnut table, butcher block   WB84/11-12:46
Maple bed, contemporary platform TV   PM84/5:92
Maple chair, two board   FW81/7-8:44
Maple cookbook/recipe shelf   WS79/11:4
Maple highboy, tall chest of drawers   WB73/1-2:36
Maple hutch, contemporary   WS81/1:4

Maple Kleenex tissue box   WS82/1:24
Maple/oak cart, kitchen butcher block top   HM84/5-6:140
Maple octagonal waste basket   WS80/1:5
Maple or birch kitchen cutting board   WS79/1:1
Maple or birch letter opener   WS80/7:7
Maple or fir knockdown Oriental table   FW80/1-2:59
Maple plywood rolltop stereo cabinet   WS81/9:6
Maple plywood sweater chest, wooden hinged   WS80/5:8
Maple plywood two drawer file cabinet   WS80/1:8
Maple rocker/high chair, child's   FW84/7-8:72
Maple spice box, four drawer   PM79/11:122
Maple telephone tower, kitchen built-in   PM84/8:102
Maple tissue box cover   WS79/3:5
Maple tray, party   HM82/5-6:48
Map reading skills   PM78/3:70
Marble game, travel   PM76/4:210
Marbleizing wood   WB75/7-8:10
Marble top sideboard, Victorian (oak)   PM83/5:102
Marble top table, Lincoln round (mahogany)   WB84/1-2:72
Marking gauge   FW77/9:77
Marking gauge   FW82/3-4:97
Marking gauge   WB76/7-8:44
Marking gauge   WS82/1:13
Marking gauge, Archimedes'   FW83/3-4:14
Marking gauge, pencil   FW78/6:76
Marking gauge, super   PM81/10:35
Marking gauge to scratch stock   WB83/3-4:77
Marking tools and valuables   PM84/3:118
Marking triangle   FW77/9:46
Mark Twain lap desk (mahogany)   PM83/10:100
Marquetry   FW80/5-6:76
Marquetry   WS83/7-8:8
Marquetry, furniture   FW83/1-2:61
Marquetry, patch pad cutting   FW76/12:38
Marquetry, patchwork   FW84/7-8:62
Marquetry, sanding   FW82/9-10:16
Marquetry corners, cutting   FW77/12:70
Marquetry cutting   FW75/12:33
Marquetry finishing   FW80/11-12:90
Marquetry fretsaw   FW83/11-12:60
Marquetry fretsaw, treadle powered   WB79/3-4:42
Marquetry game table   WB72/1-2:36
Marquetry history   FW79/5-6:67
Marquetry patching   FW78/3:18
Marquetry samples   FW84/3-4:67
Marquetry serving tray kit, Colonial   WB77/7-8:71
Masks, carving Balinese   FW80/5-6:46
Masonry   WB77/9-10:88
Masonry, insulating   WB77/7-8:4
Masonry maintenance   HM79/9:59

Masonry painting   PM78/6:144
Masonry problems   HM81/3:90
Masonry repairs   HM81/9:108
Masonry repairs   WB79/3-4:35
Masonry retaining wall planter   WB81/3-4:52
Masonry wood stove   NS84/10:74
Massachusetts lowboy, 1720 (cherry)   WB82/3-4:100
Mast, antenna or birdhouse   PM72/12:186
Matchbox toy village   PM81/11:32
Mat cutting board   PM73/9:156
Math, shop   FW80/5-6:68
Matting, picture   HM83/10:74
Matting and framing, picture   PM73/2:77
Measuring, hand   PM81/9:170
Measuring tapes   NS82/3:12
Medicine cabinet   HM82/11:51
Medicine cabinet (oak)   HM84/5-6:136
Medicine chest (redwood)   WB81/3-4:72
Mediterranean outdoor furniture   WB80/7-8:82
Mediterranean table, cabinet/lamp   WB78/9-10:70
Mediterranean table, octagonal display   WB76/3-4:86
Memo pad   PM76/6:176
Merchants desk   HM73/2:54
Mesquite Parson's table   WB83/3-4:50
Mesquite sculpture   FW79/3-4:44
Message center, wall phone   PM73/12:156
Message/phone center (oak)   PM84/8:105
Metal, sawing with plywood blade   PM84/3:68
Metal, working with sheet   HM84/4:138
Metal cleaning   WB76/7-8:14
Metal fillers   HM81/4:94
Metal finish on wood   WB79/7-8:61
Metal framing connectors   HM84/5-6:82
Metal hardness tester, shopmade   PM80/2:80
Metal heat treating   FW76/9:50
Metal lathe tool bit holder, metal   PM80/7:92
Metal lathe tool holder   PM76/4:113
Metal lathe toolpost, adjustable   PM84/5:59
Metal patio furniture repair   HM75/4:46
Metal plaques, tin can   PM79/3:118
Metal polishing   HM81/9:12
Metal sawing   WB80/7-8:45
Metal storage shed kit   HM79/5-6:28
Metal surfaces, painting   HM84/7-8:46
Metal tubing projects   PM74/3:138
Metalworking furnace   PM77/11:126
Mexican Christmas tree decorations   PM81/12:116
Mexican tile bench   WB72/5-6:8
Mexican tile patio   HM83/3:30
Micrometer, enlarging   PM79/4:52

Microscope (boxwood)   FW78/10:43
Microwave, built-in   HM80/2:52
Microwave oven, installing over range   WB84/9-10:94
Microwave ovens and pacemakers   PM81/5:88
Microwave/serving cart, kitchen (cherry)   WS82/9:8
Mildew, controlling   WB77/7-8:62
Milk paint, Colonial   FW79/3-4:67
Mill, grain   HM83/9:103
Miniature bookcase cabinet   WB82/11-12:50
Miniature cabinetmaking   FW81/5-6:58
Miniature cannon, muzzle loading   WB77/11-12:4
Miniature cannon kits   PM79/7:82
Miniature clamp, earring   WB81/11-12:93
Miniature disk sander   WB72/7-8:37
Miniature furniture   WB83/11-12:4
Miniature furniture   WB83/9-10:76
Miniature hearse, horse drawn   WB73/5-6:28
Miniature hinge   WB77/1-2:10
Miniature lathe   PM80/8:98
Miniature lead figures, painting   PM82/4:104
Miniatures, turning   PM78/2:123
Miniatures, turning   PM82/6:182
Miniatures by machine   FW83/5-6:58
Miniature shingles   FW80/9-10:19
Miniature ship building   PM74/9:70
Miniature shipwright   FW83/9-10:79
Miniature tea set, turned   WB79/5-6:58
Miniature watch grandfather case   WB76/9-10:62
Miniature workshop cabinet   PM72/2:124
Minibike, steam   PM72/5:21
Mini shelves   WB78/9-10:77
Mirror, antique dressing (cherry)   PM83/7:52
Mirror, antique dressing (pine)   PM83/7:52
Mirror, antique floor   WB84/1-2:34
Mirror, carved partridge   PM77/1:96
Mirror, Cheval full length arched (oak)   WS83/11-12:4
Mirror, Chippendale wall (mahogany)   PM83/7:52
Mirror, coat rack and hall   HM80/1:80
Mirror, Colonial   PM78/12:102
Mirror, Colonial arched and hall stand   WB82/1-2:92
Mirror, contemporary   PM80/11:130
Mirror, contemporary spice shelf   WB81/5-6:96
Mirror, contemporary wall   WS84/7-8:20
Mirror, driftwood stain   PM78/12:102
Mirror, floor   WB76/3-4:90
Mirror, free standing   HM80/11:58
Mirror, heart shape vanity   PM80/2:124
Mirror, infinity $75   PM78/12:102
Mirror, lighted three-way movie star   PM81/12:174
Mirror, Lincoln shaving   PM78/2:102

Mirror, Lincoln shaving wall (mahogany)   PM83/2:116
Mirror, makeup   WB80/11-12:28
Mirror, Mary Lincoln vanity   PM78/2:102
Mirror, round (oak)   WS80/11:10
Mirror, round top hall   WS82/5:16
Mirror, vanity   WS82/11-12:24
Mirror, vanity/shaving   WS80/7:5
Mirror, Victorian shaving stand (oak)   PM83/2:108
Mirror, Victorian wall hung shaving (pine)   PM83/2:108
Mirror, wall   NS80/11-12:62
Mirror, Williamsburg   WB79/11-12:138
Mirror, wood pendent   WB83/9-10:56
Mirror and candle shaving console, Colonial   PM72/1:140
Mirror and ceramic tile tables   HM81/1:36
Mirror and shelf, early American   WB83/1-2:37
Mirror/coat rack, antique wall (oak)   WS83/3-4:18
Mirror/coat rack, hallway   PM84/7:132
Mirrored curio stand, Victorian   WB84/5-6:46
Mirrored door vanity island, two basin   WB81/9-10:46
Mirrored room dividers   WB84/9-10:40
Mirrored wall panels   WB84/9-10:40
Mirror or ceramic tile tables   HM81/1:36
Mirrors, contemporary half round molding   PM78/12:102
Mirrors, decorating with   HM81/11:36
Mirrors, decorating with   HM82/10:78
Mirrors, four   PM78/12:102
Mirrors, silvering   WB72/3-4:10
Mirrors, three antique   PM83/7:52
Mirror sconce   PM77/11:137
Mirror top coffee table   HM81/11:74
Miter, open spline   WS84/11-12:22
Miter and spline joint   WS82/5:8
Miter and spline joints   WS80/1:11
Miter board, radial arm saw   PM79/12:110
Miter board, table saw   PM79/12:111
Miter box   WB75/3-4:52
Miter box, motorized accessories   PM82/5:117
Miter box guides   PM84/5:226
Miter box holder for vise   PM84/5:226
Miter box/sawhorse, chain saw   PM75/11:112
Miter box tips   HM84/10:28
Miter clamp, multicorner   WB79/3-4:113
Miter clamps, two   PM80/11:183
Miter clamp spur dogs, angle iron   FW83/3-4:22
Miter cutting blocks, table saw   PM78/6:86
Mitered mortise and tenon joint   WS81/7:16
Miter fixture, table saw   FW79/11-12:21
Miter gauge   WB76/3-4:64
Miter gauge, table saw   PM83/12:109
Miter gauge, table saw   PM83/7:92

Miter gauge, table saw   WB79/11-12:114
Miter gauge, table saw   WB84/1-2:82
Miter gauge hold down, table saw   PM75/12:146
Mitering, table saw   FW81/1-2:80
Mitering jig, crown molding   PM83/12:107
Mitering octagons   WS82/5:17
Miter jig, radial arm saw   FW79/5-6:14
Miter jig, radial arm saw   WB76/11-12:40
Miter jig, table saw   FW81/1-2:81
Miter jig, table saw   PM77/8:111
Miter jig, table saw   WS80/11:15
Miter jigs, table saw   FW79/11-12:24
Miter joint, routed   FW82/3-4:12
Miter joint jig, drill press doweled   PM80/11:119
Miter mathematics   WS80/11:14
Miters, oblique   FW80/5-6:71
Miters, tape and glue   FW83/11-12:34
Miter stop, table saw   PM82/12:96
Mitten and boot dryer with blower   PM72/1:142
Mixer repair, food   PM74/3:76
Mixer repair, portable   PM76/12:104
Mobile, Christmas rainbow   PM79/12:82
Mobile, Christmas snowball   WB73/11-12:52
Mobile, ocean   WB73/5-6:50
Mobile, seagull   PM75/11:170
Mobile, stained glass Christmas   PM72/12:75
Mobile home   NS80/9:22
Mobile home, solarize   NS80/9:30
Mobile home decorating   WB83/7-8:88
Mobile home landscape cooling   NS80/9:33
Mobile home solar collector, passive   WB83/7-8:92
Mobile home weatherizing   NS80/9:36
Model, plywood scale   FW78/10:73
Model building, plastic   PM78/4:106
Model cabinetmaking, miniature   FW81/5-6:58
Model car, 1915 Chevrolet   WB84/9-10:80
Model car, Stutz Bearcat from tin cans   PM79/3:118
Model cars   PM72/6:66
Model hearse, horse drawn   WB73/5-6:28
Model house, scale   WB81/1-2:50
Model maker's jointer   WB79/5-6:91
Modelmaker's workshop cabinet   PM72/2:124
Model sailboat plans to order, $12.50   PM83/1:6
Model ship building   PM74/9:70
Modern table, dining   WB81/5-6:52
Modular chair   HM84/10:114
Modular furniture   PM74/1:63
Modular storage cabinet (plywood)   WS82/7:12
Modular wall units   WS84/5-6:8
Moebius strip peg box   FW78/6:79

Moisture   WB78/7-8:34
Moisture, controlling   WB73/11-12:8
Moisture, house   PM75/9:122
Moisture, indoor   NS84/10:57
Moisture, wood   FW83/3-4:92
Moisture control   HM74/2:46
Moisture control   PM72/10:152
Moisture cures   NS84/4:74
Moisture measuring   FW77/9:78
Moisture problems, house   NS80/5-6:71
Mold, concrete block making   NS81/5-6:41
Molded mortise and tenon joint   WS82/11-12:12
Molder toolbox   WB83/1-2:87
Molding, carving Spanish   FW83/9-10:48
Molding, Chippendale reproductions   PM84/8:122
Molding, cutting   PM73/6:108
Molding, decorating with   HM84/5-6:96
Molding, decorating with   PM73/6:104
Molding, decorating with   WB84/9-10:16
Molding, decorative wood   HM77/2:30
Molding, making   PM80/11:119
Molding, ogee   FW78/9:15
Molding, picture frame   FW82/7-8:61
Molding, plastic   WB83/1-2:82
Molding, routing   FW82/7-8:18
Molding, scratch beader   FW78/6:60
Molding, sectional   FW82/9-10:18
Molding, table saw   FW82/7-8:65
Molding, wood chest   WB77/9-10:84
Molding and dowel rack, shop   PM83/12:154
Molding cutter storage   PM80/8:110
Molding geometry   FW83/7-8:57
Molding head fence, radial arm saw   PM76/4:48
Molding head storage cabinet   WB83/3-4:72
Molding making   FW79/7-8:61
Molding mitering jig, crown   PM83/12:107
Molding picture frames   HM75/1:42
Molding picture frames   PM79/8:96
Molding plane   FW82/11-12:72
Molding plane, Stanly #55   FW83/1-2:89
Molding plane, Stanly #55   HM81/12:15
Molding repair, picture frame   PM76/3:119
Moldings, decorating with wood   HM79/1:26
Moldings, entry door   WB75/11-12:32
Moldings, making   HM81/1:96
Moldings, radial arm saw curved   FW82/9-10:80
Moldings, room decoration   HM82/10:63
Moldings, routing   FW82/5-6:85
Moldings, wood   HM75/2:50
Molding tips   HM84/10:39

Molding trivets   PM74/2:147
Monk's bench/table   WB79/3-4:88
Moondial clock kit   PM75/12:98
Mortar joint repair   HM83/9:98
Mortgage, early payoff of home   NS84/11-12:28
Mortise and tenon joint   FW76/6:16
Mortise and tenon joint   FW79/3-4:46
Mortise and tenon joint   WS80/3:3
Mortise and tenon joint   WS81/1:10
Mortise and tenon joint, frame   WS83/3-4:7
Mortise and tenon joint, haunched   FW79/9-10:52
Mortise and tenon joint, haunched   WS81/11:8
Mortise and tenon joint, mitered   WS81/7:16
Mortise and tenon joint, molded   WS82/11-12:12
Mortise and tenon joint, open   WS82/11-12:18
Mortise and tenon joint, table saw   WB77/9-10:28
Mortise and tenon joint, wedged   WS81/5:12
Mortise and tenon machine   FW79/11-12:84
Mortise jig, radial arm saw   WS81/7:18
Mortise joint, slot   WS83/3-4:8
Mortise routing   FW81/9-10:90
Mortise routing   FW82/7-8:52
Mortise slot joint   WS80/3:4
Mortising, drill press   FW81/7-8:12
Mortising, horizontal   FW83/7-8:12
Mortising bits   WS83/3-4:20
Mortising chisel, hexagonal   PM82/3:70
Mortising jig, router   FW80/5-6:14
Mortising jig, table saw open   FW84/11-12:8
Mortising plane   FW77/9:18
Mortising sloping wedges and shims   FW79/11-12:95
Mortising table, drill press   FW83/11-12:10
Mortising table, radial arm saw slot   FW81/1-2:20
Mortising table legs   FW79/9-10:54
Mosaic, eggshell   WB73/3-4:60
Mosaic entry door   FW81/1-2:56
Mosaic rosettes, guitar   FW76/9:53
Mosaic tile projects   WB72/1-2:54
Mosaic tile table   WB81/3-4:130
Mother of pearl inlay   FW81/3-4:50
Motorbike maintenence   PM77/10:114
Motorcycle carrier, car   PM73/6:83
Motorcycle chain maintenance   PM79/8:114
Motorcycle maintenance   PM75/4:12
Motorcycle repair school   PM77/12:58
Motorcycle riding tips   PM78/3:64
Motorcycle saddlebags, aluminum detachable   PM74/6:164
Motorcycle safety   PM78/10:228
Motor home storage   WB83/7-8:90
Motor reversing   WB75/11-12:14

Motor reversing   WB75/1-2:14
Motor reversing switch   FW79/5-6:19
Motor reversing switch   PM76/1:104
Mouse doorstop   PM80/12:98
Movie film repair   PM83/11:158
Movie slate, director's   PM79/11:122
Movie/slide screen cabinet   PM72/9:90
Mower, buying hand   PM80/3:151
Mower, engine replacement   WB84/3-4:87
Mower accessories, riding   PM77/10:47
Mower maintenance   HM74/8:40
Mower maintenance   HM75/3:52
Mower maintenance   HM82/3:57
Mower maintenance   HM82/11:46
Mower maintenance   NS83/4:60
Mower maintenance   PM75/3:111
Mower maintenance   PM79/6:169
Mower maintenance   PM82/4:71
Mower maintenance   PM83/6:52
Mower maintenance, hand   PM80/3:146
Mower repair   HM75/4:30
Mower repair   HM83/4:83
Mower repair school   PM78/5:92
Mower tune-up   HM77/5-6:50
Mowing strips, brick   HM82/3:74
Mud room bench   NS83/5-6:56
Mud room shelves and bench   PM77/9:109
Muntin doors   PM84/12:106
Murals, photo   WB72/7-8:42
Murals, wall   HM78/1:54
Murphy knife carved signs   FW81/9-10:64
Music, American harp (mahogany)   FW81/11-12:70
Music, Aztec drum   FW77/9:72
Music, banjo/dulcimer   PM82/7:88
Music, banjo making   FW75/12:8
Music, dulcimer   FW82/3-4:68
Music, dulcimer   WB75/5-6:22
Music, dulcimer/banjo   PM82/7:88
Music, five string banjo   WB72/5-6:28
Music, Flageolet   FW77/9:80
Music, guitar   WB74/7-8:34
Music, harpsichord   WB74/1-2:34
Music, organ kit   HM76/6:34
Music, pitchfork cello   WB76/9-10:56
Music, six hole flute (cocobolo)   FW84/1-2:64
Music, thumb piano   WB74/11-12:28
Music, thumb piano   WB74/3-4:40
Music, violin making   FW79/3-4:40
Musical Christmas Creche, rotating Nativity   PM73/12:157
Musical instrument form   FW83/5-6:100

Music box, inlaid   WB80/1-2:74
Music box, inlaid   WS83/7-8:4
Music box, piano   WB82/11-12:114
Music boxes, turned   FW84/9-10:78
Music box (walnut or cherry)   WS79/11:6
Music calliope, mini pipe organ   PM82/12:102
Music center cabinet   HM78/3:38
Music/jewelry box   WB83/11-12:8
Music stand   FW81/11-12:65
Muzzle loader gun kits   PM79/10:30
Muzzle loading miniature cannon   WB77/11-12:4
Nail clinching   WB77/3-4:77
Nailing   HM83/12:10
Nailing techniques   NS83/10:22
Nailing tips   NS84/4:18
Nail polish dryer   PM74/11:107
Nail puller, cat's paw   PM82/1:60
Nails   HM81/2:62
Nails   PM80/6:137
Nails, aluminum   HM73/3:42
Nails, corrugated   PM82/7:91
Nails, driving tips   PM83/3:110
Nails, invisible joint   PM84/4:160
Nails, length and penny   WB84/11-12:117
Nails, replacing   HM75/11:53
Napkin holder   PM78/11:200
Napkin holder   PM83/2:74
Napkin holder   WB75/5-6:25
Napkin ring lathe chuck   WB82/7-8:67
Napkin rings, carved animals   WB80/1-2:24
Napkin rings, carved fish duck flower   PM83/10:98
Napkin rings, coiled rope   PM79/11:76
Napkin/tableware caddy   PM75/10:102
Nativity, musical rotating Creche   PM73/12:157
Nativity picture, laminated 3D   WB84/9-10:4
Nautical bookshelves and desk, rope   PM76/1:73
Nautical lamp, block and tackle   WB84/11-12:79
Needlepoint frames   PM83/2:72
Needlepoint jewelry box   WB81/11-12:35
Needlepoint serving tray   WB78/9-10:94
Needlework frame, deep   PM73/12:154
Nesting tables   WB76/9-10:24
Nesting tables, four   PM76/5:114
Nestled tables, inlaid (walnut)   WS83/7-8:12
Newel stair rail post, Lincoln   PM82/5:60
Newport desk, slant top   FW80/7-8:41
Newspaper fuel   NS81/10:86
Newspaper log roller   HM75/10:46
NiCd battery charger   PM82/2:62
Night light, rooster   NS80/11-12:64

Night light lighthouse   PM76/7:102
Nightstand   WB78/9-10:106
Nightstand, bedroom   WB73/3-4:36
Nightstand, contemporary   WS84/7-8:16
Nightstand, French provincial   WB82/9-10:99
Nightstand, kitchen cabinets   PM75/12:70
Nightstand, traditional (walnut)   WB84/3-4:80
Nightstand, two drawer modern   WB72/1-2:44
Nightstand (pine)   WS81/11:4
Noah's ark with animals   PM78/11:121
Noel xylophone toy   PM79/11:122
Noise, auto wind   PM73/12:146
Noise, fireplace   HM75/11:61
Noise, furnace   HM80/11:50
Noise, house   HM78/9:40
Noise, house   PM80/5:235
Noise, plumbing   PM74/2:80
Noise, plumbing pipe   PM84/1:72
Noise, reducing home   WB84/1-2:92
Noise, shop   WB78/7-8:65
Norris plane   FW83/7-8:46
Norwegian chair, 1675 painted   WB76/9-10:28
Norwegian chest   WB77/3-4:14
Norwegian chest, painted 1850   WB78/11-12:20
Norwegian chest of drawers, inlaid 1740   WB80/9-10:61
Norwegian skammel stool   PM81/3:27
Note and key board (oak)   WS81/11:24
Note box, shop   WB73/5-6:59
Note caddy   WB83/3-4:20
Note holder, duck   WB73/11-12:63
Note pad   PM76/6:176
Note pad   WB80/1-2:52
Number block toys   PM81/11:30
Numbers, drawing   PM81/1:103
Nut and bolt, wood   WB76/3-4:99
Nuts, frozen   PM77/10:116
Oak and metal park bench furniture   PM81/8:94
Oak and smoked glass modern tables   WS79/1:7
Oak antique wall mirror and coat rack   WS83/3-4:18
Oak bathroom medicine cabinet   HM84/5-6:136
Oak bench, carved hall   WB83/7-8:74
Oak bookcase, lawyer's   HM84/1:62
Oak bookcase, lawyer's   WS83/9-10:16
Oak breadbox, carved   WB83/5-6:14
Oak breadbox, rolltop   HM83/1:78
Oak cabinet, contemporary rolltop computer   PM84/2:100
Oak cabinet, contemporary stereo   PM83/9:84
Oak cabinet, early American wall   HM82/10:32
Oak cabinet, sewing   HM84/2:70
Oak cabinet and hutch, contemporary cane   WS82/7:18

Oak chair, canvas   HM81/3:54
Oak chair, contemporary   WS81/5:8
Oak chairs, green Sawyer's   FW82/3-4:50
Oak china cabinet, Victorian curved glass   WB84/9-10:56
Oak clock, schoolhouse   PM81/6:145
Oak clock, schoolhouse wall   WS82/5:4
Oak coffee table   WS83/1-2:20
Oak coffee table, simple block strips   PM80/11:130
Oak contemporary chairs   WS79/3:6
Oak contemporary table   WS81/5:4
Oak cradle   HM82/11:62
Oak desk, small rolltop   WB84/7-8:4
Oak desk/bookcase, wall hung contemporary   HM84/9:30
Oak desk sewing cabinet   WB82/5-6:4
Oak dolly   PM79/11:132
Oak dry sink, early American   HM82/10:32
Oak fern stand, antique   WB82/5-6:80
Oak file cabinet   HM84/1:63
Oak finish, ammonia fumed   FW81/5-6:70
Oak firewood holder, indoor   PM82/1:102
Oak/glass coffee table, contemporary   PM83/12:148
Oak glider swing, porch   HM84/5-6:70
Oak gun cabinet, contemporary   WB81/9-10:56
Oak hall butler, Victorian   HM83/11:24
Oak hall tree, traditional turned   WB84/11-12:40
Oak icebox   HM82/1:30
Oak icebox   WS84/11-12:4
Oak icebox bar   PM84/12:102
Oak jewelry box   HM83/12:74
Oak key and bulletin board   WS81/11:24
Oak lamp, hanging end grain   FW81/11-12:60
Oak lazy Susan, kitchen   WS82/5:10
Oak magazine rack   HM81/11:86
Oak/maple cart, kitchen butcher block top   HM84/5-6:140
Oak mirror, Cheval full length arched   WS83/11-12:4
Oak mirror, round   WS80/11:10
Oak plant stands, two   PM81/10:104
Oak refinishing   HM81/7-8:52
Oak rocking chair, child's   FW83/9-10:55
Oak serving tray   WS82/1:19
Oak shaving stand with mirror, Victorian   PM83/2:108
Oak shelf units, contemporary   WB82/9-10:96
Oak sideboard, Victorian marble top   PM83/5:102
Oak sideboard tile top   WB78/9-10:62
Oak spiral steps   FW76/3:42
Oak swing, old fashioned porch   WB81/5-6:45
Oak swing, porch   HM84/5-6:70
Oak swing, porch 1927   PM83/7:94
Oak table   WB79/5-6:24
Oak table, contemporary gate leg   FW76/6:42

Oak table, drawing   HM84/12:68
Oak table, English hayrake stretcher 1924   FW84/9-10:72
Oak table, Parson's   HM81/1:52
Oak table, round dining   PM79/7:92
Oak telephone/message center   PM84/8:105
Oak telephone shelf, rolltop under cabinet   PM84/8:107
Oak trivet, tiled   WS82/5:24
Oak TV tray tables   WS81/7:4
Oak wagon, antique toy   PM84/6:132
Oak wagon, toy with seat   HM84/3:99
Oak wall display case, wooden hinged   WS80/5:11
Oak wall shelf, dovetail tongue and groove   WS82/3:20
Oak wine rack   PM82/5:104
Oak writing desk   FW82/5-6:67
Octagonal display table, Mediterranean   WB76/3-4:86
Octagonal planter (redwood)   WS81/7:10
Octagonal wall clock frame   WS80/11:8
Octagon mitering   WS82/5:17
Office, closet   HM79/2:34
Office, computerized   PM83/8:92
Office, fold out chest   PM73/9:/6
Office, home   HM83/2:28
Office, home   PM73/9:73
Office, home   PM81/4:135
Office, home built-ins   HM84/1:41
Office, home organizer (mahogany)   PM84/8:108
Office, kitchen   PM80/12:100
Office center, his and her desks   PM81/7:97
Office desk, computer   PM81/5:114
Office file cabinet (oak)   HM84/1:63
Office furniture, home   WB72/3-4:36
Office furniture, modular   HM83/2:34
Office organizer, kitchen   PM78/4:112
Office plans to order, small portable $3.00   NS83/4:21
Ogee bracket feet   FW80/3-4:62
Ogee molding, making   FW78/9:15
Oil finishes   WB75/9-10:8
Oil finishes   WS83/11-12:12
Oil furnace   HM81/1:68
Oil furnace   HM81/2:50
Oil furnace   HM81/3:92
Oil furnace   HM81/4:48
Oil furnace, cleaning   NS83/10:26
Oil furnace, use less oil   NS80/10:49
Oil furnace maintenance   PM84/10:56
Oiling   HM74/10:40
Oil or gas fuel   NS81/9:92
Oils, coloring with penetrating   FW81/3-4:65
Oil stain finishes   WB72/3-4:40
Oil stains   HM83/4:104

Oil/varnish finish   FW79/11-12:76
Oil/varnish mix finish   FW76/3:46
One piece plywood chair   FW80/1-2:46
Opaque projector   WB73/7-8:30
Open mortise and tenon joint   WS82/11-12:18
Organ, mini calliope pipe   PM82/12:102
Organ kit   HM76/6:34
Organ kit, console   WB72/11-12:34
Oriental candle stand, chard   PM72/6:149
Oriental garden   NS81/5-6:30
Oriental garden   WB78/3-4:54
Oriental gazebo   WB80/3-4:4
Oriental jewelry, wood   WB72/11-12:44
Oriental jewelry chest   WB73/11-12:48
Oriental table, knockdown (fir or maple)   FW80/1-2:59
Oriental teahouse   WB83/5-6:64
Orienteering and map reading   PM78/3:70
Ostrich puppet   PM78/11:196
Ottoman   PM82/4:123
Ottoman, Mediterranean outdoor furniture   WB80/7-8:82
Ottoman and chair, outdoor (redwood)   HM83/4:116
Outdoor fabric covers   NS83/7-8:82
Outdoor fiberglass screen   HM72/8:52
Outdoor finishes   FW83/9-10:66
Outdoor finishes   WS83/5-6:14
Outdoor furniture   WS79/5:11
Outdoor furniture, block/wood picnic table   PM73/6:76
Outdoor furniture, cushion waterproofing   PM73/10:108
Outdoor furniture, Mediterranean   WB80/7-8:82
Outdoor play center, $250   HM79/10:60
Outdoor storage chest   WB73/3-4:52
Outdoor toolbox   HM78/2:58
Outdoor toys   WB74/5-6:30
Oval boxes, steam bent Shaker   FW82/1-2:92
Oval picture frame   HM81/2:40
Oval picture frame   WS79/9:9
Oval scribing trammel compass   PM82/12:94
Oven, solar $5   WB79/3-4:72
Overhead and pin router   FW81/7-8:65
Owl, carved low relief   WB75/1-2:44
Owl pinup   PM75/10:129
Owner builder mistakes   HM79/4:22
Owner built cabin   WB80/7-8:42
Owner built home   NS81/2:66
Owner built home   NS83/10:90
Owner built home   NS83/5-6:82
Owner built home   NS83/9:102
Owner built home   WB84/3-4:50
Owner built home   WB84/5-6:12
Owner built home   WB84/7-8:10

Owner built home, financing   NS81/2:52
Owner built home, savings   NS81/2:22
Owner built home, solar   NS82/9:68
Owner built homes   NS83/4:22
Owner built precut home   HM79/11:14
Owner built schools   HM80/3:20
Owner built schools   NS83/11-12:56
Owner built schools   WB84/5-6:107
Oyster shell veneer boxes   FW79/11-12:66
Package wrapping tying, Japanese   HM83/12:58
Pad, paint   HM83/4:47
Paddle boat, child's   WB77/3-4:58
Paddle wheel boat   WB81/7-8:16
Pagoda bird feeder   WB74/9-10:54
Paint, choosing   WB79/9-10:70
Paint, Colonial milk   FW79/3-4:67
Paint, concrete   HM80/3:40
Paint, epoxy   WB76/5-6:50
Paint, exterior peeling cure   HM84/9:67
Paint, how much to buy   HM82/4:113
Paint, interior color   HM83/12:44
Paint, marine   PM80/4:124
Paint, peeling   HM75/10:58
Paint, peeling   HM75/11:35
Paint, peelproof exterior   PM72/10:152
Paint, priming   PM84/2:24
Paint, removing from brick   HM75/4:52
Paint, roll on painted wall pattern   PM78/4:164
Paint, solar panels   NS83/4:68
Paint, stain over   WB73/3-4:20
Paint, storing   WB77/3-4:109
Paint, textured   NS80/2:16
Paint, textured wall   HM79/1:48
Paint brush, buying   HM84/5-6:18
Paint brush, cleaning   HM80/7-8:98
Paint brush cleaner   PM82/3:168
Paint brushes   HM76/9:34
Paint brushes, cleaning   PM84/11:146
Paint can sealer   WB77/9-10:20
Painted furniture   FW77/9:48
Painted Norwegian chair, 1675   WB76/9-10:28
Painting   HM81/1:34
Painting   WB83/5-6:37
Painting, car   HM83/4:128
Painting, drag sponge colorwash spatter   HM82/10:26
Painting, exterior   HM76/10:46
Painting, exterior   HM78/4:16
Painting, exterior   HM79/4:40
Painting, exterior   HM81/5-6:40
Painting, exterior   HM83/4:30

Painting, exterior   PM73/6:88
Painting, exterior   PM75/9:92
Painting, exterior   PM77/9:92
Painting, exterior   PM83/4:115
Painting, exterior   WB83/9-10:119
Painting, exterior color selection   HM82/4:70
Painting, exterior trim   HM83/9:86
Painting, house   HM77/7-8:15
Painting, house   NS82/5-6:32
Painting, interior   HM78/1:32
Painting, interior   PM73/4:186
Painting, Pennsylvania Dutch designs   PM79/12:96
Painting, preparing for interior   PM79/3:122
Painting, shopping for auto   PM75/10:56
Painting, spray can   HM83/2:29
Painting, spray can   PM74/5:112
Painting, spray can   PM83/9:88
Painting, texturing   HM82/10:45
Painting, wall graphics kits   HM78/1:13
Painting, wall preparation   WB80/3-4:106
Painting basement, airless sprayer   HM79/11:52
Painting checklist   HM79/4:54
Painting concrete   PM78/6:144
Painting concrete and metal structures   PM75/8:84
Painting furniture   WB79/7-8:46
Painting insulation scars   HM79/4:58
Painting metal surfaces   HM84/7-8:46
Painting picture frames, holder   PM82/12:132
Painting primer sealer   WB81/1-2:142
Painting problems   HM84/5-6:163
Painting problems, exterior   PM83/6:84
Painting problems, interior   PM83/7:100
Painting questions   HM81/5-6:76
Painting scaffold   PM79/5:139
Painting stucco   HM75/4:52
Painting tools   HM83/12:54
Painting tools   NS82/5-6:14
Painting tools   PM78/8:104
Painting tools, buying   HM83/4:44
Painting walls and trim   HM81/11:52
Paint on vapor barriers   NS84/4:62
Paint primer sealers   HM80/7-8:74
Paint problems   HM76/9:50
Paint remover, making   PM79/11:187
Paint removing from brass   HM75/11:56
Paint removing machine, backpack   PM74/5:152
Paint removing tools   HM81/2:8
Paint roller, buying   PM73/12:84
Paint roller, pattern designs   HM76/11:46
Paint rollers   HM76/3:32

Paint solvents   HM81/2:88
Paint sprayer, airless   HM79/11:52
Paint sprayer, airless   WB80/5-6:62
Paint strippers   HM79/11:38
Paint strippers   NS83/7-8:32
Paint stripper safety   PM83/10:65
Paint stripping   WB74/5-6:8
Paint tray, ladder   HM83/5-6:126
Paint vs. stain, house   HM82/4:77
Pan, reclaiming cast iron   HM82/1:80
Panel, cutting for raised panel door   WS79/3:10
Panel, cutting wide   WS80/3:12
Panel and frame   FW80/7-8:55
Panel and frame cabinet (pine)   WS80/3:8
Panel and frame door   WS80/3:6
Panel and frame doors   FW84/11-12:44
Panel and frame variations   FW81/7-8:59
Panel clamp, double bar   WB79/1-2:30
Paneled doors and walls, planed   FW79/9-10:84
Paneling, ceiling   WB81/11-12:82
Paneling, installing   PM75/5:88
Paneling, room diagonal   HM80/2:90
Paneling, wall   HM75/8:38
Paneling, wall   HM78/1:16
Paneling, wall   HM79/9:92
Paneling, wall   WB76/9-10:58
Paneling, wall   WB77/9-10:78
Paneling cutting jigs   PM83/3:65
Paneling repair, wood   WB76/5-6:16
Paneling walls   PM84/4:117
Panel raising planes   FW81/9-10:59
Panels, arched raised   WB77/3-4:94
Panels, edge gluing   WS84/3-4:13
Panels, radial arm saw raised   FW83/3-4:90
Panels, raised   WB78/9-10:87
Panels, raised   WS81/11:10
Panels, router cutting   FW84/1-2:56
Panels, table saw raised   WB79/11-12:136
Panel saw, plywood   FW82/3-4:90
Panel saw, plywood   WB82/1-2:67
Panel saw guide, circular portable   PM82/12:97
Panel surfacing router rail   FW80/11-12:56
Pan hanger, kitchen   HM83/2:67
Panorama picture making   PM79/4:104
Panoramic photo stand   PM81/8:134
Pan rack, kitchen   WB72/9-10:20
Pan rack, kitchen (pine)   HM80/11:32
Pan rack cabinet, kitchen   WB76/3-4:6
Pantograph   WB83/1-2:58
Pantograph correction   WB83/7-8:13

Pantry, camping   HM84/5-6:130
Pantry, closet   HM79/2:34
Pantry, kitchen   NS83/2:78
Pantry, kitchen   NS84/3:14
Pantry, roll-out food   PM83/4:145
Pantry, wall   WB75/7-8:34
Pantry door, kitchen   HM81/1:23
Pantry storage   WB79/9-10:48
Paper and hand towel rack, kitchen   PM81/2:136
Paper boring tool   PM81/10:37
Paper cutter   PM79/4:133
Paper furniture   PM72/6:132
Paper spike, desk   HM82/10:22
Paper towel holder   PM74/8:174
Paper towel holder   WB81/1-2:72
Paper towel holder, kitchen   HM83/7-8:94
Parallel spline joints (plywood)   WS80/5:9
Parcours exercise center, outdoor   PM79/9:116
Park and patio benches   PM84/6:78
Park bench, concrete   PM84/3:84
Park bench furniture (metal and oak)   PM81/8:94
Parquet floor   HM72/10:42
Parquet floor   HM77/4:26
Parquet floor   HM82/7-8:38
Parquet floor   PM76/2:118
Parquet floor   WB73/5-6:20
Parquet floor   WB81/9-10:72
Parquet table   WB81/3-4:112
Parquet wall   HM81/9:76
Parrot balancing toy   PM81/12:175
Parrot cup rack, kitchen   WB84/9-10:113
Parson's dining table   PM78/11:128
Parson's table   WB83/3-4:50
Parson's table, bridge   PM72/6:150
Parson's table, butcher block coffee   WB83/5-6:72
Parson's table, veneer   FW78/6:70
Parson's table (oak)   HM81/1:52
Particleboard   FW81/7-8:76
Particleboard   WB75/7-8:38
Partridge and dove Christmas candle holders   HM81/12:22
Partridge mirror, carved   PM77/1:96
Parts cleaner   PM76/1:91
Parts washer, garage   HM82/9:120
Passive refrigerator   NS81/7-8:36
Passive solar, basics   NS80/2:51
Passive solar, part 2   WB82/7-8:39
Passive solar, part 3   WB82/9-10:120
Passive solar collector, lean-to   PM80/7:108
Passive solar collector, mobile home   WB83/7-8:92
Passive solar house   NS80/2:56

Passive solar house, massive   NS81/10:41
Pass through, dining room   WB76/3-4:40
Pass through, louver doors   HM74/4:34
Pasta rack   HM82/12:70
Pastry tray   HM82/2:32
Patch pad cutting marquetry   FW76/12:38
Patents   HM78/9:98
Patents for inventors   PM84/5:172
Patio   NS82/4:86
Patio, brick and sand   HM77/7-8:52
Patio, brick and sand   PM73/7:78
Patio, brick three   HM84/3:54
Patio, concrete   WB81/3-4:34
Patio, fence   NS80/9:12
Patio, log sections   WB77/5-6:64
Patio, Mexican tile   HM83/3:30
Patio, portable stereo cabinet   PM73/8:82
Patio, scrap wood   WB77/5-6:56
Patio and deck ideas, nine   PM78/6:138
Patio and park benches   PM84/6:78
Patio and retaining wall, rugged   HM79/3:54
Patio and walks, paving blocks   HM80/5-6:94
Patio arbor   HM79/5-6:50
Patio arbors   HM80/5-6:18
Patio bar, latticework   PM80/6:104
Patio bar, portable wet   PM73/8:78
Patio bar/cart (redwood)   HM84/7-8:92
Patio bench   PM78/9:113
Patio blocks, sealing   HM84/9:74
Patio cart, plywood   HM80/12:19
Patio chair (redwood and cedar)   WS83/5-6:8
Patio cover   HM75/3:62
Patio cover, fiberglass   WB80/5-6:54
Patio cover, Oriental gazebo   WB80/3-4:4
Patio/deck planter   PM80/8:88
Patio door, installing   HM82/4:53
Patio door, replacing   HM79/4:33
Patio door, two surface wall   WB83/9-10:52
Patio door drapery retainers   PM84/5:192
Patio door replacement   WB81/5-6:97
Patio fence   PM75/8:92
Patio fence screen (redwood)   HM80/4:26
Patio furniture, rewebbing   HM77/7-8:43
Patio furniture, rustic willow   HM84/4:122
Patio furniture repair, metal   HM75/4:46
Patio insect vacuum   PM74/7:107
Patio lamp, post   PM75/8:92
Patio lamp (redwood)   HM80/4:22
Patio lamp (redwood)   PM75/8:91
Patio lantern lamp   HM81/2:82

Patio lounge chair   WB81/7-8:34
Patio planter   PM75/8:90
Patio putting golf green   PM75/8:55
Patio roof, hyperbolic paraboloid   WB79/7-8:79
Patios and walks, brick   PM77/5:104
Patios and walks, brick and sand   HM72/4:56
Patio screen   WB73/5-6:23
Patio screen plaques   WB75/5-6:50
Patio storage bench   HM72/8:30
Patio table   WB75/9-10:26
Patio table and benches   WB80/5-6:32
Patio table and chairs   PM79/5:142
Patio table/benches, designer   PM83/8:70
Patio table (redwood)   HM84/5-6:32
Patternmaker   FW81/1-2:82
Pattern sawing   FW84/7-8:54
Paving block walks and patio   HM80/5-6:94
Peasant art bird feeder   WB84/11-12:67
Pedal car plans to order, $6   PM80/6:124
Pedestal table, lion's paw   FW80/11-12:74
Pedestal table (pine)   WB80/7-8:54
Pediment door, front   WB76/1-2:57
PEG 1000, green wood   WB72/3-4:48
PEG 1000, green wood   WB82/3-4:106
Pegboard hooks   HM79/5-6:26
Peg box, dulcimer   FW78/6:77
PEG for green wood   FW79/11-12:68
Pelican bas relief wood carving   WB84/11-12:82
Pelican pull toy   WB72/1-2:14
Pembroke table, drop leaf (mahogany/walnut)   WS81/3:4
Pencil and card holder (scrap wood)   WS79/3:12
Pencil clothes rack, child's   PM81/11:30
Pencil gauges   FW78/6:76
Pencil holder, dowel   PM78/5:254
Pencil post bed (cherry)   FW83/7-8:54
Pendulum clock, modern (walnut)   HM83/1:82
Pendulum clock kit   PM75/12:98
Penguin pull toy   PM77/11:202
Pen holder, firewood   WB79/5-6:93
Pen ink pot, turned quill   WB76/7-8:46
Pennsylvania Dutch designs, painting   PM79/12:96
Pennsylvania Dutch tobacco drying barn   FW80/5-6:60
Pepper mill and salt shaker, hexagon   PM82/1:158
Persian window   WB77/1-2:65
Pet bed/carrier   HM77/10:42
Pewter fruit bowl   PM79/8:92
Pewter salt and pepper shakers   PM79/8:92
Pewter tableware   PM79/8:92
Pewter tankard   PM79/8:92
Philadelphia highboy   WB83/3-4:114

Philadelphia lowboy   WB83/3-4:114
Phone, antique update   WB81/9-10:114
Phone, buying   NS83/2:32
Phone, installing   PM83/5:39
Phone caddy (redwood)   PM84/7:94
Phone cupboard (pine)   PM84/8:106
Phone desk and chair   WB81/3-4:90
Phone maintenance   NS83/2:32
Phone message center, wall   PM73/12:156
Phone/message center (oak)   PM84/8:105
Phone repairs   NS84/5-6:22
Phone shelf, rolltop under cabinet (oak)   PM84/8:107
Phone speaker amp, electronic   PM74/2:132
Phone stand with drawer   PM74/7:144
Phone table, plastic laminate   PM78/6:142
Phone tower, kitchen built-in (maple)   PM84/8:102
Photo, ID   PM76/11:149
Photo calendar pinup   WB83/3-4:102
Photo close up macro light   PM81/11:24
Photo copying   PM76/3:90
Photo copying stand   PM73/7:14
Photo copying stand   PM82/12:140
Photo display screen, folding   PM73/12:48
Photo enlarging easel, borderless   PM73/2:46
Photo film dryer   PM72/12:56
Photo film washer   PM74/8:12
Photographing woodcrafts   FW82/9-10:92
Photographs, furniture from   FW79/7-8:61
Photography, high speed stop action   PM80/11:62
Photography, panorama picture making   PM79/4:104
Photography background roll   WB82/1-2:96
Photo light dolly   PM72/8:14
Photo murals   WB72/7-8:42
Photo slide copier light   PM76/1:69
Photo stand, panoramic   PM81/8:134
Photo statues   WB76/11-12:20
Photovoltaic cell mounting system   NS83/9:22
Photovoltaic electricity   NS83/9:10
Photovoltaic electricity, solar   NS82/5-6:65
Piano, thumb   WB74/11-12:28
Piano bar   PM72/9:74
Piano finish   FW84/1-2:58
Piano music box   WB82/11-12:114
Piano rebuilding, player   WB75/7-8:26
Piano restoration   WB83/11-12:70
Picket fences   NS81/7-8:63
Picket fences, four   HM82/4:30
Picket fences, wooden country   PM83/6:89
Pickup camper   PM73/3:178
Pickup camper   WB79/9-10:86

Pickup camper   WB79/5-6:46
Pickup camper plans to order   PM78/1:76
Pickup cap, wood and fiberglass   WB82/3-4:44
Pickup pass through window, installing   PM84/3:60
Pickup tailgate workbench   PM73/5:67
Picnic table   HM80/4:16
Picnic table   HM80/5-6:29
Picnic table, breakdown   PM81/6:107
Picnic table, concrete block and wood   PM73/6:76
Picnic table, designer   HM83/5-6:91
Picnic table, folding   HM80/7-8:32
Picnic table, folding   PM75/4:116
Picnic table, folding (redwood and cedar)   WS83/5-6:4
Picnic table, outdoor   PM81/4:162
Picnic table, stowaway   PM76/8:100
Picnic table/benches, designer   PM83/8:70
Picnic table/benches, sawbuck (redwood)   PM83/8:73
Picnic tray, snack   HM81/2:76
Picnic utensil caddy   WB84/3-4:66
Picture, panorama making   PM79/4:104
Picture, three in one   WB74/9-10:56
Picture frame   HM75/11:56
Picture frame   HM79/4:50
Picture frame, barn wood   PM77/2:184
Picture frame, carving running patterns   FW83/9-10:46
Picture frame, domed glass   WB73/1-2:58
Picture frame, floating   PM77/4:103
Picture frame, guilding   WB78/7-8:52
Picture frame, molding   HM75/1:42
Picture frame, molding   PM79/8:96
Picture frame, optical illusion   PM72/1:144
Picture frame, oval   HM81/2:40
Picture frame, oval   WS79/9:9
Picture frame, restoring old   WB77/5-6:60
Picture frame, turned   WB82/9-10:75
Picture frame, twenty-six   PM75/5:106
Picture frame and framing   HM83/10:65
Picture frame clamp   FW78/10:16
Picture frame clamp   FW80/1-2:16
Picture frame clamp   FW80/5-6:18
Picture frame clamp   FW80/9-10:22
Picture frame clamp   HM81/7-8:92
Picture frame clamp, bedspring   FW83/3-4:20
Picture frame holder, painting   PM82/12:132
Picture frame miter jig   PM82/12:98
Picture frame molding   FW82/7-8:61
Picture frame molding repair   PM76/3:119
Picture frame router bit   WS80/7:3
Picture framing and matting   PM73/2:77
Picture hanging   HM83/10:76

Picture heaters   HM78/1:46
Picture matting   HM83/10:74
Picture plaque   WB82/11-12:2
Pictures, copying   PM76/3:90
Pictures, flash   PM78/12:84
Pictures, making them last   PM76/4:108
Pierced tin panel Colonial pie safe   PM82/8:90
Pier curio shelf   PM75/1:112
Pie safe, pierced tin panel Colonial   PM82/8:90
Pig chair, child's   WB79/11-12:102
Pigeonhole desk   HM83/2:66
Pigeonhole desk (mahogany)   FW80/1-2:74
Pigments, dyes and stains   FW78/9:58
Pig miniature box, band sawed   PM84/5:90
Pillar and claw table   FW81/11-12:81
Pillow table plant stand (oak)   PM81/10:104
Pin and overhead router   FW81/7-8:65
Pine and cedar coffee table   WB80/3-4:76
Pine and maple bench, long Lincoln   PM80/2:126
Pine and redwood blanket chest, contemporary   WS81/7:12
Pine bed, single   FW81/5-6:68
Pine bed, traditional   HM81/9:54
Pine beehives   FW83/3-4:86
Pine bookcase and display stand   WB80/5-6:52
Pine book rack, adjustable   HM80/11:32
Pine cabinet, Colonial corner   HM82/2:30
Pine cabinet, Shaker   PM84/10:104
Pine chest, one drawer Shaker linen   HM72/8:38
Pine chest, Shaker blanket   FW81/3-4:60
Pine chest, six drawer contemporary   WS81/9:16
Pine clock, Lincoln mantle   PM81/2:130
Pine coffee table, grid   NS80/5-6:43
Pine Colonial lap desk, wooden hinged   WS80/5:6
Pine cradle, Colonial   HM84/12:64
Pine cradle, Colonial   PM83/12:130
Pine desk, Colonial trestle   PM74/10:77
Pine desk, six ft. trestle   WB82/3-4:20
Pine frame and panel cabinet   WS80/3:8
Pine furniture, antiqued   FW77/6:54
Pine furniture, Taos   FW83/5-6:79
Pine kitchen cabinets, low cost   HM82/7-8:40
Pine kitchen cooling rack   WS79/1:2
Pine lumber   FW84/5-6:62
Pine mirror, antique dressing   PM83/7:52
Pine nightstand   WS81/11:4
Pine or cherry Shaker lap desk   FW76/3:48
Pine pan rack, kitchen   HM80/11:32
Pine phone cupboard   PM84/8:106
Pine planter tray   HM83/3:87
Pine rolltop breadbox   WS79/7:6

Pine Shaker Colonial trestle table   WS79/1:3
Pine shaving mirror, Victorian wall hung   PM83/2:108
Pine shelf   PM77/11:137
Pine shelf, country strip   HM80/11:32
Pine silverware caddy   HM80/11:33
Pine spice box of drawers   WS79/11:3
Pine storage center, movable   NS80/2:59
Pine strip lantern   HM82/5-6:40
Pine table, cloverleaf top x-legs   WB80/11-12:124
Pine table, drum top and cyma curve legs   WB80/5-6:104
Pine table, inlaid round top   WB80/9-10:72
Pine table, pedestal   WB80/7-8:54
Pine table, round top modern   FW81/9-10:88
Pine table, small   WB80/3-4:50
Pine table, splayed legs with aprons   WB81/1-2:40
Pine table hutch, 1700's   PM82/7:92
Pine tie rack   WS79/1:2
Pine towel holder, kitchen   HM80/11:34
Ping pong caddy   PM76/11:200
Pin routed jewelry box   WS83/7-8:10
Pin router   FW81/7-8:63
Pin router   WS83/7-8:20
Pin router techniques   PM83/8:76
Pipe, briar   FW80/3-4:82
Pipe, briar   PM77/2:38
Pipe, copper   PM74/2:76
Pipe, frozen water   PM83/11:60
Pipe, leaking   HM83/2:56
Pipe, leaking   PM83/11:60
Pipe, making   PM77/5:225
Pipe, plastic   PM74/1:82
Pipe clamp tips   FW84/3-4:43
Pipe insulation   HM80/4:84
Pipe insulation   NS81/11-12:82
Pipe organ, mini calliope   PM82/12:102
Pipe projects, metal   PM74/3:138
Pipe rack, plexiglas   PM73/11:162
Pipe rack, smoking   WB76/1-2:24
Pipe rack and humidor drawers   PM74/11:104
Pipe rack/humidor   PM75/12:95
Pipe repairs, emergency plumbing   WB84/9-10:70
Pipe tray, smoking   PM79/4:130
Pirate treasure chest   WB80/11-12:30
Pistol, wooden 1849 pepperbox derringer   PM81/3:72
Pistol shooting tips   PM76/4:84
Pitchfork cello   WB76/9-10:56
Place mats, coiled rope   PM79/11:76
Plan and pattern sources   HM79/12:62
Plane, bench   PM84/10:62
Plane, bench   WS82/9:16

Plane, bench use   WS82/9:20
Plane, block   FW83/3-4:65
Plane, block   WB79/7-8:14
Plane, chisel rabbet   FW80/5-6:19
Plane, hand   FW75/12:22
Plane, hand   NS81/10:18
Plane, improving wood   FW79/1-2:52
Plane, Japanese   FW80/1-2:60
Plane, molding   FW82/11-12:72
Plane, mortising   FW77/9:18
Plane, Norris   FW83/7-8:46
Plane, panel raising   FW81/9-10:59
Plane, restoring Bailey   FW79/1-2:55
Plane, router   WB80/7-8:7
Plane, scraper   FW82/9-10:18
Plane, Stanly #55 molding   FW83/1-2:89
Plane, Stanly #55 molding   HM81/12:15
Plane, three wood to make   PM82/6:97
Plane, ultralight plans to order $50   PM81/11:110
Plane, using power   PM83/11:180
Plane, Vietnamese   FW82/3-4:96
Plane, wood   FW76/6:28
Plane, wood   WB73/11-12:37
Plane, wooden   WB81/5-6:6
Plane, wood toy   PM84/12:95
Plane and saw, Japanese   HM82/12:36
Plane basics, bench   FW82/7-8:84
Plane construction, wooden   FW80/1-2:65
Planed paneled doors and walls   FW79/9-10:84
Plane guide, wood   PM84/2:116
Plane guide blocks   FW83/7-8:16
Plane iron, regrinding   FW83/7-8:14
Plane iron and chisels, sharpening   FW81/7-8:67
Plane iron honing tool   FW83/9-10:10
Plane iron sharpening   FW82/7-8:20
Plane iron sharpening   WS82/9:18
Plane iron sharpening jig, carriage bolt   PM79/7:8
Planemaker's float   FW81/9-10:63
Plan enlarging by squares   WB81/11-12:94
Planer   HM83/11:62
Planer, automatic feed abrasive   FW80/7-8:65
Planer, fixed knife   FW83/1-2:94
Planer accessories, Williams and Hussey   WB83/9-10:120
Plane refurbishing   FW82/7-8:16
Planer guide boards   WB83/3-4:54
Planer hand feed, Parks   FW83/3-4:20
Planer knives storage cabinets   WB83/1-2:64
Planer lumber roller   WB83/9-10:97
Planer shavings receptacle   WB83/3-4:58
Planer toolbox   WB83/1-2:87

Plane tips, bench   PM80/8:100
Plane tips, bench   PM80/7:102
Plane tips, bench   PM80/10:122
Plane tips, block   PM80/6:116
Plane tips, power   PM83/12:50
Plans, project   WB81/11-12:36
Plans, where to buy   HM78/4:86
Plans and patterns, sources   HM80/12:45
Plant box, rolling   PM80/3:160
Plant box with dowel trellis   PM80/8:88
Plant cold frame, roll around   WB80/3-4:46
Plant cold frame and hot bed   HM78/2:26
Plant display rack   PM80/3:160
Planter, aluminum and glass window   PM79/6:60
Planter, antiqued   WB75/5-6:18
Planter, barrel   PM72/4:132
Planter, barrel   WB74/5-6:32
Planter, bathroom   PM76/5:106
Planter, bench and hanging   PM77/10:200
Planter, Bonsai   PM77/7:97
Planter, brick   HM74/8:36
Planter, concrete Chinese   WB78/3-4:58
Planter, contemporary tree   WB81/9-10:78
Planter, deck or garden   PM76/4:135
Planter, deck/patio   PM80/8:88
Planter, deck (redwood)   HM80/4:20
Planter, deck (redwood)   PM82/6:104
Planter, decorative wood and tile   WB81/3-4:4
Planter, domino   PM74/8:176
Planter, four   PM81/3:132
Planter, four tier   WB77/11-12:123
Planter, garden   NS81/5-6:46
Planter, hanging   HM79/4:68
Planter, hanging   PM77/7:98
Planter, hanging   PM81/7:96
Planter, hanging   WB72/9-10:21
Planter, hanging dowel   PM80/8:88
Planter, hanging garden   HM79/3:29
Planter, hanging heart shaped   WB83/7-8:86
Planter, hanging (scrap wood)   WS79/5:12
Planter, hanging tear drop   WB82/3-4:117
Planter, hardboard   WB81/9-10:34
Planter, octagon   PM75/8:94
Planter, octagonal (redwood)   WS81/7:10
Planter, outdoor   HM80/4:56
Planter, outdoor   WB84/5-6:100
Planter, patio   PM75/8:90
Planter, pedestal   WB81/3-4:81
Planter, plywood and plastic   HM78/10:73
Planter, plywood family room   PM79/2:132

Planter, pot (redwood)   HM82/5-6:86
Planter, raised brick   PM84/3:113
Planter, screen   WB76/3-4:59
Planter, six sides   WB78/11-12:56
Planter, strip wood   WB73/7-8:22
Planter, twelve   PM78/5:132
Planter, vertical fence   PM84/3:112
Planter, wall and book end   WB79/1-2:110
Planter, wall flowerpot   WB79/11-12:89
Planter, wishing well   HM78/11-12:86
Planter, wishing well   WB74/7-8:48
Planter, wood block   WB81/3-4:76
Planter, wrought iron window   HM78/4:38
Planter bench   PM77/3:97
Planter boxes   HM81/5-6:33
Planter boxes, animals   WB80/1-2:46
Planter box (redwood)   WS79/5:9
Planter box with trellis   PM80/3:159
Planter cabinet, room divider   HM72/12:44
Planter/divider, lighted   PM78/10:116
Planter/ letter rack   WB74/3-4:56
Planter/mailbox post   PM78/7:112
Planter molds, cut stone   HM74/8:50
Planter (redwood)   PM75/8:92
Planter (redwood or cedar)   WS79/5:3
Planter retaining wall, masonary   WB81/3-4:52
Planter/seed starter, cantilevered   NS80/3:53
Planter/table, small   PM76/10:116
Planter tray (pine)   HM83/3:87
Planter utility post cover barrel   WB79/11-12:38
Plant growth box   WB73/5-6:35
Plant hanger, double loop   HM79/7-8:89
Plant hanger, forged   PM78/6:146
Plant hanger, indoor or out (redwood)   HM80/4:24
Plant hanger, oval   WB82/1-2:119
Plant hanger/privacy fence   HM83/5-6:58
Plant holder, hanging circular   PM79/12:20
Plant hotbed   PM78/8:92
Plant hutch display   PM81/1:96
Plant ladder   WB77/5-6:40
Plant ladder, plexiglas   PM75/5:72
Plant or utility stand   WB80/1-2:83
Plant pillars (cedar)   WS79/5:4
Plant pot A-frame   HM79/3:32
Plant potting bench   HM82/3:32
Plant pot trellis, wall   PM73/2:100
Plant seed starter, indoor   NS84/1:87
Plant shelf, acrylic hanging   PM83/8:144
Plant shelf, window   PM78/12:138
Plant shelf, window   PM81/2:136

Plant shelf, window   WB77/9-10:22
Plant shelf unit   WB78/9-10:49
Plant stand   WB76/11-12:44
Plant stand   WB77/11-12:74
Plant stand   WB79/1-2:70
Plant stand, 1X12X4ft   WB81/9-10:75
Plant stand, 2X4   WB77/3-4:73
Plant stand, acrylic   PM75/12:120
Plant stand, corner pots   HM84/5-6:38
Plant stand, flower pot tree   WB78/5-6:74
Plant stand, indoor (redwood)   PM83/2:76
Plant stand, (oak)   PM81/10:104
Plant stand, park bench (metal and oak)   PM81/8:94
Plant stand, ring and spindle   WB79/9-10:77
Plant stand, scrap wood   WB78/7-8:72
Plant stand, semicircular   WB80/11-12:76
Plant stand, three legged turned   WB80/1-2:72
Plant stand, three legged turned   WB80/1-2:100
Plant stand, turned   WB76/11-12:42
Plant stand/potting bench   PM83/6:104
Plant stand (redwood)   HM80/4:24
Plant stand (redwood)   HM83/3:86
Plant stand stool   WB77/3-4:30
Plant table, modern (oak and smoked glass)   WS79/1:7
Plant table with trays (redwood)   FW84/1-2:43
Plant wagon or stand   WB75/11-12:88
Plant window box, outdoor   PM82/3:132
Plaque, carved crocodile   WB78/11-12:4
Plaque, fish   HM80/11:56
Plaque, patio screen   WB75/5-6:50
Plaque, picture   WB82/11-12:2
Plaque, tin can metal   PM79/3:118
Plaque, wall   HM78/11-12:90
Plaque, wall decal   WB75/5-6:10
Plasterboard   HM75/8:34
Plasterboard   HM83/7-8:76
Plasterboard   PM74/5:90
Plasterboard   WB78/3-4:84
Plasterboard   WB80/9-10:108
Plasterboard elevator   HM74/4:43
Plasterboard installation   HM77/7-8:22
Plasterboard installation   PM81/7:32
Plasterboard repair   HM73/4-5:66
Plasterboard repair   HM77/5-6:24
Plasterboard repair   HM83/2:54
Plasterboard repair   PM76/4:30
Plaster casting   PM75/2:64
Plaster repair   HM79/7-8:64
Plastic laminate   FW84/3-4:72
Plastic laminate   HM79/1:60

Plastic laminated boxes   WB76/9-10:46
Plastic laminate inlays   WB79/7-8:45
Plastic molding   WB83/1-2:82
Plastic pipe   HM73/3:44
Plastic pipe   PM74/1:82
Plastic pipe   PM78/11:138
Plastic plumbing   HM78/1:22
Plastic plumbing   NS81/1:40
Plastic plumbing   PM80/1:106
Plastic plumbing   WB78/7-8:62
Plastic plumbing   WB80/3-4:16
Plastic plumbing, drains   HM79/5-6:85
Plastic plumbing repairs   HM84/2:66
Plastic sheet, removing scratches   PM81/2:143
Plate, turned   WB79/5-6:4
Plate, wood sandwich   PM77/11:144
Plate butler, cupboard   PM79/11:212
Plate display racks   WB75/11-12:68
Plate holder and display stand   PM76/3:184
Plate joint   FW82/5-6:95
Plate stand   WB83/9-10:53
Plate warmer   WB83/11-12:102
Platform bed   NS81/2:61
Platform bed   PM79/8:100
Platform furniture   HM81/9:42
Play area, child's indoor   WB81/9-10:62
Playcubes, numbered   PM81/1:102
Player piano rebuilding   WB75/7-8:26
Playground equipment   HM82/5-6:84
Playground equipment   HM83/7-8:68
Playground equipment   WB80/7-8:4
Playhouse, A-frame   WB74/9-10:65
Playhouse, contemporary   WB84/5-6:42
Playhouse, cube   PM78/9:116
Playhouse, fairy tale with towers   WB84/5-6:8
Playhouse, garage tree   HM81/5-6:14
Playhouse, indoor   HM81/12:30
Playhouse, indoor door   PM75/10:146
Playhouse, Scandinavian   WB77/1-2:56
Playhouse, three   PM78/7:76
Playhouse, two story and storage   WB82/9-10:22
Playhouse and bed, fast plywood   HM78/11-12:28
Playhouse/guest cottage   HM82/5-6:66
Playhouse kitchen refrigerator sink/range   WB83/11-12:76
Playhouse puppet theater   WB83/3-4:3
Playhouse/slide   WB80/5-6:22
Playhouse/swing set, A-frame with roof   PM80/5:133
Playhouse/tower slide   PM81/6:130
Playhouse/treehouse, child's   PM80/8:92
Playing card holder   PM77/5:276

Play outdoor center, $250   HM79/10:60
Playpen and bed, baby   HM81/10:24
Play/sand box, outdoor toy   PM82/5:112
Play unit for toddlers   WB84/3-4:125
Plexiglas barometer, water   PM74/9:142
Plexiglas bookcase (walnut)   WB81/7-8:44
Plexiglas coffee table   PM75/5:72
Plexiglas cutting   FW81/7-8:18
Plexiglas cutting board   PM75/5:72
Plexiglas furniture, clear plastic   HM77/7-8:34
Plexiglas gifts   PM73/11:162
Plexiglas hat shelf/coat rack   PM75/5:72
Plexiglas heat bending   WB75/3-4:72
Plexiglas lamps, hanging contemporary   PM80/1:112
Plexiglas letter holder   PM79/6:118
Plexiglas plant ladder   PM75/5:72
Plexiglas plant shelves, hanging   PM83/8:144
Plexiglas plant stand   PM75/12:120
Plexiglas safety glass   WB74/3-4:58
Plexiglas sculpturing, etching   PM73/2:80
Plexiglas sheet, removing scratches   PM81/2:143
Plexiglas storm door repair   HM72/12:54
Plexiglas window repair   HM77/10:34
Plexiglas window replacement   PM72/3:162
Plexiglas wine rack   PM75/7:102
Plexiglas wine server   PM75/11:62
Pliers   HM76/8:46
Pliers   NS81/11-12:14
Pliers   WB74/3-4:48
Pliers, push apart   PM84/5:100
Pliers, slip joint   PM78/9:210
Plumbing   WB75/5-6:34
Plumbing   WB80/1-2:94
Plumbing, cleaning water damage   HM83/3:88
Plumbing, clogged drains   HM74/2:50
Plumbing, clogged drains   HM78/5-6:53
Plumbing, clogged showerhead   HM83/2:54
Plumbing, clogged toilet   HM78/7-8:46
Plumbing, copper   HM75/2:36
Plumbing, copper pipe   PM74/2:76
Plumbing, cutting and soldering copper pipe   HM84/12:62
Plumbing, drain unclogging   NS82/3:60
Plumbing, extra outdoor faucet   PM81/6:121
Plumbing, faucet   WB72/7-8:50
Plumbing, faucet   WB82/1-2:58
Plumbing, faucet and showerhead   HM83/7-8:56
Plumbing, faucet repair   HM72/9:44
Plumbing, faucet repair   HM79/10:78
Plumbing, faucet repair   NS82/2:49
Plumbing, faucet repair   PM75/5:11

Plumbing, faucet replacement   HM76/6:42
Plumbing, freeze proof faucet   PM84/12:64
Plumbing, frozen   HM73/1:42
Plumbing, leaky pipes   HM83/2:56
Plumbing, planning and layout   HM84/10:120
Plumbing, plastic   HM78/1:22
Plumbing, plastic   NS81/1:40
Plumbing, plastic   PM80/1:106
Plumbing, plastic   WB78/7-8:62
Plumbing, plastic drains   HM79/5-6:85
Plumbing, plastic drains   HM79/7-8:94
Plumbing, plastic pipe   HM73/3:44
Plumbing, plastic pipe   PM74/1:82
Plumbing, plastic pipe   PM78/11:138
Plumbing, plastic pipe   WB80/3-4:16
Plumbing, repairing leaking faucet   PM83/4:149
Plumbing, repairing leaking pipes   PM83/11:60
Plumbing, septic tank   HM79/9:80
Plumbing, septic tank   HM83/9:62
Plumbing, septic tank   NS81/4.00
Plumbing, septic tank maintenance   HM73/12:54
Plumbing, soldering copper   HM81/11:108
Plumbing, soldering copper tubing   NS82/1:36
Plumbing, stainless steel sink installation   HM76/10:40
Plumbing, sump pump   HM80/1:46
Plumbing, supply drains vents etc.   HM84/11:80
Plumbing, tapping copper water lines   HM76/4:42
Plumbing, thawing frozen water pipes   PM83/11:60
Plumbing, toilet repair   NS82/4:48
Plumbing, toilet seal replacement   HM83/2:56
Plumbing, toilet seating   PM74/2:72
Plumbing, toilet tank noise   HM78/11-12:72
Plumbing, toilet tank repair   HM73/3:40
Plumbing, toilet tank repair   HM74/3:48
Plumbing, toilet tank repair   HM76/11:44
Plumbing, toilet tank repair   HM80/3:36
Plumbing, toilet tank repair   HM81/9:88
Plumbing, toilet tank repair   WB82/5-6:62
Plumbing, toilet tank water valve   HM83/2:58
Plumbing, trap connections   HM78/9:90
Plumbing, tub and sink drains   WB80/3-4:87
Plumbing, tub drain repair   HM77/3:32
Plumbing, unclogging drains   PM73/11:98
Plumbing, utility sink   HM79/11:107
Plumbing, water connections   HM78/10:52
Plumbing, water hammer noises   HM79/9:109
Plumbing, water powered drain plunger   PM84/6:51
Plumbing, water supply gate and globe valves   HM79/2:72
Plumbing, workings   HM78/4:56
Plumbing advice   NS83/5-6:58

Plumbing connectors, flexible   HM84/2:68
Plumbing drainage system   HM79/4:80
Plumbing drain heat recovery system   NS84/1:68
Plumbing drains, connectors   WB81/3-4:114
Plumbing emergencies   HM79/10:92
Plumbing for washer   HM84/2:65
Plumbing noise   PM74/2:80
Plumbing noises   NS83/9:24
Plumbing pipe noises, correcting   PM84/1:72
Plumbing pipe repairs, emergency   WB84/9-10:70
Plumbing repair   HM76/2:34
Plumbing repair   HM80/2:72
Plumbing repair   HM84/1:80
Plumbing repair   PM83/11:54
Plumbing repair, leaks and clogs   PM73/2:156
Plumbing repair, plastic pipe   HM84/2:66
Plumbing techniques   WB79/11-12:104
Plumbing tree, basement   WB73/11-12:34
Plywood, edge finishing   FW80/11-12:18
Plywood, edging   HM78/7-8:37
Plywood, hardwood   FW80/7-8:76
Plywood, hinge edge   PM84/2:116
Plywood, house framing   NS84/7-8:32
Plywood, stacked shaping   FW77/3:50
Plywood basics   FW84/5-6:48
Plywood basket, folding fruit   PM74/2:140
Plywood bed/desk/chest, child's loft (FW84/5-6:52
Plywood chair, one piece   FW80/1-2:46
Plywood chairs, designer   HM79/5-6:54
Plywood coffee table, modern   HM80/12:15
Plywood construction   FW76/12:36
Plywood cutting and joining   WB79/1-2:84
Plywood cutting jigs   PM83/3:65
Plywood desk   WB84/5-6:56
Plywood desk, child's   WB75/5-6:32
Plywood desk, contemporary   WB78/11-12:86
Plywood desk and bench   HM80/12:16
Plywood desk/storage two   HM74/2:34
Plywood dining table and chairs, Colonial   PM82/4:116
Plywood dollies   FW82/3-4:12
Plywood early American furniture   WB82/5-6:95
Plywood edge, sixteen   PM74/5:96
Plywood edge banding   FW78/3:14
Plywood edge treatments   PM84/12:52
Plywood furniture, fast   HM78/11-12:28
Plywood joint, locked miter   WS80/5:10
Plywood modular storage cabinet   WS82/7:12
Plywood panel home building guide   PM84/3:139
Plywood panel saw   FW82/3-4:90
Plywood patio cart   HM80/12:19

Plywood rack   FW83/1-2:20
Plywood sofa/storage   HM81/4:14
Plywood spline joints   WS80/5:9
Plywood storage bracket   FW84/3-4:12
Plywood storage chest/box   PM74/2:146
Plywood table, dihedral-x   HM80/12:17
Plywood table, modern coffee   HM80/12:15
Plywood toy box, barn   HM80/12:14
Plywood toy race car   WS79/9:12
Plywood toy train   WS79/9:10
Plywood wall hung raised panel cabinet   WS80/3:7
Plywood wine and glass rack   HM80/12:18
Plywood wine rack   PM82/5:104
Pocket watch grandfather case   WB76/9-10:62
Podium   HM74/4:52
Poker table, folding   WB82/11-12:26
Pole and wire joinery   FW81/7-8:74
Polisher, gem   PM76/1:102
Polishing, metal   HM81/9:12
Polishing/buffing machine   WB84/7-8:28
Polishing/buffing wheels and compounds   WB84/7-8:46
Polishing wheels   HM77/10:70
Polyethylene glycol, green wood   WB72/3-4:48
Polyhedral wood puzzles   FW79/1-2:75
Poncho, rain   PM75/3:122
Pond, stone and concrete   WB81/3-4:56
Pond house table, dining   FW84/1-2:32
Pool   WB75/5-6:14
Pool, four small garden   PM84/8:94
Pool, garden waterfall and rock garden $50   HM78/9:93
Pool, indoor   NS83/11-12:46
Pool, in ground <$3000   HM83/5-6:81
Pool, lily   HM78/2:74
Pool, low cost   PM76/5:102
Pool, solar   NS82/4:66
Pool, stone and concrete garden   WB81/3-4:56
Pool, vinyl   HM76/6:40
Pool barrel, lily   HM83/5-6:64
Pool bottom, vinyl   HM72/6:54
Pool cover   PM77/8:52
Pool cue and ball rack   PM72/7:145
Pool cue rack   PM76/5:224
Pool deck   PM78/3:137
Pool filter   PM73/6:79
Pool heater, solar   PM79/5:136
Pool heater, solar   PM81/8:132
Pool kit   HM83/5-6:88
Pool maintenance   HM82/5-6:73
Pool maintenance   PM75/7:77
Pool maintenance   PM80/5:134

Pool maintenance   PM82/6:126
Pool plans to order, wooden $8   PM81/6:124
Pool storage/bench boxes   HM84/5-6:40
Pool table   PM73/1:63
Pool table, bumper   WB76/11-12:74
Pool table, miniature   WB81/11-12:60
Popcorn bowl, turned (koa)   WS83/1-2:24
Porch, adding southern style   HM84/5-6:64
Porch, live green   NS81/5-6:20
Porch, repairing   HM84/5-6:59
Porch, screened lattice   HM84/3:27
Porch, solar   NS82/10:36
Porch, Victorian lattice side   HM84/5-6:54
Porch and storage shed   WB79/5-6:60
Porch arbor   NS81/5-6:23
Porch/deck, double decker   PM82/10:118
Porch glider swing, (oak)   HM84/5-6:70
Porch post repair   HM84/9:68
Porch post replacement   HM83/9:80
Porch steps, wood   HM74/9:50
Porch swing, 1927 (oak)   PM83/7:94
Porch swing, Jimmy Carter   FW84/5-6:68
Porch swing, old fashioned (oak)   WB81/5-6:45
Porch swing and frame, old time   PM78/5:128
Porch swing (oak)   HM84/5-6:70
Portable drill stand   WB84/11-12:102
Post, coopered   FW81/5-6:78
Post, fence   HM75/2:53
Post, Lincoln turned newel stair rail   PM82/5:60
Post and beam construction   FW79/7-8:43
Post and beam cottage   NS80/3:57
Post and beam houses, insulating   NS84/9:96
Post and panel chest   FW80/7-8:53
Post ferrules   WB83/3-4:113
Post lamp   HM84/3:40
Post lamp, wood   HM78/2:34
Post puller, auto jack   PM77/8:16
Post pulling   PM79/2:80
Post pulling   PM80/6:40
Post repair, porch   HM84/9:68
Pot and pan rack, kitchen   PM82/4:166
Pot hanger, kitchen   HM81/2:18
Pot rack plans to order, kitchen   NS83/2:80
Potter's wheel   WB73/5-6:32
Potter's wheel kit   PM75/10:96
Potter's wheel tips   WB74/1-2:44
Pottery making   PM75/10:96
Pottery making   PM78/8:108
Potting bench   PM79/5:140
Potting bench   PM80/8:95

Potting bench   PM82/3:149
Potting bench, garden   PM83/3:105
Potting bench, plant   HM82/3:32
Potting bench/garden cart (redwood)   HM83/3:60
Potting bench/plant stand   PM83/6:104
Potting bench (redwood)   PM74/7:156
Potting shed, kitchen   HM81/3:66
Power hacksaw   WB77/7-8:30
Power meter/stylus timer, stereo turntable   PM81/11:85
Power tool   HM77/11-12:31
Power tool, buying   HM79/11:18
Power tool, electronic   NS84/11-12:46
Power tool, repair or replace   NS83/3:48
Power tool buying tips   PM84/12:143
Power tool maintenance   HM82/12:50
Power tool maintenance   PM83/5:106
Power tool maintenance   PM78/12:106
Power tool repair, shop   WB76/1-2:38
Power tool stand   WB72/11-12:28
Power tool stand   WB79/7-8:54
Power tool storage box   WB78/9-10:90
Precision woodworking   FW79/7-8:70
Preservatives, safest wood   NS84/7-8:64
Press, bench veneer   FW84/7-8:41
Press, cider   PM78/9:120
Press, glue   FW80/1-2:48
Press, hand arbor   PM72/9:154
Press, hydraulic   PM75/10:85
Press, hydraulic   WB76/1-2:26
Press, winemaker's   HM81/2:32
Press for veneers, shop built vacuum   FW79/5-6:52
Pressure treated lumber   NS82/3:84
Pressure treated lumber   PM80/3:162
Pressure treated lumber   WB80/7-8:97
Pricing woodworking   FW77/3:54
Primer sealer, painting   WB81/1-2:142
Primer sealers   HM80/7-8:74
Priming paint   PM84/2:24
Printed circuit board processing   PM79/3:14
Printer stand, computer   HM83/2:36
Printing Christmas cards   PM77/11:110
Projector, opaque   WB73/7-8:30
Projector, opaque letter enlarging   WB83/11-12:14
Projector, wall storage   HM76/6:38
Projector dissolve control, slide   PM74/3:120
Projector hideaway   WB78/1-2:8
Projector kit, overhead   PM72/3:115
Projector storage cabinet   WB75/11-12:78
Projector table   HM78/4:42
Propane torch   WB77/5-6:48

Propane torch holder   HM82/9:113
Protractor, framing square   WB79/11-12:20
Pull toy, bumble bee   PM73/12:166
Pull toy, circus train and animals   PM72/12:108
Pull toy, dragonfly   FW79/11-12:61
Pull toy, hatching chick   PM74/11:108
Pull toy, jumping clown   PM80/11:130
Pull toy, penguin   PM77/11:202
Pull toy, rabbit   HM82/11:24
Pull toy, seal   PM74/11:110
Pull toy, train   PM75/11:142
Pull toy, whale   PM75/11:143
Pump, basement sump   PM79/4:162
Pump, ram   PM77/4:57
Pumper, mini fire engine/motorbike   PM74/10:92
Punch, adjustable sleeve   PM73/5:167
Punch, drill press   PM80/2:130
Punch, midpoint   PM74/2:154
Punjabi weaving stool   WB78/1-2:68
Puppet, clown toy   PM81/11:32
Puppet, ostrich   PM78/11:196
Puppet theater   PM77/3:128
Puppet theater/lemonade stand, toy   HM84/7-8:86
Puppet theater playhouse   WB83/3-4:3
Puppet toy   PM77/3:133
Purfling and binding, guitar   FW81/5-6:52
Purfling router guide   FW80/3-4:13
Push stick   FW82/7-8:4
Push stick   PM76/8:96
Push stick   WB80/7-8:80
Push stick, table saw   FW77/3:53
Push stick and hold downs, table saw   WB72/7-8:16
Puzzle, box of blox   WB78/11-12:80
Puzzle, captive ring   WB78/11-12:80
Puzzle, carved little man (walnut)   FW76/6:56
Puzzle, castle   PM77/11:136
Puzzle, checkerboard   WB83/11-12:92
Puzzle, child's picture   HM84/9:137
Puzzle, classic disc   PM78/2:31
Puzzle, contour strips in box   WB78/11-12:80
Puzzle, cube   PM82/1:66
Puzzle, hen and egg   PM78/11:121
Puzzle, interlocking wood   PM72/12:150
Puzzle, jigsaw   WB84/11-12:32
Puzzle, jump a peg   PM72/3:137
Puzzle, kangaroo squirrel elephant owl   HM77/11-12:28
Puzzle, Pandora's box   WB78/11-12:80
Puzzle, peg   WB78/11-12:80
Puzzle, picture blocks   WB81/1-2:126
Puzzle, roving rings   WB78/11-12:80

Puzzle, thirteen piece furniture block   WB84/11-12:62
Puzzle, wood   WB76/3-4:16
Puzzle, wooden   FW84/11-12:38
Puzzle, wood polyhedral   FW79/1-2:75
Puzzle block table   WB77/11-12:89
PVC bicycle cart   PM80/5:132
PVC cart, bicycle   PM84/5:64
PVC drapery rings, pipe   PM82/3:167
PVC gun and rod travel case   PM74/11:178
PVC pipe cart, roll around   HM81/9:34
PVC pipe chair   HM81/9:30
PVC pipe garden cart   WB83/7-8:94
PVC pipe table   HM81/9:32
PVC pipe toy wagon   WB83/9-10:110
Quality control in production   FW80/9-10:80
Quarry tile   PM84/6:84
Quarry tile floor   PM76/4:144
Quartersawn lumber   FW80/11-12:34
Quartersawn lumber   FW84/9-10:76
Queen Anne chair   WB75/7-8:36
Queen Anne highboy chest, small   FW83/9-10:32
Queen Anne secretary desk kit   HM76/11:38
Queen Anne side chair   WB81/3-4:131
Queen Anne table   WB75/7-8:22
Queen Anne table designs   FW76/6:40
Quill pen ink pot, turned   WB76/7-8:46
Quilting frame, knocks down   WB82/9-10:124
Quilting frame, turned   WB82/9-10:84
Quilt rack   WB76/5-6:24
Quilt rack, turned   PM82/1:67
Quilt rack (cherry)   WS84/3-4:4
Rabbet and dado joint   WS80/7:9
Rabbet and dado joints   PM81/11:118
Rabbet and groove drawer joint   WS81/11:20
Rabbeting small pieces, radial arm saw   WS81/5:16
Rabbeting small pieces, table saw   WS81/5:15
Rabbit crayon holder   PM78/11:194
Rabbit hutch   WB80/3-4:60
Rabbit hutch waterer   WB81/7-8:12
Rabbit pull toy   HM82/11:24
Rabbit pull toys   PM81/4:124
Rabbit toy box   PM81/4:124
Race car bed, child's   WB79/7-8:5
Rack, door knob   WB82/3-4:9
Rack, kitchen pan   WB72/9-10:20
Rack, post and spar lumber   FW80/9-10:70
Rack, tool bigfoot   FW80/9-10:72
Racket press with ball storage, tennis   PM78/2:125
Racket rack, tennis   PM78/2:124
Radial arm saw, poor boy   FW84/5-6:12

Radial arm saw accessory cabinet   PM72/3:148
Radial arm saw auxiliary tables   WB81/1-2:131
Radial arm saw bench with storage   PM78/2:132
Radial arm saw box joint   FW81/5-6:76
Radial arm saw circle cutting jig   PM81/5:52
Radial arm saw cutoff stop   PM83/11:104
Radial arm saw doweling jig   HM81/9:126
Radial arm saw drop leaf tables   PM82/3:76
Radial arm saw dust collector, cardboard box   WB80/7-8:63
Radial arm saw dust collector/table   WB77/3-4:116
Radial arm saw dust slot   PM84/2:116
Radial arm saw extension table   PM83/11:99
Radial arm saw extension table   PM84/5:99
Radial arm saw fence   PM73/3:150
Radial arm saw fence   FW81/5-6:24
Radial arm saw fence, pivoting rip   PM80/2:130
Radial arm saw hold down   PM72/11:172
Radial arm saw jointing   FW82/1-2:14
Radial arm saw maintenance   PM83/5:106
Radial arm saw miter board   PM79/12:110
Radial arm saw miter jig   FW79/5-6:14
Radial arm saw miter jig   WB76/11-12:40
Radial arm saw molding head fence   PM76/4:48
Radial arm saw moldings, curved   FW82/9-10:80
Radial arm saw mortise jig   WS81/7:18
Radial arm saw rabbeting small pieces   WS81/5:16
Radial arm saw raised panels   FW83/3-4:90
Radial arm saw resaw jig   PM84/5:226
Radial arm saw safety accessories   WB76/3-4:4
Radial arm saw shaper   WB81/1-2:100
Radial arm saw slip joint   FW82/1-2:71
Radial arm saw slot mortising table   FW81/1-2:20
Radial arm saw table   PM79/2:122
Radial arm saw table leveling jacks   PM74/4:64
Radial arm saw techniques   PM77/9:112
Radial arm saw techniques   WB75/3-4:40
Radial arm saw turnings   WB76/11-12:92
Radial arm saw with mounted router   WB84/3-4:79
Radial saw mortise and tenon joint, mitered   WS81/7:16
Radiant heaters   NS80/11-12:45
Radiator cover   PM77/4:154
Radiator heater, hiding   NS81/9:49
Radiators, hiding   HM77/2:36
Radio, AM antenna booster   PM82/8:28
Radio, crystal   PM77/1:60
Radio, hidden auto   WB76/9-10:66
Radio booster amp   PM78/7:95
Radio controlled airplanes   PM78/8:110
Radon gas, indoor air quality   NS84/5-6:28
Raft/boat   PM76/1:96

Railroad tie steps   NS83/5-6:35
Rails and spindles   HM77/11-12:60
Rain gutters   WB77/7-8:44
Rain poncho   PM75/3:122
Raised bed garden frame   NS83/1:76
Raised panel door, cutting panel   WS79/3:10
Raised panel door frame cutting   WS79/3:11
Raised panel door joints   WS81/11:8
Raised panels   WS81/11:10
Raised panel wainscoting   WB79/3-4:16
Raised panel wall hung cabinet (plywood)   WS80/3:7
Rake, riding mower accessory   PM77/10:47
Rake, wooden garden   NS83/4:30
Ramada   HM79/5-6:50
Ram planter box   WB80/1-2:46
Ram pump   PM77/4:57
Ram swing, two person toy   PM81/11:30
Range, connecting gas   HM84/2:66
Range, repairing electric   PM75/4:144
Range, toy   PM78/11:120
Range hood, oven over   PM74/10:158
Range repair   HM73/10:42
Range repair   HM77/4:32
Range repair   NS83/5-6:66
Raspberry supports   PM84/3:114
Rasps and files, tips   HM84/3:12
Rasps and files, tips   HM84/4:18
Rattle, turned toy   FW79/11-12:58
Razor blade saw   WB75/3-4:69
Real estate, buying rural   NS81/3:92
Real estate agent   NS83/9:70
Real estate costs   NS81/2:24
Real estate investments   NS82/1:81
Reamers, socket   FW80/1-2:17
Recessed tabletop   FW80/7-8:11
Recipe box (walnut and maple)   WS80/7:8
Recipe/cookbook shelf (maple)   WS79/11:4
Recipe file box   HM83/7-8:95
Recipe holder, turned   WB79/7-8:28
Recipe holder book rack   WB82/5-6:18
Record and tape end table   WB79/7-8:22
Record cabinet, contemporary frame and panel   FW84/1-2:54
Record care, stereo   PM81/9:188
Recorder maintenance, cassette   PM79/11:34
Recorder repairs, cassette   PM72/2:110
Record storage, music   WB78/1-2:80
Recreational vehicle maintenance   PM74/3:162
Recycling   NS82/2:56
Recycling, aluminum can crusher   PM82/7:46
Recycling, can   WB75/9-10:44

Recycling center   NS82/2:45
Recycling center, kitchen   HM82/9:66
Redwood, refinishing exterior   HM83/9:92
Redwood and canvas deck chair   WS79/5:6
Redwood and canvas deck stool   WS79/5:6
Redwood and cedar garden bench   WS83/5-6:12
Redwood and cedar patio chair   WS83/5-6:8
Redwood and cedar picnic table, folding   WS83/5-6:4
Redwood and pine blanket chest, contemporary   WS81/7:12
Redwood barbecue cart   HM84/7-8:96
Redwood barbecue cart   PM84/7:94
Redwood bar/cart, patio   HM84/7-8:92
Redwood bathroom rolltop wall cabinet   WS81/9:10
Redwood bathroom vanity   WB77/11-12:20
Redwood bench/trellis   HM84/5-6:36
Redwood beverage tray   PM84/7:94
Redwood butler's tray   WS79/5:9
Redwood chair, canvas sling   PM83/6:104
Redwood chair, lawn webbing   HM72/6:52
Redwood chair, lounge   HM83/4:124
Redwood chair, lounge   PM77/6:120
Redwood chair and ottoman, outdoor   HM83/4:116
Redwood chair/table unit with umbrella   HM83/4:122
Redwood chaise lounge   PM84/7:94
Redwood deck   HM82/5-6:22
Redwood deck   PM75/4:114
Redwood deck   PM82/6:104
Redwood deck   PM84/6:90
Redwood deck   WB75/5-6:26
Redwood deck   WB84/3-4:106
Redwood deck, roofed   WB77/3-4:68
Redwood deck chair   HM80/4:18
Redwood deck planters   HM80/4:20
Redwood deck table   HM80/4:18
Redwood garden bench   WS79/5:8
Redwood garden cart/potting bench   HM83/3:60
Redwood garden center   HM80/4:22
Redwood garden shelter   HM78/7-8:14
Redwood jewelry box   WB83/11-12:8
Redwood lamp   HM75/10:42
Redwood lamp, patio   PM75/8:91
Redwood lawn furniture restoration   PM83/8:74
Redwood medicine chest   WB81/3-4:72
Redwood or cedar planter   WS79/5:3
Redwood patio fence screen   HM80/4:26
Redwood patio lamp   HM80/4:22
Redwood picnic table/benches, sawbuck   PM83/8:73
Redwood planter   PM75/8:92
Redwood planter   PM81/3:132
Redwood planter   PM84/7:94

Redwood planter, octagonal   WS81/7:10
Redwood planter, pot   HM82/5-6:86
Redwood planter box   WS79/5:9
Redwood plant hanger, indoor or out   HM80/4:24
Redwood plant stand   HM80/4:24
Redwood plant stand   HM83/3:86
Redwood plant stand, indoor   PM83/2:76
Redwood potting bench   PM74/7:156
Redwood storage building   WB78/7-8:46
Redwood storage building   WB78/5-6:113
Redwood table   PM84/7:94
Redwood table, deck   HM84/5-6:32
Redwood table, drop   HM80/4:26
Redwood table, outdoor serving   HM83/4:122
Redwood table and benches   HM82/5-6:31
Redwood table and trays, plant   FW84/1-2:43
Redwood telephone caddy   PM84/7:94
Redwood walkway and overhead trellis   PM81/8:88
Reeded pedestal table, tilt top (mahogany)   WB84/3-4:36
Reeding bedposts   FW82/11-12:34
Reeding bedposts   FW83/3-4:32
Reeding bedposts, router   FW83/1-2:4
Reel, electric extension cord   PM72/12:182
Reel, fishing bow center shot   PM73/5:153
Refectory table   PM74/3:73
Refinishing, gun stock   WB78/3-4:69
Refinishing, restoring modern antiques   WB77/1-2:95
Refinishing, stripping paint   WB74/5-6:8
Refinishing, water stain removing   WB73/11-12:44
Refinishing floors, hardwood   PM75/10:92
Refinishing floors, hardwood   PM83/1:100
Refinishing furniture   FW77/12:32
Refinishing furniture   HM75/3:64
Refinishing furniture   HM78/1:36
Refinishing furniture   HM81/9:94
Refinishing furniture   NS83/2:24
Refinishing furniture   NS83/2:27
Refinishing furniture   PM75/12:76
Refinishing furniture   PM83/11:108
Refinishing furniture   WB75/3-4:12
Refinishing furniture, finish   HM83/4:103
Refinishing furniture, outdoor   WB77/3-4:82
Refinishing furniture, stripping   HM72/9:52
Refinishing furniture, stripping   HM75/2:42
Refinishing furniture, stripping   HM83/2:80
Refinishing furniture, stripping/staining   PM75/11:114
Refinishing furniture, surface preparation   HM83/3:98
Refinishing kitchen cabinets   WB80/11-12:16
Refinishing oak   HM81/7-8:52
Refrigerator   NS81/1:34

Refrigerator, decorating   PM74/1:148
Refrigerator, passive   NS81/7-8:36
Refrigerator, sizing   PM73/11:70
Refrigerator ice maker servicing   WB82/5-6:82
Refrigerator maintenance   NS84/4:22
Refrigerator maintenance   PM80/3:132
Refrigerator repair   HM78/7-8:58
Refrigerator thermometer, outside   PM80/11:138
Regulator clock   WS84/11-12:12
Reindeer, Christmas   HM81/12:22
Reindeer Christmas table decorations   PM79/12:82
Relief carving, traditional   FW78/10:56
Remodeling, adding rooms   NS83/1:25
Remodeling, attic   PM80/2:134
Remodeling, attic   WB74/3-4:34
Remodeling, basement log cabin   WB77/11-12:118
Remodeling, bath and kitchen, Victorian   HM82/7-8:28
Remodeling, bathroom   HM83/3:39
Remodeling, bathroom and kitchen   HM83/7-8:29
Remodeling, country kitchen   WB75/1-2:32
Remodeling, dining/kitchen   HM82/7-8:35
Remodeling, fire damage repair   WB82/5-6:26
Remodeling, home   HM82/4:18
Remodeling, home   NS80/5-6:58
Remodeling, home   NS83/10:56
Remodeling, home   PM77/10:128
Remodeling, kitchen   HM83/10:44
Remodeling, kitchen   PM80/10:110
Remodeling, kitchen   WB78/11-12:38
Remodeling, opening up small house   HM78/9:16
Remodeling, removing bearing wall   PM74/8:146
Remodeling, replacing load bearing beam   WB83/11-12:82
Remodeling, room addition part 1   WB77/5-6:42
Remodeling, room addition part 2   WB77/9-10:64
Remodeling, room addition part 3   WB77/11-12:78
Remodeling, room addition part 4   WB78/1-2:40
Remodeling, room addition part 5 roof   WB78/3-4:72
Remodeling, room addition part 6   WB78/5-6:76
Remodeling, room addition part 7   WB78/7-8:56
Remodeling, room addition part 8   WB78/9-10:38
Remodeling, second story addition   NS83/1:22
Remodeling, small house   WB82/3-4:74
Remodeling, solar   HM82/2:57
Remodeling bathroom   WB78/1-2:57
Remodeling bathroom, master   HM82/7-8:53
Remodeling bathroom, two from one   HM82/9:74
Remodeling checklist, bathroom   PM82/4:178
Remodeling dining room   HM81/10:19
Remodeling garage   PM74/10:162
Remodeling loans   HM84/1:54

Remodeling with siding   HM84/4:36
Rental tools   HM78/10:30
Repairing fire damage   NS81/7-8:76
Repairing wooden chairs   FW80/1-2:79
Repair manual, home   HM82/2:37
Repair manual, home   HM83/9:71
Resawing, table saw   PM79/8:104
Resawing, table saw   WS84/9-10:21
Resawing hold in roller   FW82/1-2:14
Resawing jig, radial arm saw   PM84/5:226
Resawing jig, table saw   WS79/11:9
Resaws, Japanese   FW83/5-6:84
Restoring furniture, antique   HM83/1:51
Restoring iceboxes   WB78/11-12:118
Restoring picture frames   WB77/5-6:60
Retaining wall   HM81/5-6:44
Retaining wall   PM73/8:88
Retaining wall, broken concrete   HM76/9:38
Retaining wall, concrete   HM78/4:78
Retaining wall, dry laid   WB83/7-8:64
Retaining wall, landscaping   NS82/7-8:84
Retaining wall, planter blocks   HM83/5-6:18
Retaining wall, stone   HM82/4:100
Retaining wall, stone New England   PM82/7:84
Retaining wall and patio, rugged   HM79/3:54
Retaining wall batter board   HM82/4:104
Retaining wall planter, masonry   WB81/3-4:52
Retaining wall problems   HM81/4:76
Retaining wall tips   HM79/3:58
Retriever, bionic   PM81/10:36
Reversing belt driven tools   FW80/9-10:22
Reversing switch, motor   FW79/5-6:19
Revolving top worktable   PM77/3:68
Rewiring, electrical   WB74/11-12:8
Rifle, muzzle loader kits   PM79/10:30
Rifle kit, black powder   HM81/4:46
Rifle replica kit, flintlock   WB72/5-6:50
Ring caddy   PM80/2:124
Ring jewelry, wood   WB79/3-4:81
Ring jewelry making, silver   PM80/12:94
Rip/bevel table saw technique   WS81/7:8
Rip fence extension, table saw   FW84/9-10:8
Rip guide, table saw   PM82/12:100
Ripping roller support, table saw   FW79/9-10:22
Ripsaw tips   PM81/11:159
Rivet techniques   WB72/1-2:28
Rocker, bentwood Christmas tree decoration   PM79/12:82
Rocker, canvas with blind pivot joints   WB84/3-4:89
Rocker/high chair, child's (maple)   FW84/7-8:72
Rocking airplane toy   WB84/11-12:56

```
Rocking camel, turning split (walnut)   FW76/3:20
Rocking chair   FW83/9-10:52
Rocking chair, child's   WB82/11-12:58
Rocking chair, child's folding   WB83/11-12:40
Rocking chair, child's (oak)   FW83/9-10:55
Rocking chair, designer   HM84/10:108
Rocking chair, folding canvas   PM79/3:146
Rocking chair, giant turned   WB74/1-2:32
Rocking chair, Lincoln armless cane (walnut)   PM84/2:60
Rocking chair Christmas tree ornament   PM78/12:74
Rocking chair kit, Shaker   HM82/1:42
Rocking chair kit, Shaker   PM82/11:114
Rocking chair seat, restoring   WB79/3-4:18
Rocking elephant   HM81/10:32
Rocking horse   HM79/2:86
Rocking horse   PM77/11:138
Rocking horse   WB79/11-12:60
Rocking horse, cantilevered legs   WB81/11-12:68
Rocking horse, toddler's   WB78/1-2:97
Rocking horse, toddler's   WB81/11-12:98
Rocking horse, toddler's chair   WB79/5-6:20
Rocking horse, toy   HM82/12:62
Rocking horse, toy   HM84/11:74
Rocking horse, toy   PM79/11:122
Rocking horse, toy   WB74/11-12:38
Rocking horse, toy   WB83/11-12:96
Rocking horse, toy   WB84/11-12:8
Rocking horse candleholders   PM80/12:98
Rock polisher   PM76/1:102
Rock shop   WB72/7-8:22
Rock tumbler, wind driven   WB77/9-10:46
Roller, paint   HM83/4:44
Rolling pin   PM77/11:140
Rolling pin   PM80/11:130
Rolling pin, French   WB82/1-2:34
Rolling pin, laminated   PM76/11:126
Rolls Royce car, wood toy   PM84/12:94
Rolltop   FW78/9:52
Rolltop   WS81/9:4
Rolltop, fabric backed   FW84/9-10:54
Rolltop, shaped   FW76/9:54
Rolltop, shaped   FW78/10:64
Rolltop, wired   FW84/9-10:57
Rolltop breadbox   WB82/3-4:48
Rolltop breadbox, fake roll top   PM81/2:140
Rolltop breadbox (oak)   HM83/1:78
Rolltop breadbox (pine)   WS79/7:6
Rolltop cabinet, computer contemporary (oak)   PM84/2:100
Rolltop desk   HM75/10:60
Rolltop desk   PM76/1:80
```

Rolltop desk   WB77/3-4:64
Rolltop desk, child's   PM80/3:124
Rolltop desk, small (oak)   WB84/7-8:4
Rolltop desk chair, child's   PM80/10:212
Rolltop door cabinets   WB80/9-10:34
Rolltop door jewelry chest   WB83/5-6:104
Rolltop kitchen cabinets   FW80/11-12:78
Rolltop phone shelf, under cabinet (oak)   PM84/8:107
Rolltop stereo cabinet (maple plywood)   WS81/9:6
Rolltop strips, chamfering   FW83/3-4:22
Rolltop TV cabinet, glass door   WS83/1-2:14
Rolltop wall cabinet, bathroom (redwood)   WS81/9:10
Roman homesteaders   NS81/10:78
Roof   HM84/1:49
Roof   WB78/3-4:72
Roof   WB80/5-6:4
Roof, aluminum shakes   WB82/9-10:40
Roof, cedar shakes   HM79/5-6:46
Roof, hot tarring   NS83/3:40
Roof, hyperbolic paraboloid patio   WB79/7-8:79
Roof, leak repairs   NS84/2:24
Roof, moss protection   PM84/8:14
Roof, new   HM77/9:60
Roof, repairing flat   HM83/9:96
Roof, replacing   HM80/10:14
Roof, reshingling   PM78/4:156
Roof, reshingling   WB77/7-8:22
Roof, shingle   PM72/9:176
Roof cupola   HM78/7-8:34
Roof cupola   PM80/6:106
Roof damage repairs   PM73/5:104
Roof flashing   NS82/3:30
Roof flashing repair   HM83/9:87
Roof installation   NS82/3:18
Roof installation, shingle   WB72/5-6:14
Roof insulation   NS82/4:36
Roof leaks   HM75/11:58
Roof leaks, finding   WB80/3-4:28
Roof maintenance   HM72/8:48
Roof materials guide   PM82/4:135
Roof peak tent top   NS82/3:57
Roof products   HM83/4:35
Roof repair   HM73/9:44
Roof repair   HM76/3:42
Roof repair, shake   PM80/4:153
Roof repair, shingle   HM83/9:90
Roof repair, shingle   PM82/4:130
Roof replacement   HM76/6:28
Roof safety   NS82/3:34
Roof shingle repair   HM80/5-6:56

Roof shingles, laying   NS82/3:26
Roof shingles, wood fiber   WB83/3-4:24
Roof turbine fans   HM74/8:46
Roof ventilating turbine   HM78/9:55
Roof ventilation, vent ridge   HM81/3:8
Roof vents   HM77/3:38
Room, five in one   HM82/10:76
Room addition, warm/cool   WB78/5-6:4
Room addition part 1   WB77/5-6:42
Room addition part 2   WB77/9-10:64
Room addition part 3   WB77/11-12:78
Room addition part 4, wall framing   WB78/1-2:40
Room addition part 5, roof   WB78/3-4:72
Room addition part 6   WB78/5-6:76
Room addition part 7   WB78/7-8:56
Room addition part 8   WB78/9-10:38
Room air destratifier   NS81/1:12
Room and door trim   HM75/8:44
Room divider   WB78/3-4:36
Room divider, folding screen   HM83/10:94
Room divider, Japanese   FW82/5-6:50
Room divider, kitchen cabinets   PM75/12:70
Room divider, mirrored   WB84/9-10:40
Room divider, see through   HM81/1:21
Room divider, storage   HM81/1:20
Room divider and bed, child's   HM72/12:36
Room divider bookcase   HM80/9:21
Room divider planter cabinet   HM72/12:44
Room divider storage cabinet   WB73/9-10:54
Rooster, night light   NS80/11-12:64
Rooster cup rack, kitchen   WB84/9-10:113
Rooster weather vane   HM83/3:82
Root cellar food storage, modern version   PM82/8:94
Rope, coiled table decorations   PM79/11:76
Rope, jump   PM79/3:170
Rope bed   HM79/4:6
Rope bookshelves and desk   PM76/1:73
Rosemaling kitchen cabinets   FW80/11-12:79
Rose trellis   WB83/7-8:59
Rosette, guitar   FW81/5-6:51
Rosette cutting, radial arm saw   WB75/3-4:48
Rosewood or walnut boxes, hexagonal   FW82/3-4:63
Roto tiller maintenance   WB74/3-4:22
Rough sawn barn siding, making   PM79/1:99
Round clock, wall   WS83/11-12:10
Round dining table, contemporary (mahogany)   WS83/11-12:16
Round mirror (oak)   WS80/11:10
Round stock cutter   PM84/5:101
Round tilt top table, Chippendale (mahogany)   PM84/8:98
Round top hall mirror   WS82/5:16

Round top table, dining   WB75/1-2:36
Round top table, modern (pine)   FW81/9-10:88
Routed box joint   FW81/9-10:18
Routed drawer pull   FW79/9-10:18
Routed drawer pull   FW82/7-8:50
Routed edge joint   FW77/12:66
Routed jewelry box   WS81/1:12
Routed jewelry box   WS83/7-8:10
Routed miter joint   FW82/3-4:12
Routed signs   FW79/3-4:72
Routed signs   HM78/11-12:46
Routed snack tray, lazy Susan   WS83/7-8:16
Router   HM74/9:52
Router   HM78/11-12:60
Router, buying   WS84/1-2:16
Router, drill press overarm   WB84/11-12:128
Router, dust control   WS84/11-12:3
Router, mini hand   PM81/1:121
Router, mount on radial arm saw   WB84/3-4:79
Router, pin   FW81/7-8,63
Router, pin   WS83/7-8:20
Router, pin and overhead   FW81/7-8:65
Router adapter for drill press   PM76/1:162
Router base, auxiliary   PM80/11:118
Router base, eccentric   FW81/9-10:14
Router bit, picture frame   WS80/7:3
Router bit box   PM81/3:160
Router bits   NS80/5-6:16
Router bits, homemade   WB75/1-2:54
Router box joint jig   FW79/1-2:56
Router case   WS79/7:3
Router circle guide   FW82/11-12:22
Router circle jig   WB79/7-8:57
Router cut panels   FW84/1-2:56
Router dado guide   WB84/11-12:113
Router depth gauge   PM80/8:111
Router dovetail jig, false   WB82/1-2:104
Router dovetail joint   WS82/7:6
Router dowel making   FW80/11-12:22
Router dust collecting attachment   PM76/3:129
Routered spindles cradle   WB79/3-4:99
Router groove jig   WS83/11-12:22
Router grooving frame   WB77/9-10:92
Router guide, purfling   FW80/3-4:13
Router guide, T-square   FW84/5-6:10
Router indexing jig   WB81/3-4:54
Router inlaying   HM80/12:74
Router joints jig   PM84/1:75
Router light replacement   FW82/1-2:18
Router lumber surfacing   PM78/9:20

Router mortising jig   FW80/5-6:14
Router plane   WB80/7-8:7
Router rail   FW80/11-12:56
Router reeding bedposts   FW83/1-2:4
Router shaper table   WB84/1-2:104
Router slab surfacing jig   FW84/9-10:18
Router storage box   WB78/9-10:90
Router surfacing jig   PM83/12:112
Router table   FW79/3-4:56
Router table   WB76/5-6:14
Router table   WS79/9:6
Router table   WS82/7:16
Router table   WS82/3:18
Router table, hinged   FW81/1-2:20
Router table, poor man's   FW83/9-10:50
Router table, simple   WB81/1-2:146
Router table, table saw extension   WB74/7-8:26
Router table and cabinet   NS80/5-6:32
Router table extension   FW80/9-10:18
Router table techniques   WS80/1:10
Router techniques   WB76/5-6:10
Router techniques, part 1   HM83/2:12
Router techniques, part 2   HM83/3:12
Router techniques, pin   PM83/8:76
Router template, wing   WB78/1-2:26
Router tips   PM72/12:156
Router tips   PM73/1:138
Router tips   PM78/11:140
Router tips   PM82/10:114
Router wood threading   FW83/3-4:99
Routing, preventing rub marks or burns   PM76/4:209
Routing chisel jig   PM77/8:110
Routing cross grain jig   FW79/7-8:12
Routing for inlays   FW79/7-8:68
Routing molding   FW82/7-8:18
Routing molding   FW82/5-6:85
Routing mortise   FW81/9-10:90
Routing mortise   FW82/7-8:52
Routing on drill press   WS80/7:11
Routing slots   FW77/9:18
Routing slots   WS80/7:12
Routing splined miter joints   FW82/7-8:14
Routing tongues   FW81/1-2:22
Routing trays   WS80/7:11
Row house remodeling   NS80/2:64
Rule joint   FW79/9-10:66
Rumford fireplace   NS81/9:26
Russian troika, child's sleigh   WB83/1-2:20
Russian wood stove, brick   NS81/1:74
Rust, auto body repairs   PM84/5:114

Rust, combating   HM79/1:52
Rust, stopping auto   PM83/5:124
Rust and corrosion, stopping   HM83/4:50
Rust and corrosion fighting   PM79/6:114
Rust and corrosion rehabilitation   HM76/1:34
Rustproof finishing   WB73/5-6:40
Saber saw carpet cutting   PM84/3:144
Saber saw circle cutting   PM81/1:122
Saber saw circle cutting   PM81/2:150
Saber saw table   PM72/11:166
Saber saw tips   HM82/9:14
Saber saw tips   PM73/1:148
Saber saw tips   PM78/3:130
Saber saw tips   PM79/5:65
Saber saw tips   PM80/12:28
Saber saw tips   PM81/1:110
Saber saw tips   PM81/2:150
Saddle seat stool, caned or padded   WB84/3-4:30
Safe, Colonial cabinet home   PM79/1:84
Safe, floor   PM79/11:85
Safe, floor installation   PM79/1:86
Safety, back yard accidents   PM78/3:164
Safety, boat   PM75/12:138
Safety, boat   PM78/7:86
Safety, chain saw   WB84/1-2:64
Safety, crib and cradle   WB81/3-4:116
Safety, driving   PM80/11:87
Safety, hand tool   PM80/9:190
Safety, home   HM79/9:56
Safety, home   HM82/2:74
Safety, home   PM76/3:96
Safety, home fires   PM78/9:96
Safety, jointer   FW81/5-6:50
Safety, ladder   PM83/4:119
Safety, motorcycle   PM78/10:228
Safety, paint stripper   PM83/10:65
Safety, radial arm saw accessories   WB76/3-4:4
Safety, roof   NS82/3:34
Safety, router   PM72/12:156
Safety, sauna   NS84/2:75
Safety, scaffolding and ladder   HM83/4:42
Safety, shock detector   PM78/2:120
Safety, shop   PM78/6:136
Safety, shop   PM82/11:120
Safety, shop   WB73/7-8:65
Safety, shop   WB81/11-12:26
Safety, shop   WB82/9-10:134
Safety, stove wall shields   NS83/11-12:78
Safety, stricking tools   WB77/1-2:62
Safety, wood dust hazards   FW83/7-8:36

Safety, wood stove   PM80/10:74
Safety, woodworking hazards   FW77/12:54
Safety, woodworking injuries   FW82/9-10:84
Safety, yard   HM82/3:84
Safety glass   WB74/3-4:58
Safety products, shop   NS83/3:20
Safety switch, drill press   FW83/9-10:10
Sailboard   HM82/5-6:78
Sailboard plans to order, $7   PM81/5:110
Sailboat, cedar strip   HM81/3:78
Sailboat, toy   HM82/5-6:96
Sailboat kit   HM82/3:101
Sailboat kit   PM77/6:106
Sailboat kits   PM78/10:100
Sailboat model plans to order, $12.50   PM83/1:6
Sailboat plans to order, catamaran $5   PM78/7:116
Sailboat weather vane   PM83/3:98
Sailing, Sunfish ice skating   PM79/2:52
Sailing rigging   PM77/4:104
Salad bowl set, turned   WB79/9-10:80
Salt and pepper picnic table holder   WB83/9-10:54
Salt and pepper shaker holder   WB75/5-6:25
Salt and pepper shakers   PM84/4:104
Salt and pepper shakers, pewter   PM79/8:92
Saltbox house, solar   NS81/11-12:69
Saltmeter, electronic   PM83/2:158
Salt shaker and pepper mill, hexagon   PM82/1:158
Salt shakers, headstone   WB74/7-8:21
Salvaged lumber   HM81/7-8:82
Salvaged lumber   HM81/11:16
Salvaged lumber   NS83/11-12:42
Salvaged lumber   WB84/1-2:82
Salvaged materials   NS81/2:92
Salvaging buildings   HM82/1:22
Salvaging floor boards   HM82/1:70
Sanba thumb piano   WB74/11-12:28
Sandbox   HM80/5-6:32
Sandbox, in ground   PM81/8:87
Sandbox, roofed tractor tire   WB83/5-6:64
Sandbox, super toy   WB73/5-6:10
Sandbox, toy   HM82/5-6:100
Sandbox with roof   PM80/4:128
Sander, belt thickness sander   FW82/11-12:22
Sander, circle   PM81/12:144
Sander, contour   FW84/5-6:10
Sander, disc   FW80/7-8:68
Sander, disc and drum   PM80/10:29
Sander, disc and drum   WB81/3-4:22
Sander, drill press thickness   WB82/9-10:87
Sander, drum   WB75/9-10:47

195

Sander, edge   PM82/8:86
Sander, finishing techniques   PM75/6:92
Sander, hand   FW80/11-12:20
Sander, home built thickness   FW80/3-4:50
Sander, inflatable drum   FW80/3-4:48
Sander, jigsaw   PM84/2:116
Sander, lathe thickness   FW82/11-12:22
Sander, miniature disk   WB72/7-8:37
Sander, mount portable   PM73/4:128
Sander, oscillating spindle   FW84/5-6:59
Sander, portable   HM72/4:38
Sander, shop made belt   WB79/11-12:92
Sander, shop made belt   WB84/5-6:85
Sander, stroke   FW76/6:46
Sander, vertical belt   FW84/5-6:10
Sander, wooden drum stroke   FW81/7-8:47
Sander base, Black and Decker   WB82/7-8:69
Sander counterbalance, belt   FW82/3-4:16
Sander/grinder/sharpener, shop made   PM82/3:93
Sander/grinder technique   PM83/5:90
Sander holder, portable   WB83/9-10:135
Sander jig, belt   PM83/11:112
Sanders, buying palm   WS84/5-6:7
Sander techniques, belt   HM83/9:18
Sander techniques, finishing   HM83/10:16
Sander tips, belt   PM79/9:113
Sander tips, belt   PM82/12:112
Sanding, hand   WB79/11-12:159
Sanding, hardwood floor   HM74/6:42
Sanding, steel wool   WB79/11-12:14
Sanding and finishing, lathe   FW81/7-8:58
Sanding and sandpaper   HM78/9:46
Sanding attachments, lathe   PM83/12:109
Sanding beaded edges   FW80/11-12:19
Sanding block   PM76/4:202
Sanding block   PM77/3:138
Sanding block   PM82/12:52
Sanding block   WB84/1-2:74
Sanding block, jiffy   PM73/8:160
Sanding circle   WS80/9:12
Sanding disc jointer   FW80/3-4:47
Sanding disks   WB81/1-2:59
Sanding drum, lathe   FW80/3-4:15
Sanding drum, shaper or lathe   FW83/3-4:18
Sanding edges   FW82/5-6:20
Sanding floors   HM75/4:51
Sanding glass   HM78/1:39
Sanding glass   WS81/1:3
Sanding mop   FW80/1-2:18
Sanding table accessory, Dremel Moto Shop   PM82/8:88

Sanding tools and technique   FW78/9:79
Sanding without sandpaper   NS80/2:20
Sanding wooden wheels   FW82/5-6:20
Sandpaper   FW80/3-4:51
Sandpaper   HM76/2:40
Sandpaper   WB82/3-4:114
Sandpaper   WB82/7-8:21
Sandpaper   WS84/5-6:4
Sandpaper, folding   FW84/3-4:14
Sandpaper, using   PM84/1:111
Sandpaper basics   HM84/11:20
Sandpaper cabinet   WB81/3-4:20
Sandpaper cutting board   HM83/3:102
Sandpaper storage cabinet   PM81/11:122
Sandpaper tips   PM79/3:67
Sand/play box, outdoor toy   PM82/5:112
Sansa thumb piano, Colimba   WB74/3-4:40
Santa's boot candy cane holder, Christmas   PM79/12:82
Santa, waving   PM72/11:109
Santa Claus window hanging   PM78/12:74
Santa decoration, hanging   PM80/12:98
Santa display, animated   WB74/11-12:34
Santa door decoration   PM79/12:82
Satinwood secretary desk, 1795   WB77/5-6:38
Saucer cut, table saw   PM76/8:95
Sauna   NS84/2:73
Sauna, home (cedar)   WB82/5-6:76
Saunas, spas and hot tubs   NS82/2:20
Sauna safety   NS84/2:75
Saw, band   WB83/9-10:100
Saw, bow   FW77/9:56
Saw, bow fold-up (hardwood)   WS79/9:5
Saw, compact field   PM84/4:112
Saw, cutoff   PM76/2:109
Saw, folding camp   PM84/4:111
Saw, hand   NS81/5-6:16
Saw, hand   WB73/3-4:10
Saw, Japanese   FW80/3-4:77
Saw, plywood panel   FW82/3-4:90
Saw, plywood panel   WB82/1-2:67
Saw, portable circular   HM74/1:38
Saw, portable cutoff machine   PM74/11:150
Saw, powered hack   WB77/7-8:30
Saw, razor blade   WB75/3-4:69
Saw, rebuilt printer's   FW82/1-2:90
Saw, scroll tips   PM83/1:96
Saw, scroll tips   WB72/3-4:24
Saw, sharpening   FW80/5-6:62
Saw, shop made forty-two inch band   WB82/5-6:110
Saw, shop made scroll   WB81/7-8:66

Saw, small   FW77/9:77
Saw, small pull   FW84/9-10:8
Saw, traditional bow   WB83/7-8:4
Saw, treadle band   FW80/9-10:63
Saw, treadle powered fretsaw   WB79/3-4:42
Saw, walking beam   FW80/9-10:60
Saw and plane, Japanese   HM82/12:36
Saw basics, hand   HM77/11-12:58
Saw blade, band   WB83/11-12:36
Saw blade, carbide tipped   FW80/7-8:72
Saw blade, carbide tipped   PM77/5:59
Saw blade, carbide tipped   WS83/5-6:16
Saw blade, cleaning   PM79/8:88
Saw blade buying   WB76/1-2:56
Saw blade choice   FW82/5-6:63
Saw blade cleaning, pizza pan   PM74/11:48
Saw blade deburring jig   PM75/8:76
Saw blade sharpening, carbide tipped   WS83/7-8:19
Saw blade speeds   FW83/11-12:14
Saw blade storage cabinet, rolltop   PM72/7:158
Saw blade vise   WB75/7-8:41
Sawbuck, firewood   HM75/10:58
Sawbuck, firewood   HM79/10:102
Sawbuck, firewood   PM74/7:42
Sawbuck, firewood   PM80/10:187
Sawbuck, portable   HM84/9:136
Sawbuck/toolbox plans to order, $3.00   NS83/3:64
Saw fence   PM73/3:150
Saw guide, circular portable   PM82/12:97
Saw guide, portable   FW79/9-10:20
Saw guide, simple shop made   HM80/5-6:50
Saw handle, hand   PM78/1:99
Sawhorse   FW80/9-10:78
Sawhorse   FW83/1-2:14
Sawhorse   HM78/11-12:93
Sawhorse   HM81/11:22
Sawhorse   PM78/9:194
Sawhorse   WB73/1-2:38
Sawhorse   WB75/1-2:28
Sawhorse, folding   PM83/1:44
Sawhorse, folding   WB75/9-10:62
Sawhorse, frame and foot   FW80/9-10:79
Sawhorse, plywood   WB82/1-2:26
Sawhorse, roller top   PM78/11:131
Sawhorse, simple folding   PM78/6:44
Sawhorse, three   PM77/10:118
Sawhorse, three   WB79/1-2:92
Sawhorse, wired   WB83/9-10:89
Sawhorse, with and without shelf   PM82/4:60
Sawhorse elevators   WB81/11-12:67

Sawhorse elevators   WB83/3-4:113
Sawhorse/miter box, chainsaw   PM75/11:112
Sawhorse racks   PM82/5:112
Sawhorse toolbox   PM84/10:114
Sawhorse tool caddy   PM75/6:34
Sawhorse workbench   PM73/1:20
Sawing, hand   WB79/7-8:47
Sawing, scrolls   FW83/5-6:86
Sawing metal   WB80/7-8:45
Sawing safety   FW83/9-10:76
Saw maintenance, circular   FW78/3:80
Sawmill, band saw   FW81/3-4:86
Sawmill workings   FW79/7-8:36
Saw roller support   FW81/3-4:20
Saw roller support   WB77/7-8:10
Saw setup, shop   FW82/7-8:14
Saw sharpening   PM77/6:116
Saw sharpening   WB79/7-8:64
Saw sharpening stand   FW83/1-2:18
Saw sharpening vise   FW77/9:57
Saw support stand, caster top   HM78/2:62
Saw techniques, circular   HM82/12:20
Saw techniques, circular   HM83/1:12
Saw techniques, hand   PM77/11:8
Saw techniques, saber   PM78/3:130
Saw tips, scroll   PM83/2:98
Saw vise, hand   FW84/11-12:8
Sawyer's chairs (oak)   FW82/3-4:50
Scaffold, painting   PM79/5:139
Scaffold, rolls and folds   WB81/3-4:16
Scaffolding, renting and using   PM74/6:103
Scaffolding and ladder safety   HM83/4:42
Scale balance, decorator   WB81/5-6:33
Scale model, plywood   FW78/10:73
Scandinavian bench, storage   PM81/5:122
Scandinavian desk, standing   PM81/5:122
Scandinavian playhouse   WB77/1-2:56
Scandinavian projects, four   PM80/8:88
Scandinavian screen divider   WB75/5-6:2
Scandinavian table, coffee or dining   PM81/5:122
School, do it yourself   HM83/5-6:28
School, dome house   HM83/5-6:32
School, Foley sharpening   PM73/1:56
School, guitar making   FW79/1-2:36
School, home building   HM80/3:20
School, log home   HM83/5-6:33
School, motorcycle repair   PM77/12:58
School, owner built   WB84/5-6:107
School, owner built house   NS81/2:72
School, owner built house   NS83/11-12:56

School, professional driving   PM84/8:128
School, Shaker woodworking   HM83/5-6:30
School, small engine   PM78/5:92
School, solar home   HM83/5-6:34
School, tinsmith   HM83/5-6:31
School, woodworking   FW81/1-2:92
School clock kit   PM75/12:98
Schoolhouse clock   HM80/10:64
Schoolhouse clock (oak)   PM81/6:145
Schoolhouse wall clock (oak)   WS82/5:4
Scissors and shears   WB80/5-6:58
Sconce, candle   HM78/11-12:86
Sconce, candle   HM82/12:6
Sconce, candle   PM80/3:134
Sconce, candle with mirror   PM74/11:100
Sconce, Colonial candle (cherry)   WS79/11:5
Sconce, heart shaped candle   PM81/12:116
Sconce, mirror   PM77/11:137
Sconce, wall candle   PM78/12:74
Scooter, toddler's   PM81/11:30
Scooter/skateboard   PM78/9:181
Scraper   FW77/3:29
Scraper, glass   FW78/3:20
Scraper, hand with handle   PM82/12:95
Scraper, hook and floorman's holder   FW84/11-12:67
Scraper, sharpening cabinet   PM82/1:60
Scraper, shop made   FW78/10:13
Scraper blade sharpening   WS81/3:13
Scraper plane   FW82/9-10:18
Scraper tips, cabinet   PM84/4:108
Scrap wood box, roll about shop   PM84/11:159
Scrap wood storage   FW83/1-2:83
Scratch bead molder   FW78/6:60
Scratch stock beading tool   PM76/4:204
Scratch stock from marking gauge   WB83/3-4:77
Screen, cutting aluminum   PM81/4:42
Screen, folding   HM83/10:94
Screen, folding photo display   PM73/12:48
Screen, garage   WB76/5-6:33
Screen, hardboard folding   WB81/9-10:32
Screen, outdoor fiberglass   HM72/8:52
Screen, Scandinavian divider   WB75/5-6:2
Screen, solar   PM78/4:168
Screen, yard (cedar)   PM81/8:88
Screen and door repair, aluminum   PM73/8:90
Screen and storm window   WB81/9-10:100
Screen and window repair, storm   HM72/4:42
Screen cabinet, slide/movie   PM72/9:90
Screen divider, folder   WB79/1-2:82
Screen divider, folding   WB78/7-8:32

Screen door, stylish   WB73/5-6:24
Screen doors, slide smoothly   WB79/7-8:48
Screened deck   HM83/3:28
Screen house, garden   PM76/4:121
Screen house and deck   HM84/4:60
Screen planter   WB76/3-4:59
Screen repair   HM77/7-8:46
Screen repair   PM79/4:151
Screen repair, window   HM83/2:48
Screen trellis, deck   PM77/7:98
Screen wire, stretching taut   PM74/5:104
Screwdrivers   HM73/2:48
Screwdrivers   NS81/1:20
Screwdrivers   WB74/5-6:14
Screwdrivers, sharpening   FW84/9-10:59
Screwdriver tips   PM78/6:43
Screw hole finishing   WB74/9-10:8
Screws, removing broken   FW81/3-4:14
Screws, sheet metal   HM72/10:48
Screws, wood   WB79/11-12:40
Scribed joint   FW82/3-4:76
Scriber, duckbill   FW77/3:53
Scriber, poor boy's   FW77/6:17
Scroll saw, radial segment cutting guide   PM83/2:98
Scroll saw, shop made   WB81/7-8:66
Scroll saw circle cutting guide   PM83/2:98
Scroll saw cutting guides   PM83/2:98
Scroll saw dovetails   FW79/7-8:15
Scroll saw tips   FW83/5-6:86
Scroll saw tips   PM83/2:98
Scroll saw tips   PM83/1:96
Scroll saw tips   WB72/3-4:24
Scrub plane   PM82/6:97
Scuba diving scooter plans to order, $9.95   PM81/9:78
Scuba tow plans to order, $7.95   PM74/7:69
Scuba tow plans to order, $8.95   PM79/8:74
Sculpture, carving large   FW81/1-2:76
Sculpture, disc sander turning   FW83/11-12:66
Sculpture, interlocking wood   PM72/12:150
Sculpture, laminated   FW83/7-8:34
Sculpture, mesquite   FW79/3-4:44
Sculpture, wood   PM72/11:81
Sculpture, wooden wall butterfly   PM82/2:60
Sculpture, wood hippo   WB76/3-4:100
Sculptured pedestal table, carved   WB80/1-2:64
Sculptured wall paints   HM79/1:48
Sculpturing acrylic, etching   PM73/2:80
Sculpturing wood, hand shaping   FW76/6:24
Seagull mobile, aluminum   PM75/11:170
Sealers, finishing   WB72/11-12:50

Seal pull toy PM74/11:110
Seat caning, chair PM80/7:107
Seat restoring, antique rocker WB79/3-4:18
Seats, reclining boat PM75/3:140
Secretary, repairing old FW83/5-6:66
Secretary, Salem WB73/7-8:26
Secretary/bookcase, (mahogany) FW83/1-2:54
Secretary desk, 1795 satinwood WB77/5-6:38
Secretary desk kit, Queen Anne HM76/11:38
Security, auto HM79/9:98
Security, auto PM72/7:112
Security, auto alarm Morse code beeper PM84/1:76
Security, burglar and fire alarms WB78/3-4:10
Security, choosing burglar alarm HM75/11:42
Security, closed circuit TV HM79/7-8:54
Security, Colonial cabinet home safe PM79/1:84
Security, door locks HM78/5-6:40
Security, drain hide-a-way WB82/5-6:68
Security, electric garage door lock PM81/5:132
Security, electric garage door lock WB80/9-10;46
Security, floor safe PM79/11:85
Security, garage door opener alarm PM75/5:210
Security, hiding places PM75/9:74
Security, home HM78/5-6:8
Security, home HM82/4:85
Security, home NS83/9:42
Security, home PM75/1:97
Security, home PM79/1:87
Security, home PM81/4:149
Security, home PM82/1:110
Security, home WB80/3-4:94
Security, home WB82/9-10:4
Security, home part 2, locks WB78/5-6:50
Security, installing deadbolt lock HM84/2:62
Security, installing floor safe PM79/1:86
Security, labeling tools and valuables PM84/3:118
Security, landscape lighting HM78/5-6:68
Security, landscape lighting HM78/5-6:73
Security, peephole periscope HM82/10:82
Security, photographic inventory PM79/12:118
Security, property ID HM78/5-6:36
Security, seven bolt lock WB78/7-8:4
Security, summer home HM78/9:68
Security, ultrasonic and light detection kit PM79/4:74
Security, vacation home PM73/9:94
Security, window NS83/3:16
Security, window grate NS83/9:38
Security alarm system WB82/9-10:58
Security and insurance HM79/7-8:56
Security bars, artistic NS81/5-6:50

Security bars, window   PM83/4:166
Security dogs   HM78/5-6:28
Security equipment, home   HM78/5-6:12
Security lighting, outdoor   NS83/5-6:76
Security products   HM83/4:68
Security stand, calculator   PM80/7:95
Security system, designing burglar alarm   PM83/12:66
Security system, home   HM78/5-6:16
Security system, installing   WB84/7-8:36
Security system, trouble shooting home   PM84/4:149
Security tips, home   PM79/1:86
Security tips from burglar   HM79/7-8:62
Seedlac varnish   FW80/1-2:68
Seed starter, cantilevered window   NS80/3:53
Seed starter, indoor   NS84/1:87
Seesaw, rotating   PM72/3:140
Seesaw, toy   WB74/5-6:30
Selbermachen dowel furniture   HM80/3:48
Selbermachen dowel furniture   HM80/1:11
Selling your home   NS84/10:32
Semaphore jig, lathe   PM83/12:106
Septic tank   HM79/9:80
Septic tank   HM83/9:62
Septic tank   NS81/4:60
Septic tank maintenance   HM73/12:54
Server, Victorian marble top (oak)   PM83/5:102
Serving cart, Colonial   WB73/7-8:36
Serving cart, kitchen (walnut or fir)   FW77/3:58
Serving/microwave cart, kitchen (cherry)   WS82/9:8
Serving tray   HM83/5-6:91
Serving tray, bent (walnut and mahogany)   FW77/6:62
Serving tray, glass top (mahogany)   HM84/9:110
Serving tray, inlaid   FW75/12:41
Serving tray, laminated   PM76/11:124
Serving tray, needlepoint   WB78/9-10:94
Serving tray, tea cart   WB83/9-10:4
Serving tray, turned three tier   WB73/9-10:28
Serving tray, walnut veneer   WB77/3-4:52
Serving tray and spice rack   PM78/4:114
Serving tray kit, Colonial marquetry   WB77/7-8:71
Serving tray (oak)   WS82/1:19
Settee, Adirondack wooden lawn chair   PM82/6:116
Settee, built-in   WB80/1-2:131
Settle, Colonial storage bench   WB84/9-10:116
Settle, English pub bench   WB78/9-10:50
Sewing and magazine rack footstool   WB80/1-2:44
Sewing box, antique   WB82/7-8:62
Sewing cabinet   WB77/11-12:44
Sewing cabinet, fold-in portable   WB74/5-6:24
Sewing cabinet, French provincial   WB75/1-2:30

Sewing cabinet (oak)   HM84/2:70
Sewing caddy   PM74/8:175
Sewing caddy, turned   WB80/1-2:78
Sewing center   HM83/2:42
Sewing center   WB74/7-8:40
Sewing center, built-in   PM75/4:130
Sewing center, family room   PM79/10:130
Sewing center, island unit   PM73/3:80
Sewing center, large wall unit   PM73/3:83
Sewing center, modern compact   PM74/1:68
Sewing center, wall let down   PM73/3:77
Sewing center, wall unit   PM73/3:86
Sewing closet   HM72/2:34
Sewing closet   HM73/2:36
Sewing desk, Shaker   HM72/4:52
Sewing desk cabinet (oak)   WB82/5-6:4
Sewing spool board   WB79/1-2:123
Sewing spool cabinet, wall   PM80/3:62
Sewing spool house and clock   WB73/9-10:24
Sewing spool rack, wall   WB84/3-4:49
Sewing stand, turned English   WB83/9-10:74
Sewing storage wall   HM73/9:38
Sewing table, Colonial Sheraton   WB74/3-4:36
Sewing tape and spool rack, wall   PM83/2:70
Sewing/utility table, folding legs   WB82/9-10:18
Shades, window   WB79/9-10:52
Shades, window insulating   NS80/10:30
Shading, windows   NS80/3:38
Shading, windows   NS84/3:46
Shadow box   PM74/11:112
Shaker armchair, woven bottom   HM72/6:38
Shaker baseboard   PM84/10:109
Shaker basket (black ash)   FW80/1-2:52
Shaker bench, long   HM72/12:58
Shaker blanket chest (pine)   FW81/3-4:60
Shaker cabinet (pine)   PM84/10:104
Shaker candle stand (cherry)   WS80/9:6
Shaker chest of drawers   HM72/2:58
Shaker child's bed   WB83/9-10:66
Shaker Colonial trestle table (pine)   WS79/1:3
Shaker door trim   PM84/10:109
Shaker dovetail carrier   FW82/1-2:94
Shaker drop leaf table   WS80/9:8
Shaker dry sink   HM73/3:48
Shaker furniture kits   PM76/7:98
Shaker furniture kits   PM84/10:108
Shaker herb rack   NS82/1:70
Shaker lap desk (pine or cherry)   FW76/3:48
Shaker linen chest, one drawer (pine)   HM72/8:38
Shake roof, cedar   HM79/5-6:46

Shake roof repair   PM80/4:153
Shaker oval boxes, steambent   FW82/1-2:92
Shaker peg Colonial coat rack   WS79/3:3
Shaker peg rail   PM84/10:109
Shaker rocking chair kit   HM82/1:42
Shaker rocking chair kit   PM82/11:114
Shaker room moldings   PM84/10:104
Shaker sewing desk   HM72/4:52
Shaker shelves and peg rails   HM83/1:80
Shaker side table (cherry)   WS80/9:4
Shaker slant top desk (cherry)   WS80/11:4
Shaker stand, round (cherry)   FW77/12:68
Shaker step stand (cherry)   WS82/1:20
Shaker stool   PM81/11:32
Shaker stool, woven string bottom   HM83/12:72
Shaker storage chest, one drawer   HM72/3:52
Shaker table, dining (cherry)   HM84/10:104
Shaker table, drop leaf   HM72/10:50
Shaker table, trestle   PM76/7:101
Shaker table legs, tapered   WS80/9:11
Shaker table leg slots   FW84/5-6:10
Shaker table plans to order, $8.45   HM83/10:26
Shaker towel rack   HM73/3:48
Shaker window trim   PM84/10:109
Shaker woodworking school   HM83/5-6:30
Shaker work cabinet, drop leaf   HM72/9:48
Shaper   WB80/9-10:98
Shaper, router table   WB84/1-2:104
Shaper, shopmade   FW79/7-8:64
Shaper, shopmade   PM72/2:150
Shaper balancing   FW80/5-6:8
Shaper cutter rack   PM81/11:122
Shaper cutters and fenses   FW80/1-2:69
Shaper hold downs   PM82/12:100
Shaper kit   WB78/7-8:78
Shaper knives   FW76/12:60
Shaper radial arm saw   WB81/1-2:100
Shaper tips   WB72/5-6:35
Shaper tips   WB75/11-12:6
Sharpener, drill press honer   HM77/5-6:55
Sharpener/grinder/sander, shop made   PM82/3:93
Sharpening, grinding   FW81/7-8:66
Sharpening, jointer blade   WB82/3-4:9
Sharpening, polished edge   FW83/3-4:68
Sharpening, saw   PM77/6:116
Sharpening, scraper   FW77/3:29
Sharpening, slow speed   FW81/9-10:83
Sharpening aids   WS82/3:7
Sharpening angles   FW79/7-8:14
Sharpening auger drill bits   FW84/1-2:62

Sharpening carbide tipped saw blade   WS83/7-8:19
Sharpening chain saw   WB81/1-2:98
Sharpening chisels   FW78/9:70
Sharpening chisels   FW84/9-10:47
Sharpening chisels   PM75/2:114
Sharpening chisels and plane irons   FW81/7-8:67
Sharpening chisel turning tools   WS82/5:22
Sharpening circular saw blade   FW78/3:80
Sharpening crosscut saw tools   PM82/12:146
Sharpening equipment   FW81/9-10:76
Sharpening equipment and tips, Japanese   PM84/1:104
Sharpening fixture, jointer knife   FW81/3-4:14
Sharpening fixture for points   FW80/3-4:14
Sharpening forstner bit   HM84/11:10
Sharpening grinder cabinet   HM83/12:28
Sharpening hone, portable drill   FW84/7-8:10
Sharpening hone, shop built   FW84/9-10:52
Sharpening ice skates   PM74/2:75
Sharpening Japanese blade   FW81/7-8:71
Sharpening joiner knives   FW81/9-10:14
Sharpening jointer knifes, jig   FW82/5-6:14
Sharpening jointer knives   FW80/7-8:15
Sharpening knives   WB82/3-4:52
Sharpening oil stone, self lubricating   PM73/10:174
Sharpening plane irons   WS82/9:18
Sharpening saws   FW80/5-6:62
Sharpening saws   WB79/7-8:64
Sharpening school, Foley   PM73/1:56
Sharpening scraper blade   WS81/3:13
Sharpening screwdrivers   FW84/9-10:59
Sharpening setup on jackshaft   FW78/9:20
Sharpening setup with lineshaft   FW80/3-4:13
Sharpening stand, saw   FW83/1-2:18
Sharpening stone holder   WB79/1-2:16
Sharpening stones   FW75/12:47
Sharpening stones   FW78/9:68
Sharpening stones   NS81/2:14
Sharpening stones   WS82/3:4
Sharpening stones, diamond   WS82/11-12:7
Sharpening tips   PM73/12:86
Sharpening tips   PM81/8:82
Sharpening tips   PM82/6:100
Sharpening tips   WB84/7-8:72
Sharpening tips, chisel   WS82/3:8
Sharpening tools   HM72/8:46
Sharpening tools   HM76/2:36
Sharpening tools   HM77/5-6:40
Sharpening vise, circular saws   WB80/1-2:73
Sharpening vise, saw   FW77/9:57
Sharpening water stones, Japanese   WS82/11-12:4

Sharpening wheel, bicycle tire   FW83/7-8:14
Sharpening wire wheel   FW83/1-2:16
Shave horse, pipe clamp   FW82/3-4:12
Shaver, repairing electric   PM83/2:112
Shaving console, Colonial with candles   PM72/1:140
Shaving horse   FW78/9:46
Shaving horse   FW83/1-2:12
Shaving horse, Swiss   FW83/11-12:41
Shaving mirror, Lincoln   PM78/2:102
Shaving mirror, Lincoln wall (mahogany)   PM83/2:116
Shaving mirror, Victorian wall hung (pine)   PM83/2:108
Shavings receptacle, planer   WB83/3-4:58
Shaving stand with mirror, Victorian (oak)   PM83/2:108
Shaving tips   PM83/2:106
Shaving/vanity mirror   WS80/7:5
Shears, buying garden   PM79/3:142
Shears and scissors   WB80/5-6:58
Sheath, custom leather knife   PM79/5:29
Shed, backyard plans to order $10.50   PM83/3:102
Shed, backyard utility   PM80/3:139
Shed, firewood   PM78/10:132
Shed, firewood storage   PM81/10:114
Shed, garbage can storage lean-to   PM82/6:112
Shed, gazebo storage   PM75/8:90
Shed, lean-to all purpose   PM82/6:114
Shed, lean-to tool storage   PM82/6:113
Shed, lumber storage   HM84/2:41
Shed, small contemporary garden   PM83/8:80
Shed, solar utility   PM78/9:127
Shed, solar utility   PM81/3:136
Shed, storage   HM72/3:40
Shed, storage   NS84/5-6:90
Shed, storage   PM77/4:123
Shed, storage   WB77/3-4:46
Shed, storage building (redwood)   WB78/7-8:46
Shed, storage building (redwood)   WB78/5-6:113
Shed, storage door   HM82/12:76
Shed, storage/firewood   HM82/9:92
Shed, storage lean to   HM72/8:32
Shed, two story storage   PM72/3:55
Shed and porch, storage   WB79/5-6:60
Shed/barn plans to order, $7   PM80/8:96
Shed/greenhouse   HM72/9:40
Shed kit, metal storage   HM79/5-6:28
Shed kit, storage   HM75/9:36
Shed kit, storage   HM78/7-8:42
Shed/mini greenhouse lean-to   PM82/6:110
Sheet metal, working with   HM84/4:138
Sheet metal brake, small   WB82/3-4:64
Sheet metal brake, wood   PM73/1:170

Sheet metal brake and workbench   WB80/9-10:50
Sheet metal cutter, shop made   PM76/4:170
Sheet metal screws   HM72/10:48
Sheet metal shears   HM75/4:38
Sheetrock   HM75/8:34
Sheetrock   HM83/7-8:76
Sheetrock   PM74/5:90
Sheetrock   WB78/3-4:84
Sheetrock   WB80/9-10:108
Sheetrock, finishing   WB73/5-6:16
Sheetrock, installing   HM77/7-8:22
Sheetrock, installing   PM81/7:32
Sheetrock ceiling repair   HM77/11-12:50
Sheetrock clip fasteners   NS84/10:41
Sheetrock elevator   HM74/4:43
Sheetrock fastening anchors   NS82/1:14
Sheetrock repair   HM73/4-5:66
Sheetrock repair   HM77/5-6:24
Sheetrock repair   HM83/?:54
Sheetrock repair   HM84/3:82
Sheetrock repair   NS83/7-8:24
Sheetrock repair   PM73/1:72
Sheetrock repair   PM76/4:30
Sheetrock repair   PM79/12:95
Sheetrock repair   PM81/6:104
Shelf, bathroom tank top   PM75/1:114
Shelf, chessmen   WB74/3-4:14
Shelf, Colonial wall   PM72/3:138
Shelf, Colonial wall hung with drawer   WB84/11-12:118
Shelf, Colonial whatnot   PM73/5:96
Shelf, contemporary mirror spice   WB81/5-6:96
Shelf, cookbook/recipe (maple)   WS79/11:4
Shelf, corner   WB75/3-4:22
Shelf, corner kitchen   PM81/7:96
Shelf, cornice   WB84/3-4:97
Shelf, country strip (pine)   HM80/11:32
Shelf, curio   PM75/1:112
Shelf, diamond wall   WB76/9-10:13
Shelf, dovetail tongue and groove wall (oak)   WS82/3:20
Shelf, hanging Colonial   WB83/5-6:63
Shelf, knickknack with drawers   WB84/7-8:52
Shelf, latticework wall   WB79/1-2:48
Shelf, spindle   WB78/9-10:84
Shelf, tile accent whatnot   WB82/3-4:96
Shelf, wall   PM79/2:133
Shelf, wall   WB78/3-4:4
Shelf, wall   WB84/5-6:52
Shelf, window   WB77/9-10:22
Shelf and cabinet, bathroom   WB79/3-4:111
Shelf and mirror, early American   WB83/1-2:37

Shelf bracket, metal tubing   PM74/3:138
Shelf brackets, utility   WB79/5-6:39
Shelf/mantel, foamboard   HM78/3:31
Shelf (pine)   PM77/11:137
Shelf units, contemporary (oak)   WB82/9-10:96
Shells, carved Chippendale   FW79/3-4:76
Shelves, anywhere   PM82/9:100
Shelves, book   HM81/1:16
Shelves, boot   WB79/3-4:98
Shelves, brick and wood   WB79/3-4:66
Shelves, F. Scott Fitzgerald   HM81/2:20
Shelves, hanging   PM78/11:130
Shelves, kitchen   HM75/9:44
Shelves, kitchen   HM81/2:19
Shelves, kitchen built-in   WB84/9-10:12
Shelves, ladder   PM76/4:135
Shelves, low cost shop   PM84/5:224
Shelves, mini   WB78/9-10:77
Shelves, mud room   PM77/9:109
Shelves, ten   HM82/11:36
Shelves, turned wall   WB75/9-10:1
Shelves, variety   PM73/5:102
Shelves, wall book   PM84/7:132
Shelves, wood   WB84/1-2:43
Shelves and peg rails, Shaker   HM83/1:80
Shelving unit   WB81/3-4:6
Shelving wall unit   PM74/3:136
Sheraton bookcase   WB77/3-4:102
Sheraton sewing table, Colonial   WB74/3-4:36
Shims   PM76/4:50
Shingle repair   PM79/4:151
Shingle repair, wooden exterior   HM83/9:88
Shingle roof repair,   PM82/4:130
Shingle roof repair   HM83/9:90
Shingle roof repair   PM82/4:130
Shingle roofs   PM78/4:156
Shingles, indoor   HM74/10:36
Shingles, miniature   FW80/9-10:19
Shingles, room (cedar)   WB82/7-8:32
Shingles, splitting   FW78/9:64
Ship building, model   PM74/9:70
Ship hatch cover chairside table   WB79/11-12:130
Shipping furniture   FW84/11-12:84
Ship weather vane   WB76/3-4:88
Shipwright, miniature   FW83/9-10:79
Shirred wall covering   NS80/9:40
Shock detector   PM78/2:120
Shockproofing electrical wiring   NS83/1:80
Shoeshine box   PM81/11:30
Shoji indoor shutters   WB80/3-4:42

Shooting bench rest   PM77/11:152
Shooting board, squaring edges   PM76/4:204
Shooting box, target   PM74/6:141
Shooting silhouettes   PM81/8:85
Shooting stick stool   WB77/3-4:30
Shooting target, toy   PM72/6:146
Shooting tips, pistol   PM76/4:84
Shop, basement   WB77/11-12:100
Shop, cooperative   FW77/6:26
Shop, designing   PM82/6:94
Shop, dream   PM80/11:108
Shop, freezer panels   WB78/1-2:46
Shop, garage   HM83/12:30
Shop, lapidary   WB72/7-8:22
Shop, mobile closet   HM83/12:20
Shop, mobile home   FW80/9-10:56
Shop, small   FW80/9-10:54
Shop, small   FW80/9-10:46
Shop apron, leather   HM83/12:38
Shop built vacuum press for veneers   FW79/5-6:52
Shop cabinet, cardboard small parts   WB84/3-4:98
Shop cabinet, small movable tool   PM78/3:126
Shop cart, table saw   WS81/1:14
Shop cart and workbench   WB84/9-10:101
Shop center finder   PM80/2:130
Shop clamps rack   PM78/4:130
Shop clamp storage rack   PM83/12:158
Shop design   PM74/3:69
Shop design   PM83/11:94
Shop dowel and molding rack   PM83/12:154
Shop dust collection system   FW80/11-12:58
Shop dust collection system   WB82/9-10:82
Shop dust collector   FW78/9:76
Shop dust collector   WB75/11-12:40
Shop dust collector   WB77/9-10:91
Shop dust collector   WB78/9-10:59
Shop dust collector, cardboard box   WB80/7-8:63
Shop dust collector system   FW79/5-6:6
Shop dust collector system, plastic pipe   WB82/1-2:38
Shop dust collector tool stand   WB78/3-4:90
Shop dust exhaust fan, portable   FW83/3-4:14
Shop geometry   WB77/11-12:114
Shop ideas, fifteen   PM75/7:106
Shop layout   PM83/7:90
Shop layouts, four   PM84/11:156
Shop lazy Susan   WB76/3-4:43
Shop light, dimmer controlled   PM84/4:65
Shop light protector, chicken wire   WB81/11-12:90
Shop light stand   FW80/3-4:17
Shop lumber drying cabinet   WB82/7-8:6

Shop lumber rack   HM75/2:64
Shop lumber rack   PM81/11:122
Shop lumber rack   PM84/11:160
Shop math   FW80/5-6:68
Shop mobile work center   WB79/11-12:4
Shop noise   WB78/7-8:65
Shop note box   WB73/5-6:59
Shop organization   PM81/4:118
Shop organizer, 112 small drawers   PM80/1:103
Shop power, three phase   FW80/9-10:57
Shop power, three phase   FW81/1-2:12
Shop power tool maintenance   PM78/12:106
Shop power tool repair   WB76/1-2:38
Shop problems and solutions, eleven   PM82/5:118
Shop projects, four   PM80/2:130
Shop projects, four   PM81/1:119
Shop safety   PM78/6:136
Shop safety   PM82/11:120
Shop safety   WB81/11-12:26
Shop safety   WB82/9-10:134
Shop safety products   NS83/3:20
Shop saw setup   FW82/7-8:14
Shop scrap wood box, roll-about   PM84/11:159
Shop shelves, low cost   PM84/5:224
Shopsmith accessories   PM75/11:113
Shopsmith attachment dollies, four   PM81/12:172
Shopsmith notes   FW81/11-12:10
Shopsmith notes   FW81/7-8:4
Shop stool   WS79/7:11
Shop storage, small parts 35mm film box   WB84/11-12:51
Shop storage box   WS81/5:14
Shop storage cabinet   PM78/2:132
Shop storage cabinet   WS83/1-2:4
Shop storage cabinet, small parts   PM84/11:137
Shop storage cabinets   WB83/3-4:98
Shop storage tips   PM81/11:122
Shop table, assembly   PM84/11:160
Shop tips, ten   PM77/8:110
Shop tips, ten   PM79/8:88
Shop tips, ten   PM79/12:92
Shop tips, ten   PM79/1:96
Shop tool cabinet, mobile   PM80/2:130
Shop tool cabinet, portable   HM82/12:28
Shop tool cabinets, wall   PM82/5:114
Shop tool rack, pegboard   PM83/11:99
Shop tool repair   WB76/3-4:76
Shop tools to make, four   PM82/8:86
Shop/utility room, garage   HM83/12:26
Shop vacuum back pack   WB77/3-4:96
Shop vacuum tank   FW82/9-10:24

Shop vacuum track   WB74/7-8:56
Shop ventilation   FW84/7-8:60
Shop vise stand   WB76/11-12:48
Shop wall tool cabinet   HM81/12:20
Shop welding cabinet, arc   HM83/9:111
Shop wiring, switches and breakers   FW80/9-10:59
Shop workcenter, portable power tools   PM82/11:109
Shop worktable, wired   WB79/9-10:28
Shortwave antenna   PM80/3:84
Shotgun restocking   WB72/1-2:46
Shovel tips   PM80/9:22
Showcase cabinets   FW79/9-10:44
Shower, cedar   NS81/2:12
Shower, sun   NS81/4:49
Shower head, clogged   HM83/2:54
Shower heads, water saving   NS84/2:62
Shower heads and faucets, new   HM83/7-8:56
Shower remodeling   HM72/6:42
Shower resurfacing   HM75/10:31
Shower stall, open   WB78/5-6:56
Shuffleboard game table   PM73/12:154
Shutter, window external roll-up   HM80/9:82
Shutter, window thermal   NS83/10:40
Shutter insulation, window   WB78/5-6:86
Shutter repair   WB81/5-6:9
Shutters, indoor contemporary   PM83/1:108
Shutters, indoor raised panel   PM80/3:128
Shutters, latticework   PM80/6:103
Shutters, Shoji indoor   WB80/3-4:42
Shutters, solar reflective   PM81/4:172
Shutters, thermal window   NS80/10:61
Shutters, window insulating   NS80/10:31
Sideboard   WB77/9-10:32
Sideboard, Southern huntboard   FW83/3-4:74
Sideboard, Spanish   WB79/5-6:43
Sideboard, tile top (oak)   WB78/9-10:62
Sideboard, Victorian marble top (oak)   PM83/5:102
Side chair, Chippendale Georgian (mahogany)   WB82/1-2:64
Side chair, Queen Anne   WB81/3-4:131
Side table, Shaker (cherry)   WS80/9:4
Siding, cleaning   HM80/4:32
Siding, cleaning aluminum   HM73/4-5:59
Siding, doll house   FW83/11-12:12
Siding, house   HM78/4:28
Siding, house   HM84/1:46
Siding, house   PM79/4:144
Siding, house   WB78/5-6:30
Siding, house   WB78/3-4:24
Siding, installing house   PM74/6:96
Siding, installing vinyl   PM84/4:126

Siding, making rough sawn barn   PM79/1:99
Siding, natural   NS83/3:72
Siding, painting stained hardboard   HM84/9:83
Siding, recycling   HM83/4:56
Siding, remodeling with   HM84/4:36
Siding maintenance, wood   HM72/8:40
Siding products, home   HM83/4:35
Siding repair, clapboard   HM80/5-6:59
Siding repair, stucco   HM80/5-6:60
Siding tips   HM84/4:40
Sign letters   HM80/3:104
Signs, early American   WB72/5-6:54
Signs, Murphy knife carved   FW81/9-10:64
Signs, routed   FW79/3-4:72
Signs, routed   HM78/11-12:46
Silhouettes, shooting   PM81/8:85
Silicone rubber sealers   HM72/12:40
Sill replacement   HM83/1:70
Silvering mirrors   WB72/3-4:10
Silver jewelry   PM80/12:94
Silver solder   HM79/2:18
Silverware caddy   PM78/4:114
Silverware caddy (pine)   HM80/11:33
Silverware chest   HM83/7-8:94
Silverware chest   WB84/1-2:48
Silverware drawer organizer, acrylic   HM82/12:54
Silverware stackers, wood   WB77/11-12:107
Silverware tote   WB79/7-8:32
Sink, darkroom   PM73/3:42
Sink, repairing chipped   HM84/2:67
Sink, utility   HM79/11:107
Sink installation, stainless steel   HM76/10:40
Sink rim, lavatory   HM84/2:58
Six drawer chest, contemporary (pine)   WS81/9:16
Skammel stool, Norwegian   PM81/3:27
Skateboards   PM76/6:94
Skateboard scooter   PM78/9:181
Skates, sharpening ice   PM74/2:75
Skating rink, back yard   PM77/11:74
Sketch bench   WB74/5-6:40
Sketch pad kit, computer   PM80/2:88
Skew, turning   FW82/9-10:70
Skewers, barbecue   PM80/7:91
Ski and pole pegs   PM78/2:124
Ski boot cube   PM78/9:112
Skiing, innertube water   PM76/9:54
Skiis, cross country from old   PM75/11:102
Skiis, snow care   PM73/2:50
Ski rack   HM83/10:86
Ski rack   PM78/9:112

Skis, cross country   FW81/11-12:66
Skis, cross country   WB84/9-10:46
Skis, Norwegian cross country   FW81/11-12:68
Skis/sled   PM78/2:97
Ski workbench   PM80/1:105
Skylight   HM72/8:54
Skylight   HM82/4:58
Skylight   NS80/4:56
Skylight   NS81/11-12:78
Skylight   NS83/11-12:48
Skylight   PM76/4:138
Skylight   WB80/3-4:80
Skylight, commercial   WB80/5-6:36
Skylight, installing   HM84/9:39
Skylight, leak free   NS83/9:32
Skylight, weatherizing   PM82/12:148
Sky walls and ceilings   HM82/12:46
Slab clocks   WB83/5-6:74
Slab corrum Inhlo with clock   WB84/3-4:74
Slab lumber surfacing, router   PM70/9:20
Slabs, router surfacing jig   FW84/9-10:18
Slab top tables   WB78/1-2:62
Slant top desk, Newport style   FW80/7-8:41
Slant top desk, Shaker (cherry)   WS80/11:4
Slate floor, entry   WB82/7-8:36
Sled, Alaskan dog   WB82/11-12:30
Sled, child's wood snow   WB76/1-2:81
Sled, scooter   PM72/11:122
Sled, single runner   PM78/11:134
Sled, snow   PM80/11:110
Sled, stone hauling   PM82/7:102
Sled/skis, rescue   PM78/2:97
Sleeping bag and tent kits   WB72/3-4:50
Sleigh, child's Russian troika   WB83/1-2:20
Sleigh, horse   WB77/11-12:56
Sleigh, snow   WB72/11-12:20
Sleigh/car seat, child's   PM79/12:64
Slide, indoor toy   NS82/9:98
Slide, shoe house   WB80/5-6:22
Slide, toy   WB74/5-6:30
Slide copier light   PM76/1:69
Slide/movie screen cabinet   PM72/9:90
Slide previewer   PM80/1:102
Slide projector dissolve control   PM74/3:120
Slide/stereo cabinet, tall   PM72/9:80
Slide top box, finger joint   WS81/9:14
Slide top finger joint box   WS81/9:14
Slide viewer/table, lighted coffee   PM75/9:102
Sliding door   WB82/3-4:36
Sliding glass door insulation   PM82/1:64

Sliding screen doors, slide smoothly   WB79/7-8:48
Slip joint, radial arm saw   FW82/1-2:71
Slot, routing   FW77/9:18
Slot mortise joint   WS80/3:4
Slot mortise joint   WS83/3-4:8
Slot mortiser, table saw   FW84/11-12:8
Slot mortising table   FW82/7-8:14
Slot mortising table, radial arm saw   FW81/1-2:20
Slot routing   WS80/7:12
Smoke detectors   NS82/11-12:50
Smoke finishing   FW83/1-2:97
Smoker/barbecue plans to order, $7.95   PM79/6:13
Smoothing plane   PM82/6:97
Snack trays, turned   WB73/7-8:48
Snorkeling tow, battery powered   PM83/8:68
Snorkeling tow rig, trolling motor powered   PM73/4:96
Snowball mobile   WB73/11-12:52
Snowblower   PM78/12:94
Snowblower from leaf blower   PM76/11:57
Snowblower guide   PM75/11:82
Snowblower maintenance   HM74/1:50
Snowblower tractor cab   PM80/2:76
Snow camping   PM76/11:100
Snow camping, survival   PM79/12:84
Snow candles, free form   PM73/12:70
Snow driving   PM79/12:87
Snow melting systems   PM76/11:119
Snow rake   PM80/12:144
Snow scoops   NS82/10:18
Snowshoes, cold bending   FW84/11-12:77
Snow shovel attachment   PM79/12:37
Snow sled   PM80/11:110
Snow sled, child's wood   WB76/1-2:81
Snow sleigh   WB72/11-12:20
Snowthrower, buying and using   PM79/12:114
Snowthrower maintenance   HM72/2:50
Snowthrower maintenance   HM74/11:40
Snowthrower maintenance   PM79/11:64
Snowthrower storage   PM79/3:228
Soccer game, table   PM78/11:124
Sofa, built-in   WB80/1-2:131
Sofa, built-in and wall lights   HM75/4:36
Sofa, butcher block   PM76/12:110
Sofa, cardboard   NS83/11-12:38
Sofa, cushioned corner   PM79/2:134
Sofa, fast plywood   HM78/11-12:28
Sofa, Mediterranean outdoor furniture   WB80/7-8:82
Sofa, simple   HM80/9:18
Sofa, solid core door bottom   PM73/4:126
Sofa, Taos furniture (pine)   FW83/5-6:79

```
Sofa, three cushion   WB75/11-12:36
Sofa, upholstered Chippendale (walnut)   FW84/11-12:60
Sofa, wrap around   PM78/7:101
Sofa and chair, modern   FW80/5-6:51
Sofa and chair, upholstered   WB78/1-2:52
Sofa bed   WB79/11-12:68
Sofa/bed, caned   PM77/8:105
Sofa/bed, hidden (cherry)   FW76/9:24
Sofa/bed, modern slat   HM81/4:18
Sofa/bed, rollaway builtin   PM80/2:134
Sofa/bed, simple stackable twins   PM81/4:154
Sofa/end table, built-in   HM76/10:34
Sofa love seat, upholstered   WB82/11-12:80
Sofa sitting bench with storage   HM84/2:36
Sofa/storage, plywood   HM81/4:14
Sofa/storage unit   PM82/4:123
Soffit repair   HM80/4:44
Soffits, three   HM84/7-8:74
Soil mixer/tumbler   PM73/4:122
Solar, fans   NS82/10:38
Solar, passive part 1   WB82/5-6:40
Solar, passive part 2   WB82/7-8:39
Solar, passive part 3   WB82/9-10:120
Solar, simple   NS82/4:22
Solar add-ons for home heating, eight   PM81/9:109
Solar air collectors   NS80/5-6:40
Solar air conditioner   NS83/7-8:18
Solar air heater   NS84/9:20
Solar assisted heat pump   NS84/2:6
Solar attic   NS81/9:80
Solar bath   NS83/7-8:74
Solar breakfast counter addition, glass   HM83/5-6:54
Solar chimneys   NS84/7-8:10
Solar co-op   NS81/4:54
Solar collector   WB80/3-4:62
Solar collector, comparison   NS82/11-12:59
Solar collector, installation   HM80/9:50
Solar collector, installation   WB77/5-6:18
Solar collector, passive lean-to   PM80/7:108
Solar collector, passive mobile home   WB83/7-8:92
Solar collector, tin can   WB78/5-6:66
Solar collector, water   WB78/1-2:16
Solar collector, wood   HM77/11-12:40
Solar collector roof mounts   NS84/3:22
Solar contractor, working with   HM84/2:88
Solar dog and cat house   HM83/9:46
Solar doll house   WB80/11-12:62
Solar dryer, firewood   HM81/10:89
Solar dryer/cold frame   PM84/3:112
Solar drying kiln   FW77/6:59
```

Solar electricity, photovoltaic   NS83/9:10
Solar energy, passive basics   NS80/2:51
Solar energy, passive house   NS80/2:56
Solar energy guide   PM77/4:80
Solar family room   PM79/4:137
Solar/fireplace boiler heated home   PM80/9:117
Solar firewood dryer   NS81/9:30
Solar firewood dryer   PM83/9:122
Solar firewood dryer   WB81/9-10:82
Solar fish pond   NS84/4:16
Solar floor, radiant   NS84/9:38
Solar floors   NS82/3:88
Solar food dryer   NS81/5-6:76
Solar food dryer   PM79/1:100
Solar glass, installation   NS82/5-6:52
Solar glazings, plastic   NS82/1:58
Solar growing frame   NS81/11-12:29
Solar heated home experiences   PM77/10:84
Solar heater, lean-to   HM80/9:34
Solar heat pump   WB81/11-12:76
Solar heat storage   NS81/10:26
Solar heat storage   NS82/4:24
Solar home   HM83/5-6:101
Solar home   NS80/3:22
Solar home   NS80/7-8:68
Solar home   NS83/2:8
Solar home   NS84/9:62
Solar home   NS84/5-6:40
Solar home   NS84/2:56
Solar home   WB77/1-2:34
Solar home   WB79/1-2:20
Solar home   WB79/1-2:60
Solar home, 1940's   NS80/3:94
Solar home, A-frame   WB79/9-10:90
Solar home, active   NS82/4:20
Solar home, active   NS83/3:30
Solar home, affordable   NS83/7-8:36
Solar home, decorating   NS81/11-12:80
Solar home, double shell   NS80/9:72
Solar home, double shell   NS81/2:82
Solar home, double shell   NS82/4:28
Solar home, double shell   NS84/7-8:84
Solar home, high mass   NS84/11-12:82
Solar home, low cost   NS81/2:102
Solar home, massive passive   NS81/10:41
Solar home, new   PM84/9:80
Solar home, no furnace   PM81/4:199
Solar home, owner built   NS82/9:68
Solar home, saltbox   NS81/11-12:69
Solar home, state of the art   WB83/5-6:8

Solar home, thermal mass   NS81/10:38
Solar home, trisol   NS80/3:76
Solar home fabrics   NS80/11-12:92
Solar home fabrics   NS83/1:48
Solar home louvers   NS80/7-8:45
Solar home orientation   NS82/4:26
Solar home plans   NS81/2:56
Solar home plans   NS82/4:13
Solar home retrofit   NS80/5-6:36
Solar home retrofit evaluation   NS82/2:36
Solar home school   HM83/5-6:34
Solar hot air panel plans to order, $4.95   PM82/9:126
Solar hot air window box   NS82/10:24
Solar hot tub   PM79/3:137
Solar hot water heaters   NS80/7-8:56
Solar hot water kit   NS82/9:56
Solar hot water system part 1   WB80/11-12:88
Solar hot water system part 2   WB81/1-2:68
Solar insulation   NS81/3:41
Solarize mobile homes   NS80/9:30
Solar kits   PM78/9:151
Solar landscaping   NS84/7-8:36
Solar louver walls   NS83/5-6:10
Solar lumber drying kiln   PM77/5:273
Solar mistake, sloped glass   NS82/4:30
Solar mistakes   NS82/4:18
Solar oven, $5   WB79/3-4:72
Solar panel, air   PM75/2:102
Solar panel coatings   NS83/4:68
Solar panels   HM79/9:8
Solar panels   PM81/9:109
Solar panels, installing roof   PM83/9:96
Solar photovoltaic electricity   NS82/5-6:65
Solar pool heater, simple   PM81/8:132
Solar pool heating   PM79/5:136
Solar porch   NS82/10:36
Solar powered toy car   NS83/7-8:78
Solar remodeling   HM82/2:57
Solar retrofits   NS82/10:23
Solar room   NS80/11-12:75
Solar room   PM78/4:138
Solar room   WB84/1-2:8
Solar room, heat from clothes dryer   WB84/1-2:56
Solar room, passive kit   PM83/9:91
Solar room kits   PM83/12:54
Solar shed, utility   PM81/3:136
Solar shower   NS81/4:49
Solar shutters, reflective   PM81/4:172
Solar still, pure water   PM82/3:98
Solar storage shed   PM78/9:127

Solar sunspace   NS80/2:25
Solar sunspace   NS81/7-8:66
Solar sunspace construction   NS80/2:37
Solar swimming pool   NS82/4:66
Solar system, active   NS81/1:46
Solar system, freon   NS81/4:76
Solar thermal chimney   NS80/7-8:25
Solar trombe wall design   NS84/1:20
Solar wall   NS81/1:82
Solar water heater   HM84/12:50
Solar water heater   NS81/7-8:22
Solar water heater   NS83/7-8:10
Solar water heater   NS83/5-6:36
Solar water heater   PM81/11:64
Solar water heater   PM83/1:92
Solar water heater, batch   HM81/1:76
Solar water heater, batch   NS80/10:96
Solar water heater, batch   NS81/7-8:27
Solar water heater, buying   PM80/6:84
Solar water heater, drain back   NS81/3:46
Solar water heater, installing   PM79/9:132
Solar water heater, simple   PM82/4:164
Solar water heater, tankless hybrid   HM82/4:94
Solar water heater, tests   NS81/5-6:32
Solar water heater, thermosiphon   NS80/11-12:51
Solar water wall   NS81/10:32
Solar window films   NS84/5-6:56
Solar window installation   NS82/10:31
Solar window seat   NS84/1:36
Solar window shutter, external roll-up   HM80/9:82
Solar window sizing   NS84/10:52
Solar wood drying   FW80/5-6:56
Solar workshop, open air   HM83/2:22
Solder, silver   HM79/2:18
Soldering   HM81/11:108
Soldering, heat sink   PM82/1:18
Soldering copper tubing   NS82/1:36
Soldering electrical wiring   PM74/7:104
Soldering tip   PM79/12:37
Solder splice electronic   PM83/5:152
Solvents, buying and using   PM82/11:116
Solvents, paint   HM81/2:88
Solvents, woodshop   FW83/7-8:36
Sonotube furniture   HM79/9:115
Sound effects machine, electronic   PM82/1:68
Sound insulation   WB84/1-2:92
Spa, home   WB81/7-8:74
Spa and hot tubs   WB81/7-8:4
Spade bits, modified drill   FW84/7-8:76
Spalted wood bowls, turning   FW78/6:54

Spalted wood turning   FW77/6:50
Spanish chair and stool   WB75/5-6:44
Spanish chest, small   WB78/9-10:3
Spanish Christmas tree decorations   PM81/12:116
Spanish luthier's guitar top clamp   FW80/1-2:18
Spanish molding, carving   FW83/9-10:48
Spanish sideboard   WB79/5-6:43
Spanish table, console   WB74/11-12:44
Spanish tile bench   WB72/5-6:8
Spanish wine rack, ornamental iron   PM82/5:104
Sparkplug candlestick   PM81/2:142
Sparmaker's gouge   FW83/7-8:56
Spas, saunas and hot tubs   NS82/2:20
Speaker's lectern, portable   PM80/9:100
Speaker, installing car   PM73/9:122
Speaker, stereo   HM80/11:12
Speaker cabinet, stereo   PM76/11:120
Speaker cabinet kit   WB79/11-12:120
Speaker cabinets, cardboard   HM78/9:76
Speaker enclosures   WB73/1-2:30
Speaker hole cutter   FW82/1-2:16
Speaker kits, stereo   HM79/3:78
Speaker repair, stereo   PM83/3:170
Speargun stirrups   PM73/9:109
Speedometer, digital bicycle   PM78/2:39
Speed reducer, band saw   WB78/5-6:100
Sphere, routed wood   FW84/1-2:8
Sphere, wooden   FW79/1-2:61
Spice box, four drawer (maple)   PM79/11:122
Spice box of drawers (pine)   WS79/11:3
Spice cabinet, Colonial   WB75/11-12:64
Spice cabinet, punch pattern   HM82/2:32
Spice rack   WB77/3-4:78
Spice rack   WB81/7-8:53
Spice rack, contemporary   PM78/11:198
Spice rack, dowel   PM81/2:136
Spice rack, kitchen   NS82/11-12:48
Spice rack, kitchen   PM84/7:133
Spice rack, latticework wall   WB79/9-10:84
Spice rack, over oven   WB79/5-6:7
Spice rack, swivel   PM78/4:114
Spice rack with serving tray   PM78/4:114
Spice shelf, contemporary mirror   WB81/5-6:96
Spider leg carriage table (mahogany)   FW83/5-6:70
Spindle, spiral   WB80/9-10:4
Spindle, turning laminated   FW81/7-8:52
Spindle, turning thin   FW80/7-8:70
Spindle cradle (cherry)   FW81/11-12:72
Spindle turning   FW78/9:60
Spindle turning   FW84/11-12:81

Spindle turning   HM77/11-12:56
Spinning wheel   WB83/3-4:6
Spinning wheel, simple   PM79/9:104
Spinning wheel, vertical   WB72/1-2:31
Spinning wheel (cherry)   FW78/6:40
Spiral bookcase   WB80/9-10:30
Spiral candlesticks, turned   PM72/10:178
Spiral carving, table saw   FW82/3-4:94
Spiral lamp   WB81/1-2:60
Spiral pedestals   WB81/1-2:60
Spiral spindle desk   WB80/9-10:8
Spiral spindles   WB80/9-10:4
Spiral stairway   FW79/5-6:80
Spiral stairway   FW79/5-6:76
Spiral stairway   NS81/3:80
Spiral stairway kit   HM77/11-12:16
Spiral stairway kit   HM82/11:44
Spiral stairway kit   WB73/7-8:34
Spiral steps (oak)   FW76/3:42
Spiral step table   WB76/11-12:121
Spiral turning   FW82/3-4:92
Spline and miter joints   WS80/1:11
Spline cutting   FW80/5-6:16
Spline joints   PM79/7:85
Spline mitered joint   FW81/3-4:62
Splitting mall handle replacing   PM78/11:132
Splitting wood   FW78/9:64
Split turning, camel (walnut)   FW76/3:20
Spoke hole jig, lathe   FW79/3-4:18
Spokeshave tips   PM84/6:144
Spool and sewing tape rack, wall   PM83/2:70
Spool board, sewing   WB79/1-2:123
Spool candleholder, flax   PM77/11:142
Spool candleholder, flax   PM78/11:202
Spool display wall cabinet   WS83/3-4:4
Spool house and clock   WB73/9-10:24
Spool rack, wall   WB84/3-4:49
Spool tractor toy   PM79/5:134
Spool tractor toy   WB83/1-2:72
Spoon, carving   FW83/1-2:84
Spoon collection lamp   WB83/1-2:14
Spoon creatures   HM80/2:24
Spoon display case, wooden hinged (oak)   WS80/5:11
Spoon display racks   WB75/11-12:68
Spoon drill bits   FW83/11-12:70
Spoon jewelry   WB76/9-10:16
Spoonmaking   FW80/5-6:82
Spoon rack, Colonial   WB79/1-2:88
Sprayers, airless paint   WB80/5-6:62
Spray finishing problems   FW81/11-12:94

Sprinkler, automatic lawn   HM77/4:68
Sprinkler system   PM75/8:51
Sprinkler system   PM77/7:92
Sprinkler system, lawn   PM80/5:131
Spruce cradle, pioneer   WB72/5-6:66
Square   HM83/5-6:12
Square   HM83/7-8:18
Square   PM82/11:52
Square, carpenter's   WB73/9-10:50
Square, combination   PM77/8:14
Square, combination   PM84/11:90
Square, trueing framing   FW79/7-8:15
Square, using   PM82/10:122
Squaring edges   PM76/4:204
Squirrel cup rack, kitchen   WB84/9-10:113
Squirrel feeder   WB72/1-2:30
Squirrels in attic   PM78/11:142
Stacked plywood shaping   FW77/3:50
Stacking boxes and carriers, garden   PM82/8:96
Stacking carving   FW76/12:22
Stack of trays, swinging   PM/6/0.114
Stag weather vane   PM83/3:98
Stain, exterior   NS81/5-6:63
Stain, finishing   WB78/11-12:88
Stain, shoe polish   FW79/5-6:19
Stained glass   HM79/9:28
Stained glass   WB81/5-6:40
Stained glass, apple pepper orange pear   PM82/8:54
Stained glass, cutting   WB83/3-4:22
Stained glass Christmas mobile   PM72/12:75
Stained glass Christmas tree ornaments   PM80/12:98
Stained glass doors, kitchen cabinet   HM82/7-8:84
Stained glass fish   HM81/11:97
Stained glass hutch, frame and panel   WB81/5-6:62
Stained glass kaleidoscope, toy   PM81/1:100
Stained glass light box, Casablanca   PM80/7:96
Stained glass light box, kitchen   PM82/8:54
Stained glass mirror, dragonfly   PM80/7:96
Stained glass panel, zodiac   PM80/7:96
Stained glass projects, liquid lead   PM80/7:96
Stained glass repair   HM75/4:49
Stained glass windows   NS81/9:69
Stained glass windows   PM76/6:110
Stain finishes   PM77/12:120
Stain finishes, water   WB72/5-6:56
Staining decks, refinishing   HM84/9:91
Stain over paint   WB73/3-4:20
Stains, dyes and pigments   FW78/9:58
Stains, exterior   HM78/7-8:32
Stains, oil   HM83/4:104

Stains, removing   PM73/10:96
Stains and dyes   FW82/3-4:75
Stain vs. paint, house   HM82/4:77
Stair and floor repair   HM76/2:30
Stair bannister   WB79/7-8:58
Stair building   FW81/9-10:48
Stair closet   WB80/5-6:67
Stair closet (cedar)   WB77/5-6:25
Stair handrail   HM84/10:74
Stair layout and construction   WB77/1-2:48
Stair railing   HM82/10:70
Stair rail post, Lincoln newel   PM82/5:60
Stairs, attic   HM80/9:48
Stairs, curved   FW79/9-10:8
Stairs, handrail   PM79/2:44
Stairs, remodeling basement   HM74/1:48
Stairs, reworking   HM84/10:74
Stairs, spiral   NS81/3:80
Stairs, squeaking   HM83/2:52
Stairs design computer program   NS84/11-12:22
Stair storage   HM72/10:46
Stairway, attic   HM75/10:28
Stairway, circular   FW79/5-6:76
Stairway, spiral   FW79/5-6:80
Stairway kit, spiral   HM77/11-12:16
Stairway kit, spiral   HM82/11:44
Stairway kit, spiral   WB73/7-8:34
Stamp, cardboard   PM81/10:38
Stamp, perforating   PM81/10:38
Stamp box, carved (walnut)   FW75/12:42
Stand, blanket   WB76/5-6:24
Stand, Shaker candle (cherry)   WS80/9:6
Stand, Shaker round (cherry)   FW77/12:68
Stand with mirror, Victorian shaving (oak)   PM83/2:108
Stanly #55 molding plane   FW83/1-2:89
Stanly #55 molding plane   HM81/12:15
Staple gun   HM76/4:34
Staple gun, buying and using   PM80/4:36
Staplers   WB77/7-8:50
Staples, selecting   HM79/5-6:58
Star, Swedish   HM81/12:22
Star shaped candles   PM81/10:52
Stationery box   WB76/9-10:47
Stationery desk caddy, 1750 (cherry)   PM84/3:74
Stave chair, butcher block style   WB82/11-12:4
Staved cones   FW78/3:75
Staved container   FW79/3-4:74
Staved cylinder assemble   FW80/11-12:26
Stave joint   WS83/1-2:8
Staves, bending laminated compound curves   FW79/7-8:57

Staves, compound angled   FW78/3:73
Steam bending fixture   FW81/9-10:84
Steam bending jig   FW78/9:16
Steam bending wood   FW77/9:40
Steam bent boxes, Shaker oval   FW82/1-2:92
Steam engine kit   PM73/2:162
Steamer, pipe   FW78/3:12
Steamer, wood bending   FW78/6:9
Steam minibike   PM72/5:21
Steam powered toy truck   PM74/11:146
Steam roller, toy   PM77/11:146
Steam shovel riding toy   PM81/5:118
Steel wool   WB72/9-10:36
Steel wool pad   PM84/2:170
Steel wool sanding   WB79/11-12:14
Steeple clock kit   PM75/12:98
Stemware rack   WB78/9-10:44
Stenciling   HM82/10:62
Stenciling chairs   FW83/7-8:22
Stenciling walls   HM83/10:60
Stencils, wall   HM/6/1:52
Step, entry   PM78/4:172
Stepladder, plexiglas plant   PM75/5:72
Stepping stones, concrete   WB81/3-4:70
Stepping stones, raise and level   PM79/7:90
Step repair, brick   HM80/5-6:60
Step repair, concrete   HM80/3:56
Steps, brick and concrete   PM75/8:78
Steps, concrete   HM72/8:42
Steps, concrete   WB76/3-4:32
Steps, handrail   PM79/2:44
Steps, railroad ties   NS83/5-6:35
Steps, spiral (oak)   FW76/3:42
Steps, wood porch   HM74/9:50
Steps, worn concrete   HM73/4-5:26
Steps snow melter   PM76/11:119
Step stand, Shaker (cherry)   WS82/1:20
Step stool   HM82/7-8:74
Step stool   WB77/3-4:30
Step stool, cat child's   WB79/7-8:53
Step stool, child's   WS84/9-10:12
Step stool, conductor's   WB79/11-12:133
Step stool, library   FW79/7-8:80
Step stool, woodworkers   WB79/3-4:98
Step table, spiral   WB76/11-12:121
Stereo, installing car   PM79/10:24
Stereo, portable patio cabinet   PM73/8:82
Stereo cabinet   FW82/5-6:76
Stereo cabinet   HM75/11:38
Stereo cabinet   HM80/9:20

Stereo cabinet   HM84/2:38
Stereo cabinet   WB81/7-8:40
Stereo cabinet, contemporary (oak)   PM83/9:84
Stereo cabinet, highboy   WB83/5-6:4
Stereo cabinet, rolltop (maple plywood)   WS81/9:6
Stereo cabinet, small   WB84/11-12:14
Stereo cabinet, tall   PM72/9:80
Stereo entertainment center, contemporary   PM83/1:108
Stereo modules   HM80/11:12
Stereo record care   PM81/9:188
Stereo speaker   HM80/11:12
Stereo speaker cabinet   PM76/11:120
Stereo speaker cabinet   WB73/1-2:30
Stereo speaker cabinet, cardboard   HM78/9:76
Stereo speaker cabinet kit   WB79/11-12:120
Stereo speaker hole cutter   FW82/1-2:16
Stereo speaker kits   HM79/3:78
Stereo speaker repair   PM83/3:170
Stereo stand, 2X4   WB77/3-4:72
Stereo tape deck cabinet   WB78/1-2:76
Stereo turntable maintenance   PM83/12:61
Stereo turntable power meter/stylus timer   PM81/11:85
Stick measuring cabinet making   FW77/3:46
Still, solar water   PM82/3:98
Stilts   PM76/8:99
Stilts, tin can toy   PM81/6:52
Stockade fence   WB82/3-4:98
Stone, diamond sharpening   WS82/11-12:7
Stone, Japanese water sharpening   WS82/11-12:4
Stone, self lubricating oil sharpening   PM73/10:174
Stone, sharpening   FW75/12:47
Stone, sharpening   WS82/3:4
Stone and brick, fake wall   WB78/11-12:134
Stone fence New England   PM82/7:84
Stone sled   PM82/7:102
Stone wall   HM82/4:100
Stone wall, dry laid   WB83/7-8:64
Stone wall, insulated   NS82/3:54
Stone wall joint repair   HM83/9:98
Stool, assorted   WB77/3-4:30
Stool, child's   NS81/3:59
Stool, child's step   WS84/9-10:12
Stool, cricket   WB80/11-12:94
Stool, deck (redwood and canvas)   WS79/5:6
Stool, dowel   HM80/1:12
Stool, fireside foot   WB78/7-8:30
Stool, folding (ash and canvas)   FW82/9-10:68
Stool, gout   FW77/9:74
Stool, handy   PM82/7:138
Stool, kitchen   WB83/9-10:32

Stool, library step   FW79/7-8:80
Stool, Norwegian skammel   PM81/3:27
Stool, plywood early American furniture   WB82/5-6:95
Stool, Punjabi weaving   WB78/1-2:68
Stool, rustic slab   PM72/11:120
Stool, Shaker   PM81/11:32
Stool, shop   WS79/7:11
Stool, simple plywood   PM79/9:214
Stool, step   HM82/7-8:74
Stool, storage drum   HM79/2:82
Stool, three legged   FW77/6:35
Stool, three legged   FW82/9-10:65
Stool, tool boxes   HM82/2:54
Stool, woodworkers step   WB79/3-4:98
Stool, woven string bottom Shaker   HM83/12:72
Stool and chair, Spanish   WB75/5-6:44
Stool and table, child's lion   PM74/2:144
Stool and table, child's round   WB83/9-10:45
Stool and table, contemporary   WB84/5-6:20
Stool/bench, Colonial   PM80/11:128
Stool leg angle   FW82/9-10:67
Stool legs, turned off-center   FW79/9-10:73
Stool saddle seat, caned or padded   WB84/3-4:30
Storage, cardboard   WB83/9-10:81
Storage, garage   PM76/2:120
Storage, garage   PM77/2:122
Storage, garage   WB77/3-4:74
Storage, increasing garage   PM82/11:170
Storage, plastic pan storage in child's room   HM72/4:37
Storage, stair   HM72/10:46
Storage, workshop hardware   PM80/7:104
Storage barn kit   HM75/9:36
Storage bench   HM73/2:46
Storage bench   WB83/5-6:24
Storage bench, hall   WB76/7-8:36
Storage/bench boxes, garden or pool   HM84/5-6:40
Storage bench wall unit   HM75/1:30
Storage bin   WB80/5-6:76
Storage box, power tool   WB78/9-10:90
Storage box, shop   WS81/5:14
Storage building, disguising metal   PM74/9:146
Storage building gazebo   PM75/8:90
Storage building playhouse, two story   WB82/9-10:22
Storage building (redwood)   WB78/7-8:46
Storage building (redwood)   WB78/5-6:113
Storage cabinet, garage   HM72/4:54
Storage cabinet, garage between cars   HM74/6:34
Storage cabinet, modular (plywood)   WS82/7:12
Storage cabinet, room divider   WB73/9-10:54
Storage cabinet, shop   PM78/2:132

Storage cabinet, shop   WS83/1-2:4
Storage cabinet bookcase   WB82/1-2:79
Storage cart   HM75/11:46
Storage center, movable (pine)   NS80/2:59
Storage chest, Colonial   PM77/11:109
Storage chest, one drawer Shaker   HM72/3:52
Storage chest, outdoor   WB73/3-4:52
Storage chest bench   WB82/11-12:22
Storage chest/box, plywood   PM74/2:146
Storage/desk, built-in   HM76/8:30
Storage desk, corner   HM73/1:36
Storage/desk, two sheets plywood   HM74/2:34
Storage/firewood shed   HM82/9:92
Storage modular units, wall   WB82/3-4:90
Storage nooks   WB81/9-10:70
Storage platform, bedroom   HM76/6:26
Storage shed   HM72/3:40
Storage shed   PM77/4:123
Storage shed   WB77/3-4:46
Storage shed, lean-to   HM72/8:32
Storage shed, solar   PM78/9:127
Storage shed, two story   PM72/3:55
Storage shed and porch   WB79/5-6:60
Storage shed door   HM82/12:76
Storage shed/greenhouse   HM72/9:40
Storage shed kit   HM78/7-8:42
Storage shed kit, metal   HM79/5-6:28
Storage shop cabinet, small parts   PM84/11:137
Storage/sofa, plywood   HM81/4:14
Storage/sofa unit   PM82/4:123
Storage tips, shop   PM81/11:122
Storage unit, wall   HM72/10:36
Storage unit, wall   HM73/10:34
Storage unit, wall   HM76/8:42
Storage unit, wall   HM80/9:19
Storage unit, wall dresser   HM76/3:30
Storage unit, wall movable   HM79/12:20
Storage unit, window wall   HM74/9:36
Storage unit/desk, wall   HM77/4:19
Storage wall, perforated hardboard   HM74/1:36
Storage wall buffet   HM76/1:32
Storing paint   WB77/3-4:109
Storm door   WB75/9-10:24
Storm door, installing   HM84/9:66
Storm door, replacing   HM78/2:54
Storm door, tempered glass   PM75/2:46
Storm door and screen repair   PM73/8:90
Storm door repair, plexiglas   HM72/12:54
Storm door window replacement, plexiglas   PM72/3:162
Storm/screen door   WB83/9-10:86

```
Storm window    NS84/10:62
Storm window    WB74/9-10:58
Storm window    WB80/1-2:104
Storm window, aluminum   HM76/9:42
Storm window, building   HM79/2:60
Storm window, indoor   HM76/11:36
Storm window, plastic   NS80/10:34
Storm window, reglazing   HM73/2:38
Storm window and screen   WB81/9-10:100
Storm window and screen repair   HM72/4:42
Storm window glass repair   PM83/9:114
Storm window repair   NS84/9:32
Storm winds protection construction tips   PM80/8:66
Stove, brick Russian wood   NS81/1:74
Stove, installing coal   PM81/10:112
Stove, wood   WB78/9-10:16
Stove catalytic combustors, wood   NS84/9:90
Stove chimney, wood   NS80/2:98
Stove fires, wood   HM80/9:60
Stovehaus, wood stove heated house   PM80/8:86
Stove heated house, Stovehaus   PM80/8:86
Stove hood, oven over   PM74/10:158
Stove repair, cooking   NS83/5-6:66
Stove safety, wood   PM80/10:74
Stove spice rack, over oven   WB79/5-6:7
Stove tile wall   PM82/4:152
Stove wall shields   NS83/11-12:78
Strawberry barrel   PM73/5:88
Stretcher-to-post joint   FW81/7-8:10
Strippers, paint   NS83/7-8:32
Stripping furniture   HM72/9:52
Stripping furniture   HM83/2:80
Stripping furniture, professional   HM79/12:24
Stripping paint   WB74/5-6:8
Stroke sander   FW76/6:46
Stroke sander, wooden drum   FW81/7-8:47
Stroller, child's   WB77/11-12:52
Stucco, painting   HM75/4:52
Stucco repair   HM84/9:71
Stucco siding repair   HM80/5-6:60
Stud framing, wide   WB76/7-8:66
Stud straightening   HM83/3:106
Subcontracting   WB82/1-2:56
Subcontractors, finding   NS84/10:68
Subfloor, installing   HM84/5-6:78
Suitcase stand, folding   PM84/4:105
Summer house, large screened gazebo   NS84/4:52
Sump pump   HM80/1:46
Sump pump, basement   PM79/4:162
Sump pump, basement   WB80/3-4:78
```

Sump pump alarm, basement   PM72/12:188
Sundial, polar   PM80/5:130
Sundials   WB79/7-8:34
Sundials, four styles   WB82/7-8:49
Sunfish ice skating   PM79/2:52
Sunken bath   NS80/11-12:90
Sun/pool room   WB83/7-8:36
Sunroof kit, installing auto   PM84/4:68
Sunroom   PM78/4:138
Sunroom   PM81/1:96
Sunroom, passive kit   PM83/9:91
Sunroom kits   PM83/12:54
Sunroom plans to order, $7.50   PM79/9:138
Sunrooms   WB84/1-2:8
Sun screens   WB79/7-8:38
Sun shower   NS81/4:49
Sunspace   HM82/4:20
Sunspace   HM82/3:26
Sunspace   HM83/9:28
Sunspace   NS80/11-12:75
Sunspace   NS82/7-8:78
Sunspace   NS83/2:65
Sunspace, dual purpose   NS84/5-6:86
Sunspace, fine tuning   NS83/10:42
Sunspace, solar   NS80/12:25
Sunspace, solar   NS81/7-8:66
Sunspace construction   NS80/2:37
Sunspace design   NS83/7-8:44
Sunspace kits and plans   NS83/9:56
Support, saw roller   FW81/3-4:20
Support, saw roller   WB77/7-8:10
Support stand, caster top saw   HM78/2:62
Surface truing stock   FW78/10:50
Surfacing boards, ten methods   PM84/10:110
Surfacing jig, router   PM83/12:112
Surfacing jig, slab routering   FW84/9-10:18
Surfacing lumber, router   PM78/9:20
Surfacing panels, router rail   FW80/11-12:56
Surfacing thin stock   FW83/3-4:16
Surfboard sailing plans to order, $7   PM81/5:110
Surveyor, saving on   NS82/5-6:6
Survival, auto accidents   PM79/10:106
Survival, cold water   PM78/8:76
Survival, sled/skis   PM78/2:97
Survival, snow camping   PM79/12:84
Survival, winter   PM78/1:58
Survival, winter power failure   PM80/1:133
Survival kit   PM77/4:169
Survival life jacket   PM79/12:14
Survival skill, orienteering and map reading   PM78/3:70

Surviving cold   PM81/12:164
Suspended ceiling   HM75/8:40
Suspended ceiling   HM84/12:59
Suspended ceiling   WB77/9-10:4
Suspended ceiling   WB81/3-4:44
Suspended ceiling, invisible grid   HM73/1:56
Suspended ceiling with wood   PM83/12:102
Swag lamp (veneer strips)   WS79/3:9
Sweater chest, wooden hinged (maple plywood)   WS80/5:8
Swedish cradle Christmas card holder   PM81/12:114
Swimming dock   WB78/5-6:70
Swimming pool   WB75/5-6:14
Swimming pool, in ground <$3000   HM83/5-6:81
Swimming pool kit   HM83/5-6:88
Swimming/snorkeling tow, battery powered   PM83/8:68
Swing, dowel   PM77/7:96
Swing, hobby horse   WB78/11-12:77
Swing, horse   PM79/4:131
Swing, Jimmy Carter porch   FW84/5-6:68
Swing, old fashioned porch (oak)   WB81/5-6:45
Swing, outdoor (cedar)   NS82/7-8:43
Swing, porch 1927 (oak)   PM83/7:94
Swing, porch (oak)   HM84/5-6:70
Swing, small child's   PM76/8:99
Swing, toy   WB74/5-6:30
Swing, two person ram toy   PM81/11:30
Swing and frame, old time   PM78/5:128
Swinging ball toy, Newton's   PM74/6:152
Swing plans to order, $1.50   HM81/7-8:80
Swing set, A-frame with roof   PM80/5:133
Swing set anchor   WB78/9-10:48
Swiss alphon   FW80/5-6:4
Swiss tools   PM76/6:108
Switches, four way electric   WB73/1-2:44
Switch plates, hiding   PM78/5:123
Table, Adirondack wooden lawn   PM82/6:116
Table, antique game   FW77/9:60
Table, art deco roll-about   PM81/12:106
Table, backgammon/chess   PM78/10:65
Table, barbecue   PM77/5:107
Table, barrel   WB74/5-6:32
Table, bed   PM81/7:97
Table, book trough   WB78/7-8:44
Table, breakdown picnic   PM81/6:107
Table, breakfast   NS82/10:47
Table, bridge   PM72/9:84
Table, bulldozer sprocket   NS80/2:93
Table, butcher block   WB77/3-4:90
Table, butcher block checker   WB82/11-12:100
Table, butcher block coffee   PM76/12:110

Table, butcher block cribbage   WB82/11-12:100
Table, butcher block extendable   WB82/11-12:84
Table, butcher block (maple/walnut)   WB84/11-12:46
Table, Butler's and tray   PM75/3:90
Table, Butler's tray (walnut)   WS81/3:10
Table, Butler's tray (walnut or mahogany)   WB76/1-2:41
Table, butterfly dropleaf   WB72/5-6:48
Table, cabinet coffee   WB77/11-12:48
Table, carved pedestal   WB80/1-2:64
Table, chain saw woodcutting   PM79/12:112
Table, chess and backgammon game   WB79/7-8:70
Table, chessboard/coffee (walnut)   WB84/1-2:4
Table, chess game   PM81/2:159
Table, Chippendale tilt-top   WB81/5-6:20
Table, clear plastic coffee   HM77/7-8:36
Table, cloverleaf top x-legs (pine)   WB80/11-12:124
Table, cobbler's bench coffee   WB80/5-6:112
Table, coffee   HM76/10:34
Table, coffee (cherry)   HM81/1:57
Table, coffee (oak)   WS83/1-2:20
Table, coffee (pine and cedar)   WB80/3-4:76
Table, Colonial drop leaf (mahogany)   PM82/6:132
Table, Colonial end   WB74/7-8:37
Table, Colonial Sheraton sewing   WB74/3-4:36
Table, Colonial trestle, $75   HM79/2:36
Table, concrete block and wood picnic   PM73/6:76
Table, contemporary aquarium end   WB81/5-6:82
Table, contemporary coffee (oak/glass)   PM83/12:148
Table, contemporary cube coffee   PM82/2:106
Table, contemporary end   WB81/3-4:66
Table, contemporary game   FW77/9:63
Table, contemporary gate leg (oak)   FW76/6:42
Table, contemporary laminated legs   WB84/7-8:54
Table, contemporary (oak)   WS81/5:4
Table, contemporary three drawer coffee   WS82/1:14
Table, contemporary trestle   WS82/9:12
Table, cove cuts (koa)   FW79/1-2:65
Table, crate furniture end   HM77/4:74
Table, cribbage board two drawer   WB83/11-12:116
Table, cube coffee   PM81/1:96
Table, cutting   HM79/5-6:48
Table, deck butcher block   PM77/7:97
Table, deck (redwood)   HM80/4:18
Table, deck (redwood)   HM84/5-6:32
Table, designer picnic   HM83/5-6:91
Table, desk/drawing with adjustable height   WS84/1-2:4
Table, dihedral X-plywood   HM80/12:17
Table, dining   WB77/9-10:36
Table, dining expandable two to twelve   WB80/11-12:111
Table, dining/game   WB83/9-10:50

Table, display case   WB81/9-10:54
Table, dowel   HM80/1:18
Table, drawing   FW84/3-4:32
Table, drawing   WB79/9-10:74
Table, drawing   WB80/9-10:62
Table, drawing board and typing   WB81/5-6:4
Table, drawing (oak)   HM84/12:68
Table, drop down kitchen   HM72/12:38
Table, drop leaf   WB77/3-4:4
Table, drop leaf buffet   WB77/7-8:34
Table, drop leaf Shaker   HM72/10:50
Table, drop leaf Shaker   WS80/9:8
Table, drop leaf snack   WB83/3-4:62
Table, drop leaf triangular   WB83/1-2:110
Table, drop (redwood)   HM80/4:26
Table, drum coffee   PM73/2:164
Table, drum top and cyma curve legs (pine)   WB80/5-6:104
Table, Duncan Phyfe drop leaf (mahogany)   PM82/3:140
Table, Dutch pull-out extension dining   FW77/12:34
Table, early American tilt-top   WB75/11 12:30
Table, elliptical top Colonial tavern   WB82/1-2:22
Table, end   WB78/5-6:34
Table, English hayrake stretcher 1924 (oak)   FW84/9-10:72
Table, expanding   FW77/3:44
Table, fast plywood coffee and end   HM78/11-12:28
Table, folding card   WB82/11-12:26
Table, folding cutting   FW79/9-10:16
Table, folding drafting   PM77/5:39
Table, folding picnic   PM75/4:116
Table, folding picnic (redwood and cedar)   WS83/5-6:4
Table, folding portable   HM80/7-8:32
Table, footboard bed   PM75/9:79
Table, game/coffee   HM80/1:70
Table, garden clean-up   HM79/3:31
Table, gate leg   PM82/4:123
Table, gate leg   WB75/9-10:34
Table, gate leg   WB79/5-6:95
Table, gate leg and drop leaf   FW79/9-10:62
Table, glass top coffee (walnut)   HM81/1:56
Table, glass top contemporary   WB79/11-12:153
Table, glass top wrought iron coffee   HM76/4:44
Table, gluing   FW78/10:14
Table, greenhouse   NS81/11-12:27
Table, grid coffee (pine)   NS80/5-6:43
Table, Hepplewhite D-shaped card (mahogany)   FW84/7-8:42
Table, inlaid round top (pine)   WB80/9-10:72
Table, inlaid veneer chess/lamp   WB84/11-12:15
Table, kerfed oval coffee   WB82/7-8:56
Table, kitchen   HM81/1:54
Table, kitchen cutting   HM81/3:94

Table, kitchen or dining   WB74/5-6:20
Table, knockdown buffet   PM72/9:89
Table, leveling   PM78/8:18
Table, lighted drawing   WB80/5-6:68
Table, Lincoln's child's   HM83/11:38
Table, Lincoln round marble top (mahogany)   WB84/1-2:72
Table, lion's paw pedestal   FW80/11-12:74
Table, living room (cherry)   FW81/11-12:63
Table, long or short trestle   WB81/3-4:60
Table, low cost massive coffee   HM78/7-8:74
Table, low cost massive end   HM78/7-8:74
Table, lyre rotating top 1825 (mahogany)   WB81/3-4:78
Table, marquetry game   WB72/1-2:36
Table, mass produced   FW84/1-2:32
Table, Mediterranean octagonal display   WB76/3-4:86
Table, Mediterranean outdoor furniture   WB80/7-8:82
Table, mini/maxi gate leg   PM72/10:172
Table, mirror or ceramic tile   HM81/1:36
Table, mirror top coffee   HM81/11:74
Table, modern coffee (oak and smoked glass)   WS79/1:7
Table, modern dining   WB81/5-6:52
Table, modern end (oak and smoked glass)   WS79/1:7
Table, modern routed wood tubular   FW84/11-12:58
Table, mosaic tile   WB81/3-4:130
Table, nested country snack   HM83/7-8:26
Table, nesting   WB76/9-10:24
Table, nesting four   PM76/5:114
Table, nesting inlaid (walnut)   WS83/7-8:12
Table, occasional   WB80/3-4:118
Table, octagonal tilt-top   WB82/1-2:46
Table, Oriental knockdown (fir or maple)   FW80/1-2:59
Table, park bench style (metal and oak)   PM81/8:94
Table, parquet   WB81/3-4:112
Table, Parson's   WB83/3-4:50
Table, Parson's bridge   PM72/6:150
Table, Parson's butcher block coffee   WB83/5-6:72
Table, Parson's dining   PM78/11:128
Table, Parson's (oak)   HM81/1:52
Table, patio   WB75/9-10:26
Table, pedestal (pine)   WB80/7-8:54
Table, Pembroke drop leaf (mahogany/walnut)   WS81/3:4
Table, picnic   HM80/4:16
Table, picnic   HM80/5-6:29
Table, picnic snack   HM81/2:76
Table, pillar and claw round-top   FW81/11-12:81
Table, pillow plant stand (oak)   PM81/10:104
Table, plank top coffee   WB75/7-8:52
Table, plexiglas coffee   PM75/5:72
Table, plywood modern coffee   HM80/12:15
Table, pond house dining   FW84/1-2:32

```
Table, projector   HM78/4:42
Table, puzzle block   WB77/11-12:89
Table, PVC pipe   HM81/9:32
Table, Queen Anne   WB75/7-8:22
Table, radial arm saw   PM79/2:122
Table, radial arm saw drop leaf   PM82/3:76
Table, refectory   PM74/3:73
Table, rolling buffet/bed   PM74/6:156
Table, round coffee with mail order parts   HM78/2:52
Table, round contemporary dining (mahogany)   WS83/11-12:16
Table, round dining (oak)   PM79/7:92
Table, round lamp   WB79/7-8:62
Table, round lyre   WB83/9-10:69
Table, round top dining   WB75/1-2:36
Table, round top modern (pine)   FW81/9-10:88
Table, round traditional dining   WB79/11-12:134
Table, router   FW79/3-4:56
Table, router   WS79/9:6
Table, router   WS82/3·18
Table, router   WS82/7:16
Table, rustic end   HM78/11-12:84
Table, rustic willow furniture coffee   HM84/4:122
Table, sawbuck dining (cedar)   HM81/1:50
Table, Scandinavian coffee or dining   PM81/5:122
Table, scrap wood coffee   WB77/5-6:66
Table, set up work   FW82/9-10:90
Table, sewing/utility folding legs   WB82/9-10:18
Table, Shaker Colonial trestle (pine)   WS79/1:3
Table, Shaker dining (cherry)   HM84/10:104
Table, Shaker side (cherry)   WS80/9:4
Table, Shaker trestle   PM76/7:101
Table, ship hatch cover chairside   WB79/11-12:130
Table, shop assembly   PM84/11:160
Table, shuffleboard   PM73/12:154
Table, simple block strip coffee (oak)   PM80/11:130
Table, simple long drop leaf dining   PM82/9:104
Table, simple router   WB81/1-2:146
Table, six gate leg buffet (cherry)   WS82/3:14
Table, slab top   WB78/1-2:62
Table, slab with clock coffee   WB84/3-4:74
Table, small convenience   WB72/1-2:38
Table, small folding   PM80/1:104
Table, small (pine)   WB80/3-4:50
Table, small turned trestle   WB79/5-6:28
Table, Spanish console   WB74/11-12:44
Table, spider leg carriage (mahogany)   FW83/5-6:70
Table, spiral step   WB76/11-12:121
Table, splayed legs with aprons (pine)   WB81/1-2:40
Table, stacking tray   PM72/9:94
Table, stowaway picnic   PM76/8:100
```

Table, table saw backup   PM83/11:99
Table, tape and record end   WB79/7-8:22
Table, three under one   WB78/9-10:6
Table, tile top coffee   WB79/9-10:24
Table, tilt top reeded pedestal (mahogany)   WB84/3-4:36
Table, tough child's   HM79/10:21
Table, tray coffee (mahogany)   FW84/1-2:72
Table, trestle coffee   WB72/3-4:70
Table, trestle end   WB72/3-4:70
Table, triangular drop leaf   FW80/11-12:61
Table, triangular drop leaf   WB72/9-10:40
Table, triangular end storage   PM82/2:106
Table, turned end (walnut)   WB74/3-4:66
Table, TV tray (oak)   WS81/7:4
Table, two drawer and secret compartment end   WB83/9-10:102
Table, two height coffee/dining   WB79/3-4:4
Table, veneered hexagonal   WB79/5-6:82
Table, veneering   WB80/1-2:80
Table, veneer Parson's   FW78/6:70
Table, wagon seat coffee   WB72/9-10:44
Table, wall dressing   HM79/12:68
Table, welding   NS80/3:87
Table, welding   WB80/11-12:105
Table, wine rack base and glass top   WB80/1-2:70
Table, wood strip coffee   PM80/9:103
Table, workbench drawing   PM79/3:126
Table, woven top coffee   WB77/11-12:96
Table accessories, coiled rope   PM79/11:76
Table and benches, butcher block   PM72/7:140
Table and benches, outdoor   PM81/4:162
Table and benches, patio   WB80/5-6:32
Table and benches (redwood)   HM82/5-6:31
Table and chair, child's   WB76/11-12:100
Table and chairs, card cabinet   WB82/3-4:26
Table and chairs, Colonial drop leaf   PM82/4:116
Table and chairs, Contemporary trestle   PM76/9:104
Table and chairs, hexagonal patio   PM79/5:142
Table and seat, plastic laminate phone   PM78/6:142
Table and stools, child's lion   PM74/2:144
Table and stools, child's round   WB83/9-10:45
Table and stools, contemporary   WB84/5-6:20
Table and terrarium, contemporary coffee   WB81/1-2:4
Table/bench   HM75/3:42
Table/bench, designer patio   PM83/8:70
Table/bench, foyer   PM79/6:112
Table/bench, Monk's   WB79/3-4:88
Table/bench, picnic sawbuck (redwood)   PM83/8:73
Table bench, trestle   WS82/9:24
Table centerpiece, lollipop tree   PM80/12:98
Table chair, child's   WB83/7-8:50

Table decorations, Christmas reindeer   PM79/12:82
Table design, trestle   FW83/9-10:42
Table designs, Queen Anne   FW76/6:40
Table/desk, drop leaf dining   PM82/11:112
Table drop leaf hinges   WS81/3:8
Table feet, adjustable   FW81/1-2:22
Table hutch, 1700's (pine)   PM82/7:92
Table/hutch/chair, Colonial   PM73/7:96
Table joint, drop leaf   WS80/9:10
Table lamp   NS81/10:60
Table lamp, art deco   PM81/12:106
Table lamp, cobbler's bench   PM73/5:92
Table lamp, dovetail   WS82/7:24
Table/lamp, turned pedestal   WB83/11-12:66
Table legs, Cabriole   FW79/9-10:80
Table legs, cabriole   WB78/5-6:42
Table legs, mortising   FW79/9-10:54
Table legs, tapered laminated   FW79/1-2:48
Table legs, tapered reed   FW81/11-12:85
Table legs, tapered Shaker   WS80/9-11
Table leg slots, Shaker   FW84/5-6:10
Table/magazine rack, Colonial doughbox lamp   WB84/3-4:4
Table modules, coffee   HM80/2:28
Table napkin holder   PM83/2:74
Table (oak)   WB79/5-6:24
Table plans to order, Shaker $8.45   HM83/10:26
Table/planter, small   PM76/10:116
Table (redwood)   PM84/7:94
Table refinishing, drop leaf   HM83/10:52
Table saw, cutting circle   FW80/9-10:24
Table saw, homemade combination   FW80/1-2:36
Table saw, large panel support   PM81/3:159
Table saw, miter jig   FW81/1-2:81
Table saw, portable   FW82/3-4:20
Table saw, portable   WB75/7-8:42
Table saw, resawing   PM79/8:104
Table saw, small parts   FW80/3-4:16
Table saw, tenons   FW80/7-8:14
Table saw, wooden   FW83/7-8:28
Table saw antisplit device   PM82/6:98
Table saw backup table   PM83/11:99
Table saw basics   FW82/5-6:61
Table saw bench for portable circular saw   PM79/11:136
Table saw blade height gauge   PM81/8:115
Table saw blade height scale   PM76/8:96
Table saw box joint   WS81/9:12
Table saw circle cutter   PM81/7:130
Table saw cove cutting   WS84/11-12:11
Table saw cove cutting jig   WS80/11:16
Table saw cutoff box   FW79/11-12:21

Table saw cutoff box   PM84/5:98
Table saw dolly   FW81/7-8:16
Table saw dolly   PM74/8:56
Table saw dovetails   FW83/11-12:50
Table saw edge truing jig   WB84/1-2:84
Table saw extension   FW80/9-10:18
Table saw extension, router table   WB74/7-8:26
Table saw fence, add-on   PM79/7:114
Table saw fence, scissor jack   FW83/3-4:18
Table saw fence stop, self locking   PM83/11:106
Table saw finger joint jig   FW80/1-2:13
Table saw frame miter jig, picture   PM82/12:98
Table saw guard   FW82/3-4:14
Table saw guard   FW83/5-6:14
Table saw height gauge   PM83/11:112
Table saw helpers   HM78/9:36
Table saw hold down   PM83/11:114
Table saw hold down clamps   WS79/1:6
Table saw hold downs and push sticks   WB72/7-8:16
Table saw hold in   FW82/9-10:20
Table saw jig, repetitive cuts   PM79/8:88
Table saw jig for tenoner   FW79/9-10:16
Table saw kit   HM83/12:34
Table saw kit, AMT   PM78/7:92
Table saw maintenance   PM83/5:106
Table saw marking inlay   PM84/11:140
Table saw miter board   PM79/12:111
Table saw miter cutting blocks   PM78/6:86
Table saw miter fixture   FW79/11-12:21
Table saw miter gauge   PM83/7:92
Table saw miter gauge   PM83/12:109
Table saw miter gauge   WB79/11-12:114
Table saw miter gauge   WB84/1-2:82
Table saw miter gauge hold down   PM75/12:146
Table saw mitering   FW81/1-2:80
Table saw miter jig   FW79/11-12:24
Table saw miter jig   PM77/8:111
Table saw miter jig   WS80/11:15
Table saw miter stop   PM82/12:96
Table saw molding   FW82/7-8:65
Table saw mortise and tenon joints   WB77/9-10:28
Table saw open mortising jig   FW84/11-12:8
Table saw pattern sawing   FW84/7-8:54
Table saw push stick   FW77/3:53
Table saw push stick   PM76/8:96
Table saw rabbeting small pieces   WS81/5:15
Table saw raised panels   WB79/11-12:136
Table saw resawing   WS84/9-10:21
Table saw resawing jig   WS79/11:9
Table saw rip/bevel technique   WS81/7:8

Table saw rip fence extension, two   FW84/9-10:8
Table saw rip guide   PM82/12:100
Table saw ripping roller support   FW79/9-10:22
Table saw roller support   PM75/11:150
Table saw saucer cut   PM76/8:95
Table saw shop cart   WS81/1:14
Table saw sliding crosscut fixture   FW79/11-12:16
Table saw slot mortiser   FW84/11-12:8
Table saw stand   WB72/11-12:28
Table saw support roller   PM74/1:147
Table saw taper/bevel technique   WS81/7:11
Table saw taper jig   WS79/9:4
Table saw taper jig   WS79/1:6
Table saw tenoner   PM76/8:96
Table saw tenoner   PM79/2:130
Table saw tenoning jig   PM83/11:104
Table saw tips   HM84/2:16
Table saw tips   HM84/1:18
Table saw tips   PM/2/7.162
Table saw tips   PM72/10:166
Table saw tips   PM78/8:18
Table saw tips   PM79/8:104
Table saw tips   WB78/7-8:39
Table saw twist carving   FW82/3-4:94
Table/slide viewer, lighted coffee   PM75/9:102
Table soccer game   PM78/11:124
Table/sofa, built in end   HM76/10:34
Table tennis caddy   PM76/11:200
Table top, knockdown with dovetails   FW80/1-2:57
Table top, recessed   FW80/7-8:11
Table top, rounded on lathe   FW82/1-2:18
Table top construction   WS81/5:6
Table top edge shaping   WB77/7-8:28
Table top end boards   WS80/5:7
Table top finish   WB75/11-12:24
Tableware caddy   PM78/4:114
Tableware caddy, picnic   WB84/3-4:66
Tableware chest   WB84/1-2:48
Tableware/napkin caddy   PM75/10:102
Tableware tote   WB79/7-8:32
Table with trays, plant (redwood)   FW84/1-2:43
Taboret plans to order, $3.50   NS83/1:74
Tachometer, gear shifting   PM79/6:37
Tailgate party organizer   PM79/10:116
Tailgate workbench   PM73/5:67
Tall case clock, 18th century   FW81/1-2:67
Tambour   FW78/9:52
Tambour, fabric backed   FW84/9-10:54
Tambour, rolltop   WS81/9:4
Tambour, shaped   FW76/9:54

Tambour, shaped   FW78/10:64
Tambour, wired   FW84/9-10:57
Tambour breadbox   WB82/3-4:48
Tambour breadbox, fake tambour   PM81/2:140
Tambour breadbox (pine)   WS79/7:6
Tambour door cabinets   WB80/9-10:34
Tambour door jewelry chest   WB83/5-6:104
Tambour kitchen cabinets   FW80/11-12:78
Tambour stereo cabinet   WB81/7-8:40
Tambour stereo cabinet (maple plywood)   WS81/9:6
Tambour strips, chamfering   FW83/3-4:22
Tambour TV cabinet, glass door   WS83/1-2:14
Tambour wall cabinet, bathroom (redwood)   WS81/9:10
Tankard, pewter   PM79/8:92
Tank top shelf, bathroom   PM75/1:114
Tantalus wine case   WB76/3-4:54
Taos furniture (pine)   FW83/5-6:79
Tape and record end table   WB79/7-8:22
Tape cartridge storage cabinet   WB83/9-10:36
Tape deck cabinet   WB78/1-2:76
Tape dispenser   HM80/3:75
Taper/bevel table saw technique   WS81/7:11
Tapered grooves   WB76/5-6:69
Tapered laminated table legs   FW79/1-2:48
Tapered reed table legs   FW81/11-12:85
Tapered table legs, Shaker   WS80/9:11
Tape repairs   PM76/10:102
Taper jig   WB78/7-8:39
Taper jig, table saw   WS79/9:4
Taper jig, table saw   WS79/1:6
Tapes, adhesives   HM75/2:38
Tapping copper water lines   HM76/4:42
Taps and dies, threading metal   PM84/12:98
Tap wrench   PM78/1:99
Tap wrench, turnbuckle   PM80/2:65
Target, BB   PM78/11:208
Targets, shooting silhouettes   PM81/8:85
Target shooting box   PM74/6:141
Tavern table, elliptical top Colonial   WB82/1-2:22
Tavern tray kit, Colonial marquetry serving   WB77/7-8:71
Tea cart, Chinese Chippendale   WB79/5-6:52
Tea cart, drop leaf and tray   WB83/9-10:4
Tea cart, traditional   WB76/3-4:60
Teahouse/gazebo   WB83/5-6:64
Teahouse plans to order, $4   HM82/5-6:112
Teak light fixture, contemporary   PM82/4:166
Tea set, turned miniature   WB79/5-6:58
Tee game   PM76/2:34
Tee game solution   PM76/7:6
Teeterboard, elephant   FW80/5-6:77

Telephone, antique update   WB81/9-10:114
Telephone, buying   NS83/2:32
Telephone, installing   PM83/5:39
Telephone, removing rotary dial   PM81/3:32
Telephone cabinet, corner   HM83/10:126
Telephone caddy (redwood)   PM84/7:94
Telephone chest (walnut)   FW76/3:56
Telephone cupboard (pine)   PM84/8:106
Telephone desk and chair   WB81/3-4:90
Telephone maintenance   NS83/2:36
Telephone message center, wall   PM73/12:156
Telephone/message center (oak)   PM84/8:105
Telephone organizer, kitchen wall   PM81/2:136
Telephone repairs   NS84/5-6:22
Telephone shelf, rolltop under cabinet (oak)   PM84/8:107
Telephone speaker amp, electronic   PM74/2:132
Telephone stand with drawer   PM74/7:144
Telephone table, plastic laminate   PM78/6:142
Telephone tower, kitchen built in (maple)   PM84/8:102
Telescope from camera lens   PM74/11:138
Temple lantern, garden   WB78/3-4:56
Tennis caddy, table   PM76/11:200
Tennis court, backyard mini   PM73/9:160
Tennis racket press with ball storage   PM78/2:125
Tennis racket rack   PM78/2:124
Tennis racket restringing   PM74/7:166
Tenoner, table saw   PM76/8:96
Tenoner, table saw   PM79/2:130
Tenoner, table saw jig   FW79/9-10:16
Tenoning jig, table saw   PM83/11:104
Tenon jig   WB82/1-2:24
Tenon joint   WS83/3-4:10
Tenon joint, twin   WS80/11:12
Tenon joints   WS80/3:5
Tenons, bandsaw chair rung   FW81/3-4:18
Tenons, round on slats   FW81/3-4:18
Tenons, table saw   FW80/7-8:14
Tent and sleeping bag kits   WB72/3-4:50
Termites   NS83/5-6:44
Termites   PM78/4:128
Termite treatment   PM72/3:124
Terrarium, glass Tiffany   PM78/5:66
Terrarium and coffee table, contemporary   WB81/1-2:4
Tester, audio/video cable   PM84/3:154
Tester, dry cell batteries   PM81/2:142
Tester, shopmade metal hardness   PM80/2:80
Tetherball game   PM76/8:99
Textured paint   HM82/10:45
Textured wall paints   HM79/1:48
Theater, puppet   PM77/3:128

Thermal chimney   NS80/7-8:25
Thermal shutter, window   NS83/10:40
Thermal shutters   NS80/10:61
Thermometer/clock, desk   WS84/5-6:18
Thermosiphoning hot air panel   NS82/10:25
Thermosiphon solar water heater   NS80/11-12:51
Thermostats, setback   HM78/10:40
Thermostats, setback   HM80/12:52
Thermostat setback   NS80/11-12:66
Thicknesser, veneer   FW78/9:18
Thickness planing, jointer   FW84/9-10:8
Thickness sander, drill press   WB82/9-10:87
Thickness sander, homebuilt   FW80/3-4:50
Thickness sander, lathe   FW82/11-12:22
Thimble collection lamp   WB83/1-2:14
Threading metal   PM84/12:98
Threading tools, wood   FW77/9:65
Threading wood, router   FW83/3-4:99
Threads, metal for wood   WB75/9-10:30
Threads, wood   WB76/3-4:99
Threads, wooden   FW77/3:22
Threads, wooden   FW81/3-4:20
Three dimensional wall decoration   HM75/2:34
Three legged stool   FW77/6:35
Three legged stool   FW82/9-10:65
Three phase shop power   FW80/9-10:57
Three phase shop power   FW81/1-2:12
Three wheeler toy   WB82/5-6:50
Thumb piano   WB74/11-12:28
Thumb piano, Colimba or Sansa   WB74/3-4:40
Tie and belt rack, door mounted   WB80/11-12:80
Tie rack   WB84/3-4:96
Tie rack (pine)   WS79/1:2
Tiffany terrarium, glass   PM78/5:66
Tile, ceramic   HM80/1:73
Tile, ceramic   NS80/3:47
Tile, ceramic   PM84/6:84
Tile, ceramic bathroom   PM84/4:141
Tile, ceramic designer tips   HM84/3:68
Tile, ceramic floor   HM80/11:20
Tile, ceramic wall   HM73/3:50
Tile, floor   HM75/8:36
Tile, floor   HM76/6:44
Tile, floor   WB74/11-12:48
Tile, Mexican masonary   HM83/3:30
Tile, pregrouted ceramic   HM74/10:38
Tile, quarry   PM84/6:84
Tile, self-sticking ceramic   HM74/8:48
Tile, using and installing   PM84/6:84
Tile, wood parquet   PM84/6:84

Tile and laminate countertops   PM83/2:102
Tile and mirror tables, ceramic   HM81/1:36
Tile and wood planters   WB81/3-4:4
Tile bathroom, ceramic   HM82/7-8:57
Tile bathroom, ceramic   PM78/6:134
Tile bench, Mexican   WB72/5-6:8
Tiled trivet (oak)   WS82/5:24
Tile fireplace   PM79/4:160
Tile floor   HM74/3:34
Tile floor   HM78/1:26
Tile floor, ceramic   HM72/4:44
Tile floor, ceramic   HM84/4:85
Tile floor, clay   PM76/12:106
Tile floor, installing ceramic   HM84/4:96
Tile floor, quarry   PM76/4:144
Tile floor covering, resilient   WB80/11-12:73
Tile graphics, floor   PM79/2:134
Tile grout, ceramic   HM84/2:58
Tile mailbox update   HM80/3:59
Tile projects, mosaic   WB72/1-2:54
Tile repair, ceramic   HM74/3:46
Tile repair, ceramic   HM84/2:54
Tile repair, ceramic   NS84/11-12:18
Tile repair, ceramic   PM75/5:193
Tile table, mosaic   WB81/3-4:130
Tile top coffee table   WB79/9-10:24
Tile top sideboard (oak)   WB78/9-10:62
Tile wall, wood stove   PM82/4:152
Tiller maintenance   HM82/3:64
Tiller maintenance   WB74/3-4:22
Tiller tips, garden   PM78/3:160
Tilt top table, Chippendale   WB81/5-6:20
Tilt top table, Chippendale (mahogany)   PM84/8:98
Tilt top table, early American   WB75/11-12:30
Tilt top table, octagonal top   WB82/1-2:46
Tilt top table, reeded pedestal (mahogany)   WB84/3-4:36
Timber frame cottage   NS80/3:57
Timbers, building with heavy   FW79/7-8:43
Timer, darkroom   PM72/6:122
Timer, electronic egg   PM75/5:209
Timer, stereo turntable stylus   PM81/11:85
Tin can car, model Stutz Bearcat   PM79/3:118
Tin can Christmas tree   PM73/12:72
Tin can lantern   PM79/3:118
Tin can metal plaques   PM79/3:118
Tin can recycling   WB75/9-10:44
Tin can toy train   WB75/11-12:39
Tin Christmas tree ornaments   PM81/12:116
Tinkertoy child's chair, canvas   PM80/11:128
Tin safe, pierced panel Colonial   PM82/8:90

Tinsmith school   HM83/5-6:31
Tires, car   HM84/4:147
Tissue box cover (maple)   WS79/3:5
Tissue box (maple)   WS82/1:24
Tissue/magazine rack, Colonial bathroom   WB84/1-2:79
Toenailing tips   NS84/4:18
Toilet, clogged   HM78/7-8:46
Toilet, composting   HM82/9:48
Toilet, composting   NS80/11-12:102
Toilet, waterless   WB78/3-4:59
Toilet repair   NS82/4:48
Toilet seal replacement   HM83/2:56
Toilet seating   PM74/2:72
Toilet tank noise   HM78/11-12:72
Toilet tank repair   HM73/3:40
Toilet tank repair   HM74/3:48
Toilet tank repair   HM76/11:44
Toilet tank repair   HM80/3:36
Toilet tank repair   HM81/9:88
Toilet tank repair   PM83/11:59
Toilet tank repair   WB82/5-6:62
Toilet tank water valve   HM83/2:58
Toilet tissue holder/magazine rack, bathroom   PM75/4:134
Tomato cage, horizontal   PM84/3:114
Tomatoes, ten growing tips   HM84/4:114
Tomato ladder   PM84/3:114
Tomato tower   PM80/3:159
Tomato tower with water hole   PM83/6:132
Tomato trellis   PM82/6:138
Tongs, kitchen   PM76/3:188
Tongue and groove, plywood and solid wood   WS84/5-6:20
Tongues, routing   FW81/1-2:22
Tool, cat's paw nail puller   PM82/1:60
Tool, impact driver   NS80/7-8:16
Tool, multi one piece sheet steel wrench   PM82/8:87
Tool, power maintenance   HM82/12:50
Toolbox   NS82/11-12:47
Toolbox, buying metal   PM79/11:129
Toolbox, contemporary wood   PM80/11:116
Toolbox, equipping   PM84/10:116
Toolbox, old fashioned   HM79/1:36
Toolbox, open top tray carpenter's   PM81/11:128
Toolbox, outdoor   HM78/2:58
Toolbox, stocking basic   HM79/5-6:40
Toolbox, two   PM84/10:114
Toolbox (cherry)   PM81/11:128
Toolbox (cherry)   PM83/4:108
Toolbox/sawbuck plans to order, $3.00   NS83/3:64
Toolbox sawhorse   PM84/10:114
Toolbox stools   HM82/2:54

Tool buying tips, powered   PM84/12:143
Tool cabinet, cabinetmaker's   FW81/9-10:56
Tool cabinet, mobile   PM80/2:130
Tool cabinet, mobile   PM81/10:122
Tool cabinet, portable   HM82/12:28
Tool cabinet, shop wall   HM81/12:20
Tool cabinet, small movable   PM78/3:126
Tool cabinet, trifold   WB81/3-4:102
Tool cabinet, wall   PM82/5:114
Tool caddy, tin cans   PM80/5:54
Tool caddy sawhorse   PM75/6:34
Tool carousel   FW80/9-10:53
Tool carrying modules, portable workshop   HM78/10:76
Tool cart, garden   NS80/7-8:41
Tool chest, double   PM84/11:131
Tool chest, joiner's   FW80/9-10:76
Tool chest, portable   PM84/11:131
Tool chest, roll about   PM84/11:131
Tool chest, woodworker's (mahogany)   NS81/7-8:45
Tool chest (cherry)   PM79/11:132
Tool dolly   PM81/3:52
Tool dolly, garage   PM82/10:132
Tool ferrules   FW80/9-10:22
Tool handles, turned   PM82/2:106
Tool handles, turning   PM83/12:104
Tool heat treating   FW76/9:50
Tool holder, fiberglass   WB83/1-2:107
Tool holders   FW80/9-10:20
Tool holders, hardware cloth   PM81/1:119
Tool holder (scrap wood)   WS79/7:12
Tool kits, powered   HM83/12:34
Tool maintenance, power   PM83/5:106
Tool maintenance, garden   PM78/3:168
Tool mistakes, hand   PM80/9:190
Tool rack, bigfoot   FW80/9-10:72
Tool rack, pegboard   PM83/11:99
Tool rack, tin can   PM81/11:122
Tools, airpowered   FW79/1-2:70
Tools, antique   FW76/3:39
Tools, buying power   HM79/11:18
Tools, eight shop built   PM76/4:202
Tools, electronic project   PM82/1:106
Tools, hand   WB73/1-2:10
Tools, investing in   PM75/11:104
Tools, Japanese   PM76/11:114
Tools, Japanese woodworking   WB83/1-2:75
Tools, old hand   HM81/12:13
Tools, screwdrivers   NS81/1:20
Tools, seven shop built   PM81/10:35
Tools, sharpening   HM76/2:36

Tools, toy PM80/11:128
Tools, wheel PM81/7:84
Tools for toolbox PM84/10:116
Tool sharpening HM72/8:46
Tool sharpening HM77/5-6:40
Tool shed, lean-to PM82/6:113
Tool shed/mini greenhouse lean-to PM82/6:110
Tool stand, lathe WB81/3-4:129
Tool stand, power WB72/11-12:28
Tool stand dust collector WB78/3-4:90
Tool stand support WB77/5-6:29
Tool tote PM72/6:116
Tool tray, open shelf PM81/11:122
Toothbrush holder WB80/7-8:59
Toothbrush holder, child's WB83/1-2:86
Top, old fashioned toy HM82/11:27
Torch, propane WB77/5-6:48
Torque wrench PM75/8:80
Torsion box FW82/1-2:96
Tortoise shell paint finish WB74/11-12:66
Towel and cup holder, bathroom hands PM79/11:122
Towel bar, bathroom HM82/11:52
Towel rack NS80/2:62
Towel rack, kitchen HM83/7-8:94
Towel rack, kitchen (pine) HM80/11:34
Towel rack, paper WB81/1-2:72
Towel rack, paper and hand PM81/2:136
Towel rack, recessed ladder WB82/1-2:106
Towel rack, Shaker HM73/3:48
Towel rack, suspended WB78/7-8:83
Towel rack, wall WB79/5-6:66
Towel rack and cabinet, recessed bathroom HM76/9:46
Towel racks PM78/3:128
Tower, antenna or birdhouse PM72/12:186
Toy, Amtrak riding PM78/11:194
Toy, ball and cup PM78/12:74
Toy, bumble bee pull PM73/12:166
Toy, button and string PM78/12:74
Toy, circus train and animals PM72/12:108
Toy, doll house furniture WB77/11-12:86
Toy, dragonfly pull FW79/11-12:61
Toy, educational learning frames PM81/11:30
Toy, funny car PM78/11:194
Toy, Newton's swinging balls PM74/6:152
Toy, old tire elephant NS80/5-6:68
Toy, pull car shapes WB75/9-10:64
Toy, pull chicken and egg WB83/3-4:70
Toy, pull hatching chick PM74/11:108
Toy, pull jumping clown PM80/11:130
Toy, pull rabbit HM82/11:24

Toy, pull seal   PM74/11:110
Toy, teeter totter/ slide   WB77/11-12:68
Toy, tetherball game   PM76/8:99
Toy, three wheel kiddie truck   PM76/12:16
Toy, whirly antique   PM83/5:207
Toy airplane   PM76/4:118
Toy airplane   WB79/11-12:70
Toy airplane, biplane   WS84/9-10:8
Toy airplane, Fokker triplane tricycle   WB83/7-8:26
Toy airplane, motor and line   PM77/2:192
Toy airplane, radio controlled CO2 model   PM72/2:144
Toy airplane, rocking   WB84/11-12:56
Toy airplane, SST   WB82/11-12:35
Toy animals, prehistoric   WB81/11-12:95
Toy axles, wood   FW82/9-10:16
Toy balance beam   PM83/6:98
Toy balance beam, 2X4s   PM76/4:18
Toy banks, wooden cat clown and baboon   PM81/1:94
Toy barn, red   WB79/5-6:31
Toy biplane, wood   PM84/12:95
Toy blocks, numbers   PM81/11:30
Toy blocks box   WB81/5-6:111
Toy block village   WB75/1-2:16
Toy boat, freighter   WB82/9-10:45
Toy boat, herring fishing   WB82/11-12:48
Toy boat, lobster   WB82/11-12:48
Toy boat, riding toy   WB79/11-12:72
Toy boats, tug and barge   WB78/5-6:46
Toy bookends, Crayon   PM81/11:30
Toy boomerang   FW84/3-4:61
Toy bouncing jet   WB72/11-12:22
Toy box, boxcar   WB80/11-12:45
Toy box, eighteen wheeler   WB83/11-12:94
Toy box, elephant   WB79/1-2:94
Toy box, lion   WB78/11-12:72
Toy box, plywood barn   HM80/12:14
Toy box, rabbit   PM81/4:124
Toy box/bench, Scandinavian   PM81/5:122
Toy box blanket chest   WB82/11-12:72
Toy box circus wagon   PM75/11:120
Toy box circus wagon   WB80/11-12:64
Toy box/doll crib   WB74/5-6:26
Toy box/dollhouse   PM81/6:94
Toy box playcubes, numbered   PM81/1:102
Toy bucking horse   WB79/11-12:60
Toy building logs   WB84/5-6:4
Toy bulldozer   WB79/11-12:26
Toy bulletin/chalkboard   PM81/5:118
Toy butterfly, push action   WB84/11-12:122
Toy camera   WB77/7-8:20

Toy car, 1915 Chevrolet   WB84/9-10:80
Toy car, solar powered   NS83/7-8:78
Toy car garage and suitcase   WB81/11-12:42
Toy cars, block   PM75/12:96
Toy cars, wood   WB75/11-12:54
Toy cars and truck   PM78/11:194
Toy cars and trucks, blockmobiles   PM73/11:169
Toy cat and dog, pull   PM79/11:122
Toy chest   NS81/3:59
Toy chest   WS83/9-10:4
Toy chest, circus wagon   HM79/1:21
Toy chest, Colonial   PM79/1:94
Toy chest, simple   WB77/5-6:4
Toy chests, alphabet pirate trunk Pa. Dutch   PM78/1:100
Toy climbing bear   PM79/5:134
Toy counting box, child's   PM73/11:175
Toy cradle, Hoover doll   WB84/11-12:89
Toy crane, high rise   WB79/11-12:96
Toy crayon holders, bunny elephant duck   PM78/11:194
Toy dice jumbler   WB81/1-2:66
Toy dog, pull   HM83/11:76
Toy dog, pull   PM73/11:168
Toy doll cradle, Colonial   PM81/5:118
Toy doll high chair   WB84/11-12:86
Toy dollhouse   PM75/11:122
Toy dollhouse, gingerbread $10   HM79/1:84
Toy dollhouse roof, Victorian   WB73/9-10:42
Toy doll table and chair, Barbie   WB80/11-12:42
Toy duck, waddling   NS82/11-12:46
Toy ducks, pull   PM73/11:166
Toy dump truck   HM83/12:68
Toy earth mover   WB73/11-12:22
Toy finishing   WB73/7-8:44
Toy flying helicopter   HM82/11:27
Toy flying machine, helicopter   PM79/5:134
Toy front end loader, wood   PM84/12:97
Toy furniture, doll   WB76/11-12:52
Toy go cart plans to order, Mini Indy II   PM78/5:110
Toy gun cardboard shooter   PM80/8:36
Toy handsaw   PM78/11:196
Toy helicopter   WB79/11-12:66
Toy helicopter, large   WB82/11-12:10
Toy helicopter, wood   HM84/12:72
Toy hobby horse, auto spring   WB84/5-6:16
Toy horse and wagon   FW80/11-12:61
Toy horse bench   PM78/11:121
Toy horse swing   PM79/4:131
Toy hutch   HM82/11:26
Toy jump rope   PM79/3:170
Toy kaleidoscope   PM81/1:100

Toy kitchen appliances   PM73/11:172
Toy kitchen refrigerator sink/range   WB83/11-12:76
Toy kites   PM77/8:96
Toy kites, bicentennial   PM76/3:98
Toy kites, building   PM75/3:114
Toy kite winder   HM82/5-6:98
Toy lemonade stand   PM79/8:86
Toy lemonade stand/puppet theater   HM84/7-8:86
Toy locomotive   WB73/11-12:32
Toy logs, building   FW84/5-6:12
Toy monkey bars, indoor   PM79/7:80
Toy Noah's ark with animals   PM78/11:121
Toy parrot, balancing   PM81/12:175
Toy pedal car plans to order, $6   PM80/6:124
Toy pelican, pull   WB72/1-2:14
Toy penguin, pull   PM77/11:202
Toy playcubes, numbered   PM81/1:102
Toy play equipment, backyard   PM83/6:98
Toy playhouse, A frame   WB74/9-10:65
Toy playhouse, contemporary   WB84/5-6:42
Toy playhouse, cube   PM78/9:116
Toy playhouse, fairy tale with towers   WB84/5-6:8
Toy playhouse, indoor   PM75/10:146
Toy playhouses, three   PM78/7:76
Toy playhouse/tower slide   PM81/6:130
Toy play/sand box, outdoor   PM82/5:112
Toy play unit for toddlers   WB84/3-4:125
Toy puppet   PM77/3:133
Toy puppet, clown   PM81/11:32
Toy puppet, ostrich   PM78/11:196
Toy puppet theater   PM77/3:128
Toy rabbit, pull   HM82/11:24
Toy race car   PM81/5:118
Toy race car (plywood)   WS79/9:12
Toy range   PM78/11:120
Toy rattle, turned   FW79/11-12:58
Toy rocking horse   HM79/2:86
Toy rocking horse   HM82/12:62
Toy rocking horse   HM84/11:74
Toy rocking horse   PM77/11:138
Toy rocking horse   PM79/11:122
Toy rocking horse   WB74/11-12:38
Toy rocking horse   WB83/11-12:96
Toy rocking horse   WB84/11-12:8
Toy rocking horse, cantilevered legs   WB81/11-12:68
Toy rocking horse, toddler's   WB78/1-2:97
Toy Rolls Royce car, wood   PM84/12:94
Toys, backyard   NS80/5-6:66
Toys, kid made   FW79/11-12:98
Toys, outdoor   WB74/5-6:30

Toys, pull rabbits   PM81/4:124
Toys, six Christmas   PM75/11:118
Toys, wood   WB81/11-12:96
Toy sailboat   HM82/5-6:96
Toy sandbox   HM82/5-6:100
Toy sandbox, in-ground   PM81/8:87
Toy sandbox, super   WB73/5-6:10
Toy sandbox with roof   PM80/4:128
Toy scooter/skateboard   PM78/9:181
Toy seesaw, rotating   PM72/3:140
Toys from the past   PM79/5:134
Toy shooting target   PM72/6:146
Toy sky hook   PM79/5:134
Toy sled, scooter   PM72/11:122
Toy sled, single runner   PM78/11:134
Toy slide, indoor   NS82/9:98
Toy soldier Christmas tree ornament   PM80/12:98
Toy soldier lamp, child's   WB77/11-12:16
Toy soldiers and cannon   HM78/11-12:86
Toy space ship   WB78/11-12:108
Toy spool tractor   PM79/5:134
Toy spool tractor   WB83/1-2:72
Toy steam roller   PM77/11:146
Toy steam roller   WB79/7-8:26
Toy steam shovel, riding   PM81/5:118
Toy stick horse   PM80/11:128
Toy stick horse   WB82/5-6:53
Toy stilts   PM76/8:99
Toy stilts, tin can   PM81/6:52
Toy swing, two person ram   PM81/11:30
Toy swing set, A-frame with roof   PM80/5:133
Toy three wheeler   WB82/5-6:50
Toy toolbox   PM78/11:196
Toy tools   PM80/11:128
Toy top, old fashioned   HM82/11:27
Toy top, (walnut)   PM80/11:128
Toy tops   PM78/12:74
Toy trailer truck   HM82/11:62
Toy train   PM75/11:143
Toy train, Child's pull   WB78/11-12:50
Toy train, diesel   WB79/11-12:23
Toy train, diesel with crane car   WB83/11-12:60
Toy train, pull   PM75/11:142
Toy train, small wood   PM84/12:97
Toy train, steam   WB79/11-12:56
Toy train, tin can   WB75/11-12:39
Toy train, wood   HM82/12:60
Toy train, wood   PM79/11:122
Toy train, wood   WB83/9-10:62
Toy train locomotive, large   WB80/11-12:38

Toy train (plywood)   WS79/9:10
Toy tree house   PM80/8:92
Toy tricycle, toddler's   PM81/11:30
Toy tricycle, wood   PM80/11:128
Toy truck   PM77/11:136
Toy truck, double trailer tank   WB79/11-12:90
Toy truck, dump   PM76/6:116
Toy truck, dump   WB77/3-4:92
Toy truck, dump   WS84/9-10:4
Toy truck, man's steam powered   PM74/11:146
Toy truck, wood dump   PM84/12:96
Toy truck, wood log   PM84/12:96
Toy truck pedal car plans to order $9.95   PM82/8:62
Toy trucks, auto carrier and delivery van   FW79/11-12:64
Toy tug boat   WB82/11-12:90
Toy village, Matchbox   PM81/11:32
Toy wagon, antique (oak)   PM84/6:132
Toy wagon, little red   WB82/5-6:54
Toy wagon, PVC pipe   WB83/9-10:110
Toy wagon with seat (oak)   HM84/9:90
Toy whale, pull   PM75/11:143
Toy wheelbarrow   WB81/11-12:32
Toy wheelbarrow   WB82/5-6:52
Toy wheel cutter   FW80/9-10:34
Toy wheel maker   WB84/9-10:44
Toy wheels   FW81/9-10:16
Toy wheels   FW82/11-12:22
Toy wheels   FW83/5-6:6
Toy wheels   WB81/11-12:52
Toy wheels, wood   WB84/9-10:52
Toy wheels, wooden   FW82/5-6:20
Toy whimmydiddle, belt balancer   PM79/5:134
Toy whistle, sliding metal tubing   PM74/3:138
Toy whistle, wood   PM75/10:144
Toy working gnome windmill weathervane   WB82/9-10:116
Toy xylophone, Noel   PM79/11:122
Tracing table, lighted   WB80/5-6:68
Track lighting   HM75/1:36
Track lighting   HM78/9:84
Track lighting   PM76/9:100
Track lighting   WB75/11-12:85
Traditional desk   WB79/3-4:38
Trail bike carrier, car   PM73/6:83
Trailer, garden   HM84/3:99
Trailer, utility   HM84/3:98
Trailer, utility/boat   HM80/11:60
Trailer hitch weight scale   PM78/10:32
Trailer maintenance, utility   PM84/2:74
Train, diesel toy   WB79/11-12:23
Train, diesel with crane car toy   WB83/11-12:60

Train, pull toy   WB78/11-12:50
Train, small wood toy   PM84/12:97
Train, tin can toy   WB75/11-12:39
Train, toy   PM75/11:143
Train, toy (plywood)   WS79/9:10
Train, toy steam   WB79/11-12:56
Train, wooden toy   HM82/12:60
Train, wooden toy   PM79/11:122
Train, wooden toy   WB83/9-10:62
Train and animals, pull toy circus   PM72/12:108
Train Christmas tree decoration   PM79/12:82
Train jewelry box   HM82/12:63
Train locomotive, large toy   WB80/11-12:38
Train pull toy   PM75/11:142
Train weather vane   PM83/3:98
Train weather vane   WB73/9-10:40
Trammel, shop built   PM74/1:150
Trammel/compass, oval scribing   PM82/12:94
Trammel point, Dremel hand grinder   PM81/1:120
Transistor tester, electronic   PM74/3:124
Trap, animal   PM76/5:86
Trap connections, plumbing   HM78/9:90
Trash compactor, homebuilt   PM72/11:162
Tray, bent serving (walnut and mahogany)   FW77/6:62
Tray, beverage (redwood)   PM84/7:94
Tray, ceramic tile cheese   PM75/12:95
Tray, coin sorter   WS80/7:6
Tray, cracker   PM76/4:172
Tray, folding stand (ash and canvas)   FW82/9-10:68
Tray, glass top serving (mahogany)   HM84/9:110
Tray, hobby   HM84/11:78
Tray, inlaid serving   FW75/12:41
Tray, needlepoint serving   WB78/9-10:94
Tray, party (maple)   HM82/5-6:48
Tray, pastry   HM82/2:32
Tray, routed lazy Susan snack   WS83/7-8:16
Tray, serving (oak)   WS82/1:19
Tray, tea cart serving   WB83/9-10:4
Tray, walnut veneer serving   WB77/3-4:52
Tray, wine and cheese   HM83/5-6:91
Tray and butler's table   PM75/3:90
Tray and spice rack, serving   PM78/4:114
Tray coffee table (mahogany)   FW84/1-2:72
Tray kit, Colonial marquetry serving   WB77/7-8:71
Tray routing   WS80/7:11
Trays, stack of swinging   PM76/6:114
Trays, turned snack   WB73/7-8:48
Trays and table, plant (redwood)   FW84/1-2:43
Tray/wine rack   PM76/12:109
Treadle band saw   FW80/9-10:63

Treadle lathe   FW79/3-4:60
Treadle powered fretsaw   WB79/3-4:42
Treasure chest, pirate   WB80/11-12:30
Treasure chest jewelry box   PM75/12:97
Treasure chest jewelry box   WB73/9-10:47
Treated lumber   PM80/3:162
Treated lumber, treating with preservative   PM84/4:170
Tree care   HM84/3:123
Tree Christmas tree ornament   PM80/12:98
Tree felling   PM73/9:90
Tree felling, chain saw   PM79/10:126
Tree house, child's   PM80/8:92
Tree house, indoor bed and desk   WB72/3-4:32
Treeman's knot   PM80/2:6
Treen, English   FW76/12:58
Tree of life, candleholder   PM78/12:74
Tree planting   HM83/3:68
Tree repair   HM79/3:42
Trees, energy savers   HM79/5-6:38
Trees, lightning rod   HM78/7-8:64
Trees, repairing splitting   HM79/11:102
Trees, selecting and planting   HM84/9:54
Trees, solar landscaping   NS84/7-8:36
Tree stump chair   WB77/5-6:6
Tree turnings, lamp   WB77/3-4:118
Trellis, A-frame garden   HM79/3:30
Trellis, arch   PM81/8:88
Trellis, arched lattice garden   PM84/6:74
Trellis, bean   PM84/3:130
Trellis, bicycle wheel   NS80/2:96
Trellis, cucumber   PM84/3:114
Trellis, dowel and plant box   PM80/8:88
Trellis, folding   PM77/7:99
Trellis, garden   NS83/1:79
Trellis, garden   PM83/6:104
Trellis, plant pot wall   PM73/2:100
Trellis, porch   NS81/5-6:22
Trellis, rose   WB83/7-8:59
Trellis, string   PM80/3:158
Trellis, tomato   PM82/6:138
Trellis, wood freestanding   PM80/3:158
Trellis and walkway, overhead (redwood)   PM81/8:88
Trellis/bench (redwood)   HM84/5-6:36
Trellises   NS81/5-6:25
Trellis screen, deck   PM77/7:98
Trestle bench   WB83/9-10:32
Trestle coffee table   WB72/3-4:70
Trestle desk, Colonial (pine)   PM74/10:77
Trestle desk, six ft. (pine)   WB82/3-4:20
Trestle end table   WB72/3-4:70

Trestle table, Colonial $75   HM79/2:36
Trestle table, contemporary   WS82/9:12
Trestle table, desk/drawing   WS84/1-2:4
Trestle table, long or short   WB81/3-4:60
Trestle table, Shaker   PM76/7:101
Trestle table, Shaker Colonial (pine)   WS79/1:3
Trestle table, small turned   WB79/5-6:28
Trestle table and chairs, Contemporary   PM76/9:104
Trestle table bench   WS82/9:24
Trestle table design   FW83/9-10:42
Triangle marking   FW77/9:46
Triangular drop leaf table   FW80/11-12:61
Triangular drop leaf table   WB72/9-10:40
Triangular table, drop leaf   WB83/1-2:110
Trickle irrigation   PM79/3:140
Tricycle, toddler's   PM81/11:30
Tricycle, wood   PM80/11:128
Tricycle triplane, Fokker   WB83/7-8:26
Trim, room and door   HM75/8:44
Trimmer maintenance, hedge   HM82/3:64
Triplane tricycle, Fokker   WB83/7-8:26
Trivet, heart   HM82/2:32
Trivet, tiled (oak)   WS82/5:24
Trivets, molding   PM74/2:147
Trombe wall design   NS84/1:20
Trophy case, in-wall   WB78/7-8:28
Trowels   WB82/3-4:88
Truck, toy   PM77/11:136
Truck, toy   PM78/11:194
Truck, toy auto carrier and delivery van   FW79/11-12:64
Truck, toy double trailer tank   WB79/11-12:90
Truck, toy dump   HM83/12:68
Truck, toy dump   PM76/6:116
Truck, toy dump   WB77/3-4:92
Truck, toy dump   WS84/9-10:4
Truck, toy steam powered   PM74/11:146
Truck, toy three wheel kiddie   PM76/12:16
Truck, toy trailer   HM82/11:62
Truck, toy wooden dump   PM84/12:96
Truck, toy wooden log   PM84/12:96
Truck camper   PM73/3:178
Truck camper   WB79/9-10:86
Truck camper   WB79/5-6:46
Truck camper plans to order   PM78/1:76
Truck cap, wood and fiberglass   WB82/3-4:44
Truck pass through window, installing   PM84/3:60
Truck pedal car toy plans to order $9.95   PM82/8:62
Truck tailgate workbench   PM73/5:67
Truing stock   FW78/10:50
Trundle bed, boy's   PM79/9:112

Trundle bed/sofa, rollaway builtin   PM80/2:134
Trunks, alphabet pirate trunk Pa. Dutch   PM78/1:100
Trunks, restoring   HM79/1:80
Truss framing   PM79/6:164
Tub, hot   HM82/5-6:24
Tub, solar hot   PM79/3:137
Tub, stone walled   NS82/3:53
Tub, whirlpool   HM83/7-8:40
Tub and shower, fiberglass panels   HM76/9:40
Tub and shower kit   HM80/1:51
Tub and shower unit installation   HM74/11:54
Tub drain repair   HM77/3:32
Tubing projects, metal   PM74/3:138
Tub kit, hot   HM79/5-6:15
Tub kit, hot   WB81/7-8:46
Tubs, hot and spas   WB81/7-8:4
Tub to shower updating   WB83/1-2:94
Tubular table, modern routed wood   FW84/11-12:58
Tumbler, wind driven   WB77/9-10:46
Tumbler cabinet, rock   WB/L/7 0:??
Tung oil, polymerized   WS84/3-4:7
Tung oil finish   FW78/10:55
Turned balance scale, decorator   WB81/5-6:33
Turned barometer frame   WB73/9-10:39
Turned bed, Apolinere enameled   FW84/7-8:56
Turned bells, wooden guest   WB82/7-8:85
Turned bowl   FW82/1-2:54
Turned bowl, fruit   WB73/5-6:63
Turned bowl, inlaid fruit   PM75/2:116
Turned bowl bottoms   FW84/3-4:64
Turned bowl finish, salad   WB72/1-2:26
Turned bowls, boards   WB74/5-6:50
Turned boxes, small   FW77/12:72
Turned bud vase   PM74/11:102
Turned candelabra   WB77/5-6:36
Turned candleholder   PM74/11:102
Turned candleholder   PM77/11:146
Turned candleholder   PM78/11:198
Turned candleholder   PM79/5:290
Turned candleholder   WB77/9-10:41
Turned candleholder   WB79/11-12:112
Turned candleholder, adjustable   PM77/12:121
Turned candleholder, floor   WB75/9-10:59
Turned candleholder (walnut)   HM82/12:64
Turned candle sconce   PM80/3:134
Turned canister   WS81/3:14
Turned canister set, kitchen (walnut)   WS83/1-2:10
Turned chandelier   WB77/9-10:6
Turned chandelier, classical   PM74/2:158
Turned chess set, deluxe   WB76/11-12:78

Turned compote and candlestick   WB77/9-10:24
Turned desk caddy   WB81/11-12:24
Turned end table (walnut)   WB74/3-4:66
Turned floor lamp   WB84/5-6:38
Turned flute, six hole (cocobolo)   FW84/1-2:64
Turned fruit bowl   WS82/5:18
Turned hall tree, traditional   WB84/11-12:40
Turned handles, ferruled   WB74/9-10:42
Turned inlaid box   WB75/7-8:48
Turned laminated bowls   FW80/1-2:14
Turned lamp table, pedestal   WB83/11-12:66
Turned picture frame   WB82/9-10:75
Turned plant stand   WB76/11-12:42
Turned plant stand   WB79/1-2:70
Turned plant stand, ring and spindle   WB79/9-10:77
Turned plant stand, three legged   WB80/1-2:100
Turned plant stand, three legged   WB80/1-2:72
Turned popcorn bowl (koa)   WS83/1-2:24
Turned post, Lincoln newel stair rail   PM82/5:60
Turned quill pen ink pot   WB76/7-8:46
Turned quilting frame   WB82/9-10:84
Turned quilt rack   PM82/1:67
Turned recipe holder   WB79/7-8:28
Turned rocking chair, giant   WB74/1-2:32
Turned rolling pin   PM80/11:130
Turned salad bowl set   WB79/9-10:80
Turned serving tray, three tier   WB73/9-10:28
Turned sewing caddy   WB80/1-2:78
Turned sewing stand, English   WB83/9-10:74
Turned snack trays   WB73/7-8:48
Turned spiral candlesticks   PM72/10:178
Turned stair bannister   WB79/7-8:58
Turned table lamp   WB79/9-10:59
Turned table lighter   WB74/11-12:32
Turned tea set, miniature   WB79/5-6:58
Turned tilt top table, early American   WB75/11-12:30
Turned tool handles   PM82/2:106
Turned toy rattle   FW79/11-12:58
Turned toy top, (walnut)   PM80/11:128
Turned trestle table, small   WB79/5-6:28
Turned wall shelves   WB75/9-10:1
Turned whatnot shelf, corner Victorian   WB81/11-12:56
Turned wood bottle lamps   WB72/5-6:26
Turning, ornamental   FW76/9:46
Turning, spindle   FW78/9:60
Turning, split camel (walnut)   FW76/3:20
Turning, twist   FW82/3-4:92
Turning blank clamp   FW81/5-6:20
Turning bobbins   FW80/7-8:70
Turning bowl, inside   FW77/6:41

Turning bowls, Ethiopia   FW80/3-4:54
Turning bowls, giant   FW83/7-8:48
Turning bowls, grain designs   FW81/11-12:75
Turning bowls, matched set   FW83/1-2:70
Turning bowls, taped faceplate   FW79/5-6:14
Turning centerfinder, plexiglas   FW83/1-2:16
Turning checkered bowls   FW75/12:16
Turning chisel rack   WB80/9-10:107
Turning chisels   FW79/9-10:70
Turning chisels   WB75/5-6:61
Turning chisels, small   PM78/2:122
Turning chuck, bowl   FW84/9-10:10
Turning decoration   FW80/7-8:16
Turning duplicates   FW82/7-8:14
Turning Flageolet   FW77/9:80
Turning flutes   FW83/7-8:12
Turning fundamentals   WB79/5-6:33
Turning gauge, duplicate   FW80/11-12:24
Turning gauges   FW79/11-12:74
Turning gauges, go/no go   FW79/11-12:21
Turning goblet (cherry or koa)   WS82/9.4
Turning goblets   FW83/1-2:72
Turning gouge, bowl   FW76/12:55
Turning green bowls   FW76/6:37
Turning head, tapered   FW78/9:16
Turning inlaid bowl   FW79/1-2:69
Turning jig, drill press   PM83/12:106
Turning laminated bowls   FW78/3:70
Turning laminated bowls   FW78/10:48
Turning laminated spindles   FW81/7-8:52
Turning lamp, tree   WB77/3-4:118
Turning lamp bases   FW80/11-12:24
Turning long tapers   FW79/11-12:22
Turning miniatures   PM82/6:182
Turning music boxes   FW84/9-10:78
Turning off-center legs   FW79/9-10:73
Turning ringed objects   FW80/7-8:16
Turnings, geometric   FW81/7-8:54
Turnings, hollow   FW79/5-6:62
Turnings, inlaid   FW81/7-8:56
Turnings, radial arm saw   WB76/11-12:92
Turning scratch pattern   WB77/3-4:40
Turning sculpture, disc sander   FW83/11-12:66
Turning segments   FW80/3-4:56
Turning skew   FW82/9-10:70
Turning spalted wood bowls   FW78/6:54
Turning spindles   FW84/11-12:81
Turning spindles, thin   FW80/7-8:70
Turning splated wood   FW77/6:50
Turning squares or checkered parts   PM82/3:76

Turnings without screw holes   FW80/11-12:82
Turning tall slender objects   WB82/3-4:66
Turning thin bowls   FW80/7-8:60
Turning tips   FW79/11-12:72
Turning tips   FW82/11-12:91
Turning tips   PM79/5:144
Turning tips, wood   FW84/1-2:40
Turning tool handles   PM83/12:104
Turning tools   FW83/5-6:92
Turning tool sharpening   WS82/5:22
Turning without lathe   WB82/1-2:68
Turning with PEG   FW79/11-12:68
Turning wood, metal lathe   FW82/5-6:98
Turntable, grooming bonsai   PM80/3:174
Turntable, TV   PM74/2:142
Turntable maintenance, stereo   PM83/12:61
Turtle miniature box, band sawed   PM84/5:90
TV, closed circuit security   HM79/7-8:54
TV, giant screen from kit or scratch   PM80/2:107
TV antenna, installation   HM77/4:40
TV antenna, replacing broken   PM83/1:28
TV antenna in attic   HM80/10:58
TV antenna installation   PM73/10:104
TV antennas   PM79/6:102
TV bed, contemporary platform (maple)   PM84/5:92
TV cabinet, Colonial dry sink   WB84/3-4:122
TV cabinet, rolltop glass door   WS83/1-2:14
TV cabinet, uses for old   WB84/9-10:63
TV cabinet and firewood storage   WB81/11-12:102
TV cart   WB78/5-6:40
TV commercial silencer   PM80/1:162
TV entertainment center, contemporary   PM83/1:108
TV reception interference   PM80/6:88
TV repair   HM81/11:62
TV stand, contemporary   HM81/9:84
TV tray tables (oak)   WS81/7:4
TV turntable   PM74/2:142
TV/video recorder stand   WB83/9-10:138
Twain lap desk (mahogany)   PM83/10:100
Twist carving, table saw   FW82/3-4:94
Twisted lumber   FW80/5-6:16
Twist turning   FW82/3-4:92
Two board chair (maple)   FW81/7-8:44
Typewriter stand and cabinet   WB72/3-4:36
Typing table drawing board   WB81/5-6:4
UL   WB79/1-2:32
Ultralight airplane kits   PM82/5:94
Ultralight airplane plans to order $50   PM81/11:110
Umbrella table and chair unit (redwood)   HM83/4:122
Underground home   HM80/2:12

Underground home   HM82/11:120
Underground home   HM83/1:30
Underground homes   HM80/7-8:44
Underground homes   NS84/11-12:6
Underground house   NS80/10:44
Underground house   NS81/5-6:60
Underground house   NS82/1:18
Underground house   NS82/5-6:84
Underground house   NS83/9:98
Underground house   NS84/1:46
Underground house   WB79/3-4:92
Underground house   WB81/1-2:80
Underground house, owner built   NS82/1:23
Underground house, Texas   NS82/1:27
Underground house, waterproofing   NS82/1:30
Underground house guidelines   NS80/2:74
Underground house roof support   NS82/1:33
Underground houses   WB79/1-2:104
Underground houses, twelve   PM80/5:114
Underground tubes   NS81/11-12:48
Upholstered chair   WB76/7-8:32
Upholstered sofa, Chippendale (walnut)   FW84/11-12:60
Upholstered sofa and chair   WB78/1-2:52
Upholstered sofa love seat   WB82/11-12:80
Upholstered wing chair   WB80/9-10:6
Upholstering, chair   HM79/1:82
Upholstering, chair   PM77/11:128
Upholstering, chair seat   HM83/4:18
Utensil caddy, picnic   WB84/3-4:66
Utensil rack, dowel kitchen   PM84/1:112
Utensils, carved kitchen   WB82/1-2:32
Utility/boat trailer   HM80/11:60
Utility post cover, barrel planter   WB79/11-12:38
Utility room remodeling   PM77/1:92
Utility room/shop, garage   HM83/12:26
Utility shed   NS84/5-6:90
Utility sink   HM79/11:107
Utility trailer   HM84/3:98
Utility trailer maintenance   PM84/2:74
Vacation home, small   HM82/7-8:87
Vacation home projects, five   PM81/7:92
Vacation home security   PM73/9:94
Vacuum back pack, shop   WB77/3-4:96
Vacuum cleaner repair   PM75/12:86
Vacuum dolly, tip proof   PM80/5:55
Vacuum extension   WB77/7-8:33
Vacuum gauge manometer   HM81/3:93
Vacuum press for veneers, shop built   FW79/5-6:52
Vacuum system, built-in   HM83/12:48
Vacuum system, central   HM78/3:26

Vacuum system, central   WB83/3-4:32
Vacuum track, shop   WB74/7-8:56
Valentine gifts, four   PM80/2:124
Valet, dresser top   PM75/12:97
Van camper   PM72/5:154
Van camper plans to order, $15   PM79/3:48
Van conversion, camper   WB73/3-4:56
Vanity, bathroom   HM75/9:40
Vanity, bathroom   HM82/11:54
Vanity, bathroom   WB76/11-12:64
Vanity, bathroom (redwood)   WB77/11-12:20
Vanity, drawers   WB77/5-6:16
Vanity, shop built bathroom   WB79/1-2:52
Vanity, two basin mirrored door island   WB81/9-10:46
Vanity, well lighted   PM74/1:71
Vanity mirror   WS82/11-12:24
Vanity mirror, Mary Lincoln's   PM78/2:102
Vanity/shaving mirror   WS80/7:5
Vans, customizing mini   PM84/7:88
Vapor barrier, ceiling   NS84/9:14
Vapor barrier and insulation   WB78/1-2:32
Vapor barriers   NS80/5-6:71
Vapor barriers, paint on   NS84/4:62
Varnish, rubbed on   FW84/3-4:39
Varnish, seedlac   FW80/1-2:68
Varnish, water based   FW84/7-8:65
Varnishes, early   FW82/7-8:54
Varnish finish   PM78/2:134
Varnish finish, outdoor   WB73/9-10:22
Varnishing   HM83/4:110
Varnish/oil finish   FW79/11-12:76
Vase, cut glass bottle   PM72/12:104
Vase, turned squares or checkered   PM82/3:76
Vases, free form   PM77/11:140
V-block, better   FW78/3:16
V-block clamp   PM82/8:89
Vegetable bin, country kitchen   HM82/9:58
Velvetizing   PM74/11:158
Veneer   FW76/9:33
Veneer, bench press   FW84/7-8:41
Veneer, repairing curved   WB84/3-4:40
Veneer boxes, oyster shell   FW79/11-12:66
Veneer chair   FW79/5-6:52
Veneer corner cutting   FW78/10:4
Veneer cutting jig   FW84/7-8:64
Veneering   FW84/5-6:36
Veneering   PM77/5:110
Veneering   WB81/5-6:24
Veneering, hammer   FW78/3:52
Veneering, table   WB80/1-2:80

Veneering cylinders   FW78/9:15
Veneering table tops   WB76/11-12:118
Veneering tips   FW83/9-10:74
Veneer knife check repair   FW78/9:83
Veneer laying   FW84/7-8:37
Veneer Parsons table   FW78/6:70
Veneer press, shop built vacuum   FW79/5-6:52
Veneer repair   HM83/1:54
Veneer repairs   HM80/3:80
Veneer strip lamp   WS79/3:9
Veneer strip thicknesser   FW78/9:18
Veneer trimmer   FW77/6:16
Veneer trimming   FW78/3:16
Venetian blinds   HM79/1:54
Venetian blinds, repair   HM77/11-12:68
Ventilation, home   HM81/11:82
Venting heaters   NS82/10:66
Vertical blinds, covering   HM77/10:74
Vestibulus, milling   PM83/11:100
Victorian bench, fireplace   HM80/11:32
Victorian china cabinet, curved glass (oak)   WB84/9-10:56
Victorian curio stand, mirrored   WB84/5-6:46
Victorian doll house/jewelry chest   WB79/1-2:113
Victorian hall butler (oak)   HM83/11:24
Victorian kitchen and bath, remodeling   HM82/7-8:28
Victorian porch, lattice side   HM84/5-6:54
Victorian shaving mirror, wall hung (pine)   PM83/2:108
Victorian shaving stand with mirror (oak)   PM83/2:108
Victorian sideboard, marble top (oak)   PM83/5:102
Victorian whatnot shelf, turned corner   WB81/11-12:56
Video/audio cable tester   PM84/3:154
Video camera kit   PM81/5:22
Video game cabinet   PM84/3:110
Video recorder/TV stand   WB83/9-10:138
Vietnamese planes   FW82/3-4:96
Village, Matchbox   PM81/11:32
Village mantel Christmas decorations   PM81/12:114
Vinyl floor, seamless   HM75/10:50
Vinyl floor, seamless   PM75/9:100
Vinyl floor, sheet   HM84/9:45
Vinyl flooring   WB84/3-4:86
Vinyl floors   HM78/1:43
Vinyl floors   HM79/1:18
Vinyl gutters   WB80/7-8:72
Vinyl pool   HM76/6:40
Vinyl pool bottom   HM72/6:54
Vinyl siding, installing   PM84/4:126
Violin case   FW83/7-8:20
Violin making   FW79/3-4:40
Vise   FW80/11-12:30

Vise, auxiliary   FW80/11-12:21
Vise, bench   FW82/11-12:24
Vise, bicycle repair   PM83/7:96
Vise, hand saw sharpening   FW84/11-12:8
Vise, horizontal   FW81/5-6:18
Vise, leg   FW78/6:16
Vise, leg   FW80/9-10:66
Vise, saw blade   WB75/7-8:41
Vise, saw sharpening   FW77/9:57
Vise, sharpening circular saws   WB80/1-2:73
Vise, shoulder   FW80/9-10:68
Vise, welding   PM81/10:37
Vise, wooden workbench   FW80/9-10:69
Vise, workbench end   PM79/5:40
Vise, workbench top   PM77/2:60
Vise clamp   PM81/4:121
Vise drum stand   WB79/9-10:105
Vise extension   PM78/4:130
Vise fixtures, machinists'   WB79/9-10:94
Vise handle, long   PM81/5:51
Vises, workbench   HM78/11-12:83
Vise stand   WB76/11-12:48
Volkswagon Beetle Woody plans to order, $14.95   PM83/7:137
Voltmeter, auto   PM80/5:42
Voltmeter/burglar alarm, auto   PM82/3:24
Volt ohm meter   HM79/7-8:24
Vulcan fibre board   WB79/1-2:114
VW Beetle Woody plans to order, $14.95   PM83/7:137
Waffle iron repair   HM82/1:78
Wagon, antique toy (oak)   PM84/6:132
Wagon, horse drawn model hearse   WB73/5-6:28
Wagon, little red toy   WB82/5-6:54
Wagon, mower pulled garden   WB78/5-6:80
Wagon, PVC pipe toy   WB83/9-10:110
Wagon, toy with seat (oak)   HM84/3:99
Wagon and horse, toy   FW80/11-12:61
Wagon seat chest   WB75/3-4:60
Wagon seat coffee table   WB72/9-10:44
Wagon toy box, circus   WB80/11-12:64
Wagon wheel, spoked   WB76/3-4:72
Wainscot, wall   PM84/6:80
Wainscoting   HM79/11:65
Wainscoting, raised panel   WB79/3-4:16
Wainscoting chair rail   PM84/6:83
Walk and driveway repair, concrete   HM75/3:24
Walking beam saw   FW80/9-10:60
Walking cane, ladies   WB78/7-8:55
Walks and patio, paving blocks   HM80/5-6:94
Walks and patios, brick   PM77/5:104
Walkway and overhead trellis (redwood)   PM81/8:88

Walkway lamp   HM84/3:52
Walkways and decks   HM84/5-6:45
Wall, broken concrete retaining   HM76/9:38
Wall, curved   PM84/3:122
Wall, decorative removable   WB77/1-2:82
Wall, draped   WB77/9-10:18
Wall, insulated stone   NS82/3:54
Wall, parquet   HM81/9:76
Wall, removal   NS80/2:71
Wall, removal   WB75/5-6:17
Wall, removing bearing   PM74/8:146
Wall, sky   HM82/12:46
Wall, solar   NS81/1:82
Wall, stone retaining   HM82/4:100
Wallboard   HM75/8:34
Wallboard   HM83/7-8:76
Wallboard   WB78/3-4:84
Wallboard   WB80/9-10:108
Wallboard, installing   PM81/7:32
Wallboard, taping   WB73/5-6:16
Wallboard elevator   HM74/4:43
Wallboard installation   HM77/7-8:22
Wallboard patching   PM79/12:95
Wallboard patching   PM81/6:104
Wallboard repair   HM77/5-6:24
Wallboard repair   HM83/2:54
Wallboard repairs   HM84/3:82
Wall bookcase   HM76/4:28
Wall bookcase, built-in   WB80/1-2:87
Wall bookcase unit   PM74/4:166
Wall cabinet, bathroom rolltop (redwood)   WS81/9:10
Wall cabinet, contemporary   HM84/2:70
Wall cabinet, spool display   WS83/3-4:4
Wall cabinet unit   PM82/4:123
Wall clock, octagonal frame   WS80/11:8
Wall clock, round   WS83/11-12:10
Wall clock, schoolhouse (oak)   WS82/5:4
Wallcovering, selecting   HM84/9:60
Wallcoverings   HM82/10:38
Wall coverings   NS80/9:40
Wallcoverings   WB80/1-2:54
Wall decoration, three dimensional   HM75/2:34
Wall decoration graphic   PM78/11:130
Wall decorations, wood strips   HM76/2:26
Wall desk, drop leaf   PM73/9:73
Wall/desk clock (walnut and maple)   WS80/7:4
Wall display case, wooden hinged (oak)   WS80/5:11
Wall dressing table   HM79/12:68
Wall entertainment unit   HM81/12:26
Wall fasteners   PM76/9:120

Wall flowerpot planter   WB79/11-12:89
Wall framing   WB78/1-2:40
Wall graphics, tape   PM82/4:166
Wall hanger, duck head   PM80/8:51
Wall heater, installing   PM81/9:142
Wall hung cabinet, raised panel (plywood)   WS80/3:7
Wall hutch, Colonial   WS81/11:16
Wall insulation   HM78/9:22
Wall lamps   HM73/2:56
Wall lantern, English candle   WS84/11-12:16
Wall light bracket, adjustable   WS80/5:4
Wall mirror   NS80/11-12:62
Wall mirror, Chippendale (mahogany)   PM83/7:52
Wall mirror, contemporary   WS84/7-8:20
Wall mirror/coat rack, antique (oak)   WS83/3-4:18
Wall murals   HM78/1:54
Wall painting graphics kits   HM78/1:13
Wall paneling   HM75/8:38
Wall paneling   HM78/1:16
Wall paneling   WB76/9-10:58
Wall pantry   WB75/7-8:34
Wallpaper   HM74/6:38
Wallpaper   HM78/1:48
Wallpaper   HM80/10:104
Wallpaper   WB75/11-12:46
Wall paper, buying and using   PM78/1:96
Wallpaper, hanging   NS82/7-8:64
Wallpaper, hanging   PM74/1:78
Wallpaper, professional removal   HM79/9:64
Wallpaper, removing   HM73/10:38
Wallpaper, roll on painted pattern   PM78/4:164
Wallpapering   HM83/10:54
Wallpaper pasting board   PM81/6:24
Wallpaper remodeling   HM80/1:56
Wallpaper squares   HM76/6:32
Wall partition, movable   WB77/9-10:58
Wall phone message center   PM73/12:156
Wall planter   WB79/1-2:110
Wall plant pot trellis   PM73/2:100
Wall plaques, fish   HM80/11:56
Wall rack, kitchen   WB74/5-6:62
Wall room divider   PM75/2:84
Walls, carpeted   NS81/1:70
Walls, decorating with wood   HM84/11:59
Walls, hanging anything   PM80/4:164
Walls, load bearing   HM81/1:72
Walls, moving   HM84/11:26
Walls, repairing or hiding   HM82/10:48
Walls, retaining   PM73/8:88
Walls, water leak damage repair   HM79/5-6:62

Walls and doors, planed paneled   FW79/9-10:84
Walls and floors, insulating   NS80/9:90
Wall sculpture, wooden butterfly   PM82/2:60
Wall shelf   PM79/2:133
Wall shelf   WB78/3-4:4
Wall shelf, diamond   WB76/9-10:13
Wall shelf, dovetail tongue and groove (oak)   WS82/3:20
Wall shelf, latticework   WB79/1-2:48
Wall shelf, small   WB84/5-6:52
Wall shelf with drawer, Colonial   WB84/11-12:118
Wall shelves   PM84/7:132
Wall shelves, turned   WB75/9-10:1
Wall shelves, wood   WB84/1-2:43
Wall shelving unit   PM74/3:136
Wall spice rack, latticework   WB79/9-10:84
Wall stenciling   HM83/10:60
Wall stencils   HM76/1:52
Wall storage modular units   WB82/3-4:90
Wall storage unit   HM73/10:34
Wall storage unit   HM76/8:42
Wall storage unit   HM80/9:19
Wall storage unit, dowel   HM80/3:48
Wall storage unit, kitchen cabinets   PM75/12:70
Wall storage unit, movable   HM79/12:20
Wall storage unit, wood panel   PM72/1:122
Wall storage unit/desk   HM77/4:19
Wall switch plates, hiding   PM78/5:123
Wall towel rack   WB79/5-6:66
Wall unit, contemporary   PM84/4:136
Wall unit, entertainment   WB84/9-10:66
Wall units, modular   WS84/5-6:8
Wall wainscot   PM84/6:80
Wall wainscoting, raised panel   WB79/3-4:16
Wall workshop   PM83/4:126
Walnut, finishing   WB78/1-2:98
Walnut and mahogany serving tray, bent   FW77/6:62
Walnut and maple desk/wall clock   WS80/7:4
Walnut and maple fishing net, laminated   FW80/1-2:56
Walnut and maple kitchen knife case   WS80/7:7
Walnut and maple recipe box   WS80/7:8
Walnut and maple table, butcher block   WB84/11-12:46
Walnut and plexiglas bookcase   WB81/7-8:44
Walnut armchair, high back 17th century   WB78/3-4:32
Walnut armoire   PM81/3:140
Walnut bureau, four drawer 1848   WB84/5-6:74
Walnut Butler's tray table   WS81/3:10
Walnut cabinet, four panel door chair side   WS82/11-12:14
Walnut camel, turning split   FW76/3:20
Walnut candleholders, turned   HM82/12:64
Walnut canister set, turned   WS83/1-2:10

Walnut chair, Lincoln armless cane rocking   PM84/2:60
Walnut chest of drawers   WB84/7-8:57
Walnut chisel case   WS82/11-12:20
Walnut clock, mantel wood and crystal   HM84/11:70
Walnut clock, modern pendulum   HM83/1:82
Walnut cradle, antique   HM78/11-12:84
Walnut desk, cabriole legs   WB84/11-12:48
Walnut end table, turned   WB74/3-4:66
Walnut footstool, Colonial   PM75/1:110
Walnut jewelry box, contemporary   WS82/11-12:20
Walnut lamp, floor   WB77/5-6:68
Walnut/mahogany drop leaf Pembroke table   WS81/3:4
Walnut nestled tables, inlaid   WS83/7-8:12
Walnut nightstand, traditional   WB84/3-4:80
Walnut oil bowl finish   FW83/1-2:71
Walnut or cherry music box   WS79/11:6
Walnut or fir kitchen serving cart   FW77/3:58
Walnut or mahogany table, Butler's tray   WB76/1-2:41
Walnut or rosewood boxes, hexagonal   FW82/3-4:63
Walnut puzzle, carved little man   FW76/6:56
Walnut sofa, upholstered Chippendale   FW84/11-12:60
Walnut table, glass top coffee   HM81/1:56
Walnut table chessboard/coffee   WB84/1-2:4
Walnut telephone chest   FW76/3:56
Walnut toy top   PM80/11:128
Walnut veneer serving tray   WB77/3-4:52
Walnut wardrobe   PM81/3:140
Wardrobe (walnut)   PM81/3:140
Warm/cool room   WB78/5-6:4
Warming plate, cup and bowls   WB83/11-12:102
Warped floor repair   HM83/2:65
Warped furniture repair   HM83/1:56
Washer, plumbing for   HM84/2:65
Washer, replacing belt   PM84/5:62
Washer and dryer installation   HM84/2:47
Washer and dryer laundry room, built-in   HM77/10:20
Washer outlet box installation   HM84/3:18
Washer repair   HM78/2:48
Washer repair   NS80/4:68
Washer repair   PM73/1:66
Washer repair, solid state   PM79/8:102
Washer repairs   HM84/9:96
Washer repairs   NS84/1:24
Washstand, harp rack Colonial   WB82/3-4:67
Waste basket, contemporary   WB81/1-2:6
Wastebasket, hardboard   WB81/9-10:34
Waste basket, octagonal (maple)   WS80/1:5
Watch, pocket grandfather case   WB76/9-10:62
Watch stand, lighted   PM72/6:148
Water, potable   NS80/4:24

Water, rain cistern   NS80/4:34
Water alarm, basement   PM80/7:56
Water alarms, basement   PM82/4:84
Waterbed   WB81/9-10:86
Waterbeds   NS81/11-12:11
Water check valve, hot   NS83/3:54
Water cistern, above ground   HM82/9:60
Water closet repair   NS82/4:48
Water closet repair   PM83/11:59
Water conservation   NS80/7-8:50
Water damage, cleaning up   HM83/3:88
Waterer, rabbit hutch   WB81/7-8:12
Water filter, carbon   NS80/4:33
Water filter, installation   PM78/5:136
Water filter, refrigerated   PM84/11:48
Water filters   HM82/11:30
Water filters   NS83/10:82
Water gilding, gold   FW84/5-6:82
Water hammer noises   HM79/9:109
Water hammer noises   NS83/5:04
Water heater, batch solar   NS80/10:96
Water heater, batch solar   NS81/7-8:27
Water heater, buying solar   PM80/6:84
Water heater, drain back solar   NS81/3:46
Water heater, heat pump   NS83/4:54
Water heater, heat pump   NS83/9:12
Water heater, heat pump   PM83/1:92
Water heater, heat pump   WB83/7-8:78
Water heater, installation   HM79/1:38
Water heater, installing solar   PM79/9:132
Water heater, insulate gas   NS83/2:60
Water heater, insulating   HM76/10:50
Water heater, insulation kit   HM80/2:36
Water heater, simple solar   PM82/4:164
Water heater, solar   NS80/7-8:56
Water heater, solar   NS81/7-8:22
Water heater, solar   NS83/7-8:10
Water heater, solar   PM81/11:64
Water heater, solar   PM83/1:92
Water heater, solar batch   HM81/1:76
Water heater, solar batch   NS83/5-6:36
Water heater, solar part 1   WB80/11-12:88
Water heater, solar part 2   WB81/1-2:68
Water heater, solar tankless hybrid   HM82/4:94
Water heater, solar tests   NS81/5-6:32
Water heater, tankless   HM83/5-6:16
Water heater, tankless   HM84/12:50
Water heater, tankless   NS81/3:69
Water heater, thermosiphon solar   NS80/11-12:51
Water heater, three   HM84/12:50

Water heater, well water assisted   PM83/1:92
Water heater and pipe insulation   HM77/10:46
Water heater and radiator, fireplace   HM74/3:38
Water heater maintenance, electric   HM73/10:48
Water heater repair   NS84/3:26
Water heater repair   PM73/9:84
Water heater sediment cleaner   PM82/4:138
Water heating, solar kit   NS82/9:56
Water heating cost reduction   NS80/9:63
Water leak damage repair   HM79/5-6:62
Water leaks, basement   PM80/2:163
Water level   PM76/3:187
Water pipe noises, correcting   PM84/1:72
Water pipes, thawing frozen   PM83/11:60
Water power, miniature hydroelectric plant   PM81/2:122
Waterproofers, basement   NS81/4:38
Waterproofing underground houses   NS82/1:30
Water saving shower heads   NS84/2:62
Water source heat pump   PM80/9:155
Water stain finishes   WB72/5-6:56
Water stains, removing   WB73/11-12:44
Water still, solar   PM82/3:98
Water supply valves, gate and globe   HM79/2:72
Water treatments   NS84/9:58
Water wall, solar   NS81/10:32
Wax, emulsified   FW80/11-12:95
Wax French polishing finishing   FW82/3-4:73
Weatherizing   HM72/12:48
Weatherizing   HM73/2:44
Weatherizing   HM74/2:38
Weatherizing   HM76/1:46
Weatherizing   HM77/9:16
Weatherizing   HM78/9:44
Weatherizing   HM78/3:80
Weatherizing   HM79/9:46
Weatherizing   HM83/10:96
Weatherizing   NS80/4:76
Weatherizing   NS81/10:44
Weatherizing   NS82/10:52
Weatherizing   NS84/10:56
Weatherizing   PM75/10:90
Weatherizing   PM76/10:112
Weatherizing, air leak detector   PM79/2:194
Weatherizing, fan air leak detector   HM81/10:60
Weatherizing, home   PM78/9:142
Weatherizing, home   PM84/9:84
Weatherizing, home   WB80/1-2:4
Weatherizing, mobile home   NS80/9:36
Weatherizing crawl space   HM84/9:86
Weatherizing doors/windows   PM78/9:158

Weatherizing electrical system   HM80/2:92
Weatherizing skylights   PM82/12:148
Weatherizing tips   HM84/10:86
Weatherizing tips   PM83/10:48
Weatherizing windows   HM80/9:66
Weatherizing windows   PM83/4:132
Weather station   WB74/7-8:32
Weather stripping   HM76/11:48
Weatherstripping   NS83/1:34
Weatherstripping   WB78/11-12:121
Weathervane, flying duck   PM72/3:144
Weather vane, ship   WB76/3-4:88
Weather vane, train   WB73/9-10:40
Weather vanes   NS80/7-8:66
Weathervanes, biplane or rooster   HM83/3:82
Weather vanes, deer ship Indian or train   PM83/3:98
Weathervane windmill, working gnome   WB82/9-10:116
Weaving, Punjabi   WB78/1-2:68
Weaving loom   PM77/2:118
Wedged loom joint   FW82/5:116
Wedged mortise and tenon joints   WS81/5:12
Wedge/tenon joint   FW79/9-10:10
Weed trimmer maintenance   HM82/3:62
Weed trimmers   NS82/7-8:12
Weed trimmers   PM79/8:162
Weight bench, exercise   PM73/12:152
Welding, arc   HM81/12:56
Welding, electric arc   WB80/9-10:114
Welding, gas and arc   HM81/1:10
Welding, introduction to arc   NS80/3:83
Welding and cutting, gas   WB80/11-12:102
Welding cabinet, arc   HM83/9:111
Welding kits   NS80/3:12
Welding table   NS80/3:87
Welding table   WB80/11-12:105
Welding tips   PM74/1:144
Welding vise   PM81/10:37
Well, barbecue   PM80/8:130
Well, decorative cistern   WB79/3-4:56
Well, gutter downspout   WB79/9-10:44
Well water assisted water heater   PM83/1:92
Whale chair, child's   WB78/11-12:74
Whale napkin ring, carved   WB80/1-2:24
Whale pull toy   PM75/11:143
Whatnot, corner   WB84/3-4:88
Whatnot shelf, Colonial   PM73/5:96
Whatnot shelf, tile accents   WB82/3-4:96
Whatnot shelf, turned corner Victorian   WB81/11-12:56
Wheel, potter's   WB73/5-6:32
Wheel, simple spinning   PM79/9:104

Wheel, spinning   WB83/3-4:6
Wheel, spinning (cherry)   FW78/6:40
Wheel, spoked wagon   WB76/3-4:72
Wheelbarrow   PM77/3:98
Wheelbarrow, toy   WB81/11-12:32
Wheelbarrow, toy   WB82/5-6:52
Wheel blocks, auto   HM84/5-6:150
Wheelchair ramps   HM84/2:10
Wheel maker, toy   WB84/9-10:44
Wheels, toy   FW83/5-6:6
Wheels, toy   WB81/11-12:52
Wheels, toy wood   WB84/9-10:52
Wheels, wooden   FW82/5-6:20
Wheel tools   PM81/7:84
Wheel truing jig, bicycle   PM83/7:96
Whetstones   FW78/9:68
Whirlpool bath   WB83/1-2:49
Whirlpool tub   HM83/7-8:40
Whirly toy, antique   PM83/5:207
Whistle, sliding metal tubing   PM74/3:138
Whistle, wood   WB81/11-12:96
Whistle toy, wood   PM75/10:144
Whole house fan   HM79/5-6:43
Wicker furniture, restoring   HM84/5-6:123
Wicker repair   PM81/8:93
Wildflower and grass lawn   NS80/5-6:20
Williamsburg mirror   WB79/11-12:138
Willow furniture, rustic patio   HM84/4:122
Winch, auto   PM81/3:128
Wind, increase building resistance   WB84/5-6:6
Wind chimes, metal tubes   WB83/3-4:59
Wind driven tumbler, rock   WB77/9-10:46
Windmill energy   NS80/11-12:24
Windmill weathervane, working gnome   WB82/9-10:116
Wind noises, auto   PM73/12:146
Window, aluminum storm   HM76/9:42
Window, bay   WB79/7-8:18
Window, bay installation   HM84/4:49
Window, bay replacement   WB82/9-10:70
Window, broken sash cord replacement   HM83/2:84
Window, building inside storm   HM79/2:60
Window, double pane   NS80/10:39
Window, framing basement   PM84/3:176
Window, glass block   WB72/9-10:25
Window, greenhouse   HM81/9:28
Window, indoor storm   HM76/11:36
Window, installing bay   PM84/4:130
Window, insulating   NS80/10:26
Window, latticework   PM80/6:105
Window, lattlicework   WB79/9-10:14

Window, Persian   WB77/1-2:65
Window, pickup pass through installation   PM84/3:60
Window, plastic covering   NS80/10:34
Window, reglazing   PM84/9:118
Window, reglazing storm   HM73/2:38
Window, repairing glass   HM84/10:24
Window, replacement   WB80/7-8:56
Window, replacing   HM74/3:42
Window, replacing   HM80/5-6:62
Window, replacing double hung   HM83/9:40
Window, replacing double hung   PM84/4:133
Window, replacing old   WB84/7-8:40
Window, replacing with energy efficient   WB84/7-8:16
Window, restoring sash   HM82/1:72
Window, sealing   WB77/1-2:20
Window, shading   NS84/3:46
Window, stained glass   NS81/9:69
Window, stained glass   PM76/6:110
Window, storm   NS84/10:62
Window, storm   WB74/9-10:58
Window, storm   WB80/1-2:104
Window, weatherizing   PM83/4:132
Window and door drip caps   NS84/11-12:26
Window and screen repair, storm   HM72/4:42
Window and screens, storm   WB81/9-10:100
Window awnings, canvas   HM82/5-6:92
Window blinds, vertical   WB80/5-6:64
Window box, outdoor   PM82/3:132
Window box, solar hot air   NS82/10:24
Window channel replacement   WB74/11-12:43
Window/door, weatherizing   PM78/9:158
Window films   NS84/5-6:56
Window frame repair   NS83/4:36
Window glass, efficient   NS81/9:43
Window glass, replacing   HM79/4:74
Window glass repair   HM77/7-8:58
Window glass repair   HM83/2:52
Window glass repair   PM73/2:152
Window glass repair, storm   PM83/9:114
Window glass replacement   HM73/12:44
Window greenhouse   HM77/7-8:49
Window greenhouse   HM82/4:64
Window greenhouse   NS82/3:45
Window greenhouse   PM75/9:54
Window greenhouse   WB79/5-6:56
Window grillwork   WB74/5-6:48
Window installation   HM75/9:46
Window installation, solar   NS82/10:31
Window insulation   NS80/10:36
Window insulation   NS82/2:8

Window insulation   PM81/4:175
Window insulation   PM81/9:24
Window insulation, low cost   WB81/11-12:72
Window lambrequins, covered frame   HM77/11-12:75
Window moisture damage repair   HM83/2:48
Window planter, aluminum and glass   PM79/6:60
Window planter, wrought iron   HM78/4:38
Window plant shelf   PM78/12:138
Window plant shelf   PM81/2:136
Window putty removing   HM73/4-5:66
Window putty repair   PM79/4:151
Window remodeling   WB75/7-8:62
Window remodeling   WB79/9-10:14
Window repair, plexiglas   HM77/10:34
Window repair, storm   NS84/9:32
Window replacement   HM76/3:36
Window replacement   PM78/9:160
Window replacement, plexiglas   PM72/3:162
Window screen repair   HM77/7-8:46
Window screen repair   HM83/2:48
Window seat, solar   NS84/1:36
Window seat/firewood box pass through   NS84/1:16
Window security   NS83/3:16
Window security bars   PM83/4:166
Window security grate   NS83/9:38
Window seed starter, cantilevered   NS80/3:53
Window shades   WB79/9-10:52
Window shades, insulating   NS80/10:30
Window shading   NS80/3:38
Window shading   PM81/7:88
Window shelf, over   WB77/9-10:22
Window shutter, external roll-up   HM80/9:82
Window shutter, thermal   NS83/10:40
Window shutter insulation   WB78/5-6:86
Window shutters   NS80/10:61
Window shutters, indoor raised panel   PM80/3:128
Window shutters, Shoji indoor   WB80/3-4:42
Window sizing, solar   NS84/10:52
Window storage unit   HM74/9:36
Window trim   WB80/7-8:64
Window trim finishing   WB82/11-12:108
Window weatherizing   HM80/9:66
Wind power   NS83/4:44
Wind power   PM78/5:116
Wind protection construction tips   PM80/8:66
Windshield repair   HM82/10:24
Windsor chair   WB79/1-2:66
Windsurfer plans to order, $7   PM81/5:110
Windsurfing   HM82/5-6:78
Wine and cheese tray   HM83/5-6:91

Wine and food cellar, underground   HM83/9:114
Wine and glass rack, plywood   HM80/12:18
Wine bottle rack   PM80/8:88
Wine case   WB76/3-4:54
Wine glass/bottle rack   WB83/9-10:124
Wine glass rack   PM77/11:144
Wine/glass rack   WB83/1-2:99
Wine glass rack, hanging   WB83/3-4:45
Winemaker's press   HM81/2:32
Wine rack   HM81/9:104
Wine rack   PM75/11:173
Wine rack, Spanish ornamental iron   PM82/5:104
Wine rack, stackable units   WB81/5-6:89
Wine rack, twenty-four bottles   HM78/9:52
Wine rack base and glass top table   WB80/1-2:70
Wine rack/cart   PM77/11:135
Wine rack door   PM83/1:95
Wine rack (oak)   PM82/5:104
Wine rack (plywood)   PM82/5:104
Wine racks, stackable   HM83/11:02
Wine racks, three   PM75/7:102
Wine racks, three   PM82/5:104
Wine rack/tray   PM76/12:109
Wine server, acrylic   PM75/11:62
Wine stemware rack   WB78/9-10:44
Wing chair, upholstered   WB80/9-10:6
Winter driving   PM72/12:98
Winter driving   PM78/12:70
Winter driving tips   PM75/11:74
Winter emergencies   HM75/1:34
Winter emergency driving kit   PM80/10:150
Winterizing checklist, home   NS83/10:46
Wires, splicing   PM73/3:138
Wire wheel sharpening   FW83/1-2:16
Wiring, aluminum   HM81/3:20
Wiring, light and power circuits   HM84/9:104
Wiring, soldering electrical   PM74/7:104
Wiring, surface mounted electric   WB83/9-10:75
Wiring, switches and outlets   HM84/7-8:72
Wiring circuit update   HM79/10:46
Wiring electric outlets   PM73/2:154
Wiring hardware, installing   HM83/11:45
Wiring lights   HM83/10:37
Wiring lights   PM76/9:102
Wiring repairs, electrical   PM83/10:34
Wishing well grill   WB80/7-8:24
Wishing well planter   WB74/7-8:48
Wood, basic primer   PM84/11:120
Wood, green   FW79/5-6:48
Wood, green and polyethylene glycol   WB72/3-4:48

Wood, marbleizing   WB75/7-8:10
Wood, pressure treated   NS82/3:84
Wood, treated   PM80/3:162
Wood, weather and rot protection   NS82/3:72
Wood box, fireplace   WB78/9-10:92
Wood butcher   FW77/3:20
Wood carving   FW76/9:35
Wood carving   PM77/1:94
Wood carving   WB75/1-2:40
Wood carving tips   FW84/3-4:58
Wood chisel holder   PM79/3:70
Wood/coal bin   NS80/9:53
Wood cutting table, chain saw   PM79/12:112
Wood doors, solid   FW79/7-8:78
Wood drying   FW76/12:40
Wood drying kiln   FW77/3:39
Wooden balls, small   FW80/7-8:10
Wooden bar clamps   WS79/9:3
Wooden cabinet hinge, inlaid   FW82/7-8:52
Wooden clamps   FW77/9:64
Wooden hinge, 18th century   FW84/7-8:45
Wooden hinged Colonial lap desk (pine)   WS80/5:6
Wooden hinged sweater chest (maple plywood)   WS80/5:8
Wooden hinged wall display case (oak)   WS80/5:11
Wooden hinge jewelry box   WS80/5:5
Wooden plane construction   FW80/1-2:65
Wooden sphere, routed   FW84/1-2:8
Wooden threads   FW77/3:22
Wooden toys   PM84/12:94
Wood fillers   WB73/1-2:42
Wood floors, refinishing hardwood   PM83/1:100
Wood glue   FW83/11-12:62
Wood grain, reading   FW83/11-12:45
Wood identification   FW82/9-10:76
Wood insects   NS82/4:56
Woodlot management   FW82/3-4:82
Wood moisture   FW76/9:20
Wood moisture   FW83/3-4:92
Wood parquet tile   PM84/6:84
Woodpecker damage   PM84/3:32
Wood preservatives   NS82/3:76
Wood preservatives, safest   NS84/7-8:64
Wood splitters   NS80/10:18
Wood stove   NS80/10:76
Wood stove   WB81/9-10:16
Wood stove, brick Russian   NS81/1:74
Woodstove, buying   HM78/10:22
Wood stove, Finland masonary   NS83/1:50
Wood stove, fireplace   NS81/9:32
Wood stove, masonry   NS84/10:74

Woodstove buying guide to clean burning NS84/10:86
Wood stove catalytic combustors NS83/9:50
Wood stove catalytic combustors NS84/9:90
Wood stove catalytic converter NS81/9:35
Wood stove cooking NS84/10:84
Wood stove fender, copper tubing HM81/10:72
Woodstove fires HM80/9:60
Wood stove/furnace piggyback HM77/10:38
Wood stove heated house, Stovehaus PM80/8:86
Wood stove heat shield NS80/10:87
Wood stove inserts NS81/9:37
Wood stove installation NS80/10:78
Wood stove maintenance NS82/10:40
Wood stove safety PM80/10:74
Wood stove tile wall PM82/4:152
Wood turning tips PM79/5:144
Woodwind Flageolet, turning FW77/9:80
Woodworker's tool chest (mahogany) NS81/7-8:45
Woodworking for children HM83/12:62
Woodworking guide PM84/11:117
Woodworking injuries FW82/9-10:84
Woodworking machine, homemade combination FW80/1-2:36
Woodworking machine construction FW80/3-4:43
Woodworking machine maintenance FW78/10:66
Woodworking machinery, used FW78/9:82
Woodworking machines, making portable FW82/7-8:22
Woodworking precision and accuracy FW79/7-8:70
Woodworking pricing FW77/3:54
Woodworking schools FW81/1-2:92
Woodworking tips, nine PM80/11:118
Woodworking tips, ten PM83/3:106
Woodworking tips, thirty-six PM84/11:138
Woodworking tips, twenty-three PM76/2:110
Woody VW Beetle plans to order, $14.95 PM83/7:137
Workbench FW76/9:40
Workbench FW79/5-6:72
Workbench FW82/9-10:88
Workbench HM81/12:18
Workbench HM84/12:36
Workbench PM72/10:89
Workbench PM80/11:114
Workbench PM84/11:126
Workbench, $30 WB77/11-12:40
Workbench, assembly PM82/11:106
Workbench, child's PM80/11:115
Workbench, child's adjustable WB76/3-4:28
Workbench, compact PM84/1:114
Workbench, craftsman's PM81/11:126
Workbench, double top FW80/9-10:70
Workbench, folding portable PM84/4:109

Workbench, garage   PM82/10:128
Workbench, hand tool   WB76/1-2:44
Workbench, heavy duty   WB81/11-12:22
Workbench, hinged tool storage   HM79/11:50
Workbench, hobby center   WB83/9-10:57
Workbench, inexpensive   FW81/1-2:24
Workbench, mini   HM79/4:62
Workbench, movable   NS81/11-12:51
Workbench, on the job   PM82/2:169
Workbench, outdoor   FW82/3-4:18
Workbench, portable   FW82/11-12:30
Workbench, portable   HM82/12:26
Workbench, portable shop   WB81/9-10:120
Workbench, rollaway workshop   PM73/9:162
Workbench, sawhorse   PM73/1:20
Workbench, simple   HM77/5-6:46
Workbench, small   FW78/3:86
Workbench, small fold down   HM84/12:42
Workbench, softwood   FW80/9-10:66
Workbench, tailgate   PM73/5:67
Workbench, tool clamp on   HM82/12:29
Workbench, traditional   WB73/3-4:42
Workbench clean-up bag   PM82/6:140
Workbench dog, self-locking   FW83/1-2:12
Workbench dog, wooden   FW83/11-12:10
Workbench dogs, round   FW80/1-2:15
Workbench dogs, wood   FW83/1-2:20
Workbenches   PM76/3:124
Workbench holding hook   PM76/4:202
Workbench hook bending jig   PM76/2:117
Workbench kits   HM78/11-12:54
Workbench sheet metal brake   WB80/9-10:50
Workbench shoulder vise and clamping dogs   FW80/9-10:68
Workbench stop, self locking   PM77/8:110
Workbench top vise   PM77/2:60
Workbench update   WB83/7-8:44
Workbench vise, end   PM79/5:40
Workbench vise, wooden   FW80/9-10:69
Workbench vises   HM78/11-12:83
Workcenter, home   PM80/12:100
Workcenter, mobile   WB79/11-12:4
Workcenter, portable power tools   PM82/11:109
Workshop, closet sized   PM79/11:140
Workshop, converting shack   WB81/3-4:96
Workshop, dream   HM79/4:26
Workshop, garage   WB72/9-10:26
Workshop, open air solar   HM83/2:22
Workshop, portable   HM78/10:76
Workshop, roll away workbench   PM73/9:162
Workshop, small roll away   PM74/10:70

Workshop/bench, two minis   PM76/1:98
Workshop clock   PM78/11:200
Workshop design   PM72/10:85
Workshop design   PM84/11:124
Workshop in the wall   PM83/4:126
Workshop layouts, three   HM84/12:25
Workshop storage, hardware   PM80/7:104
Workstation, computer   PM83/8:92
Worktable   WB81/9-10:42
Worktable, hobby corner   HM76/11:34
Worktable, revolving top   PM77/3:68
Worktable, rolling   FW82/7-8:20
Worktable, tough child's   HM79/10:21
Worktable, wired   WB79/9-10:28
World globe, wood   FW79/1-2:61
Woven bottom Shaker armchair   HM72/6:38
Woven cane   FW80/1-2:49
Woven chair bottom, split sapling   WB81/3-4:106
Woven slat cabinet doors   WB80/11-12:96
Woven string bottom Shaker stool   HM83/12:72
Woven top coffee table   WB77/11-12:96
Wrapping paper center   HM83/11:70
Wrapping tying, Japanese   HM83/12:58
Wreath, wooden Christmas   PM81/12:114
Wreath Christmas decoration   PM78/12:74
Wreaths, Christmas   PM72/12:75
Wren birdhouse, gourd and coconut   WB76/5-6:22
Wrench, multi one piece sheet steel tool   PM82/8:87
Wrenches   HM74/11:42
Wrench tips   PM78/12:110
Writing desk (oak)   FW82/5-6:67
Wrought iron firewood holder, indoor   PM82/1:102
Wrought iron railings, installing   PM73/7:82
Wrought iron rails and columns   HM77/7-8:60
Wrought iron table, glass top coffee   HM76/4:44
Wrought iron window planter   HM78/4:38
Wrought iron window planter, aluminum   PM79/6:60
Xylophone, Noel toy   PM79/11:122
Yard, grassless   WB83/9-10:92
Yard games   PM76/8:97
Yard light, installing post lamp   PM74/4:176
Yard light, post   PM76/5:108
Yard light, wiring and installing   PM73/5:100
Yardlights, four   HM84/3:39
Yard screen (cedar)   PM81/8:88
Yarn bin, family room   PM79/10:130
Zebra rocking horse   WB78/11-12:75
Zodiac stained glass panel   PM80/7:96